THE CHRISTIAN LIFE

THE
CHRISTIAN LIFE

Church Dogmatics IV,4
Lecture Fragments

BY

KARL BARTH

TRANSLATED BY

GEOFFREY W. BROMILEY

WILLIAM B. EERDMANS PUBLISHING COMPANY
Grand Rapids, Michigan

Translation of unpublished lecture fragments
of *Kirchliche Dogmatik* IV,4:
Das christliche Leben,
Basel

Library of Congress Cataloging in Publication Data

Barth, Karl, 1886-1968.
The Christian life.

Translation of Das christliche Leben.
1. Christian ethics—Reformed authors.
2. Reconciliation. I. Title.
BJ1253.B3413   241   80-39942
ISBN 0-8028-3523-6

CONTENTS

TRANSLATOR'S PREFACE

When Karl Barth retired at the age of 75, he was at work on the continuation of Volume IV of the *Church Dogmatics* and it was hoped that the fourth part of this, the "Ethics of Reconciliation," would soon appear. Various factors combined to frustrate this hope. Barth interrupted his normal course to give the series on *Evangelical Theology*, which he then repeated in part on his American tour. After his return, retirement disrupted his established routine. Medical problems then sapped him of the vigor and concentration he needed for more exacting tasks. He was also not satisfied that he had found the best way to organize his material in the important central sections between baptism as the foundation of the Christian life and the Lord's Supper as its renewal. He hesitated in particular between faithfulness as the leading concept, invocation of God, which would produce an exposition of the Lord's Prayer, and gratitude, which would enable him to develop his thoughts according to the familiar fourfold relation to God, others, self, and the world.

In the event, then, Barth prepared for official publication only the section on baptism, which appeared in the series of the *Church Dogmatics* as a Fragment of Volume IV,4. For the rest, he was unable even to complete the central sections, let alone revise them to his satisfaction, and he never even began the concluding eucharistic section. Nevertheless, he left behind several hundred pages of typescript, and with the decision to publish a complete Swiss edition of all his writings these were finally made available to the public and are now presented in this English translation.

The translation reproduces faithfully and, it is hoped, readably, the reflections of the later Barth on the relation between ethics and reconciliation and then on the Christian life as invocation according to the address and the first two petitions of the Lord's Prayer. It should be noted, however, that there has been some compression of the very competent and painstaking editorial work done in the original version. Only a sampling is given (in the first pages) of the mostly minor variations in the available text, some of the more indirect allusions have not been documented, and while biblical and non-biblical references not given by Barth have usually been supplied in special brackets [ ] or in footnotes, full quotations that Barth did not include in his own text have been eliminated. Naturally this implies no criticism of the excellent Swiss editing; it simply avoids an expansion which is hardly necessary when scholars who might be interested in such matters have the data at hand in the original. The translation of the Swiss Preface will facilitate an understanding of the editorial procedures adopted and the apparatus is reproduced in full in the pieces that comprise the Appendix.

For general readers, it is hoped that even though fragmentary, and not wholly satisfactory to its author, this discussion of the Christian life as invocation will both document and promote the concerns of the later Barth for the church's work and witness in the power and context of the reconciling work of God.

Pasadena
Michaelmas 1980   GEOFFREY W. BROMILEY

PREFACE

Karl Barth did not finish his *Dogmatics*. He never wrote the projected Volume V, which would have expounded the doctrine of redemption; also missing is the greater part of the ethics of reconciliation, which would have completed Volume IV. A self-contained fragment of IV,4, which was planned as "The Command of God the Reconciler" and would have constituted Chapter XVII, was published in 1967 under the title "Baptism as the Foundation of the Christian Life" (E.T. 1969). Further fragments of this ethical chapter are to be found in the literary remains, although even with the doctrine of baptism they would have formed less than half of *CD* IV,4. These fragments are published in the present volume.

We have first an introduction to the ethics of reconciliation in the section "Ethics as the Task of the Doctrine of Reconciliation" (§74). Following the doctrine of baptism (§75) is the torso of an exposition of the Lord's Prayer, which breaks off after the second petition (§§76– 78). This exposition of the Lord's Prayer, which would have been the heart of the ethics of the Christian life, was to have been followed by a concluding section on the Lord's Supper. The three parts of the theory of Christian conduct in terms of the doctrine of reconciliation would have come together as a whole under the guiding concept of calling upon God. The doctrine of baptism, which precedes the exposition of the Lord's Prayer, ends with an understanding of water baptism as the prayer for the Holy Spirit, which is the foundation of the Christian life, while the doctrine of the Lord's Supper, which would have concluded the chapter, was to have shown this to be the thanksgiving — *eucharistia* — which renews the Christian life. Barth did not originally envision this arrangement of the ethical chapter of the doctrine of reconciliation; it arose by way of a self-correction which he felt he should make when he had already delivered §74 and §75 in lecture form. The process is instructive concerning Barth's mode of working, and some hints may be given regarding it.

1. Barth broke off his normal work on *CD* with the end of his lecturing. He was prevented from continuing, first by the American trip, then by a series of illnesses. But half in jest and half in earnest he had often pointed out that even the continuation of *CD*, let alone its conclusion, was threatened by the removal of the "salutary pressure" of having to prepare lectures. One may see in this an indication of the great importance that the author attached to his work as a teacher in Basel. It was as a professor that he

was a doctor of the church. The texts of *CD* came into existence first in connection with the lectures, in which students would be introduced in a given semester to some portion of dogmatics or ethics. This shaped the sub-sections of *CD*, the parts being so planned in relation to the whole that students could always have the whole in view. It is thus no accident that the exposition of the Lord's Prayer found in the remains breaks off at the point where Barth ended his lectures, while the already completed lectures on baptism were later revised and prepared for publication. In the year before his death, Barth often considered doing further work on the doctrine of the Lord's Supper, though he left no drafts of this. As he said verbally, he would have liked to present his view of the so-called sacraments within the context of *CD*. In contrast, however, there were no plans for the con-tinuation of the exposition of the Lord's Prayer. The pieces found in the remains certainly have technical markings for printing, but they had not been revised for publication. Apart from uncorrected slips, there are many external indications of this, for example, the use of colons and dashes, which is so much greater than is customary in Barth's other writings.

2. One fact merits special attention. After the introductory section (§74) had been delivered in lecture form in the 1959/60 winter semester (and that on baptism in the summer semester of 1960), Barth subjected it to a radical revision with a view to what he now regarded as a necessary revision of the arrangement of the whole chapter. One might speak in this connection of a totally new conception of IV,4, not unlike the complete revision of the *Romans Commentary* in the second edition, or the replacement of the false start of the Prolegomena of the *Christian Dogmatics* by *CD* I,1. Within *CD* there is a comparable — though less significant — self-correction in the con-text of the doctrine of creation, in which Barth omitted much material from his manuscript (and lectures?) when he published *CD* III,1 and III,2.

In the present instance §74 is revised with a view to the necessary rearrangement of the whole chapter. Barth had originally planned to bring the whole ethics of reconciliation under the rubric of the faithfulness which determines the Christian life. The arrangement would then have been as follows (cf. p. 288):

There are thus six areas of discussion. We shall be dealing (1) with the foundation of Christian faithfulness and baptism as its first and once-for-all human act confirming its divine foundation, (2) with the Chris-tian's faithfulness to the Holy Spirit which determines and delimits all that follows, (3) with his faithfulness in the community, (4) with his faithfulness to himself, (5) with his faithfulness in the world, and (6) with the renewal of Christian faithfulness and the Lord's Supper as the human action in which the Christian may and should continually con-firm its divine renewal.

The considerations behind this arrangement are presented in the Appendix ("First Version of the Conclusion of §74").

The revision of the lecture manuscript which Barth undertook in the summer semester of 1960 may be traced to some extent in his letters. In a letter to Dorothee Hoch dated August 8, 1960, he consents to the distribution of a transcript of the lectures only "with hesitation and reservations" because he had revised and at times added a good deal to the original manuscript, of which she had a copy. This can hardly refer to less than a material reconstruction of the whole chapter. In the same letter, though, Barth says that there has been no material alteration but that everything is now, he hopes, more precise and complete. The new beginning necessitated by the revision of the introduction is referred to for the first time four weeks later. In a letter to his son Markus dated September 5, Barth says that he has been busy at his desk, although for the moment he has only been moving backward, namely, in replanning IV,4 in terms of the invocation of God. On September 18 he writes to his son Christoph that as the new semester approaches he has fortunately finished the doctrine of baptism in the summer semester and is now coming to the true theme of IV,4, namely, an attempt to portray the Christian life, which he will do under the controlling concept of calling upon God with the Lord's Prayer as a model. Having only just achieved clarity in the matter, he has had to go back and do a lot of revising and refining during the vacation and can only now get down to preparation for the semester along the right lines. God has wrought a beneficial change. Writing again to Christoph on October 26, Barth says that the section on "Our Father in Heaven," which follows baptism and begins the ethics proper, is going fairly well. Writing to Markus again on December 24, he says that the course of IV,4 is very different from what it was in the manuscript known to Markus. He has given a new direction to the sections after the one on baptism and has oriented the introductory one to the concept of invocation. The guiding thread is the Lord's Prayer, which is examined in relation to the imperatives contained in the petitions. With this and the Lord's Supper, Barth expects to have his hands full during his retirement.

The self-correction, then, is that Barth now conceives of the ethics of reconciliation, or the command of God the Reconciler, in terms of the command of Psalm 50:15: "Call upon me." The living of the Christian life in obedience to that command is understood as an invocation of God. The foundation and renewal of the Christian life are to be dealt with in the doctrines of baptism and the Lord's Supper, and between these the Christian life itself is to be portrayed in an exposition of the Lord's Prayer. What Barth did in execution of this plan is now published in full in this volume. It should be noted that pp. 31–35, apart from some minor alterations, are identical to Barth's essay "The Command of the Gracious God" in the Festschrift for K. H. Miskotte, entitled *Woord en Wereld* (Amsterdam, 1961, pp. 280–286).

3. No evaluation of the content of this volume will be given here, but one observation may perhaps be permitted. Not the least reason why special attention should be given to the fragments of the exposition of the Lord's

Prayer is that they bring out more sharply the eschatological orientation of the doctrine of reconciliation than do the corresponding discussions in IV,3. The commonly expressed view that there can be no eschatology proper in the course of *CD* is thus shown to be even more unfounded than it previously was. In fact, indications to the contrary are innumerable. It is not without significance that the last sentence of the unfinished *CD* formulates as follows the promise for every person (and not just the Christian): "Jesus Christ is his hope too."

The text of this volume is based on a typescript and the dictated original and on a manuscript in Barth's own hand, of which the conclusion of §77 and two pages of §78 are no longer available. (Both manuscript and typescript may be found in the Karl Barth-Archive in Basel.) For much of §77 and §78, comparison can also be made with recordings of the corresponding lectures.

In general, the printed version follows the typescript that Karl Barth dictated to his secretary, Charlotte von Kirschbaum, on the basis of his manuscript. In this process he often altered the original text, usually by small, but sometimes by bigger, changes and expansions. The text also underwent what were at times substantial handwritten corrections and expansions either before the lectures or on the typescript after them. One of these corrections may be mentioned here. The second sentence of §74 originally read: "The doctrine of reconciliation should also close with an ethical chapter (and so, too, when it is time, the doctrine of redemption)." In the typescript Barth changed the manuscript "is" to "comes": "when the time comes." The text resulting from these various processes is what is here designated the typescript.

In this edition we cannot undertake to distinguish all the different stages of its evolution. The texts in the Appendix offer at the most some examples for comparison with the corresponding portions in the main version. An account must be given, however, of the cases in which the editors deviate from Barth's typescript.

As indicated, the typescript is provided with technical instructions for composition, though these are not definitive. At two points alterations have been necessary as compared with these and with the volumes of *CD*. According to the editorial guidelines for the *Gesamtausgabe*, italics are used instead of interspacings, except in Greek quotations. Thus foreign expressions can no longer be printed in italics to distinguish them from the rest of the text, and insofar as they are quotations they are placed in quotation marks.

According to the same guidelines, occasional doublings are removed, unusual abbreviations are eliminated, and inconsistencies in spelling and punctuation are brought into line with the general practice in the text and in *CD*. In those cases in which a stress has to be supplied for the sake of consistency (as in parallel concepts), it has usually been possible simply to go back to the manuscript version.

Going back to the original has been very important in the not infrequent cases in which errors and misunderstandings have crept in through dictation, as, for example, when the typescript reads: ". . . the one commanding of the one God to whom man is gracious in Jesus Christ" (p. 9); or when the text of the manuscript, "Prayer and (*und*) hearing are two different things even when it is pure prayer" is rendered in the typescript: "Prayer for (*um*) hearing are two different things" (p. 246); or finally, when the typescript has: "[God] who knows about (*um*) their needs better than they themselves," and the manuscript reads: "[God] who knows about (*um*) them and (*und*) their needs" (p. 51). As a rule, the slips are grammatical and involve case and number, which are not clear at first glance in the manuscript, since Barth seldom writes final syllables plainly. When unintentional deviations from quotations arise through writing or dictation slips, or when grammatically imperfect sentences occur, these errors are quietly corrected from the manuscript. This is also done when nonsense results, as in our first example. Sometimes corrections have the support of marks that Barth himself put in the margin, as in the case of the incorrect use of "befreite" for "befreiten" on p. 104.

The typescript also contains some syntactical errors which could be put right only by insertions in brackets. The notes (in the German text) show when the manuscript could be used for this purpose.

These additions by the editors have been kept to a minimum. There has obviously been no alteration of Barth's style: his use of older grammatical forms has been respected; the particular form used in liturgical and biblical quotations has been left as it is; insertions in brackets have been made only in the case of errors. When it has not been possible to decipher a word in Barth's text, an insertion with a question mark has been made in brackets. In sum, alterations of the typescript are not indicated only when, on the basis of the manuscript, they set aside errors that destroy a statement grammatically. In other instances, necessary insertions are always in brackets, and notes show where they are taken from the manuscript. Other alterations are also indicated in the notes, even corrections which the meaning of a statement demands, as in the examples.

In the notes that give information on the differences between the printed version and the originals, it should be observed that to make reference easier, the editors have printed the deviations in italics. For this reason, italics for the sake of emphasis are omitted in these notes (cf. p. 36, n. 9 of the German text). To achieve greater clarity, the notes sometimes repeat adjoining phrases that are in agreement, though not now in italics. The editors have always consulted the manuscript, though they have used it only when the relevant passage is in it and did not come in at a later stage, or when the manuscript can be deciphered. Sometimes the manuscript version is offered when the typescript does not demand alteration but the manuscript version is to be preferred (cf. p. 230, n. 24 of the German text). On the other hand, the editors have refrained from making what might seem to be desirable changes or additions when the manuscript and typescript are in agreement, for example, on p. 460 (lines 22ff.) where both manuscript and typescript use the present tense (*wird*) and not, as one might have expected, a future (*wird . . . sein*).

Finally, the textual notes include three proposals of the editors for the correction of passages that seem to stand in need of emendation, namely, p. 337, n. 89; p. 400, n. 42; p. 464, n. 129 (German text). (For the full textual apparatus, readers should consult the German original, since it has not been reproduced in the English translation.) The other notes supply materials for quotations and allusions in the text. They are the work of the editors; Barth's text contains no footnotes. In the case of historical materials, extracts are given where Barth refers to a particular text or the works are not readily available. Perhaps some will think too much has been done in this regard. The editors share with them the hope that the days of ignorance will never come in which the comprehensive apparatus resolved upon for the volumes of the *Gesamtausgabe* will be needed everywhere. Nevertheless, the trouble which some of the references gave the editors leads us to suspect that many of the notes will already be useful to readers today. (Since the extracts are mostly German, only the references have been given in the English translation.)

In order not to make the notes unnecessarily bulky, references are simply repeated in many cases where the text itself refers to what precedes. For the same reason, the relevant excursuses in *CD* are indicated in the case of theological concepts. In common expressions and catchwords, no notes are provided when examples might be adduced but no true source can be named, at least none to which Barth is plainly referring. Thus there is no note in the case of "Perhaps, and perhaps not," where Barth might have had in mind a passage in the second edition of his *Romans*, or might be alluding to an anecdote in his letter to E. Thurneysen dated May 30, 1921, or might be simply quoting in abbreviated form from G. Büchner's *Leonce und Lena*, Act I, Scene 2. Where Barth quotes from the Bible or alludes to biblical expressions without giving a reference, the reference has been supplied in brackets. In some cases where Barth gives a reference and uses "f." but more than one verse follows, the "f." has been replaced by "ff." The abbreviations of the books of the Bible are as in *CD*, while RGG[3] is taken as a guide for other abbreviations. *SL* should be added to these for *Series Latina* in the *Corpus Christianorum* (German text).

Thanks are due to Dr. Hinrich Stoevesandt and his wife for the critical and constructive attention with which they have accompanied the labors of the editors. Mrs. Gerlinde Berutti-Hühn has rendered good service in preparing the indexes. Readers are indebted to Mrs. Gerta Hüffmeier and Mrs. Hanne Dicke for their laborious technical work. Nor should it pass unnoticed that the University of Tübingen has in its own way helped forward the work on this volume.

In conclusion we should mention the names of those whom Barth himself wished to acknowledge in the Preface to *CD* IV,4. In the notes he made when, in preparing this volume, he read "the New Testament again from A to Z and word by word" (letter to Markus Barth, September 27, 1959), the following entry appears: "Preface to IV,4: G. Merz — P. Schempp — H. Iwand."

TÜBINGEN, *December 5, 1975*   HANS-ANTON DREWES
                                                EBERHARD JÜNGEL

CHAPTER XVII

THE COMMAND OF GOD
THE RECONCILER

§74

ETHICS AS A TASK OF THE
DOCTRINE OF RECONCILIATION

In the context of the doctrine of reconciliation, special ethics serves to demonstrate how far the command of the one God is centrally the command of the Lord of the covenant, in which the action of sinful man is determined, ordered, and limited by the free grace of the faithful God manifested and operative in Jesus Christ.

1. THE CENTRAL PROBLEM OF SPECIAL ETHICS

A chapter on ethics as the general doctrine of the command of God concluded the doctrine of God at an earlier point in the *Church Dogmatics* (II,2). Another chapter on ethics as the special doctrine of the command of God the Creator concluded the doctrine of creation at a later point (III,4). The doctrine of reconciliation (and also, if we reach it, the doctrine of redemption) must now be brought to an end with a similar chapter on ethics.

Comprehensively, ethics is an attempt to answer theoretically the question of what may be called *good* human action. Theological ethics such as is attempted here finds both this question and its answer in God's Word. It thus finds it where theological dogmatics as the critical science of true church proclamation finds all its questions and answers. Theological ethics can be understood only as an integral element of dogmatics (cf. *CD* I,2 § 22,3). The Word of God, with which dogmatics (and consequently theological ethics) is concerned at every point as the basis, object, content, and norm of true church proclamation, is, however, Jesus Christ in the divine-human unity of his being and work. In God's Word, then, we are dealing both with God and with man: with God acting in relation to man and with man acting in relation to God; or, to put it in terms of the ethical problem, with the sure and certain goodness of the divine action and the problematical goodness of the human action. At every point in true church proclamation it must and will be a matter of both. And the Word of God is the command of God to the extent that in it the sure and certain goodness of God's goodness confronts the problematical goodness of man's as its standard, requirement, and direction. And as the command of God, it is the source and norm of theological ethics. Described very generally on this presupposition, the human action is good which is commanded by God in his Word and is obedient to him. Precisely for this reason, ethics cannot be understood and ventured as an independent discipline working on its own presuppositions

3

and according to its own methods, but only as an integral element in dogmatics.

At issue here is a chapter on special ethics; there is also a general ethics. It was unfolded earlier in the *Church Dogmatics* as the general doctrine of the command of God: as the doctrine of the functions in whose fulfilment it has and manifests its essence, namely, the claim, decision, and judgment of God which in his Word become evident as the command confronting human action. Primarily, though not exclusively — this is why, like the doctrine of election, it belongs to the doctrine of God — the statement about general ethics is a statement about God.

In special ethics we shift emphasis, following the command of God with particular reference to the man to whom he turns in it. In the statement about it — without losing sight of the primary thing, the character of the command as God's act — we deal with its significance and outworking in the life of the man to whom it comes, with the freedom for good action which is demanded of him but also granted, granted to him but also demanded, as God commands him. Special ethics looks at man as this particular man at this particular time and place, who yesterday selected and decided and acted on the basis of the possibilities available, who does the same today in different circumstances, and who will do the same tomorrow in different circumstances again. It is concerned to see and show how far this specific, concrete, special, and even very special action of man can or cannot be called a good action, that is, an action that corresponds to the divine claim, agrees with the divine decision, and conforms to the divine judgment.

We may briefly recall here two safeguards which were expressly grounded and explained earlier (*CD* III,4 § 52,1):

1. At issue is the relation of human action to *God's* command. God himself, God alone is good, and he decides what human action may be called good or not good. As the Word of God in general is the speaking of the *living* God, so the command of God in particular is his commanding. Special ethics has to point to the concrete meaning of his commanding and the willing, choosing, and acting that corresponds to it or contradicts it. It may not infringe upon — "the Spirit blows where he wills" (Jn. 3:8) — either the free disposing of God regarding the concrete meaning and content of his commanding or the free responsibility of the action of man. It has to respect the directness of the dealings between the commanding God and the man who obeys or disobeys him. Hence it cannot adopt as self-evident presuppositions any supposed natural or rational truths or any timeless truths supposedly taken from the Bible or the Christian tradition. It cannot for its part proclaim any such truths, for they would obviously come between God and man. It cannot adopt and proclaim any general rules whose detailed and concrete exposition and application remain an open question, to answer which in individual cases is the task of special ethics. God's command, and what it means for man as claim, decision, and judgment, is not the timeless truth of a general principle, or a collection of such truths, but the specific content of what is always a special event between God and man in its

historical reality. Where and when it goes forth and finds an answer in man's obedience or disobedience, it is a precise and filled-out direction and not, therefore, an empty form that still needs filling out and preciseness. Special ethics, then, must resist the temptation to become legalistic and casuistic ethics. Its task is to point to that event between God and man, to its uncontrollable content.

2. Also at issue is the one command of the one God in all the concrete forms of the command over against all concrete human actions and in all the dealings of the one God with all men. Special ethics has to consider and indicate the sovereignty of the divine commanding, but also its constancy, the faithfulness of God to himself and to man; the uniqueness and singularity of each individual act of human obedience or disobedience, but also the continuity of human being, attitude, and action; the event-character of every encounter of God with man and man with God, but also the fact that this event takes place in the history of God with this man but also with all other men. His encounters with men are individual yet not on that account isolated points, but points on a line. Special ethics must not fail to bring out the character that is always distinctive in the divine commanding, in the impulsion of the Holy Spirit in contrast to that of all other spirits. It must not fail to bring out the standard by which human action is always measured as regards its rightness or wrongness. It must not describe the free commanding of God as if there might be at work in it the requirements and impulses of a plurality of gods and ideas and forces. Nor must it describe human action as if it might consist of an uncontoured plenitude of accidental or arbitrary individual acts. Special ethics has to direct and instruct responsible man precisely with a reference to the ever-new event of his encounter with the living God. It has to lead him to reflect on this encounter. If it cannot be a legalistic and casuistic ethics, nor can it be an obscure ethics of the *kairos* in general. Its task is to expound *this kairos* — that of the event between God and man.

We have to steer a course between that Scylla and this Charybdis. Neither the free commanding of God nor the action of freely responsible man can be shut up in a general law which we control. The event between them cannot be understood and presented in a series of applications of such a law. God and man are not for us unwritten pages or unknown quantities. The particular facticity of the event between them is not the only thing we can know and say about it. Who the commanding God is and who responsible man is — God in the mystery of his commanding and man in the mystery of his obedience or disobedience — is not hidden from us but is revealed and may be known in the one Jesus Christ: God *and* man, if not in their essence, at least in their work and therefore in their manner; God *and* man, accessible to human apprehension, if not expressible in human words, at least describable and attestable. If special ethics does what it should do as theological ethics and clings to true God and true man as they declare themselves in Jesus Christ, then good care is taken that it will move within the limits of respect for the immediacy of the dealings between God and man, that it will not violate the freedom of God and the freedom of man but will honor them. It will then certainly not become legalistic or casuistic ethics. Good care will also be taken that God and man in the reality of their dealings will always be relatively perceptible and apprehensible for it, so that it will not have to rest content with indefinite references to their specific facticity in each instance. Similarly, it certainly cannot degenerate into an indefinite ethics of the *kairos*. Regarding the fact that God *and* man are not unknown but are known to us in Jesus Christ, reference to the event — the many events — of the encounter between the commanding God and the man who acts can and must become a formed and contoured reference, yet nothing more than a reference, which at least approximates to the concretion of that event. It may thus be of service to the ethical instruction with which special ethics must be concerned.

Who is the *God* who commands in royal freedom?[1] If we hold fast to God's self-declaration in Jesus Christ, then we may resolutely answer in the negative: he is not in any case a general or neutral god, however lofty, who owes his closer definition to the intrinsically nonobligatory surmising or thinking of some human religion or metaphysics, even though it be that of the Christian faith. He is not in any case empty transcendence whose possible filling out can be provided only by human existence. And we may no less resolutely answer in the positive: in any case, no matter how it may be with the faith or unbelief, the obedience or disobedience of the man who confronts him, he is the one without whom this man would not even be. He is the one who has created him. No matter what many may think of it, God is the one who has reconciled man to himself when as a sinner man became his enemy. He is the one who in the concluding manifestation of his love wills to redeem man, and will redeem him from the discord in which he now exists. He is the partner of man as the Initiator and Lord of this history of his dealings with him. It is with him, with this one as outlined thus, that acting man comes to have and has dealings in that event of his encounter with God's command. The encounter is in any case determined and limited by the work and therefore by the manner of this Lord. It takes place in the sphere of the Father, the Son, and the Holy Spirit, who is man's Creator, Reconciler, and Redeemer.

And who is the man who acts in free responsibility in his relationship to this God? If now we also hold fast to the self-declaration of man in Jesus Christ, then we must answer negatively here too: certainly not a being that is superior to God, or equal, or independently existing on the same plane. Man is not a being whose existence has any hope apart from God. He is also not a being that can in any respect be left to its own devices. And therefore here again we must answer positively: man is the creature of God, the creature among all others that is elected, determined, and endowed for covenant with him. And he is the being that, in spite of its own unfaithfulness and therefore not according to its merits but by the faithfulness of God, is a participant in his grace, is justified before God, sanctified for him,

---

[1] In the typescript (hereafter referred to as TS) this and the next paragraph are marked by a red **X**, perhaps to show that they are recapitulations of *CD* III,4 §52,1, pp. 24–26.

and called to his service. He is, finally, the child of God to whom as such it is promised that God's eternal light will shine upon him and he will live for ever. In all cases this being is God's partner, on and with whom God is at work in the history he inaugurates and governs, in every encounter between them. The man who acts for good or ill in his confrontation with the claim, decision, and judgment of the divine command has this three-fold character corresponding to the nature of God. His encounter with the command of God does not take place on his side in a sphere that is indefinite and infinite but in one that is fixed and limited.

It is with this knowledge of God and man that we are to denote, under-stand, and describe the divine commanding in its relation to human action, with full respect for the freedom, directness, particularity, and uniqueness with which it takes place between God and this or that man at this or that time and place. To be sure — and in what sphere of theological knowledge is it any different? — this can be done only with relative, and not absolute, validity. It certainly cannot be done exhaustively. The final mystery of the encounter has still to be brought out more clearly. Nevertheless, in contrast to an empty reference to the mere point of reality, which contains no definite statements, it can be done in such a way that certain lines emerge which are at least distinctive to the event. From this knowledge of God and man, without human speech trying to crowd out or replace the divine, there result certain directives that can serve as witnesses to the Word of God as the divine command which God alone speaks to man. These directives may help man on to ethical reflection and action, to the finding, studying, hon-oring, and, God willing, the keeping of the commandments; that is, to his conversion from disobedience to obedience in relation to the divine com-manding as it comes precisely to him. To draw these lines, to give these directives, is, in a general way, the task and theme of special ethics.

In what follows we shall present *one* chapter of special ethics. But there is not just one chapter, nor an indefinite number of chapters; there are three chapters of special ethics. The knowledge of God and man disclosed in Jesus Christ, on which, as shown, special ethics is based and becomes possible and necessary, is not simple, nor indefinitely multiple, but triple. In itself, of course, it is one: Knowledge of the one, total God and the one, total man. But as one it is differentiated and structured:

it is knowlege of God as Creator and man as his creature;

it is knowledge of God as Reconciler and man as a sinner referred to his grace and a participant in it;

it is knowledge of God as Redeemer and man as his child and future heir.

It is knowledge of the Father, the Son, and the Holy Spirit. Accordingly, the understanding and description of the divine commanding in relation to man and his acts, the presentation of those lines and directives which is the task of special ethics, can also be attempted only with differentiation and structure — not arbitrarily, but in the triple distinction that is indicated by the triply distinct knowledge of God and man. Distinction does not mean division. That God is essentially Father, Son, and Holy Spirit does not mean that his being is inwardly split, but that it is triply active and rich in its unity. And that in his work he is Creator, Reconciler, and Redeemer does not mean the division of his work into the activities of three different departments — "the external works of the Trinity are not divided"[2] — but that this work of his is triply free and loving and glorious in its unity. All this, *mutatis mutandis*, applies analogically to the man who is created by him, is reconciled with him, and is to be redeemed as his child. In the event of his encounter with the God who commands him, man in undivided totality exists in triple determination before God and with him. In this event God commands and man acts, not in conjunction and succession, but each time in all three spheres and fields and areas, with distinction but not separation.

The present issue is that of knowing, understanding, and describing this event. It should be remembered that our knowledge is achieved as a pilgrim theology in the light of grace and not of glory, in the light of the *parousia* of Jesus Christ, which begins with his resurrection, continues in the presence and action of his Holy Spirit, but has not yet reached its goal. Hence this knowledge does not yet match the knowledge with which God knows himself and us. Thus our understanding and description of this event — truly as pilgrim theology — has to follow step by step the one history whose course is reflected in the distinction of the three spheres: creation, reconciliation, and redemption. Always and everywhere it has to see them together: the first article of the Creed in the light of the second and moving toward the third, the second the presupposition of the first and the third, the third the final word to be said on the basis of the second and also the first. Each of God's three modes of being implies in itself a relationship to the other two, and similarly each of God's three works in itself relates to the other two. An understanding and description that modestly follows that one history, however, will refrain from attempting to mix or even identify the three spheres in which it takes place. It could only fail in such an attempt. It would have to admit that it found nothing to understand or describe. It should not be afraid of the succession and conjunction of an evaluation of the event which does not divide it but distinguishes between the three standpoints presented to it in the knowledge of God and man. Special ethics has to speak about the one totality of the event in three chapters corresponding to the threeness of these standpoints. What it comes to see and has to show can only be at each step something particular, provisional, and passing, which will be followed by something else. This something else has to follow, always in a particular form, the one command of the one God to the one man. Its knowledge, understanding, and description can only be inadequate, but precisely in this inadequacy it is commensurate with the theme within the limits of pilgrim theology.

In this respect the doctrine of creation concluded with a chapter on "The Command of God the Creator" (*CD* III,4) — not on the view that there is a special command, or complex of commands, different and separate from

---

[2]This phrase, which goes back to Augustine (e.g., *De trin.* I,iv,7; V,xiii,14), is described by Barth as "the theological rule with respect to the Trinity" (*CD* I,1, p. 375).

the others, but on the view that the one command of the one God, and in relation to it the one undivided action of man, has also in this totality the special character and aspect that it has to be understood and described as the command which God the Creator has given to his creature. Thus the first chapter of special ethics in the particular context of the doctrine of creation had to show how far the one commanding of the one God who is gracious to man in Jesus Christ is (not only, but also) the command of his Creator and determines, orders, and limits (not only, but also) his creaturely action and inaction as such. In the same way the doctrine of redemption (what is called eschatology) will have to close with a chapter on "The Command of God the Redeemer"—again not on the view that there is an independent command of this name, but on the view that the one command of the one God who is gracious to man in Jesus Christ has (not only, but also) an eschatological form and that it (and human action too) has thus to be evaluated, understood, and described in this special way once again.

The one command of the one God, "who is gracious to man in Jesus Christ"—this definition of the divine Commander is basic and decisive for his action and commanding as Creator and Redeemer and also for man's understanding. With it we have reached the central theme of special ethics: the theme of the chapter upon which we are now entering. The expression "the God who is gracious to us in Jesus Christ" paraphrases the shorter "God the Reconciler." The divine command is also the command of God the Reconciler and is directed also to the man who by him is reconciled to God, the sinful man to whom as such God is faithful in Jesus Christ and gracious in his faithfulness. Here too we have to say that the one command of God has the form of "not only, but also." Both behind and before we have to remember that it is also the command of God the Creator and the command of God the Redeemer, so that special ethics has the two corresponding tasks as well. Nevertheless, it has a special task here too. And here in the doctrine of reconciliation, as in general so also ethically, we stand before the center, the source of all the reality and revelation of God and man—Jesus Christ, who is not only the ontic but also the noetic basis of the whole of Christian truth and the Christian message. There is no center without a circumference, no second article of the Creed without the first and the third. But the center establishes the circumference and not the reverse. It is from the second article, "I believe . . . in Jesus Christ, the only Son of God, our Lord" and so forth, that the first and third articles receive meaning and have the distinctive sense in which they too are Christian confession, and not the reverse. There thus follows the central position, the material primacy, of the task of this second chapter of special ethics in relation to the first and third. That God is Lord of the covenant of grace is materially the first thing by which his being and work, and therefore his speaking and commanding, as Creator and Redeemer are also determined and stamped. And that man moves from and to him as Lord of the covenant of grace is what characterizes (positively or negatively) man's being and action as also the creature and the future heir of God, not the reverse. The core of every statement in the first and third chapters of special ethics will thus consist of statements taken from the second, of specific christological and soteriological statements. In the second chapter, on which we now embark, we have to deal with the center, core, and origin of the totality as such.

The theme and content of the witness of the Old Testament and New Testament is the connected history of unique and singular encounters between God and man. This history, and the individual encounters in which it takes its course, has an absolute beginning and an absolute goal, an Alpha and Omega, to use the words of Revelation (1:8). It comes from God, who as Creator is Lord of this history, and from man, who as his creature is the partner of this Lord. Again it goes to God the Redeemer, who as such determines its *telos*, and to man as his child, whom he conducts to its *telos*. This "from him" and "to him" (Rom. 11:36) are made a history (rather than a static relation), and characterized as such by the "through him" which stands between them and is bracketed by them. In the biblical testimony to this history—which not accidentally begins with the Book of Genesis and ends in Revelation—they are occasionally discussed explicitly (sometimes the whence and sometimes the whither, sometimes with a reference to God and sometimes to man). They are also implicit—and this is the rule—in all other biblical statements as the presupposition of what is directly expressed in them. The God of whom the prophets and apostles speak would not be God if he were not God the Creator at the beginning and God the Redeemer at the end. The man whom the biblical witnesses have in view as God's partner in this history would not be man if he were not under God's lordship from that beginning on to that end. And how could the history (especially this history) be history if it did not have a beginning and an end, this beginning and this end? Thus creation and redemption are indispensable elements in the biblical witness to this history. This is what, on a biblical basis, imperiously imposes on dogmatics (and in this context, ethics) the triple structure of a prologue, a main statement, and an epilogue. No one of these, not the prologue nor the epilogue, can be left out. In their own ways, all of them are of decisive significance for the whole of Christian knowledge and Christian confession. Only in its threeness is the totality the theme of the Christian message and Christian faith.

All the same, there can be no doubt that what the Old Testament and New Testament witnesses have directly before them is the history of the dealings and fellowship between God and man as such: always including (whether explicitly or only implicitly) the whence and the whither, but not (even in explicit references) the whence and the whither as such. If the whence and the whither of God's way with man are always in the field of vision, this field is not everywhere filled by these events as such.

The Old Testament deals with Yahweh's action and speech in relation to the men of his people and the problematical answer that these give to his action and speech. This answer is positive, corresponding to the purpose of Yahweh, only in the sense that their being and work is at all events confronted and engaged by his claim, decision, and judgment. From the standpoint of these men, it is always the answer of their unfaithfulness and disobedience. The Old Testament bears witness to the ensuing acts of this contradictory drama. Primarily in this form the biblical witness points back to the beginning of the history of God and man, to creation, which is above the contradiction and resists it from the very first.

In the New Testament witness this covenant history as the national history of Israel is replaced (or followed and completed) by covenant history as the history of Jesus Christ and in it the history of the race intended already in that national history.

Yahweh and Israel, God and man, are now alongside one another; indeed, they are one. The God who had glorified the covenant of his grace in the first form of his faithfulness to the many unfaithful men of Israel is the God who glorifies it now in its new form by introducing the one faithful and obedient Israelite in whom Israel's justification, sanctification, and vocation are unproblematically enacted by its God. And in the person of him who comes on the scene as the one Israelite who faithfully keeps the covenant with Israel there stands — in keeping with the sending of Israel to the whole world — the man in whom the whole human race is set in the light of God's grace and in relation to whom the whole human race is to be told that God's name is already hallowed in its midst, God's kingdom has already come, and God's will in and with it is already done. This history of completed fellowship between God and man, not merely commencing on one side but established on both, is the theme and content of the New Testament witness in strict unity with that of the Old Testament. And primarily in this form the biblical witness looks ahead to the goal of the history of God with man, to God the Redeemer and the man who is to be redeemed by him.

The witness to this history, or to the Word of God spoken and audible in it, may be found in the Bible side by side with the witness to its beginning and the witness to its goal. It does not cancel these, nor does it render them superfluous, but gives them their dignity, importance, and illuminating force. It does not merely stand in the middle of them, however, but forms the center around which they are only the necessary circumference. It is the main statement of the biblical message, the one that governs everything. As such it is inseparably joined to the statements about creation and redemption. It includes them. It thus points unmistakably back to the one and forward to the other, so that alongside and with it (whether explicitly or implicitly) they too are always made. But at every point they are made only as prologue and epilogue, as presupposition or implication of the main statement. What commands the original, direct, and decisive attention of the biblical witnesses in those two forms is the history of the covenant of grace. It is in the knowledge of this, as hearers of the Word of God spoken in this, that they always think and speak, even when they unfold their knowledge backwards and forwards. At its core their word is in the Old Testament the confession that Yahweh is Israel's God and Israel Yahweh's people, and in the New Testament the confession that Jesus is Kyrios, namely, the Messiah of Israel and as such the Redeemer of the world. From no biblical texts can we gather that the individual or collective authors thought in the reverse sequence, as though their statement about the history of the covenant of grace were important simply as the implication of an independently attained knowledge of creation or as the presupposition of an independently attained knowledge of redemption, of resurrection and eternal life in a future aeon; as though their witness were primarily and properly related to an Alpha or Omega of all things. This kind of shift in emphasis was reserved for later speculations (abstract mythologies of creation and redemption), which may always be recognized clearly enough as deviations from the biblical witness. An order of rank prevails in the biblical witness. According to this order, the statement about the history of God's covenant of grace certainly contains and states the other two. Yet it does not follow them but precedes them. It is the main, central statement of the biblical message. If dogmatics, and in this context ethics, is to be faithful to its orientation to Holy Scripture, it must stick to this, even though it may follow the order of the Creed, as we have done and are still doing.

With this insight, we regard the task of special ethics in the present chapter, in which we are dealing with the command of God the Reconciler, as its central task. Where God as the one who has reconciled the world to himself in Jesus Christ encounters man, who belongs to this world, as the one who has been reconciled to God in Jesus Christ, and where it is a matter of the commanding of God and the responsibility of man in this particular encounter, we stand as it were before the model of all that takes place between God and man. Whatever else may have to be seen is to be seen from this point. Whatever else may have to be said is to be said as the prologue or epilogue to the main statement which is to be made here.

Looking backward, then, we were not being arbitrary when in relation to the command of God the Creator we did all we could to provide a christological and soteriological foundation for all the relevant discussions. What can the Christian say that is true and important about the encounter between God the Creator and man his creature in its ethical character if he does not receive light from the point where this encounter may be seen as an event in the covenant of grace set up between God and man, and therefore in its primal form? And when we come to deal with the command of God the Redeemer in the third and last chapter of special ethics, we shall keep our eyes strictly on the priority of the problem we are now tackling.

It need only be pointed out in conclusion that in this field, if anywhere, the closest attention and care is required.

2. THE GRACIOUS GOD AS THE COMMANDING GOD

In this second section of our attempted introduction our task is to give a general and comprehensive sketch of the encounter between the commanding God and responsible man from the special standpoint of the divinely instituted covenant of grace. We shall later have to investigate and describe its detailed contours. So that we may not view the details under consideration capriciously, but according to the correctly determined basic line,[3] we need to begin with a survey of the whole. In what form are (1) God and (2) man to be considered and grasped according to the normative center of the biblical testimony? Of what kind (3) is the situation in which they encounter one another, especially from the standpoint of its ethical character? And what is it (4) that God requires of man in this situation, and what is to be done by man in obedience? These are the questions we must answer here in preparation for all that follows.

We are combining with them point by point at least an indication of the New Testament presuppositions of the answers that are to be given here, and ultimately of our whole undertaking.

The question is (1) that of the commanding God. Since this governs everything, it has to come first. But we are also asserting that this is an

[3]The TS originally added: "and according to the materially required selection, sequence, and meaning," but this was later erased.

answered question in Jesus Christ, exclusively in him, but in him clearly, solidly, exhaustively, and definitively; in him authentically and validly for all men of all times and places in the whole cosmos. For in him God has spoken and acted, still does so, and will do so again; in him God is active and manifest in his activity. Hence in the question of the commanding God we cannot look back behind him or forward ahead of him. There is no prior time in which the commanding God was not the one he is in Jesus Christ, and no later time in which he will not be so. He is never and nowhere any other than the God who acts and speaks in him. In him and through him he also commands. To encounter God is to encounter Jesus Christ. He who hears him hears God. To obey him is to obey God, to enter into his discipleship; not to obey him is not to obey God. In good or bad, wittingly or unwittingly, man is subject to *his* claim, *his* decision, and *his* judgment when he confronts God and is responsible to God.

He is "at the right hand of God," or, as Hebrews says (1:3; 8:1), "at the right hand of the Majesty on high" (μεγαλωσύνη). God's throne is also his, the Lamb's (Rev. 5:6). That is, *he* is God in the fulfilment of his divine will, the use of his divine power, the revelation of his divine purpose. To him God the Father has committed all things (Mt. 11:27; 28:18; Jn. 3:35; 13:3). Him he loved before the foundation of the world (Jn. 17:24). Through him the world came into being (Jn. 1:3, 10; 1 Cor. 8:6; Col. 1:16); through him as his mighty Word it is upheld (Heb. 1:3); and in him God has reconciled it to himself (2 Cor. 5:19; Col. 1:19f.). He, then, is the bread of life (Jn. 6:35), the good shepherd (Jn. 10:11), the light of the world (Jn. 8:12), the way, the truth, and the life (Jn. 14:6). All that belongs to the Father also belongs to him (Jn. 16:15; 17:10). The Father is in him and he in the Father (Jn. 10:38; 14:10); he and the Father are one (Jn. 10:30; 17:11). Those who see him see the Father who has sent him (Jn. 12:45; 14:9). Those who believe in him believe not only in him but also in him that sent him (Jn. 12:44). There is nothing that is not subject to him as to the Father (Heb. 2:8). To the glory of God the Father, he is the bearer of the name which is above every name and at the hearing of which every knee shall bow: the Lord Jesus Christ (κύριος Ἰησοῦς Χριστός, Phil. 2:9ff.). Thus the gospel in which he proclaims himself and in which the community proclaims him is as such the gospel of God (εὐαγγέλιον τοῦ θεοῦ, Mk. 1:14; Rom. 1:1). The kingdom of God can sometimes be called without reservation the kingdom of Christ (Col. 1:13; 2 Tim. 4:1; 2 Pet. 1:11). He himself is not just ἴσα θεῷ ὤν (Phil. 2:6), but also at times very simply and directly God (θεός, Jn. 1:1; Heb. 1:8, 9; Tit. 2:13). Undoubtedly God commands as he, Jesus Christ, commands.

The basic significance of this is that the commanding God is himself historical, that among and with and for and to men he acts and speaks as himself man. If we think we know him at a quiet distance, in the loftiness and silence of some divine beyond and apart, we do not know him at all. To seek God there is not to find him but to find another. It is not to find his commanding Word but to confuse it with human postulates. The God who is and acts, who makes himself known and commands in Jesus Christ, is the living God who for all his otherworldliness works in this world, in time. He is the Lord who lives in heaven but also on earth. He is the God who has disclosed himself and constantly does so in all the mystery of his

Godhead, moving out of naked Godhead and into the human world that was created by him, that is lost without him, and that is to be saved and renewed by him; confirming the lordship over it that was called into question by the arrogance, folly, falsehood, and the ensuing misery of man; and establishing his honor by giving himself to and for this world to its salvation. This action of his is the event in which God wills to be God and is God. Thus he is the God who comes in this will of his that no one and nothing can arrest or break, the God who is, and who is present to his creation, in this sovereign coming. Revealing and glorifying his name, maintaining and validating his right to this creation, he is the free and different and new God compared to all the truths it knows and acknowledges, compared to all the gods and forces that are at work in it and that it admires and fears and hates and venerates. In this new action he encounters man. To him who is engaged in this new action man becomes and is responsible. In this new action God commands, and he does so unmistakably and incontrovertibly.

That his eternal Word was made flesh and tabernacled among us (Jn. 1:14) means that the hour of God's new rule (βασιλεύειν) has dawned, filling time and teleologically determining all that is in it. His kingdom has drawn near. This means that he, seizing and using the power pertaining to the Creator, has in his own person closed in on man, and indeed the whole cosmos, in fulfilment of his superior will, putting an end to the evasions and digressions of the creature and making its conversion to him necessary (Mk. 1:15): ἔφθασεν ἐφ' ὑμᾶς (Mt. 12:28; Lk. 11:20). It means that as the Lord in the midst (ἐντὸς ὑμῶν, Lk. 17:21) he is irresistibly at work to create obedience to himself. Thus Jesus speaks as one who has power (Mk. 1:22, etc.). He frightens not only demons (Mk. 1:24, etc.) but also men (Mk. 5:15, etc.). He does not command repentance, faith, discipleship, and service merely in general terms, but he does so concretely in a way that can cause hurt, upsetting vested interests. He ruthlessly demands that his direct instructions be obeyed. The gospel of Jesus Christ includes the bitter chapter of Matthew 23, the accounts of the cursing of the fig tree (Mk. 11:12ff.), and the by no means gentle cleansing of the temple (Mk. 11:15f. and par.). Revelation 1:12−17 describes him as follows: "His feet were like burnished bronze, refined as in a furnace, and his voice was like the sound of many waters; . . . from his mouth issued a sharp two-edged sword, and his face was like the sun shining in full strength. When I saw him, I fell at his feet as though dead." As God's kingdom is his act, it is always and everywhere a new and free reality, his own reality that cannot be domesticated. Flesh and blood (man of and with his own will and power) cannot and will not ever inherit it, claiming it as its own possession and for its own use (1 Cor. 15:50). No one can or will ever take it by force (Mt. 11:12); we can only pray for its coming (Mt. 6:10). But again, as it is God's act, it has and is power (δύναμις, 1 Cor. 4:20), an unshakable exercise of dominion (Heb. 12:28). Like the seed the farmer entrusts to the earth, it grows of itself (αὐτομάτη, Mk. 4:28) without human cooperation. It is like the germinating grain victoriously competing with all other plants (Mk. 4:30ff.). Like a net cast in the sea, it reaches and gathers men of all kinds (Mt. 13:47f.). Like the little bit of leaven it permeates the whole lump (Mt. 13:33 and par.). Necessarily, like the treasure hid in the field, or the most valuable pearl (Mt. 13:44ff.), it casts all other goods in the shade. Whatever else man may expect or seek in fulfilment of legitimate needs, he will do it only in observance of this (irreversible) ranking—and only in this way (Mt. 6:33). For the King of this kingdom, who is at work on and among men in this seizure and exercise of power, is the King of kings and Lord of lords (1 Tim. 6:15 and par.), the Almighty (παντοκράτωρ, Rev. 1:8 and par.), to whom as such all owe everything, but who himself owes nothing. Thus none can precede him, nor bind him, nor put him under obligation (Rom. 11:35). His mind (νοῦς), the principle of his free will, decision, and action, is unsearchable (1 Cor. 2:10; Rom. 11:34); his judgments, being final, are unfathomable; and his ways, as he selects them, are incomprehensible (Rom. 11:33). He alone is and knows a priori. Hence in Hebrews (12:29) he, "our God," can be described as a "consuming fire." It can also be said (10:31) that it is fearful (φοβερόν) to fall into his hands, the hands of the living God. Note that this is said about God not by those who find the "Holy" or the "Fascinosum" in religion, but by the New Testament community. This is the God with whose commanding man has to deal precisely in the knowledge of the covenant of grace.

His ruling, however, is a definitely shaped and qualified action. To be sure, as it takes place and is revealed in Jesus Christ, it also has quite simply in its sovereignty[4] that no less fascinating than mysterious character of power. Nevertheless, we cannot stop for a moment at this statement. As we orient ourselves further to that being of God in Jesus Christ, the concept of the kingdom of God, of the divine seizure and exercise of power, of the commanding God himself, discloses itself to us at once in its unequivocally distinctive fulness. His powerful action is the great and active Yes of his free and gracious address to the world created by him, and to man who is at the heart of it. God reigns unequivocally by pronouncing this Yes and putting it into action in the instituting, upholding, executing, and fulfilling of his covenant with man. This takes place with right and power, but also with the concrete mind and purpose of him who is Lord of man but also man's Father and Brother. It thus takes place in opposition and conflict with man's alienation from God, from his fellows, and not least from himself. It resists man's fall from his true determination and nature. The coming of the kingdom of God certainly means the breaking of judgment on the man who violates it. Yet it does not strive against him but for him: against the perversion of his thinking and willing and being; against the darkness and confusion of his situation; against the destruction of his whole creaturely being of which man is guilty because of his transgression but by which he is also punished and smitten; against the power of chaos and nothingness to which he has delivered himself up and to whose threat he is exposing all creation. God is wrathful with him because he is so urgently concerned about him. He judges man because his fall violates God's own honor and carries with it man's perdition. He judges him by rushing powerfully to his aid to create right for him, that is, to put him in the right against all forces, and not least of all, but decisively, himself, to acquit him, and to save him from corruption, so that man may not be lost but live for ever through him, in inaugurated fellowship with him, and therefore for him. He thus judges him to his salvation. This is what takes place in the mighty proclamation

---

[4]TS: "its sovereignty also has quite simply that fascinating character of power."

of his name, the mighty coming of his kingdom, the mighty doing of his will on earth as in heaven. The righteousness of his kingdom is something totally inconceivable from man's standpoint. What takes place with it is for man something absolutely new and unexpected. For man is not worthy that God should speak this Yes to him and put it in action. He has not earned this; he cannot do it himself nor help to make it true and actual. There takes place here the work of the almighty grace of God. God himself in free goodness gives himself to and for him, taking his place, the place where man could only perish before him, making good what he did badly in order that man might be able to be and remain his man and to be made totally new. The Yes that God speaks to him and puts into action has its basis only in God himself, only in his resolve and purpose, only in his willing in no circumstances to be God merely in isolation and therefore without man, only in his willing in all circumstances to be God only in fellowship with man, the God who is holy precisely in his grace and righteous precisely in his mercy. He sets up his covenant and upholds it and carries it to its goal by justifying man before himself, sanctifying him for himself, and calling him to his side in his service. The friendship with which he answers man's enmity consists in his making man for his part his friend. He thus reconciles man to himself. The fascinating and mysterious power of the dawning of his hour, the rude incursion of his kingdom, serves this reconciling. It is in this form, manner, and purpose — no other — that he is Pantokrator, the Almighty. The God who rules thus in Jesus Christ, the gracious God, is the God who commands.

"The times of ignorance God overlooked, but now he commands all men everywhere to repent, because he has fixed a day on which he will judge the world in righteousness by a man whom he has appointed," says Paul in Athens (Acts 17:30f.). "He will baptize you with the Holy Spirit and with fire. His winnowing fork is in his hand, and he will clear his threshing floor and gather his wheat into the granary, but the chaff he will burn with unquenchable fire," says John the Baptist according to Matthew 3:11f. Obviously, Jesus came as Judge, comes as Judge, and will come again as Judge in his final, universal, and definitive manifestation: to kindle a fire on earth (Lk. 12:49) and to bring a sword (Mt. 10:34). But equally clearly the judgment he has executed, and is still to execute, has very definitely a positive meaning and purpose. "God sent the Son into the world, not to condemn the world, but that the world might be saved through him" (Jn. 3:17; cf. 12:47). And clearly again what is judged by him, burned with fire, and slain with the sword is the sin that remains in the flesh (ἐν [τῇ] σαρϰί), the race and humanity in their alienation from God (Rom. 8:3). And no less clearly the manner and purpose of his judging, burning, and slaying is that "he himself bore our sins in his body on the tree, that we might die to sin and live to righteousness" (1 Pet. 2:24); or, more strongly: "[God] made him to be sin who knew no sin, so that in him we might become the righteousness of God" (2 Cor. 5:21); or, if possible, even more strongly: "Christ redeemed us from the curse of the law, having become a curse for us" (Gal. 3:13). He judges, burns, and slays as the Lamb of God, who takes to himself, bears, and bears away the sin of the world (Jn. 1:29). He judges the enmity of man against God in his own flesh (Eph. 2:14). He judges by giving his body, himself, as a ransom (λύτρον) for many (Mk. 10:45 and par.). He judges as the ἱλαστήριον (Rom. 3:25) provided by God himself, as the expiation (ἱλασμός) for our sins, and not for ours only but for the sins of the whole world (1 Jn. 2:2). He judges, then, not in victorious feud with sinful man, nor as the avenger of his fall and offenses, but by separating man from his sin and therefore from his shame and corruption. By God's will he rescues him from the present wicked aeon (Gal. 1:4), reconciling him, God's enemy, and the whole alienated cosmos to its Lord (Rom. 5:9, 11; 2 Cor. 5:18; Col. 1:20, 22). He destroys the works of the devil (1 Jn. 3:8) and opens the gates of death and Hades (Rev. 1:18). He frees those who in fear of death were slaves all their lives (Heb. 2:15), and he opens up for them access to the Father (Eph. 2:18; cf. Rom. 5:2). "By the grace of God he tasted death (ὑπὲρ παντός) for every one" (Heb. 2:9). It is thus that he judges. Hence his message, and the message about him, is not a mixture of εὐαγγέλιον and δυσαγγέλιον, but in the telos of all it says it is unequivocally εὐαγγέλιον, the message of the grace of his judgment: "He has anointed me to preach good news to the poor. He has sent me to proclaim release to the captives, and recovering of sight to the blind, to set at liberty those who are oppressed, to proclaim the acceptable year of the Lord" (Lk. 4:18f.). "He went about doing good and healing all that were oppressed by the devil" (Acts 10:38), for "he is Lord of all" (οὗτός ἐστιν πάντων κύριος), as we read in the same context (v. 36). It is thus that God was and is in Jesus Christ. Therefore, we may read from the same slate who and what he, the commanding God, is. It is true, and should not be suppressed, that whether the world accepts it or not he judges the world (Rom. 3:6), even to the most hidden things of men (Rom. 2:16) and without being led astray by the apparent differences between men (Rom. 2:11; 1 Pet. 1:17). It is true that in this judgment his Word is sharper and more cutting than a two-edged sword (Heb. 4:12f.). It is true that every plant he has not planted will be rooted up (Mt. 15:13). But he is the God of the Jews *and* of the Gentiles (Rom. 3:29), and he judges through Jesus Christ (Rom. 2:16) and therefore according to the gospel. His righteousness revealed in the gospel (Rom. 1:17) is not the empty distributive justice of a world judge scrutinizing, assessing, rewarding, and punishing people from a distance. Rather, it consists of his own work in the establishment of his divine right and therefore in assisting, protecting, and helping the right of mankind against all his near and distant enemies, and primarily against the nearest of them all, namely, himself. As the righteous one, the δίκαιος δικαιῶν (Rom. 3:26) acts in this way: God is who he is. He loves the world (Jn. 3:16) in defiance of it, and therefore in consuming and killing love, yet not to its merited hurt but to its unmerited salvation. In this way he confirms, renews, and empowers his covenant. His perfection (Mt. 5:48) is that he meets his enemies in this way (Rom. 5:10), causing his sun to shine on the good and the bad and his rain to fall on the just and the unjust (Mt. 5:45). He is not just occasionally but essentially — not just partially but totally — love (1 Jn. 4:8, 16). His distinctive divine goodness and lovingkindness (χρηστότης καὶ φιλανθρωπία) appeared (Tit. 3:4), his disciplining grace to all men (Tit. 2:11f.), for in himself he is no other and nothing other than the (one) God our Savior (θεὸς σωτήρ, 1 Tim. 1:1; Jude 25), "the Father of mercies and God of all comfort" (2 Cor. 1:3), "the God of peace" (Rom. 15:33, etc.), and therefore "the God of hope" (Rom. 15:13). "He who did not spare his own Son but gave him up for us all, will he not also give us all things with him?" (Rom. 8:32). This God, the gracious God, is the commanding God.

A final point along these lines is that there is in God's act in Jesus Christ, whether in its character as an act of power or its character as an act of grace, no trace of caprice, contingency, or mutability. No nonbeing corresponds to his divine being; nonbeing can be only meaninglessly and unsuccessfully ascribed or attributed to him. His act, and in his act his being, is that of the absolutely reliable God who is faithful to himself, and therefore to creation and man. God in Christ is the God who rules out and makes totally impossible any doubt, uncertainty, or mistrust in relation to himself, since there is in him no basis for this. For he is the one God (1 Cor. 8:5f.), beside whom there are many lords and gods but no other God, so that in face of him there may be caprice on man's side but there can be only one right choice, the true and practicable choice that corresponds to his own choosing and electing. He is also the true God, that is, the one who, without needing to demonstrate his Word by the standard of other words, speaks directly and incontrovertibly for himself as none of those other lords does or can do. No one can take up the stance apart from him that would be needed for a discussion of his reality, power, and grace. To discuss—and even to deny—these is not really to have them in view but to be talking about the reality of those other supposed lords and gods. No theoretical or practical atheism or polytheism can have him in view or touch or affect him—his being, power, or grace. One can think and will and talk past him; this is constantly done without his Word and the power of his Spirit. The sin that brings man's misery, both at its root and also in all its forms, is that of trying to slip by God on a thousand secret paths. But no one can do this, not even the worst and most deliberate and hardened sinner, idolater, or ungodly person. For there is none to whom he has not come first, long before the flight began. There is none whom he does not precede from all eternity. Even for the wildest atheists and believers in demons, and for them unrestrictedly and unchangeably, he is the one he is in his power and grace. In relation to him there may be all kinds of atheistic and polytheistic experiments and games, but these cannot touch, let alone change, either what he is in himself or what he is for the world and man. He is special and different for each man and in each time and situation for each man, but he is never other than himself for any man or in any time or situation of any man. The multiplicity of his ways is endless, but his will and resolve in all his ways is one and the same. Hence one can and should and must count on it that God makes no mistakes, that his power never fails, even though it be ever so deeply hidden—and when is it not?—that his grace can never yield or fall, even though it be felt and experienced ever so slightly or not at all. And who among us can boast of always feeling it, of ever having experienced it in all its depth? There are riches in God, but no antithesis, contradiction, or dialectic. Thus we can count on it that his action in the glorifying of his name, the coming of his kingdom, and the doing of his will, will never break off. Even though it be in the most alien form and manner, it will always continue as the living and life-giving basis of every relation to him, even the most inconstant, the most broken, and the most negative. Always and everywhere he will be for everyone the one he wills to be according to his good pleasure, but always the one he is, in the power of his grace and the grace of his power. This faithful God is in Jesus Christ. As the one true God, he is also the God who commands.

He is the θεὸς ἄφθαρτος (1 Tim. 1:17), "the Father of lights with whom there is no variation or shadow due to change" (Jas. 1:17). As Paul told the volatile Athenians, "he is not far from each one of us, for in him [i.e., in his sphere] we live and move and have our being" (Acts 17:27f.). His kingdom is impregnable (Heb. 12:28), and his gifts and grace and calling are irrevocable (Rom. 11:29); for he is himself essentially πιστός: faithful, constant, and reliable. As such he is credible, the limit of all the temptation that overtakes us (1 Cor. 10:13); faithful even when we are unfaithful (2 Tim. 2:13), and therefore greater than our heart that condemns us (1 Jn. 3:20), so that he will strengthen us and keep us from evil (2 Thess. 3:3). Because he is faithful, the word of the apostle cannot be Yes *and* No (2 Cor. 1:18). The basis and source of all these statements is clear. It is not to be found in any certainty or constancy of any faith in God, love of God, hope in God, or abstract speculation about God, of which those who speak thus about God might boast. God's Son, Jesus Christ, is not Yes *and* No, but what took place in him was simply Yes. The promises of God given to us in him are Yes and Amen (2 Cor. 1:19f.). He was before Abraham was (Jn. 8:58). He became a man and lived and suffered and rose again in time, but he was in the beginning (ἐν ἀρχῇ) with God (Jn. 1:1f.). What was executed in his existence was God's eternal choice and πρόθεσις before the foundation of the world (Acts 2:23; 1 Pet. 1:20; Eph. 1:4). He did what he did once for all (ἄπαξ, ἐφάπαξ, Rom. 6:10; 1 Pet. 3:18; Heb. 7:27; 9:26; 10:10). It took place in his death that all things were fulfilled (παντά[5] τετέλεσται, Jn. 19:28, 30). Yesterday, today, and for ever he is the same, αὐτός (Heb. 13:8). The priestly office is unchanging, in whose fulfilment he can fully (εἰς τὸ παντελές) save those who come to God by him, ever living to represent them (Heb. 7:24f.). Thus "Amen" is his name as the "true and faithful witness" (Rev. 3:14; cf. 19:11) to whom God for his part bears his sure and certain testimony (1 Jn. 5:9). He, the one Mediator between God and man (1 Tim. 2:5), is as such the Guarantor and Revealer of the one true God and therefore of the faithful God. And this God is the commanding God.

We now come (2) to the man who is responsible to this commanding God. Here again we must begin by stating that this is the question that is answered in Jesus Christ. One cannot emphasize enough that in him true man as well as true God is present and manifest. There is no abstract humanity and therefore no correspondingly abstract human self-understanding. Man is no more, no less, no other than what he is through and with and for Jesus Christ. Authentic (as distinct from all fictional) and assured (as distinct from all hypothetical) human understanding is that in which man knows, sees, and understands who and what he is on the basis of Jesus Christ, together with him, and in orientation to him. For in Christ he is constituted as man by God, he is claimed by God, decision is made by God concerning him, and he is judged by God. Without Christ he would not be man at all. The first and last word about man as well as God is spoken in him. He who hears this word knows man, naturally not just himself personally, but with himself his fellow man who perhaps does not hear this word or hear it correctly—every man, man as such. In this word it is seen as in a mirror who and what man was as God's creature and

[5]MS and TS: τὰ πάντα.

therefore in his original human nature, who and what he still secretly is, and also who and what he will be as a child of God in the consummation of the work of God: who and what he already secretly is. In this word there may be seen primarily and centrally, however, who and what he now is in the middle between that beginning and that end of his existence, participating as God's partner in the history of the covenant of grace instituted and executed by God. What would we know of the covenant of grace, and of man as God's partner in its history, if we knew nothing of Jesus Christ? In him the history begins and proceeds. He, or God through him, makes man a partner in this covenant. Together with him, as one whom God has set at his side and exalted to be his brother, man is this partner of God. He is so in order to serve God by serving Jesus Christ. In his history God acts exemplarily and fruitfully on and to all men. So each man as such — not just the man who knows him but also the man who scarcely knows him or knows him not at all — has a part in his history and without it would have no history of his own. He could not know his own history as human (in distinction from purely natural) history apart from his share in the history of Jesus Christ. As the true God is the God who is and acts and reveals himself in Jesus Christ, so true man is the man who is bound to him and set over against him in Jesus Christ. He is the man about whom we are asking — the man who is responsible to the commanding God.

As in the New Testament — and in a different way but in the same sense the same may also be said of the Old Testament — there is no general picture of God, so there is no general picture of man, formed in arbitrary abstraction: there is no man responsible to God who is defined and described and addressed, no man who is interesting, apart from his confrontation with the gracious God, that is, concretely, with Jesus Christ. In this confrontation, and in no other way, man is what he is. The New Testament is exclusively the document of the history of man sharing in some way, closely or at a distance, on the right hand or the left, in the history of Jesus Christ. It sees and measures man by what God is and has done and still does for him in Jesus Christ. In this variously ordered relation to him man is noteworthy and interesting inasmuch as every other understanding of man that might possibly be maintained is completely overshadowed by it. "The old has passed away" (2 Cor. 5:17). This is true in its own way of the man who in the New Testament does not recognize Jesus Christ, is not bound by faith to him, and is opposed to him in unbelief: even the Pharisees and scribes, even the men of the obstinate synagogue, even the Samaritans, and later the men in the wider world of the nations, Judas and false teachers in the community, even Pilate who condemned Jesus and the soldiers who tortured and killed him. "From now on, therefore, we regard no one from a human point of view" (2 Cor. 5:16): no one according to the measure of a general human understanding or the standard of the manner in which he understands and presents himself; all are what they are or are not in a circle around him. Naturally this is true especially of the men who dominate the New Testament field of vision, who, awakened to knowledge of faith in him, become his disciples and apostles, or are summoned into his community by them. It is of these men that the New Testament writings speak and to them that they are addressed. This is done on the clear presupposition that they are to be addressed on the basis of the fact that their existence — this is why they are and are called Christians — stands or falls with that of Jesus Christ, with what he is for them, with the model of his obedience, suffering, and love, with his life and death and resurrection, and with his self-declaration. They have not chosen him, but he has chosen them (Jn. 15:16). He did not do it today or yesterday but before the foundation of the world (Eph. 1:4). They live as they put him on (Rom. 13:14), as they eat his flesh and drink his blood (Jn. 6:53), as he lives in them so that the only thing for them to do is to believe in him (Gal. 2:20), as they do not live, then, to themselves but to him (2 Cor. 5:15). His death includes theirs, his resurrection theirs (Rom. 6:3f.). He is in them and they in him (Jn. 14:20). He is the vine and they are the branches that without him[6] can do nothing (Jn. 15:5). So they know themselves only as and so far as they know that he is in them (2 Cor. 13:5). In the New Testament this is said directly of these men only. It speaks of the special relation into which they—and provisionally only they—are put by the awakening, quickening, and enlightening Holy Spirit. But the history of Jesus Christ, to which that of Christians stands in this special relation, is not a divine segregation in favor of these men, and their history in its special relation to his is not a private or group affair. These men now exist in the context of the uniting (ἀνακεφαλαίωσις) of all things, which has taken place in Jesus Christ (Eph. 1:10). He to whom they are called by the power of the Holy Spirit, and with whom they may stand in that special relation, is he in whom God has created not only them but the whole cosmos and all men within it (Jn. 1:3, etc.). He is the image of the invisible God and also the πρωτότοκος or archetype of all creation (Col. 1:15), the offering for the sins of the whole world (1 Jn. 2:2); the one—yet not the only one, but the first—the firstfruits of the endless host of the dead (Col. 1:18). As such he is the one to whom all power belongs in heaven and on earth (Mt. 28:18; Phil. 2:9f.; Eph. 1:21), the light which shines on all men (Jn. 1:9), the Son to whom the Father has given power over all flesh (Jn. 17:2). "Come to me, all who labor and are heavy-laden" (Mt. 11:28) is his message. For the community which is the body of this Head, this means that it is filled by him who fills all in all (τὰ πάντα ἐν πᾶσιν, Eph. 1:23). It cannot want to be an end in itself; it exists "for the praise of the glory" of God (Eph. 1:12), in the sign—the manner and function—of the angel which, flying in the zenith, has to proclaim the everlasting message of peace to all nations, tribes, languages, and people (Rev. 14:6). The people gathered in it, that is, Christians are "brought . . . forth by the word of truth," "redeemed from mankind as the first fruits" (ἀπαρχή) of the creatures of God for him and for the Lamb (Jas. 1:18; Rev. 14:4). This means that in their special relation to Jesus Christ they are pro-totypes, examples, and representatives, anticipating the true being of all men who are not yet as they are but will be, anticipating that which they already are before God according to his will and resolve from all eternity, namely, those who are adopted into fellowship with his Son (1 Cor. 1:9). In the light of his special relation to Jesus Christ, in analogy to it, the Christian has no option but to see and under-stand and define and describe the non-Christian, man as such, in this way. Only on the assumption that Jesus Christ is his Lord too can he approach his fellow man. He can wish to have dealings with him only as a designated brother. That this other does not hear the voice of Jesus Christ, or alleges he does not hear it, in no way alters the fact that he belongs to him. That he does not accept him in no way alters the fact that he too is his possession, to which Jesus Christ is coming (Jn. 1:11). The decision concerning his true human being was taken from all eternity and also in time on Golgotha, long before he is ready (or not ready) to recognize it and to honor it with his own decision. Thus the Christian view of man in all its particularity is

---

[6]MS and TS: "without whom they"

basic and normative for the view of man in general and as such. What the Christian knows about himself he has to attest to the non-Christian as valid also for him, namely, that Jesus Christ is the origin and goal of his existence too. This characterizes every man as a man who is responsible to the gracious God.

If we understand the situation of human existence in terms of Christian existence, we infer that the man who is responsible to the gracious God is the man who is affirmed and loved and elected by God. He is so either actually or virtually as a member of the people or community of God. He lives by what God is, by what he is in the word of his grace for this people and therefore also for him. He thus lives by God's eternal mercy, whose power is that God, faithful to his affirmation, love, and election, has in the freedom of his lovingkindness made him also free. To have freed him is to have reconciled him to himself; to have reconciled him is to have justified him so that he can stand before him; to have sanctified him, so that he can live with and for him; and to have called him, so that he can serve him as his witness. He has the freedom to be this man who is justified before God, sanctified for him, and called by him. He has only this freedom — everything else called freedom is unfreedom — but he really has it. He has it in the fulfilment of his destiny by creation whereby he is from God and to God. He has it in the order of his being by creation whereby he is fellow man of fellow man. He has it as the content of his structure by creation as soul of his body. He has it as the meaning of his existence by creation in his restricted time. Whoever he may be, he has it in all circumstances, in every conceivable condition and situation in which he may find himself. As man he is always and everywhere to be addressed in terms of it. He may and can be this man, and as he makes use of this freedom, he is this man. He does not have this freedom of himself, however; he has it only as God's gift. He thus has it independently of the degree to which he recognizes it, or practices it, or honors it, and above all independently of the degree to which he experiences, feels, and discovers it. He has it through and with and for Jesus Christ. But through and with and for him he has it — and has it inalienably. For in him, in the power of what God in him has willed and has done, and wills and does for man, he is the man whom God has affirmed. He as such is the man who is confronted by the gracious God and is responsible to him, the God who commands him.

"By the grace of God I am what I am" (1 Cor. 15:10). "I live; yet not I, but Christ lives in me" (Gal. 2:20 KJV). People of this kind are known by God before they know him (Gal. 4:9; 1 Cor. 8:3; 13:12); they are loved by him before they love him (1 Jn. 4:10); they are reconciled with him even when they are enemies (Rom. 5:10). Thus the righteousness of God — the establishment and execution of the right which God has to all men, and therefore to them too, and which all men, and therefore they too, have before him and through him — is theirs freely (δωρεάν, Rom. 3:24). They are not saved by their own power; God's free gift saves them, not the merit of their works; hence no one can boast (Eph. 2:8). Their sanctification is that they can have their origin in God with Jesus Christ who sanctifies them — that Jesus Christ is not ashamed to call them brethren (Heb. 2:11) They are clean through the Word he has spoken to them (Jn. 15:3). As he has given them the power for it, they become the children of God (Jn. 1:12). As such they have and retain peace. Peace, which is coupled with grace in apostolic greetings (Rom. 1:7, etc.), means their being before God with their fellows and themselves according to the order of the divine grace of reconciliation. This ordered being is the root of their freedom as the basic and comprehensive determination of their attitude and action. It is the freedom of those who are justified before God, sanctified for him, and called to his service: their freedom to exist as such, and no other freedom but this authentic freedom. The truth, that is, God's Son, which is its creative ground, makes them free (Jn. 8:32, 36). They become and are free only where the Spirit of the Lord is, because where the Spirit of the Lord is, there is freedom (2 Cor. 3:17). These men are called into this freedom. They are not private people. They stand in public service. They are called into this service in order to be the salt of the earth and the light of the world (Mt. 5:13f.), in order to "declare the wonderful deeds of him who called you out of darkness into his marvelous light" (1 Pet. 2:9), in order to put their persons (their bodies, σώματα) at God's disposal as "a living sacrifice, holy and acceptable to God" (Rom. 12:1), in order that, "bought with a price," they may "glorify God" in their bodies (1 Cor. 6:20). We note the plural in all these and similar passages. The people in them are certainly individuals, but they are so as those who are called to peace and freedom by grace. As individuals they are members of the body of Jesus Christ, living stones built up with many others into him, *the* living stone. Because they are in fellowship with him, they are in fellowship with all the others who are comforted and exhorted and responsible with them, with all the other members of a "chosen race, a royal priesthood, a holy nation, God's own people," which as such shares the grace of God, peace with him, and freedom for him, and thus carries his commission in the world (1 Pet. 2:4f., 9). We do not forget that all these things are ascribed to believers. The man who knows Jesus Christ, who is awakened to the obedience of faith (Rom. 1:5) and perseveres in it, the apostle, the Christian, is the man of this kind. These passages, then, refer to Christian people, the members of the community. If, however, Christians are to understand themselves as firstfruits (ἀπαρχή), we cannot avoid the conclusion that in and with what is said primarily and directly to them, and to them alone, there is said something prophetically, exemplarily, and proleptically about the whole race as Christ's people *in spe* (in hope) and therefore about everyone. All men are to be addressed in anticipation precisely in terms of the special responsibility of Christians.

That man is what he is through the Yes of God's grace means, of course, that he is not worthy to be affirmed and loved and elected by God, to be reconciled by him, to be justified, sanctified, and called, to have and to retain peace, to be a free man. He stands in absolute need that all this should happen to him. It happens to him that he may be this man apart from and even in opposition to his own deserts and capacities, in and in spite of his impotence, even though he is not worthy of it but completely unworthy. As it happens to him, it may be seen who and what he is and would have had to remain if it had not happened to him, the enemy of God, his neighbor, and himself, completely unrighteous and unholy and uncalled, without peace, not free but bound. If by God's grace he may accept God's Yes and live by it, he obviously finds himself accused of being one who apart from this and in himself deserved and could receive only God's No, under whose consuming force he would have perished. It is not abstract law, but rather the event in which reconciliation, peace, and freedom are secured, the saving judgment in which God establishes and executes his own right and that of man. It is the redeeming death and passion in which Jesus Christ—the one obedient one—has as the Lamb of God taken to himself and borne away the sin of the world and of everyman. This is also the fearful revelation of sin and the unequivocal assertion that man does not owe its pardon or his adoption as a child of God in any way to himself. In this connection it should also be noted that the grace of God—as grace totally without man's cooperation or merit, in the royal freedom of the pure goodness of God—could not really and effectively come upon man without his at once being genuinely shown up and exposed for the first time in all the inappropriateness of his response, in all the shattering poverty of his thanks, in all the inaccessibility of his attitude to the gift of peace and his use of the freedom that is promised and made available to him. He finds himself shown up in the dubious way in which, obscuring and even obfuscating everything, he is what he may be, and really is, by the grace of God: the man justified, sanctified, and called by him. Must not and will not precisely the Christian acknowledge, recognize, and confess that after what has been done and has taken place once and for all for the world—and therefore for him too—in the death and passion of Jesus Christ, he can never lift up hands that are any other than very weak, very dirty, and always very empty? How can the one who can boast earnestly, sincerely, and in full assurance of the grace of God that has come to him, take any pleasure in knowing or boasting about his corresponding being and thought and action? Would he have a true understanding of himself if even for a moment he could forget or secretly deny that what has happened and still happens to him is God's free grace in the face of which he must renounce—indeed, may gladly renounce—all glory of his own? Can he truly understand himself, and be in truth the one he is, without humbly but resolutely accepting this renunciation again and again, putting himself in the place where with other sinners he can only look to God's grace and pray for it? The people who knows and acts thus in relation to the grace of God is the people elected, loved, and affirmed by him. The one who as a member of this people is forced to recognize and ready to confess his solidarity with all other sinners is the man who is responsible to the God who commands him.

No unprejudiced reader of the New Testament can miss the fact that when it presents the man of the fall, of unbelief, sin, and transgression, it has in view almost exclusively the man of the community, Christian man, except when it follows the line of the Old Testament prophets and speaks of Israel's transgression, as John's Gospel does when it refers to the Jews. To be sure, the whole world is in the power of the evil one (1 Jn. 5:19). It is corrupt by nature. This is always presupposed and is evident enough, for example, in the visions of judgment in Revelation. Sometimes it is dramatically portrayed, as in the figure of Pilate in the Gospels, or of Herod in Acts (12:21ff.), or, again in Acts, of Elymas the sorcerer (13:8ff.), or of the Ephesians who shouted for two whole hours about the greatness of their goddess Diana (19:23ff.). Nevertheless, it is an exception when Romans 1:18–32 specifically mentions it as a subsidiary theme, remarkably without expressly naming the nations (ἔθνη) or Hellenes (Ἕλληνες), although undoubtedly with reference to them, just as the reference is to the Jews in 2:1ff. The New Testament knows very fully and with great exactitude what goes on outside, but basically it does not look or talk through the window (*"You* who are evil," Mt. 7:11). For the New Testament writers the interesting sinner is not the worldly man but the Christian: Peter, who is not on God's side but man's and has to be rebuked (Mk. 8:33); Peter again, whose conversion is not behind him but still ahead (Lk. 22:31ff.), and who is well able to deny his Lord; Judas, who is elected and called like the other disciples but who betrays the Lord (Mk. 14:44f.); the hardened hearts of the disciples (Mk. 6:52; 8:17), who forget so easily of what Spirit they are children (Lk. 9:55), who, when Jesus speaks about the traitor, all very remarkably have to ask: Is it I? (Mk. 14:19), and who all leave him and flee when the passion comes (Mk. 14:50), especially the naked youth who is perhaps to be identified as the evangelist Mark (14:51f.). They and not the crowds (ὄχλοι) of Galilee who are addressed as a "faithless and perverse generation" ("how long am I to be with you and bear with you?" Lk. 9:41). Even in the epistles the apostle is no saint but one who is always coming back to the fact that he originally persecuted the community (1 Cor. 15:9, etc.). And the people who transgress the Ten Commandments, and who are vividly portrayed in the lists of vices, are not worldlings but Christians. It is not pagan but Christian Corinth that is attacked. The reference is not to the Hellenistic philosophers and mystery devotees of the age but to enthusiasts, sectarians, false teachers, pseudo-apostles, nomists, antinomists, Judaizers, syncretists, and all the more or less blatant and recognizable "enemies of the cross of Christ" (Phil. 3:18) who live and work in the community, in the honest or dishonest view that they belong to it and should speak in its name. According to the New Testament, judgment begins in the house of God (1 Pet. 4:17). The apostle finds sin dwelling in himself (Rom. 7:17, 21). Woe to the Christian who says he has no sin, for he leads himself astray, the truth is not in him, and he makes Jesus Christ a liar (1 Jn. 1:8ff.). Connected with this is the fact that in the New Testament man himself and as such is accused and condemned with the offensive sharpness which always distinguishes Christian thinking about mankind, when it is true to itself, from all non-Christian thinking. "Sin came into the world through one man" (Rom. 5:12); by his disobedience many, that is, all, are made sinners (5:19). "Every man is false" (Rom. 3:4). "All men . . . are under the power of sin" (3:9). "None is righteous, no, not one; no one understands; no one seeks for God. All have turned aside, together they have gone wrong; no one does good, not even one" (3:10ff.). "There is no distinction . . . all have sinned and fall short of the glory of God" (3:22f.). "No human being can boast in the presence of God" (1 Cor. 1:29). He who boasts can boast only in the Lord (v. 31; 2 Cor. 10:17), or boast only of the evidences of his own weakness (2 Cor. 11:30; 12:9), or boast that mercy has been shown him (2 Cor. 4:1). Hence the response, "Father, I have sinned against heaven and before you; I am no longer worthy to be called your son; treat me as one of your hired servants" (Lk. 15:18f.). The Christian knows and says this first and decisively about himself and only then about others. In relation to its own humanity the community confesses that it lies under this judgment. Only as it precedes the world in bowing under judgment does it have the insight and courage that permit it and command it to proclaim that the judgment applies to all. Nor does it do this in ethical pessimism and defeatism, but in the knowledge of the reconciling grace of God which has come to it and therefore as an example to the world. In repenting it has in its ears the "I say unto you" (Mt. 5:22, etc.) which opens up the kingdom of heaven and leaves all legalistic zeal behind. As it repents it sees the event of salvation in the event of the crucifixion of Jesus Christ. It proclaims the revelation of the wrath of God as the reverse side of the revelation of his righteousness which creates order, peace, and freedom (Rom. 1:17f.). Primarily this is an unmasking of the unbelief, disobedience, and transgression of which it knows it is itself guilty, and with it all men. By this, its own boasting and that of all men is shattered. In it, judgment is executed on humanity and therewith the sentence concerning it is spoken. In the light of the event of Golgotha the only option for the Christian and for all men is the confession of the prodigal son or the prayer of the publican: "God, be merciful to me a sinner" (Lk. 18:13). The man for whom this is the only option is the man who is responsible to the gracious God who commands him.

But if this is not the first thing to be said about man, neither is it the last; for as the fact that man is condemned and judged by God is not the original and basic determination of his existence, neither is it the last and definitive determination. It is not true that he is now determined by his unbelief and disobedience, that he has left the dominion of the gracious God, that he has excluded himself from the covenant with him, that he can no longer respond to the grace addressed to him, that he is released from responsibility to God. Nor is it true that his existence is now to be seen and understood — in a poor interpretation of the slogan "at the same time both sinner and righteous" (*simul iustus et peccator*) — as one which is two-sided, ambivalent, and fluctuating in the light of the grace of God on the one hand, and the shadow of his own sin on the other, so that there may be ascribed to him only a partial and limited responsibility for his own being and acts. We cannot restrict in this way the lordship of Jesus Christ, through whom, with whom, and for whom man is who he is. As man's contradiction and fall take place in relationship to God, he cannot emancipate himself from God and posit himself absolutely over against him. The lordship of Christ in its positive nature and character too — and in these especially — is as superior to man as is the eternal will and counsel of God which is executed in it. Man's contradiction and fall do not limit it, but it limits them. They do not triumph over it, either partially or totally, but it over them. No matter how gross and serious man's sin may be, the grace addressed to him is per se greater and more weighty. It qualifies and characterizes his transgression as something that in all its gravity and horror is still an episode. It is the free grace of the faithful God which, as it is not evoked by the being and work of man, cannot be destroyed or even restricted by him. It goes before man on his way and also overtakes him to go before him again. It does not leave him to the meaninglessness and misdeeds of which he is guilty on the way. But neither does it allow him to come to terms with the meaninglessness of his existence or to persist and continue in his misdeeds. It is the same on both sides of the incident, on both sides an offer and the gift of a new beginning [TS: "task"], on both sides the promise, hope, comfort, admonition, life, and power which forbid and make impossible for man all the doubt and frivolity that arise. Grace is God's superior answer to man's sin. It is salvation from even the deepest and final lostness, for it is the grace of Jesus Christ. As such it is the creation and revelation of the man who at the same time *was* the sinner and *will be* righteous. In sum, the man who, as the great sinner he is, is visited tirelessly and inescapably with strict kindness and kind strictness by the God who encompasses him on every side, is the man who is responsible to God as his commanding God.

As the Christian sees and understands every other man in his own person as a believer, man is the prodigal son who, keeping swine in the far country and wanting their food, comes to himself, is seen by his father coming home even when "he was yet at a distance," has been dead but is alive again, has been lost but is found (Lk. 15:16ff.). He is the man who, as his heart accuses and must accuse him, cannot alter the fact that God is greater than his heart (1 Jn. 3:20), that his own unfaithfulness cannot erase God's faithfulness (Rom. 3:3), that even his unrighteousness must confirm God's righteousness and his lie God's truth (Rom. 3:5, 7). He is the man in the face of whose mighty sin God's grace is even mightier (Rom. 5:20)—not because at its root the sin is really not so bad or dangerous after all, nor because he can contest its character as pride, sloth, and falsehood, nor because he can break its power or at least relativize it conceptually. Rather, it is because man, miserable man, whom no one and nothing can redeem from his being of death (Rom. 7:24), has even in this deepest of depths no one and nothing to fear, no ever-so-righteous accusation or merited destruction. This is because Jesus Christ, who gave himself and died and rose again for him, is at the right hand of God and intercedes for him, because he cannot be separated from his love and therefore from God's love; for, no matter how it may stand with him, God is not against him but for him (Rom. 8:31–39). Jesus came specifically to call sinners (Mk. 2:17), to seek and to save the lost (Lk. 19:10): the lost sheep, the lost coin, the lost son (15:3ff., 8ff., 11ff.). He received publicans as sinners and ate with them (Lk. 15:2). When we were still sinners, he died for us (Rom. 5:8); when we were still God's enemies, he reconciled us through the death of his Son (Rom. 5:10). With this the last word about man—and it agrees with the first—is spoken. With this the definitive decision about his existence is made. His transgression is not minimized. The threat and danger to which he has exposed himself are not made innocuous. In themselves these are all infinite. But first and last we have to see and understand man, not in the light of these things, but in the light of that superior decision, in the light of the love of Jesus Christ, which is above all knowledge. It is in this light that we are to see and understand man's responsibility to the gracious God and his command.

From the knowledge of God and man there follows (3) the situation in which they stand over against one another. Let it be asserted primarily that God and man are two subjects in genuine encounter. God and man do in fact confront one another: two partners of different kinds, acting differently, so that they cannot be exchanged or equated. God cannot be compared, confused, or intermingled with man, nor man with God. They are totally unlike and remain so not only in their relationship as Creator and creature but also, with specifically sharp contours, in the relationship which now concerns us, their relationship in the covenant of grace and its basis in the action whereby God reconciled the world to himself. God is gracious to man, not man to God. And man is responsible and indebted to God, not God to man. Any reversal or obscuring of the distinction between the two is impossible. It is true that God is an object to man, as man is to God. Yet man's faith can no more dissolve into a divine act than God can dissolve into the human act of faith. Even in their unity in Jesus Christ himself,

God does not cease to be God nor man to be man. Their distinction even in their unity in Jesus Christ typifies the qualitative and definitive distinction between God and every other man.

The intensity with which it can be said of God's love that it is shed abroad in our hearts by the Holy Spirit (Rom. 5:5), and of God's grace that in the grace of the one man Jesus Christ it has flowed over or into the many (Rom. 5:15), does not mislead any of the New Testament writers into understanding the togetherness of God and man as any other than one of distance and distinction. The few places in which the barrier seems at first glance to be lifted are at John 10:34, quoting Psalm 82:6: "I say, you are gods" (ἐγὼ εἶπα· θεοί ἐστε), though here verse 35' at once explains: "He called them gods (θεοί) to whom the word of God came" (πρὸς οὓς ὁ λόγος τοῦ θεοῦ ἐγένετο); and at Acts 17:28, quoting the Greek poet Aratus: "For we are indeed his offspring" (τοῦ [θεοῦ] γὰρ καὶ γένος ἐσμέν). In the context this is simply a warning against idolatry as the tendency of man, who derives from God, to make an impossible equation of God with some precious creaturely object. One might also refer to another quotation from a Hellenistic source at 2 Peter 1:4, where the promises of Jesus Christ are said to be given to Christians that they might "become partakers of the divine nature" (ἵνα διὰ τούτων γένησθε θείας κοινωνοὶ φύσεως). The exhortation that follows shows plainly that the author here is not speaking of anything more than the practical fellowship of Christians with God and on this basis the conformity of their acts with the divine nature. For the rest, the men of the New Testament are just as far removed from any divine mysticism as are those of the Old Testament. They are kept from this by their knowledge of the gracious God as Judge of the world (Rom. 3:6) and by their knowledge of themselves as those who have passed to life only through death (Jn. 5:24; 1 Jn. 3:14), whose life is thus hidden with Christ in God (Col. 3:3), whose true life is indeed identical with the life of Christ as their representative (Phil. 1:21; Col. 3:4). Thus their God is always their Father in heaven (Mt. 6:9). They can seek and think of themselves as children of this God, of their living and moving and having their being in his kingdom (Acts 17:28), only as things above (Col. 3:1f.), looking ahead to the manifestation of this divine sonship of theirs (Rom. 8:19; Col. 3:4). Connected with this is the fact that they must renounce all swearing (Mt. 5:33ff.; Jas. 5:12). Thus their relation to God can be realized only in their faith in his Word, and this faith only in the spreading of their requests (αἰτήματα) before him (Phil. 4:6), their "supplications, prayers, intercessions, and thanksgivings" (1 Tim. 2:1), their participation in the *proskynesis* (adoration) of all heavenly and earthly creatures as described in Revelation 4:10 and 5:14. In this asking, seeking, and knocking (Mt. 7:7), in this *proskynesis*, man cannot possibly exchange or confuse God with himself or himself with God. What would responsibility mean if the man who is responsible to God did not truly and genuinely stand *over against* him?

But now, describing the situation further, we must add at once that as any identification, comparison, or interchange of God and man is ruled out, so is any separation between them. In the covenant of grace they are distinct partners, but precisely in their distinction they are partners who are inseparably bound to one another. In all its freedom God's grace is his reliable grace for the man to whom it is addressed. It would be blasphemy to think of God and say that he might be other than the God who is gracious to man. Similarly, if man's responsibility to God is free, in his relation to God he can be no other man and therefore — since he is free by God's grace alone — he cannot shake off or get rid of this responsibility. "If I take the wings of the morning and dwell in the uttermost parts of the sea, even there thy hand shall lead me, and thy right hand shall hold me" (Ps. 139:9f.). The unity of God and man in Jesus Christ guarantees the fact that God and man and man and God belong together, are bound together, and are in fellowship with one another. In him the covenant has its irrevocable basis. In him it cannot be broken.

Apposite here is what Hebrews (6:13f.; 7:20f.) says about the oath with which God — swearing by himself in default of anyone higher — confirmed the promise he had given to Abraham and with which he also instituted Jesus Christ to be "a priest for ever, after the order of Melchizedek" (7:17). In "two unchangeable things" — the author has in view the Old and New Testament forms of the history of the covenant, both vouched for in the same way by God himself — we thus have "strong encouragement," our hope being the anchor that reaches "into the inner shrine behind the curtain" (6:18f.). Necessarily then, and not accidentally, God and man belong together, just as in all their hiddenness, and clearly for all the distinction, father and child belong together. No a priori theology, anthropology, or even christology, but Jesus Christ himself is the basis of this assurance. This accounts for the astonishingly natural way in which the New Testament always speaks of God in practical relation to man and of man as claimed in practice for God. In his whole nature and its perversion man belongs from the very first to God.

The fellowship of God with man — we are again looking at its original in Jesus Christ — is fellowship in a specific and irreversible order of before and after, above and below. God unconditionally precedes and man can only follow. The free God elects and wills. The free man must elect and will what God wills and elects. God is the giver and man the recipient. Man is an active, not an inactive recipient, yet even in his activity he is still a recipient. In the present context the decisive point is that God directs, demands, orders, and commands, while man can exercise his responsibility only by obeying God's command. That God might withhold his direction and man his obedience is not foreseen in the covenant of grace. These are excluded possibilities. Also excluded is that in the dealings between God and man there might be something other than command and obedience, namely, negotiable arrangements and agreements reached on the same plane, a kind of contract or fellowship in which the definite order of first and second is either eliminated or even reversed.

One whole aspect of Johannine christology is normative in this regard. It consists of a development of the prayer in Gethsemane recounted by the synoptists: "Father . . . not my will, but thine, be done" (Lk. 22:42 and par.). "The Father is greater than I" is the confession of Jesus in John 14:28. There need be no fear that this will call into question the unity of the Son with the Father. Indeed, in the form of subordination in coordination it confirms it. Jesus has come from the Father and goes back to him (16:28). He lives as the Father lives (6:57), not to do his own will (5:30; 6:38), but rather — this is His food — to do the will of him who sent him (4:34). He works as the Father works (5:17); he does what he sees him do (5:19); he speaks as he hears him speak (8:28). It is thus that he is one with the Father (10:30). Precisely in this relation to his Father the Son can and must require that he too be heard and obeyed as he himself hears and obeys. In view of the starting point, the force of the divine command ("Hear, O Israel," Dt. 6:4) and the human duty of obedience ("Speak, Lord, for thy servant hears," 1 Sam. 3:9f.) are, if possible, even more sharply contoured in the New Testament than in the Old. What Jesus wants from his disciples he demands in the form of an ultimate control and direction as one who has authority (ἐξουσίαν ἔχων, Mt. 7:29). We cannot call him "Lord" without doing what he says (Lk. 6:46). Even if proper understanding is needed, no one should ever deny that he authors and proclaims a new law that does not cancel but fulfils the law of Moses (Mt. 5:17f.). Galatians (6:2) speaks specifically of the law of Christ (νόμος τοῦ Χριστοῦ), and in John 13:34 and 1 John 2:8 we read of his new commandment (καινὴ ἐντολή). Again Paul describes himself as "under the law of Christ" (ἔννομος Χριστοῦ, 1 Cor. 9:21). The parable of the two houses, the one built on the rock of hearing and doing and the other on the sand of hearing without doing (Mt. 7:24ff.), speaks clearly of the binding way in which man is claimed for action corresponding to the Word of Jesus. Faith in him that is not the obedience of faith (Rom. 1:5) cannot be faith in him.

The purpose of fellowship between God and man, and therefore of the relationship of command and obedience that characterizes it, is determined in the covenant of grace by the fact that God's glory and man's salvation, while they are so different, are not two things but one. God validates his own glory in his love, in being God as man's Father and Savior, in being kind to man. It is up to man for his part to acknowledge the being, will, and act of God, and therefore as his beloved and elect child, judged, saved, healed, carried, and led by him, to praise him and to give him and him alone all the glory. God's free kindness alone is the point of his demanding and ordering and commanding. Hence the point of the obedience that man owes him can be only the demonstration of his free gratitude. In the relationship determined in this way, God and man are one in Jesus Christ. On this basis this is how it is with the fellowship between God and everyman, between everyman and God. This is the last and decisive thing that is to be said about the situation in which they confront one another.

This is pregnantly described in the song of praise which, according to Luke 2:13f., "a multitude of the heavenly host" sang on the night of the nativity of Jesus Christ. The purpose and result of the reconciliation effected in him, the covenant of grace in its final actualization, is that there took place together as one and the same thing, on the one side the glory of God in the height of his sovereignty and holiness and in the depths on earth, and on the other side the peace created by him for men of his good pleasure, their peace with God, with one another, and within themselves. To speak with Ephesians 1:9f., the revealed mystery of the will of God, his eternal purpose executed according to his plan in fulfilled time, is that all things in heaven and earth, the breach between them being overcome, should be united (ἀνακεφα-λαιώσασθαι) into one, into an inseparable whole, in Jesus Christ. The petition which he laid on the lips of his disciples and which they were to repeat ("Thy will be done on earth as it is in heaven," Mt. 6:10) is already heard and fulfilled in him even before it is uttered, although this does not make it superfluous but rather gives it its real meaning as a petition. What a superior authority enjoins on man in this situation is not, for all its strictness, the demand of an abstract God insisting in some kind of lofty egoism on his due, his rights, his honor. To be sure, a yoke is laid on man (Mt. 11:28ff.) and a burden must be carried. Yet this does not make his labor and load heavier; it does not make them infinite as an obligation to serve that lofty God who looks out for his own interests. Instead, when the man who labors and is heavy-laden is summoned to obedience, it creates for him ἀνάπαυσις, sabbath refreshment, rest. He is to honor God and serve him by letting himself be given this rest. Hence it can be no alien thing to render the required obedience. He takes upon himself an easy yoke and a light burden. Growing on the good tree that God has planted, he has simply to bring forth the expected fruit as a branch of the vine Jesus Christ (Jn. 15:1f.; Mt. 7:17f.; Rom. 7:4): the fruit of conversion (Mt. 3:8), of righteousness (Phil. 1:11; Heb. 12:11; Jas. 3:18), of the Spirit (Gal. 5:22; Eph. 5:9). The God who wills this and commands this from him is the God who is gracious to him. Man is responsible for bearing this fruit, for glorifying God by exercising this responsibility, for putting into practice (κατεργάζεσθαι), the salvation (σωτηρία) that God has given him, and that with fear and trembling (μετὰ φόβου καὶ τρόμου, Phil. 2:12). As the work of his gratitude (εὐχαριστία) corresponding to the grace (χάρις) of God shown to him, it can only be the work of his obedience.

Taking up our real task, we now move on to (4) the question of the command that God gives to man in this situation. How does it run, what does it say and require, in the special form in which we have now to understand it as the command of the God who has reconciled the world to himself? What does the God who is gracious want from the man who is responsible to him, to him alone, but to him directly and unavoidably because he is the God who is gracious to man? In discharging our true task, everything — the line we must take and the decisive points we must make — depends on a clear and pertinent answer to this question.

Naturally this is not the sham question ("What shall I do?" [Lk. 12:17]) of the rich farmer, who knows very well what he wants to do. Rather, it is the open question of those who hurried to John the Baptist at the Jordan, the people, the publicans, and the soldiers who, frightened by the announcement of coming judgment, asked him: "What then shall we do?" (Lk. 3:10ff.). It is the open question of the rich young ruler who ran to Jesus (Mk. 10:17) and bowing before him asked, "Good Teacher, what must I do to inherit eternal life?" and whom Jesus loves, as we are expressly told later. It is the open question of those who, when they heard Peter proclaim in his sermon at Pentecost that God had made Jesus, whom they crucified, both Lord and Christ, were pierced to the heart and cried, "Brethren, what shall we do?" (Acts 2:36f.). It is also the open question that Saul put to Jesus when he suddenly appeared to him on the Damascus road: "What shall I do, Lord?" [Acts 22:10]. It is obviously the same open question that Paul wants to lead Christians to ask when, at the head of his description of the required transformation by the renewal of the mind, he asks them to learn and test and discover and know (δοκιμάζειν) what is the will of God, the commanded action that is good and acceptable and perfect to him (Rom. 12:2; cf. Phil. 1:10; Eph. 5:10, 17).

If this is to be an authentic and therefore a fruitful question, it cannot be asked in a vacuum but has to be asked in the situation already depicted. It has to grow out of knowledge of this situation and the underlying knowledge of God and man. The kingdom of God has drawn near. It has impinged on people. They see themselves set in the circle of the covenant of grace. At this place it is clear to them that they are summoned and impelled to a reaction corresponding to God's action. It is no longer or not yet clear to them, however, what this reaction must be if it is made responsibly. They are sure that they cannot give themselves directions to this effect, that they must be given an order or a command instructing them. This is how the question arises: "What shall we do?" It is no rhetorical question. Those who ask it do not expect the answer to be simply an echo of the answer they have long since given themselves. Yet it does not have either an indefinite origin or an indefinite goal. It is not the question of men who are left to themselves; it is not put contingently or capriciously; it is not put out of a more or less urgent curiosity, nor out of a need, but with no obligation, to seek out and find information about what perhaps ought to be done. It cannot inquire, then, what might be suggested to man by some higher power or idea, by some principle or model of his own, by a court that must still, perhaps, be set up and investigated and defined, so that its authority is open to question and discussion. At this point man *asks* because he *is asked*. Being asked, he must have an answer, but he knows no answer. He asks for information about the authority by which he is asked. Put as an authentic question in this sense — and it is inauthentic in any other sense — the question of the command of God, of what man must do according to God's will, is as such the beginning of the human reaction appropriate to God's action. As man asks it, therefore, he is already on the way to obedience. The divinely grounded and established fellowship between God and man is upheld as man, obviously reached and seized by God, does not continue to adapt to his destiny or the contingency or self-autonomy of human action in accordance with what those in his nearer or more distant background regard as right or with his own capricious impulse to do this or that. He has now found his Master and knows he is under obligation and responsibility to this Master. He has also found that he can only very dubiously — or even not at all — reconcile his previous acts with his encounter with this Master and the resulting obligation and responsibility. He is shaken when he sees, to his disquiet, the possibility of acts that correspond better to the situation in which he finds himself. He cannot be content simply to be asked. He must make the question his own and put it as his own. With this question he must turn to the point from which it is put to him, as the people of Jerusalem turned to John the Baptist and to the apostles, and as the rich young ruler, and later Saul, turned to Jesus himself. Man obviously does this on the basis of a new determination of his existence compared to what he was, or thought he was, before. It is plain, however, that the question is and will always be put to him once and for all, so that even if he has found an answer, and gone some way on the path of the demanded action, he cannot leave it behind as outdated, but must always let it be put to him again as a question. How could it be his genuine question if he ever thought it was no longer necessary to put it afresh? When does he not need to take new steps on the path of obedience and therefore to ask for new directions?

When can there ever be anything but a continuation of obedience in the relationship between the free and gracious God and the free man who is bound and under obligation and responsibility to him as such? When can there ever be anything but a reaction that corresponds continually to the divine action? This is obviously the point of the words addressed in Romans 12:2 to those who are already Christians. Does not the beginning, and therefore the question of the will of God, always have to be a new event? The continuity of obedience can be guaranteed on man's side only if he is not too proud always to begin again at the beginning with this question. Those who already have an answer to this question — this is a basic law of the situation in which alone they can have it — will always see themselves as directed to the point where they must, or may, hear it again and again, and therefore ask concerning it again and again.

A reminder of basic importance must be inserted here. The concept of the command of God denotes a dynamic reality. The command is that of the living God. Thus the concept speaks of God's action to the extent that this is also a specific Word directed to man. The expression "the command of God" means that the gracious God, acting as such with and for and on man, does not keep silent but says something to man, telling him what he wants from him, what he for his part is to do. The concept speaks of the directing and demanding and ordering of God which takes place in and with his action and with which he appeals to the freedom that he has given man as his Creator and Reconciler. The command of God is the event in which God commands. It is a specific command of God in each specific form of his dealings with man, in each specific time, in relation to the presuppositions and consequences of each specific existence of each man. It is the one very definite thing that God demands from this or that man. Thus the command of God is not a principle of action revealed to man and imposed upon him. It is not a collection of such principles which man, if he is to see and do what is right in detail, must expound and apply to the best of his knowledge and conscience, or according to the advice, or in submission to the authority, of others. Precisely with reference to the nature and direction of his concrete action here and now he would in this case be abandoned to destiny or chance or his own judgment or opinion or that of others. God in his command, however, tells him very concretely what he is to do or not do here and now in these or those particular circumstances. God accompanies man's way with ever new and living and specific direction. He is always the free God who has chosen the good for man and made it known to him as a matter for his choice too. What free man has always to do is to receive God's command as his concrete claim, decision, and judgment, and thus to repeat God's choice, practicing what God has elected as the good. For this repeating of God's choice man is responsible in his own knowledge, will, and act. Thus the question, "What shall I do?" asks about God's choice of the good today, the direction in which God makes this known so that it may be kept. It asks about the very concrete and specific form and manner of the action that God wants from man. Hence the action in which man must follow God's commanding step by step must also be very specific: either specific obedience insofar as it proceeds from right hearing of the divine order and does what is ordered, or disobedience insofar as it either does not proceed from such hearing or does not do what is heard as is commanded. Either way, in the encounter and togetherness of God and man we do not have a static confrontation whose form and manner are fixed for good and all. Since it is the free God and free man who encounter one another and are together, we always have some part of a common history, a specific, concrete, once-for-all, and unique event, or an ongoing and interconnected series of such events. Hence the question, "What shall I or we do?" can never become outdated. No ethics can anticipate that event or series of events. Their form and manner will always be the mystery of the commanding God and obedient or disobedient man. Ethics can and should indicate that always and everywhere there has been and will be that event or series of events between God and man. It cannot, either in advance or subsequently, decide what God wills from man. Hence it cannot try to answer the question, "What shall I do?" God's command as it discloses itself to man here and now is the answer to it. Nor can any ethics try to decide about man's obedience or disobedience. The commanding God, he alone, decides and judges this. Ethics can only indicate that in the here and now the obedience or disobedience of man has also taken place, and does and will do so, in relation to God's command. Ethics, then, cannot itself give direction. It can only give instruction, teaching us how to put that question relevantly and how to look forward openly, attentively, and willingly to the answer that God alone can and does give.

In the preceding sketch we have simply been recapitulating theses from the general doctrine of God's command as this is worked out in *CD* II,2 (especially in the subsection on "The Definiteness of the Divine Decision," pp. 661–708). There is no need for another exposition of these theses here. Similarly, we need not repeat but may presuppose the biblical grounding and elucidation of the matter which was attempted in II,2. The command of God, being identical with the free and living commanding of God, is always and everywhere a definite, even a very definite command.

Ethics, however, can point to the event of the encounter between God and man, to the mystery of the specific divine ordering, directing, and commanding and of the specific human obeying or disobeying. It can give instruction in the art of correct asking about God's will and open hearing of God's command. It can do this because, for all the specificity of his commanding here and now, it is always the gracious God who in the situation of the covenant which now commands our interest encounters the man who is responsible to him as such. Thus the mystery of his encounter with man is not one of a darkness in which anything might be possible and might become actual. The very specific thing which the free God wants done here and now by free man, the content of his command, is wholly and utterly a matter of his particular disposing. But this free and particular disposing always takes place in the context and order which are laid down by the fact that he is not a dark and formless numen but the almighty Lord who wills the best for the man who is responsible to him, who seeks his own glory by being man's Savior. It is as such that he is his Lord; it is as such that he claims him, decides concerning him, and judges him; and it is as such that he commands him. We can and should count on it that in all cases, always and everywhere, his free commanding is characterized by his being this and no other God. Similarly, the man who encounters this God is no unwritten page, nor is his responsibility a neutral and indefinite one, in the discharging of which he has to do in obedience today what was disobedience yesterday, or has not to do as disobedience today what was obedience yesterday. The path on which he must follow God's free commanding with ruthless openness and readiness is a very specific path to the extent that what he must do or not do according to God's command he will do or not do only as the man who is bound and under obligation to God as the gracious God and no other. Thus the concrete direction which God gives man here and now cannot be replaced by the exposition and application of any general principles that are either handed down, self-invented, or prescribed by others. Nevertheless, there is a criterion by which the direction God has given man in his command may be clearly distinguished from man's own insights or the suggestions of other spirits and forces. The command of God may always be recognized as such because, as the command of Jesus Christ, the one Mediator between God and man, it encounters man in the form of grace: not as the exponent of man's own fantasies, wishes, and desires, nor as the dictate of an unknown deity coming upon him as an alien or enemy, but as the direction of him who, apart from and even in opposition to man's own acts and merits, loved him from all eternity, who understands him better than man does himself, who intends better for him than he does for himself, who with this better knowledge and intention, for his salvation, reminds him of his freedom, takes him seriously in this freedom, and summons him to make the only possible use of it. The command of God will infallibly make itself known as the law of the gospel. No insights of man's own, no whisperings or promptings of other spirits, can stand up against a strict application of this criterion. For no eye has seen, nor ear heard, nor has it entered any human heart, that the God who has reconciled the world to himself in Jesus Christ is the true God, and that the man reconciled to God in him is true man — God has prepared this for those who love him (1 Cor. 2:9). The meaning in this context is that God's command is prepared for those who, because God has first loved them (1 Jn. 4:19), may love him in return. Ethics has to adopt this criterion and apply it here and now to that event, to the mystery of God's commanding and man's response.

One may rightly wonder why more frequent and energetic use is not made of this criterion in the debates between Christian ethics and all other ethics. For what is it that distinguishes Christian instruction in the doing of what is right and necessary and good, when what is commanded of man is presented just as clearly and earnestly by the teachings that are also plainly given in this matter by the animistic religions, by Islam and Buddhism, by Judaism, and last but not least by the substitute religions of nationalism, humanism, and socialism? Is it not simply this, that in the Christian understanding, God's requirements of man can be no other than the sharply contoured imperatives of the love that is freely addressed to him, that freely affirms him, and that freely wills and accomplishes his salvation? And on the other side, what differentiates (from all other teachings) the Christian understanding of the conduct expected of man if it is not that from the very first and in all cases this can be no other than the work of man's free gratitude for the grace displayed to him? If there has to be debate with proponents of other ethical systems, why is not the debate conducted on this premise, as it unequivocally and resolutely should be? Why is not issue joined with the alienation of the commanding authority and responsible man in all other systems, with the abstract legalism of all other ethical conceptions? The reason why this is not done is perhaps connected with the existence of so much ostensibly Christian ethics that has stopped measuring itself by this criterion. Such ethics will fare poorly in relation to other ethics if in its distinctive positions it does not take its origin, or to a large degree takes it only confusedly, in the insight that the command of God is the law of the gospel, which shows itself to be authentic by the fact that always, even as the strictest claim, the most sovereign decision, and the most holy judgment, it is the form of the grace that summons man to freedom. A Christianity and community oriented to this fundamental distinctive need not worry about the originality of its message. Really oriented to it, it can be certain that it will speak to the rest of mankind, which is ethically interested and motivated but finally trapped in every kind of dead legalism, the new and special thing, the specifically Christian thing, which at root it clearly and forcefully expects to hear.

The command of God is in all cases the command of Jesus Christ and therefore the law of the gospel, the form of grace. This is the mark by which this command is distinguished from all the other imperatives that may also seem to be, or really are, both serious and urgent. But we must now take from it its content, what man is commanded in it, beginning with the general directive, if we are to know what God demands of man and what man must always do in obedience to God. We must inquire into this general directive in this last part of the introduction. Understanding it will give us the relevant structure of this part of special ethics. What is the one thing in the midst of the truly and not just apparently many things that the gracious God commands man? In the face of the unity of the commanding God on the one side and of responsible man in all his different times, places, and situations on the other, or, decisively, in the face of the unity of the living Mediator between God and man, we have to presuppose that all along the line this one thing is at issue. We are now asking what is the most relevant term for this one thing, the most appropriate concept in which it can be understood as the basis of all our further deliberations. Various possibilities suggest themselves. A choice has to be made, and it must not be made arbitrarily. As we venture it, we cannot focus sharply enough the point at issue. The choice will always be a venture which can vindicate itself only when it is made, for of the concepts in question there is none that does not commend itself from some standpoints and none that imposes itself as absolutely necessary to the exclusion of all others. We can seek only a relative and not an absolute concept, only the one that characterizes the matter at issue, and embraces it in all its multiplicity, with what seems to be approximately the greatest clarity.

The general concept of the "Christian life" suggests itself first. This whole part of special ethics might in fact be regarded as a tractate on the life of the Christian (Calvin, *Inst.* III, 6). If it is, the hardworn, heavily freighted, and ambivalent adjective "Christian" will have to carry the sense of "grounded in the knowledge of God in Jesus Christ and oriented to the effected justification, sanctification, and vocation of man in him." As it is thus grounded and oriented, human life is a Christian life. The gracious God demands this life from man as his covenant-partner. Man must live it in obedience to God. God does not just demand it from the "Christian," but demands it from him as an example. As an example, the Christian can and should be obedient in this life. Whether man recognizes it or not, God's command has always and everywhere this content. And wherever and whenever a man's life is lived in obedience to God, it is consciously or unconsciously a Christian life. But what does "a Christian life" mean?

The basic concept in *CD* III,4, the first part of special ethics worked out as the final part of the doctrine of creation, was the concept of "freedom." It was especially adapted to play a dominant role there because our task at that point was to describe the command and obedience in relation to the determinations of human existence which, as we learned from the Word of God, are posited at creation. It is such a rich and beautiful and fruitful concept, and it occurs in such important places in the basic discussions of God and man in the covenant of grace which are just behind us, that one might well ask whether we are not permitted and commanded to continue along the same lines, to put ethics as the crown of the doctrine of reconciliation under the same promising sign, and to develop ethics here too—if with a rather different application—as the ethics of freedom. In theology, however, there must be no tyranny of concepts. For this reason alone, to avoid any danger or even any harmful appearance in this direction, it is advisable to look for a new basic concept for this second part of special ethics. A decisive reason, however, is that while the concept of freedom is, as we have seen, illuminating enough as a term for the matter at hand, the command of the gracious God and the obedience of the man responsible to him, it does not adequately bring out its special characteristics. We shall have to keep it in mind and time and again give it its due. But in the present context we need to find a more precise basic concept.

Not a little might be said in favor of the concept of "repentance," which in the New Testament is so important in denoting what God requires and man must do under the sign of the imminent kingdom of God. In this context we are thinking of repentance as the conversion which is grounded, and has to be carried through, in an awareness of the situation: conversion from an old manner and orientation of life, which has been overtaken and outdated in this situation, to a new one which corresponds to it better. The radical and universal nature of the divine command, and of the human obedience for which it calls, is brought out with classical clarity in this concept so long as it is understood with sufficient depth and comprehensiveness. It might undoubtedly be the concept that we need. It too we shall have to keep in view and time and again recall. We may widen our search and pass by, without wholly neglecting it, a related concept that is so precious to the existentialist theological thinking of our time, that of the "decision" which is constantly demanded and has constantly to be made in new ventures. This is because, while it excellently brings out the formal point that the question of the nature and content of the command and obedience is left open, what we want is not just a formally clear concept, but also one that is filled out materially, one that tells us *what* is the conversion that is according to God's will, *what* is the decision to which man is summoned by it.

Why, then, do we not adopt the great and simple concept of "faith"? Is faith not the Alpha and Omega of what God expects and requires of man? Is it not the imperative of all Christian imperatives? Can decision mean anything other than the decision of faith? When this concept is expounded as man's venture of trust and obedience in relation to the God revealed to him by his Word in his work of grace, does it not embrace everything that God wants done by the man who knows him in his goodness and severity? We certainly do better not to join Luther in calling faith the "creative divinity" even "in us," since this might easily be stated and understood in unfortunate proximity to Feuerbach.[7] But who can oppose Luther when elsewhere, if still a little dubiously, he describes faith as the "captain" of all good works? Is it not that? Can an ethics that is specifically oriented to God and man in the covenant of grace want anything other or better than to be an ethics of faith? But does there not threaten here a new tyranny of concepts deriving from the opposition to Judaizing in Galatians and Romans and its interpretation by Luther and his generation, and in modern times especially by the existentialists? Against the elevation of faith as the central ethical concept do we not have to say of faith as well that it describes what God commands and man must do only formally and not materially, so that it has to be filled out in a specific way if it is to say something that has ethical content?

First Corinthians 13 could not easily be changed from a hymn in praise of love (ἀγάπη) to a hymn in praise of faith (πίστις). The same may be said of Paul's statement that love is the fulfilment of the law (Rom. 13:10), which reminds us very clearly of what is called the "new commandment" in the Johannine writings [Jn. 13:34; 1 Jn. 2:8]. If faith is to be the central ethical concept, do we not have to bear in mind the misunderstanding to which, as "mere" faith, it was already exposed in the New Testament communities (Jas. 2:14), and has always been exposed since? Do we not have to understand it more precisely, along the lines of the saying that occurs already in Galatians (5:6), as the faith that works by love? To avoid a new fideism, or fideimonism, that threatens today (cf. G. Ebeling, *Das Wesen des [christlichen]*

[7]Cf. *WA*, 40, I, 360, 5f. for the phrase "Fides est creatrix divinitatis . . . in nobis" (quoted by Feuerbach in *Gesammelte Werke*, V; Berlin, 1973, pp. 229f.) and *WA*, 6, 213, 13f.; 234, 1-3 for the description of faith as the "heubtman . . . aller anderer werck."

Glaubens, 1959),[8] do we not finally have to define it explicitly as faith in Jesus Christ or the like?

Certainly in all that we say about our theme, it must never be forgotten that there can be no other obedience than that of faith. Nevertheless, it is still advisable not to think that our question is disposed of by pointing to this concept.

As another fine possibility, why not "thanksgiving"? To give thanks is to recognize an unobligated and unmerited favor. It is to show that one recognizes the favor as a favor, and as a free one at that. It is to express this in act and attitude toward the one who does the favor. As a concept that is both formally clear and materially important, standing as it does in excellent relation to man's encounter with God in the covenant of grace, this seems to be fairly exactly the concept we are seeking.

A good linguistic argument supports the choice of this concept, namely, the obvious correspondence and analogy between εὐχαριστία and χάρις, gratitude and grace. There is also an historical argument, for if we adopt the concept, we shall be following the material and linguistic example of the Heidelberg Catechism, whose third, ethical section, which is so typical of the Reformed side of the Reformation, bears the familiar title: "Of Gratitude." Christ, who has bought us with his blood, renews us by his Holy Spirit, "so that in our whole life we may show ourselves grateful to God for his blessings and he may be praised through us" (Qu. 86; cf. 32, 43, 64).

We might accept this rich and living concept joyfully and with no reserve. Gratitude, or, more concretely, thanksgiving, does in fact give us precise and exhaustive information about what is commanded of man in his relationship to the gracious God, and therefore about what is decisively and comprehensively commanded of him.

The same is true — and in relation to biblical thought and speech this choice might be even better — when we look at the concept of "faithfulness." God activates and reveals his own faithfulness in Jesus Christ. What he thus wills and requires of man is that he manifest and attest a similar faithfulness for his part. Faithfulness is a steady and lasting perseverance in thought, word, attitude, and act. It is endurance and persistence in a union, commitment, and obligation that is laid upon man with both kindness and strictness. Faithfulness characterizes in preeminent fashion the situation of the covenant — of the covenant of grace between God and man in which God himself, in spite of everything that might argue against it, constantly unites and commits and pledges himself to be man's God, to be his wisdom, righteousness, sanctification, and redemption (1 Cor. 1:30), and then demands of man that he not be any other than the one to whom he

---

[8]For Barth's comments written on his copy of this book, see the German, K. Barth, *Das christliche Leben*, *Gesamtausgabe* (1976), p. 59, n. 20.

has bound and committed and pledged himself, and therefore that he respond with his own faithfulness to the faithfulness of God.

Faithfulness, deeply linked to the concepts of truth, righteousness, and mercy, is the basic category in which the Old Testament understands and presents both the being and action of Yahweh in his covenant with the people elected and called by him, and also that which he expects of this people, its commitment. "Yahweh your God is God, the faithful God who keeps covenant and steadfast love with those who love him and keep his commandments, to a thousand generations" (Dt. 7:9). He always remains himself in his relationship to this people: himself (with the same goal of salvation) as the God of the progenitor Abraham, but also of Isaac, Jacob ("all live to him," Lk. 20:38), and his descendants; the God who does not merely perform the unique act of power in the exodus from Egypt with which the common history of Yahweh and this people begins, but continues his work in the people's life in the wilderness, in the complicated events of the conquest on both sides of the Jordan, in the hard struggle to maintain it, and then in the leading of David and his house. This faithful action of his, perceived and proclaimed by Moses and the prophets, is the Word in which he commands Israel to become and to be and to remain faithful to him in its own response of faithfulness. Israel does this only in a transitory way. It displays it concretely only in certain very fragile forms. Its history as a whole is that of ever new forms of unfaithfulness, a long history, from the standpoint of its acts and attitudes, of defection from the covenant of Yahweh. Nevertheless Yahweh, not Israel, set up this covenant, so that Israel can neither destroy nor evade it. What can Israel's unfaithfulness accomplish over against God's faithfulness (Rom. 3:3)? Only that Yahweh's ongoing direction takes on a predominantly and even exclusively penal character! Yet Yahweh still loves his people even when he accuses and condemns and smites it. It is because he loves it so much that he deals with it so severely. In so doing he does not cease to bear witness to it that he is its Lord, that he watches over it, that he has not turned from it in weariness and disenchantment, that he is not looking for another partner. He does not accept its unfaithfulness. As though nothing had happened, he continues to call it back to the only appropriate stance of faithfulness and therefore to remind it of the salvation he still purposes for it. His eyes, the eyes of the faithful God, still "look with favor on the faithful in the land" (Ps. 101:6).

Again, if we are to understand the New Testament concept of faith, it is important to remember that the adjective πιστός (also the noun πίστις in Rom. 3:3) can often denote a quality or attitude of God. He first is πιστεύων. He first has shown himself constant and persistent in what he has done for the world and everyman in Jesus Christ. Thus faith in its usual sense as a term for the human act, and the verb πιστεύειν, notwithstanding its meaning elsewhere, are to be understood basically as the faithfulness of man responding to this faithfulness of God. In faith man sticks it out with God because he sees that God as his God, and to his advantage, first willed to stick it out with him, and did in fact do so. This human faithfulness which responds and corresponds to the faithfulness of God is obedience, the venture of trust in God. Is not perhaps this readiness of the human partner to stick it out with the divine partner the meaning and nerve of all the other New Testament imperatives? Do not these speak frequently and urgently of the command that Christians endure, remain, stand fast, be established, hold on, and persevere, as though everything depended on this? That they should begin and continue with this trust, that there should be this response of human to divine faithfulness, is, of course, taken for granted in the New Testament sphere when the acts of Christians are in view. Why, then, do we find that the awakening of faith and the entry into freedom to persevere with God seem to be surrounded with an aspect of the extraordinary? Why do we find exhortations in which there is a continual summons to the required response of faithfulness and therefore to holding fast to God? Why is there continual reference to the obviously not yet attained perfection of perseverance? Failure at this decisive point, that is, unfaithfulness, is obviously a danger that seriously threatens the Christian and even the apostle. To avert it, the elect, the called, the believers stand in need of intercession and must call on God themselves. One decisive change, however, has come about in the New Testament, as compared with the Old, which alters the whole picture. The open contradiction in the Old Testament between the faithfulness of God and the unfaithfulness of man has now at the decisive point been successfully removed for the whole sphere of human existence. In *one* person the covenant of grace has been confirmed and fulfilled on man's side also. Staying by God, πίστις, πιστεύειν has become an event or work of human obedience. Constantly threatened by the possibility that they might fail and become unfaithful as continually unfaithful Israel did, New Testament πιστεύοντες look, and their πίστις refers, to the *one* person in whom the covenant of grace is fulfilled, kept, and established, not only as God's act but also as man's, and therefore in faithfulness on both sides: to the "pioneer and perfecter of our faith" (ἀρχηγὸς καὶ τελειωτὴς τῆς πίστεως, Heb. 12:2), who is set before them as the firstborn Brother who has persevered for all of them, who has been faithful in their place, and who has thus become the pioneer (Heb. 2:10; Luther, "duke") of their salvation (ἀρχηγὸς τῆς σωτηρίας), whose faithfulness is their comfort in every hour, but by whom they are also called to orient themselves to this faithfulness of his. Believing now means — and this makes the requirement imperious but also liberating — not only staying with God but also staying (because with God, with this man too) in fellowship with him: believing in Jesus Christ. This is the decisive and comprehensive new thing in the demand for faithfulness and therefore in the central ethical problem in the New Testament.

The faithfulness which the self-motivated God promises to man, and keeps with man, is free. It is also unconditional, for it could vacillate or fade only if God were unfaithful to himself and thus ceased to be God. It is also total, with no reservation, interruption, or end. The command that he has given man to be faithful is in keeping with all this. It is a matter of man's persistence with God according to the measure and manner of God's persistence with man: free, unforced faithfulness from the heart, unconditional faithfulness not linked to any claims on God, total faithfulness to be kept with no reservations. What is demanded here is not something inappropriate, but simply that man as a clear mirror encounter God as God encounters him. He may do this not only because God commands him; God also frees and empowers him to do so as a partner in the covenant of grace set up by him and fulfilled in Jesus Christ. Man has no reason to meet God except in faithfulness. But will he do so? Will he constantly keep in view that he may and should and can do so, that he really has no other choice than actually to do so? He might have forgotten this, either completely or in part. He might not be a clear mirror of the divine faithfulness, but a covered mirror. He is always in danger of faltering, stumbling, falling, or lying down somewhere on the appointed and open and directed path. Sin still couches at the door, and he has a desire for it (Gen. 4:7). Or, more strongly, it still dwells in him (Rom. 7:17, 20). The faithfulness with which he turns to God is unlike that with which God turns to him to the point of nonrecognition. Yet this man is taken into account when faithfulness corresponding to his situation in the covenant of grace is required of him, when he is summoned and admonished to display it, when he is constantly reminded of it, and it is etched upon him, as something new to him. He needs the command of the gracious God that demands this adjustment. God wills that man be faithful to him. This order is the content of the command of God the Reconciler.

But we are still seeking a word or concept that will express the fact that some human *action* is at issue in the obedience which the gracious God commands of man. Certainly we shall not only have to keep constantly in mind but emphatically validate and honor all the concepts so far considered: the Christian life, freedom, conversion, decision, faith, thanksgiving, and especially faithfulness. Certainly in all of them, when rightly understood, we have to think of a specific human action. But what is not clearly enough underscored by them is that in the obedience demanded by the gracious God, and achieved by the man who recognizes and confesses him, we have to do with more than a certain form of human life (which might well be construed passively) and the disposition or attitude corresponding to it. What God expects and wills from those in whose hearts he has caused the light of the knowledge of his glory in the face of Jesus Christ to shine (2 Cor. 4:6) is the action of obedience accomplished as their Christian life. We must now ask concerning the relatively best understanding of this action and its title. We venture the following discussion and choice.

This action must (1) be distinctive to man as the partner of God in the covenant of grace established by him. It must derive and proceed from the fulfilment of this covenant in Jesus Christ. It must also grow out of man's awareness of fellowship with him and receive its form from this. It must be practiced in accordance with his direction and guidance.

This action must also (2) be one for which man finds himself empowered only by the free grace of God, so that in it he can use only this empowering but also has no choice other than to make use of it.

This action, grounded in the divine empowering, must be (3) an authentically and specifically human action, willed and undertaken in a free human resolve and carried out concretely as man's rising up and lying down, coming and going, eating and drinking, working and resting. No less serious in his place than God in his, man must be present and at work in it according to the measure of his human capacity.

As this particular human action, this action must (4) have central significance and import for all man's other being and acts. It must precede, accompany, and follow the whole of his life's work. For all its particularity, it must be representative of all he does and give it meaning, direction, and character.

In this action man (5) will find himself wholly referred to the gracious God as his only helper in distress and the only source and giver of all good things. In what he does he will be able to give active expression only to his own willingness and readiness in relation to the gracious God.

In it, then, he must (6) act as one who does not regard himself as worthy to encounter God and answer him, who can have no thought of making himself worthy, who may and must and will dare no more than to present himself as a partner and to act as such.

But he must do this (7) as one who in the face of the initiative that God has taken regarding him may and must and will actually venture to do this with complete confidence, with no reservation, doubt, hesitation, or vacillation.

Insofar as all the concepts considered come to actualization and are not just empty concepts, they do so in this action. It is an action that characterizes the event of the Christian life. It controls it in all its dimensions. In it man as a Christian acquires his freedom, and in it consists the exercise of this freedom: his conversion and decision. It is the work of his faith and gratitude. His faithfulness is his persistence in the repetition of this action. It is the epitome and common denominator of all that the gracious God expects and wants of man and of all that comes into question as man's obedience to the gracious God. God commands this action, and in performing it man does what is right and good before him.

We are speaking of the humble and resolute, the frightened and joyful *invocation* of the gracious God in gratitude, praise, and above all petition. In the sphere of the covenant, this is the normal action corresponding to the fulfilment of the covenant in Jesus Christ. Man is empowered for this, and obligated to it, by God's grace. In it man in his whole humanity takes his proper place over against God. In it he does the central thing that precedes, accompanies, and follows all else he does. In it he acts as the one who is referred wholly to God and has absolute need of him. In it he ventures the turning to God for which no worthiness qualifies him. He does it in fearless hope on the basis that God has turned to him and summoned him to this venture. We thus understand calling upon God — in all the richness of the action included in it — as the one thing in the many that the God who has reconciled the world to himself in Jesus Christ demands of man as he permits it to him. It is, therefore, the general key with which we may enter upon the task that is before us.

In the title of his chapter on prayer (*Inst.* III, 20) Calvin calls invocation of God the "chief exercise of faith." Then, before doing anything else, he speaks about the fourfold law in which man must come before God with reverence (4– 5); that he cannot be pleased with himself (6– 7) but can only confess his guilt (8– 10) and trust in God's kindness alone; and that the action can thus be performed only as the prayer of faith and with absolute certainty that this prayer will be heard and answered (11– 12). Of all the offices of piety, none is more urgently commended to us in Scripture. Not to pray is rebellion against God and is definitely unbelief (13). Calling on God is the chief thing in worship, while offering sacrifices to God is set below it (27). Along similar lines the Heidelberg Catechism (Qu. 116) calls prayer the chief part of the gratitude that God demands of us. Long before Calvin, Luther (in the introduction to his exposition of the Lord's Prayer in the Larger Catechism of 1529) had spoken to the same effect. We owe it to the command of God to pray. We are bidden to do so with the same strictness as we are forbidden to have other gods, to kill, or to steal. No one, then, should think it is up to himself whether or not to pray. We should and must pray if we are to be Christians. This is a work of obedience which man has to do, not for the sake of his own worthiness, but for the sake of the command. The command that was relevant for Paul is relevant for me too. And my prayer is just as precious, sacred, and pleasing to God as that of Paul or the greatest saints, for I rest my prayer on the command on which all the saints rest their prayers. The first and most necessary thing is that all our prayers should be based on and should stand on God's obedience. And we should realize that God will not smite in jest but will be angry and punish us if we do not pray, just as he punishes all other disobedience, since he will not let our prayers be in vain and lost. For if he would not hear us, he would not call upon us to pray or give such a strong command to do so.

We thus understand the command, "Call upon me" (Ps. 50:15), to be the basic meaning of every divine command, and we regard invocation according to this command as the basic meaning of all human obedience. What God permits man, what he expects, wills, and requires of him, is a life of calling upon him. This life of calling upon God will be a person's Christian life: his life in freedom, conversion, faith, gratitude, and faithfulness. It is this command, and the human action corresponding to it, that we shall have to investigate and present in this part of ethics.

The arrangement according to which we must proceed on this presupposition is self-evident. In our discussion and presentation we shall simply follow the course of the prayer which has come down to us in Matthew 6:9–13 and Luke 11:2–4: the prayer that Jesus Christ himself prayed, that he prayed first and then told his disciples to pray after him. The order that is given at this absolutely and exclusively authorized place — the order that we should call on God thus and not otherwise — encloses within itself point by point the criterion of a life, action, and work that is determined by this prayer, by the One who as the representative of all men before God, prayed this prayer to him.

It is a breviary of the whole gospel (Tertullian, De oratione I,6). It binds the whole man. "Lord, teach us to pray" (Lk. 11:1) means finally, "Lord, teach us to believe" (Ernst Lohmeyer, Das Vater-Unser, 1947[2], pp. 11,12).

That in considering this criterion we might miss the essential thing is as little to be feared, so long as we follow the criterion, as that the nonessential might lead us astray from the sure path of knowledge and destroy and scatter us. From this incomparable text, familiar to Christianity in every age, we learn not only that we should pray, but also what we should pray and how we should pray. We also perceive what, as those who may and should pray thus, we have to know about shaping our life as Christians.

A study of the special themes suggested by the Lord's Prayer will be the center of this chapter of special ethics. But this center has a circumference which is just as clearly laid down for us and which we shall have to deal with extensively as the natural framework of the main portion.

God not only displays but makes known his grace to man, and in so doing he permits and orders him to call upon him, and man's calling upon God becomes an event on this basis; yet in each individual case all this can be only a special history played out in the light and power of the basic event between God and man in Jesus Christ, and totally determined by this event. It is by no means self-evident that this history should take place, that we can thus refer to a divine permission and commanding and a responsive human obeying, which apply to specific people, and that it is thus incumbent on us to reckon with the fact that God is there for specific people and that these people may and will be there for him too. It is by no means self-evident that we may count on the Christian life's being a reality. There thus arises the question of its foundation. How does the history begin in which alone it can become and be a reality, whether from the standpoint of the God who is gracious to man and who commands him as the gracious God, or from that of the man who is responsible and obligated to this God? How does it come about that the grace of God is manifest to a man, that his permission and command to call upon him, using the order of Jesus Christ ("Pray then like this"), acquires validity and force in the life of a man, becoming a factor that determines this life? And how does it come about that this fact is confirmed on man's side, that this order begins to win for itself his hearing and obedience? There also arises the question of the continual renewal of the Christian life. How can and will the history continue once it has begun? On God's side, how will the new factor in a person's life, the faithfulness of God and the command of Jesus Christ to call upon him as he directs, newly acquire and maintain its actuality? On man's side, in what movement will he follow the march of God's speech and action, in what new obedience will he be able to correspond to God's new command, always remaining faithful afresh in fresh invocation? Ethics in the context of the doctrine of reconciliation obviously cannot refrain from taking up both these questions, that of the beginning of the history, the foundation of the Christian life, and that of its continuation, the renewal of the Christian life. We shall answer the first question before the detailed discussions that follow the Lord's Prayer as a guide, and we shall answer the second question after these discussions. This is how they will form a framework to the main portion.

It is by no means arbitrary if in the circumference of our central discussion of the Lord's Prayer we deal with two other themes that belong constitutively to the life and teaching of the church, namely, baptism (in the prologue) and the Lord's Supper (in the epilogue). Both of these are human actions that follow emphatic divine commands and ordinances: the giving and receiving of baptism and the celebration of the Lord's Supper. Baptism in particular refers to the foundation of the Christian life, and the Lord's Supper to its renewal. Both are connected with the history played out between the gracious God and obedient man. In this regard baptism relates especially to the beginning of the history, to man's entry into a life determined by calling upon God, while the Lord's Supper relates especially to the continuation of the history, the sustaining of man in the fellowship of that life and therefore in calling upon God. Thus baptism and the Lord's Supper belong to ethics, and especially to ethics as it is to be worked out in the special light of God's reconciling action.

In dealing with baptism and the Lord's Supper only incidentally in the three preceding parts of the doctrine of reconciliation, and discussing them precisely in the present context, we have presupposed a decision that needs to be established, but can only be indicated here, regarding their basis, goal, and meaning. In brief, this decision is as follows. Baptism and the Lord's Supper are not events, institutions, mediations, or revelations of salvation. They are not representations and actualizations, emanations, repetitions, or extensions, nor indeed guarantees and seals of the work and word of God; nor are they instruments, vehicles, channels, or means of God's reconciling grace. They are not what they have been called since the second century, namely, mysteries or sacraments. With all that the community of Jesus Christ and its members are and say and do, they belong to something that God has permitted and entrusted and commanded to Christians, namely, the answering, attesting, and proclaiming of the one act and revelation of salvation that has taken place in the one Mediator between God and man [1 Tim. 2:5], who himself directly actualizes and presents and activates and declares himself in the power of his Holy Spirit. Like the Christian life in invocation of God, they are actions of human obedience for which Jesus Christ makes his people free and responsible. They refer themselves to God's own work and word, and they correspond to his grace and commands. In so doing they have the promise of the divine good pleasure and they are well done as holy, meaningful, fruitful, human actions, radiant in the shining of the one true light in which they may take place and which they have to indicate in their own place and manner as free and responsible human action.

We must now begin with a discussion of the foundation of the Christian life, that is, with the doctrine of baptism. We shall then go on to present the Christian life according to the guidance of the Lord's Prayer. We shall close the chapter with a discussion of the renewal of the Christian life, in other words, the doctrine of the Lord's Supper.

§75

THE FOUNDATION OF THE
CHRISTIAN LIFE[1]

A man's turning to faithfulness to God, and consequently to calling upon him, is the work of this faithful God which, perfectly accomplished in the history of Jesus Christ, in virtue of the awakening, quickening, and illuminating power of this history, becomes a new beginning of life as his baptism with the Holy Spirit.

The first step of this life of faithfulness to God, the Christian life, is a man's baptism with water, which by his own decision is requested of the community and which is administered by the community, as the binding confession of his obedience, conversion, and hope, made in prayer for God's grace, wherein he honors the freedom of this grace.

[1]Barth revised the text of this section and published it as *KD* IV,4: *Das christliche Leben (Fragment). Die Taufe als Begründung des christlichen Lebens*, Zurich, 1967; E.T. *CD* IV,4: *The Christian Life (Fragment). Baptism as the Foundation of the Christian Life*, Edinburgh, 1969.

§76

THE CHILDREN AND THEIR FATHER[1]

The obedience of Christians follows from the fact that in Jesus Christ they may recognize God as his Father and theirs, and themselves as his children. Obedience is their action to the extent that it is ventured in invocation of God, in which, liberated thereto by his Holy Spirit, they may take God at his word as their Father and take themselves seriously as his children.

1. THE FATHER

Our task is that of Christian ethics as an attempt to portray Christian life under the command of God. We have already discussed its foundation: God's free act in his turning to man, that is, baptism with the Holy Spirit, which can only be God's work; and man's free act at the beginning of his turning to God, that is, baptism with water as the work in which he begins to respond to the work and Word of God. We now ask what the Christian life is in the light of this foundation. What are the decisive signs or marks that distinguish it in its outworking?

"Christian life" as we use it here means the life of Christians. We are not now thinking of Christians in their quality as members of variously ordered and directed Christian fellowships, nor of Christians as the more or less devout and convinced representatives of personal Christian piety, let alone of Christians as representatives of a so-called Christian outlook and practice. What we have in view are Christians in that which in fact makes them such, in their relation to Jesus Christ, and especially in the obligation and commitment that derives from this relation. What we have in view is their life in its relation to the divine command as it is given to them as those who are thus obligated and committed to Jesus Christ. We are asking in what sense and measure their life can be understood as one of obedience to this command.

The general answer to this question, which we will put before all the detailed things we shall have to say, runs as follows. The life of Christians is one of obedience to this command to the extent that it is a human life whose purpose, will, and work focuses always on the one action of invocation of God, and which in its deepest and highest needs and desires, in terms of its achievements, is to be understood in its totality as a life in

---

[1]In the TS a handwritten note above the title of this section reads:
Thanks, praise, prayer
Spiritual life.

49

invocation of God. That Christians call upon God, that they do everything
they do in this calling upon God, is what is expected of them as those who
are obligated and committed to Jesus Christ. It is the command they must
keep if their action is to be obedience.

The path that we must take in our investigation and presentation, the
path on which we must develop and expound the details, is laid down for
us at every point by the progression of the prayer which in the first and
third Gospels of the New Testament is handed down as the prayer which
Jesus himself prayed, and which he prayed before his disciples so that they
too might learn to pray it. As we have already noted, as a prayer the Lord's
Prayer is, in the words of Tertullian, a breviary of the whole gospel. It
invites us in unique fashion to apply the old adage that the law of prayer
is the law of faith. We shall here accept this invitation by understanding
the law of faith that is implicit in the law of prayer, and is to be taken from
it, as a law of life, a criterion by which to answer our question concerning
the obedience required of Christians.

The very first words of the prayer give us concrete direction. It has been
rightly said of the address that it already includes all that follows as petition
and praise. As an invocation in the narrower sense it characterizes the
Lord's Prayer in its totality as an invocation of God: "Our Father who art
in heaven." Those who pray thus do so as those who for their part are called
upon to do so. They do not do it by reason of their own desire or need or
taste. They are directed to do so. Invocation of God — as real invocation of
the real God — is not an action that may or may not be undertaken at will,
but one that follows an absolutely superior command. They are also instructed in it. It is not an action that may be capriciously undertaken in this
way or that, but one whose direction and form are prescribed. It is the
commanded and ordered action of certain people. This is the standpoint
from which it is to be evaluated, both as a totality and in all its parts,
including the introduction.

Οὕτως, "thus," are you to pray (or worship) — you, my disciples, who are associated with me as members of the end-time people of God, or as those who are
destined and about to become members — so said Jesus according to Matthew 6:9.
Materially, Luke 11:2 is to the same effect: "When you pray, say . . . ," except that
here the demand of Jesus is his answer to a request put by one of the disciples (v. 1):
"Lord, teach us to pray, as John taught his disciples" — a request which in context
seems to be motivated less by the example of the instruction John gave his disciples
than by the fact that the disciples of Jesus had been witnesses of his own prayers:
"He was praying in a certain place, and when he ceased, one of his disciples said
to him, Lord, teach us to pray." In both Gospels the direction and instruction of
Jesus have first of all the character of liturgical instruction, but in both cases the
emphasis lies on material teaching. In Matthew (6:7f.) the "pray like this" is meant
to distinguish the prayer of the disciples from the empty speaking (βαττολογία, like
that of the Gentiles) that is charged against certain circles, the idea being that by
using many words (ἐν τῇ πολυλογίᾳ) they can secure a hearing from a God who is
far from them. What Jesus is telling the disciples is this: fewer words, but the correct
ones, are necessary. These words are correct on the presupposition that God is your
Father, the Father of those who are praying; that he is near to them, that he knows

their needs in advance, that he does not need from them any detailed rehearsals or entreaties, but he simply wants them to turn and cling to him in all their well-known need, calling upon him as the needy people they are. When they pray in this way, simply calling upon God, simply asking him as the one who knows their needs better than they do themselves, then they can and should count on the hearing for which those who pray like the Gentiles exert themselves in vain—this is where the emphasis lies in Luke. When people have God himself in view and call upon him, when they pray for the Holy Spirit (Lk. 11:13), then they cannot fail. The giving follows the asking, the finding the seeking, the opening the knocking (vv. 9f.). What they do can no more be in vain than the unabashed midnight request for three loaves (vv. 5ff.), or the request for a fish or an egg with which a hungry child approaches his father (vv. 11f.). In both cases it is the Father who is at issue, the Father who is near at hand even in all his majesty, seeing those who call upon him according to Matthew, answering their calling upon him according to Luke. He is "Father" alone in Luke 11:2, "Our Father who art in heaven" in Matthew 6:9, the introit which is also as such the sum of the Lord's Prayer and the ethical imperatives implicit in it.

Father! When used in Christian thought and speech as a term for God, the word "Father" is always to be employed and understood in precisely the same sense that it has here in the introit to the Lord's Prayer, namely, as a vocative. This can and must be called the fundamental rule of its Christian use and understanding. This rule must be remembered whenever the word is employed, not in direct address, but in statements, so that the One so called is not expressly addressed in the second person, but in the third person, as is unavoidable in practice, and as happens constantly in the New Testament itself. If the word is to have a Christian meaning and content, even in third-person statements it must be used in such a way that the function of the nominative as a *locum tenens* for the vocative is kept in mind and is indeed brought out in the nearer or more distant context of the statements concerned. If it is a matter of God, then seriously, properly, and strictly Christians cannot speak *about* the Father but only *to* him. They will certainly recognize that even before they speak, and quite apart from their doing so, he is the Father himself. They will not think that he becomes the Father only in and in virtue of their address. When we are thinking and speaking as Christians, "Father" cannot be just a human existential factor any more than "God" can. Yet Christians have to put into active practice their knowledge of God's being as Father. They have to do this in the form and power of their confession (not about him but to him): I believe in one God, the Father. They have to do it in response to the Word in which he declares himself as the One he is in himself. "The Father," we say; but what we have in mind, and must have in mind, when we dare to apply this word to God, to speak it and even to think it in relation to him, is: "O Father!" Father as a vocative, whether expressed or not, is the primal form of the thinking, the primal sound of the speaking, and the primal act of the obedience demanded of Christians. In other words, it is the primal act of the freedom Christians are given, the primal form of the faithfulness with which they may correspond to his faithfulness. They necessarily forget or deny that they are Christians if they leave out this vocative in what they think and say, if their life is not seriously and finally sustained and determined by this vocative. Or, positively, all that they do in obedience can consist only in a repetition, application, and concrete expression of this vocative: "Father!"

Certainly the Spirit—the living power of the work and word of Jesus Christ, the Spirit whom God has shed abroad in the hearts of Christians (Rom. 8:15), whom they have received from him and who has made them Christians—discloses to them objectively the truth that God is the Father and is their Father, and what this means. But he does so by subjectively impelling them, by himself crying "Abba, Father" according to Galatians 4:6, or, more cautiously but more vividly, by empowering them to call upon God in this way. As those who are enlightened by the Spirit to know the truth of God's fatherhood per se, they are at once driven (ἀγόμενοι) by him to act thus. The Spirit of God is the Spirit of sonship, in whose presence and under whose lordship and direction they have no other possible relationship to God, but they really do have this possibility—and they cannot help but make use of it—of turning to God with this vocative. They would not have the Spirit of Christ, they would not be Christ's or belong to his people (Rom. 8:9); the spirit impelling them would be a totally different spirit from him whom they are given and whom they have received: a spirit of bondage, the slavish spirit of fear of a remote and terrible God of human invention; they would not be Christians at all if with the cry, "Abba, Father," they would not accept God and take him seriously as the One he is, as the One who has spoken to them as such. How could they ever forget that this cry activates the freedom they are given and therefore the obedience required of them, the epitome of all Christian ethos? How could the word "Father," with reference to God, ever pass through their minds or over their lips without this cry to him echoing as the basic note in all their unavoidable (and justifiable) objectivizing thoughts and statements, without its determining their whole action as a direct response to him?

Father! God is this independently of the attitude or disposition with which other beings encounter or do not encounter him. He is it absolutely *for* them and in no sense *through* them. He is it essentially, in all his inner and outer glory, and he acts and speaks as such. This explains the need for thought and speech about him that can seriously, truly, and finally take place only in this vocative, that can consist only of calling upon him as Father. One thing must be clear and self-evident to those who become and are obedient to his command (which corresponds to his most proper being), that is, to Christians: in him they do not have to do with a final reality of neutral character, whether it be described, conceived, or postulated positively or purely negatively. In him they do not have to do with a "He" that is a mere cipher ascribed with more or less knowledge to an "It" concealed behind it, which is simply a bit of etiquette appended to it with more or less conviction and skill. The Father invoked by Christians is not just called such when deep down and in truth he is no more than an idea or epitome of fatherhood. Deep down and in truth he is really Father. He is thus a speaking and hearing subject, a subject that acts personally. He is more than a powerful and efficacious object; he is an object only to the extent that a person, an independent subject, can also be an object—that is, by making itself an object to others without ceasing to be a subject. To put it epigrammatically and objectively, in himself he is not an object. Whatever may be meant by fatherhood, it stands or falls by whether or not it is the distinction and revelation of the nature of this person, the manifestation of his inner and outer glory, and not by whether this person is simply the personification of what is truly and properly a neutral fatherhood. Here Kierkegaard is right: subjectivity is truth. With the "Father" thought and uttered and lived out by Christians, the One thus invoked is centrally and not incidentally, absolutely and not relatively, definitively and not provisionally addressed as subject, as a fatherly "Thou." He is thus affirmed as a fatherly "I" and taken seriously and literally as such. An "It," even though it might be the supreme "It," the Holy or Wholly Other (Otto), the Encompassing (Jaspers), could not be addressed as a "Thou" and afffirmed as an "I," or could be so only symbolically, so that this would not be the "Thou" or "I" that Christians have in mind when they speak of God. The vocative that Christians are empowered and required to think and utter and live out is a vocative with no conditions or mental reservations. It is invocation of the self-acting Subject-Father, and only thus is it invocation of God.

In the New Testament, as we have seen, invocation of the Father is a crying (κράζειν) according to Romans 8:23, a sighing (στενάζειν) according to Colossians 3:16 and Ephesians 5:19, a singing (ᾄδειν), or, according to Luke 10:21, a rejoicing (ἀγαλλιᾶσθαι). Materially it is a thanksgiving, a praising, and above all a praying and interceding, so that it is always an expressed or unexpressed speaking. Since it is a speaking, it obviously presupposes the personal being not only of the one who speaks but also of the one addressed. The former counts upon it that the latter hears, that in invoking the latter he is responding to the latter's prior invoking of himself. Thus the one invoked is no mere thing, no deaf and dumb idea, however lofty, nor in any sense a something; but in all his otherness he is a he, who as such does what no neutral thing can ever do and lets the one who calls upon him speak with him. This is he whom Christians invoke as Father.

Father! Understood as a vocative and used in Christian thought and speech, this word gives the required precision, the appropriate fullness, and the authentic interpretation to a word that in itself is indefinite, empty, and ambivalent, namely, the word "God." God himself, the one true and real God, obviously does not need this in order to avoid indistinctness, emptiness, and ambivalence. But the word "God" in all human languages does need it, for it can mean everything for some, this or that for others, and even nothing at all, or a mere illusion, for others. It can denote a mystery, or *the* mystery, beyond the totality of the time-space cosmos known to people or sensed by them. It can denote a particular mystery, ostensible or real, within this cosmos. Or it can denote the mystery of the unity of the cosmos as such. It can be used in the singular or in an arbitrary plural. Under its sign the existence of God or the gods can be affirmed or denied and the nature of God or the gods expounded in different ways. In relation to the word "God," the question is unavoidable: who among all those who have it in their minds or express it on their lips can claim that their picture or concept of God is wholly and exclusively correct? Might it not be that the establishment of a peaceful pantheon, which includes an altar to the unknown God, is the most suitable solution to the problem posed by the presence of that word? Or might it not be simpler to consign the problem to an historical museum by fundamentally renouncing any serious use of the word? Christians, however, move through this misty territory invoking the Father with crying, sighing, singing, and rejoicing, praising the Father, thanking the Father, and above all praying to the Father, their life being a life in this vocative. They do not do this with the claim that of themselves they know better than everyone else. They do not do it as those who, on the grounds of their religion and tradition, in their kerygma and dogma, in their special theology and philosophy, offer to all the others a patent solution on a platter, who carry off the prize amid so much authentic and inauthentic certainty and uncertainty, so much imaginative and unimaginative fantasy, so many areas full or free of problems, so many necessary and unnecessary conflicts and compromises on the part of those who think and utter the word "God." Christians know that they are in too great solidarity with all other men not to have to admit that even when they think and utter it, the word "God" will always need afresh the genuine precision, fullness, and interpretation that come to it. And they know much too much about the one true and real God not to be clear that authentic interpretation cannot come to the word "God" by any human defining, meditating, or speculating — not even their own — but comes only when the Word of God aids the intrinsically impotent word "God" and gives it the only possible and correct content. They are not made Christians by greater perspicacity or profundity but simply by being enabled to be those who perceive the Word of God. Thus they have not come out victors in the battle about the meaning of "God." It is just that, being the people they are, they cannot ignore or deny that God himself has spoken and speaks and that this means the end of all discussion concerning the word "God." "My children," they hear him say, and with this he becomes and is knowable to them as the one true and real God. "God speaks well about God" (Pascal). In responding to this with the invocation "Our Father," they recognize and confess him as the one he is. Hence the indefiniteness, emptiness, and ambivalence of the word "God" lies irrevocably behind them. They can and should take this word on their lips in a childlike, confident, peaceful, and merry way, because they now know what they are saying when they use it. They know because they are taught by God himself.

We take this connection between "God" and "Father" primarily from the New Testament Epistles, in which "Father" (πατήρ) is used when there is a desire to stress the Christian qualification of the word "God" (θεός) and to characterize the term in accordance with this purpose. This need can be especially, though not exclusively, present when the meaning of θεός is not at once apparent in the context, for example, in the introductions to letters with their greetings and good wishes to the community and their thanking (εὐχαριστεῖν) or praising (εὐλογεῖν) of God which leads on at once to all that follows. Who or what unites the writers to those to whom they write? God — yet not a general deity, nor this or that God, but the one who in his self-declaration has shown himself to be Father and in this sense God. "God the Father" (ὁ θεὸς καὶ πατήρ) — this expression, since it occurs in 1 Thessalonians 1:3 and 3:11, is probably the original form of the designation, and it can still be used sometimes in later Epistles (2 Cor. 1:3; cf. 11:31; Eph. 1:3; 1 Pet. 1:3). That πατήρ is an interpretation of θεός is especially clear in 1 Corinthians 8:6 and Ephesians 4:6, where εἷς θεός, not more closely defined as such, is equated with εἷς πατήρ in the broadest sense (and even more expressly "who is above all and through all and in all," Eph. 4:6). As a rule, however, the characterization of God is achieved in the formula θεὸς πατήρ. Naturally, since the order is irreversible, a father is not defined as God but God as Father. Christians know, recognize, and confess as God the God who is Father. In relation to this God, with wishes that call upon him, the apostles greet their communities. It is in knowledge of him that they are united to their communities and their communities to them. God the Father — defined as "our Father" in the Lord's Prayer, is the one who has given Paul his apostleship according to Galatians 1:1 [cf. v. 3]. "Grace and peace from God our Father" (we shall have to deal separately with a decisive expansion of this formula) becomes a stereotyped greeting to those to whom he writes. One reads of the glory (δόξα) of this God the Father in Philippians 2:11, of his πρόγνωσις in 1 Peter 1:2, of the thanks Christians should offer him in Colossians 3:17. "God and the Father" occurs twice in James (1:27; 3:9), and the equation is obvious when, as the source of all good, he is called the Father of lights in 1:17 and the Father of spirits who is above all human fathers in Hebrews 12:9. The word θεός, being obviously integrated into πατήρ and implied in it, can also be omitted, as in the invocation in Galatians 4:6, Romans 8:15, and as also in the statement in Romans 6:4 (materially equivalent to Gal. 1:1) that Christ was raised up by the glory of the Father. It is just the Father who in Colossians 1:12 adapts Christians for participation in the inheritance of the saints. It is just to the Father that Jesus Christ has opened up access (Eph. 2:18). It is just before the Father — the Father from whom every family is named — that the apostle bows his knees (Eph. 3:14). Along with the much more common θεός or ὁ θεός, and without any visible connection with it, "Father" also plays a significant role in 1 John. The same applies especially in the four Gospels. The Fourth Gospel stands out because here the use of "Father" is more than double that of "God." Here too the terms are plainly connected only in four passages (5:18; 6:27; 8:41; 20:17). In the Synoptics the use of "God" predominates, and no connection is made between it and "Father." Here, as in John, we have the strongest confirmation of the critical function of "Father" in relation to "God," for the word occurs only in the Lord's own sayings. In distinction from Paul's use, only Jesus is said to address as Father him whom others call God. Even statements about the Father come only from his lips. Consistently in John, at the Johannine-sounding Matthew 11:27 and par., but in other places in the Synoptics as well, the Father is the Father of Jesus, and as such, according to the characteristic Matthean phrase, he is the "heavenly" Father or the Father "in heaven." According to the Gospels, it is for Jesus alone to proclaim the Father as also "your" Father, or, in the Lord's Prayer, "our" Father. We shall have to come back to this. It must be mentioned here, however, because the christological significance of the word "Father," which is plain in the Epistles, may already be seen unmistakably in the Gospels, and with it the critical function of the term in its relation to "God."

Father! But what is the precision, fullness, and interpretation that are given to the word "God" in this vocative? When God is called Father, does this mean, as the term at once suggests, that he is the founder and head of a family, of a society of beings who are related by nature, physically, to him and to one another, and who thus belong to him and to one another? Although we shall have to be more precise, the word certainly points in this direction. The word "Father" defines God as the one without whom the reality distinct from himself would not exist; through whom, however, it does exist, so that it owes to him its existence, form, and meaning, and therefore its unity and interconnection. Nevertheless, the word "Father" as used by Christians moves on at once far beyond the boundaries of this immediate significance. In distinction from a family, the fellowship of which God is founder and head is not a fellowship alongside which there might be others with other founders and heads. It embraces everything and all things, all the reality distinct from God. Since it is totally dependent on him, since it totally coinheres in him and therefore in itself, he and it are not alike but unlike. There is no natural or physical relationship between them. He is not its genitor. "Father" in the mind and on the lips of Christians means indeed the source and raison d'être of all other reality. It means, therefore, being with it. It means its coinherence with itself on the basis of its common origin in him. But it also points to God as its absolutely superior origin, as its Creator, and to itself as his creation. Supremely transcending the most immediate sense of the term, it denotes God as the one true Father whom all creaturely fatherhood (Eph. 3:15), whether creaturely fathers know it or not, must attest and confirm, but can do so only in a likeness, and not with equality.

The ancient Greeks could also call Zeus "Father," but he is father of the gods only as their genitor and therefore as the first among equals, not as their creator. Nor does one glean the sense of creator from Plato's references to the father of all or of all things. In the mystery religions, we find the idea of a brotherhood of initiates united in the cult of their particular God, but in context this seems to denote their supposedly common physical origin in the one they worship, and therefore their oneness with him by nature. The same has to be presupposed when the Stoics find the fatherliness of the deity in the fact that it gives to man a share in the logos — something that G. Schrenk has not sufficiently taken into account in his otherwise very instructive article in *TDNT* V, pp. 945ff. "The Father from whom are all things" (1 Cor. 8:6), "one God and Father of us all, who is above all and through all and in all" (Eph. 4:6), "the Father from whom every family in heaven and on earth is named" (Eph. 3:15) — all these, along with this quotation from Aratus: "We are indeed his offspring" (Acts 17:28), may well be conscious reminiscences from the thought and speech of the surrounding Hellenistic world whose formulations the New Testament authors could adopt, but in so doing, as may be seen clearly from the contexts in which they are used, could in the very same words have in view, and say to their readers, something very different from what the words meant and said in their original setting. The one whom the New Testament authors called "God the Father," and as such the origin of everything and all things, is certainly not a God who stands in a natural relation with the world and with men as their genitor. In distinction from all such gods, he is the one (εἷς) who is characterized not only by his freely originating but also by his having a complete power of disposal over all that is and was and is to come outside him. Thus in principle he is both transcendent over it and immanent to it at one and the same time. If as the ground and master of a distinct reality he is comparable to other fathers, as the free ground and perfect master of this distinct reality he is Father in a different sense from all other fathers. As is emphasized in Matthew, and consequently in the Matthean version of the Lord's Prayer, he is the Father "in heaven," the "heavenly" Father of everything and all things. Similarly, the descriptions in Ephesians 3:15 and 4:6 remind us no less of his absolute superiority over all things than of his absolute presence to all things in this superiority. Heaven is both unattainably distant from everything and all things on earth and also at the same time unavoidably present to them. In the New Testament the Father is the Creator, the God who both distinguishes himself from everything and all things and also unites himself to them, the God who in relation to them exists simultaneously in this transcendence and immanence, the God who cannot be mastered but can only be invoked by his creature, yet can and may and should be invoked by it.

Father! It is obvious that this vocative points, but does so in a very special way, to a place where the one who calls on God knows that he himself, along with everything and all things, is absolutely dependent and conditioned. It points to this place too, so that there can be no contradicting Schleiermacher's definition of God as the "source of the feeling of absolute dependence." All the same, this definition is unsatisfactory because the source might finally be a neuter, an original "It" or "Something." For Schleiermacher this is what it actually was — an interpretation which, as we have seen, is ruled out by the personal address "Father." If the source is God as a "Thou," and hence as a subject, then obviously much more is meant than that God as Father in heaven is the origin of the world and of people. What is meant is God in the function grounded in his fatherhood as absolute origin, in the exercise of his authority over everything and all things; God in his work as Father of the household who provides and teaches, but God also as Lord, King, and Judge in his kingdom and possession. He is the one who as Creator, in free power of disposal, tirelessly, uninterruptedly, and reliably bears and practices full responsibility for the continuity of the being, the life, the past, present, and future of his creation, as the one who is also its commander, whose will and purpose it must follow, whose legislative, executive, and judicial power it must respect, and to whom it is responsible in all that it does or does not do. "Father" is the vocative of absolute respect before this God, a respect which even the most mighty neuter, even in its quality as creative origin, could not evoke from man. On the lips of Christians, of course, this vocative, when applied to God the Lord, King, and Judge, denotes something specific in his being and action. Thus the final word concerning the preciseness, fullness, and interpretation of the word "God" cannot be spoken even by describing and understanding God as the household Father, Regent, and Judge who watches and rules over everything and all things, right and necessary though it undoubtedly is to describe and understand him first in this general way. There are all kinds of household fathers, regents, and judges, some of them self-seeking, slovenly, arrogant, and even tyrannical and wicked. Who knows with what mind or in what manner a father of this kind, even in the most eminent sense, might rule and govern everything and all things? What it means to call on him as the Ruler of all things will be very much conditioned by the spirit in which this Ruler of all things exists and works. Hence we need to probe more deeply.

The idea that a father should be not only a genitor but also a household father, a provider, instructor, lord, king, and judge is obvious. No less obvious was and is the corresponding conception of the deity as a postulate and fantasy of pre- and extra-Christian humanity, though this idea, while a familiar one, is not well founded or certain, and above all it does not entail respect or trust. Rather, it is more incidental than necessary, more speculative and aesthetic than practically effective. Now New Testament man also knows God in this fatherly function. He lives with the knowledge that in God he has to do with the all-pervasive Pantocrator in great and little things alike (Rev. 1:8, etc.). "Abba, Father, all things are possible to thee," is the form of address in the prayer of Jesus in Gethsemane (Mk. 14:36). "My Father is working still" (ἕως ἄρτι), up to this hour — to the eschatological hour of the work of the Son and beyond — is the saying of Jesus in John 5:17, and this too might well refer to God's almighty work as the Father. God is the Father who feeds the birds that neither sow nor reap nor gather into barns (Mt. 6:26), who arrays the lilies, which neither toil nor spin, in a glory greater than that of Solomon (6:28), without whom not a sparrow falls to the earth, who has counted even the hairs on the heads of his people (6:8, 32), and who knows their needs long before they ask that they be met: reason enough why they not only need not be anxious about their lives or their bodies (6:25, 31), but why such anxiety should be forbidden them as pagan disobedience unworthy of the children of this Father. As their Father, however, God also sees into their hidden being and rewards them according to what he sees there (6:4, 18). They call upon him as Father who, as 1 Peter 1:17 reminds Christians, judges them without respect of person, each according to his works. All these statements have general validity and application. They are made both esoterically and exoterically. They are made with reference to members of the community, but since these are the Father's witnesses to all other men who, without knowing it, also belong to the Father's house, have their home in him, and are subject to his law, they are made also with reference to all men. If, however, these statements are to be heard and understood in New Testament terms, they need to be elucidated according to the context of the New Testament message. What is described in them is not the work of an unknown Almighty who can be pictured at will, but that of a very definite Almighty, whose work has a concrete character, the work of the Father who wills to be and can be invoked, not in fear but in respect, that is, in a fear of God which is not frightened of him but honors him, in the authentic fear of trust in God. God is the Father who is the "Father in heaven" not merely as the living Lord of everything and all things but also as the one who is this with a specific intention, disposition, and purpose in relation to his household.

Father! In the minds and on the lips of Christians the vocative signifies the "dear" Father. The phrase "the dear Lord" has been greatly watered down and abused. Not without reason it arouses suspicion and derision. Nevertheless, we cannot avoid it. Note that it is not a more precise definition that Christians have to wrestle through and on which they have to decide. They know a God who is not just the dear Lord in the thoughts and wishes of those who revere him, but who is dear in himself, the God who is free, almighty, and sovereign in his love, and not otherwise. They know this God as the Creator and Lord of men and things. They ascribe nothing to him when they thank and praise him. His own nature and work lay on them the inescapable demand that they should approach him thus. Similarly, the confidence with which they come to him as petitioners is not their own postulate or venture but their due acknowledgment of his being as the Creator who is good to his creatures, as the Lord, King, and Judge who wills and achieves the best for all the members and inhabitants of his house, as the majestic subject to whom they may say a familiar "Thou" because he has first said a familiar "Thou" to them, standing over against them as an "I" in the incomparable seriousness of a friendliness which cannot be defeated by any indifference or even hostility on their part. For this reason their thanksgiving, praise, and prayer are not forced but joyful, nor are they threatened by any doubt but are certain of their cause, not because in their human minds and mouths they cannot be skeptical and sullen since unbelieving, but because in relation to him to whom they are offered they can have no other character than that of a free and supremely cheerful and peaceful action, because he himself evokes and awakens this character in them. He has acted toward them, and also spoken to them, in fatherly goodness, and he still does so — in a free fatherly goodness with which he does not have to approach them but does in fact approach them, because this alone is his mind and attitude toward them — a fatherly goodness that is a vital necessity for them (for how could they live if he were to withhold it?), but which they have not earned, to which they have no claim, and of which they have never in any way whatever shown themselves worthy. That he should lavish this upon them, and handle them with it, they can experience and record only as the one great and incomprehensible wonder of their lives. As those who receive and know it, they find themselves chosen for it with no ability, cooperation, or right of their own. But they *do* find themselves chosen for it — this is what makes them Christians. They would not yet be Christians, or would be so no longer, if they could not call upon God in his majesty as Creator and his function as Lord, King, and Ruler of his house, if they could not call upon him as all these things (which he *is*) with experience and knowledge of his free fatherly goodness, in the way appropriate to this qualification of his nature, being, and action — if their calling upon God had not yet begun or had ceased to be a joyful and assured praising, thanking, and praying, They would then be dealing still, or once again, with a self-chosen and self-created God. Christians are those who find that the world and they themselves are loved in all the unbridgeable distance from God which God himself has bridged, so that now they too can and may and should love him in return — they who are far from him, him who is near to them, crying "Abba, Father" to him — they who are far from him as those who are now very near to him.

We do not see the forest for the trees if we think we should omit the New Testament qualification of God's fatherhood as fatherly goodness. It is, of course, true and remarkable enough that in the relatively far fewer Old Testament passages in which Yahweh is spoken of as Father, this theme is more explicit than in the many New Testament texts in which θεός is interpreted or replaced by πατήρ. This fact seems strange at first, but there is good reason for it, since in the New Testament the qualification is an integral part of the controlling statement on which we have already touched and to which we shall have to return later, namely, that God is Father because and insofar as Jesus Christ is his Son and he is the Father of Jesus Christ. Alongside this statement there is, as a rule, little need to lay special stress on the Father's love, goodness, grace, and so forth, since it contains within itself all that need be said about the character of the divine Creator and Father as the fount and origin of all good things (Calvin, *Inst.* I, 2, 2). To the best of my knowledge there are only two passages where this rule is broken: James 1:17, where God is called "the Father of lights" from whom comes down "every good endowment and every perfect gift," and 2 Corinthians 1:3, where the formula used also at Colossians 1:3 [and Rom. 15:6; 2 Cor. 11:31; Eph. 1:3; 1 Pet. 1:3], "God the Father of our Lord Jesus Christ," parallels "the Father of mercies and God of all comfort," that is, the Father who as such is the basis and origin of mercy and from whom, therefore, all true comfort and admonition are to be expected. This description of God is perhaps a reminiscence of Psalm 103:13 and therefore of the Old Testament conception of God as the Father of Israel: "As a father pities his children, so the Lord pities those who fear him." The God of Israel is the one who has mercy on Israel as its Father, and it lives as it may continually experience, invoke, and expect his fatherly mercy in its history. In the free choice of his love he has established the relationship—not a natural but an historical relationship—between himself and this people, and then in particular his relationship to the eschatological heir of the throne of David, electing and determining himself to be its Head, Guarantor, and Guardian. "You are my son, today I have begotten you" (Ps. 2:7), is the declaration of his will with specific reference to the coming king. "He shall cry to me, 'Thou art my Father, my God, and the Rock of my salvation' " (Ps. 89:26). "I will be his father, and he shall be my son. . . . I will not take my steadfast love from him" (2 Sam. 7:14f.). Whether the special relationship between Yahweh and this eschatological son of David is a reflection of his relationship to the chosen people as such, or whether it is the original of that relationship, is hard to decide and perhaps foolish to ask. There are undoubtedly very similar, even parallel passages in the Song of Moses that relate to Israel as such: "Is he not your father, who created you, who made you and established you?" (Dt. 32:6). We may also consult Hosea 11:1, 8: "When Israel was a child, I loved him, and out of Egypt I called my son. . . . Is not Ephraim my son?[2] How can I give you up, O Ephraim! How can I hand you over, O Israel! . . . My heart recoils within me, my compassion grows warm." Jeremiah 31:20, which is perhaps independent of the Hosea reference, is to the same effect: "Is Ephraim my dear son? Is he my darling child? For as often as I speak against him, I do remember him still. Therefore my heart yearns for him; I will surely have mercy on him." So is the invocation in Isaiah 63:15–17: "Where are thy zeal and thy might? The yearning of thy heart and thy compassion are withheld from me. For thou art our Father, though Abraham does not know us and Israel does not acknowledge us; thou, O Lord, art our Father, our Redeemer from of old is thy name. O Lord, why dost thou make us err from thy ways and harden our heart, so that we fear thee not?" The final saying is a significantly palpable element in the context of all these passages apart from the two about the eschatological Son of David. The fatherly being and action of Yahweh are those of his free mercy to his people, whose own being and action do not correspond to his but contradict

---

[2]In the MS, Barth seems to have mixed up the Hosea and Jeremiah passages, and in correcting the mistake he failed to strike out the phrase "Is not Ephraim my son?" from the Hosea quotation.

them. It is a corrupt and crooked generation, a foolish and unwise people — children who have broken faith with their Father (Dt. 32:5f.). "But they did not know that I healed them. I led them with cords of compassion, with the bands of love" (Hos. 11:3f.). This people speaks of him and invokes him as its father, the friend of its youth — and it does evil (Jer. 3:4f., 19f.). "If then I am a father, where is my honor?" (Mal. 1:6). This is the situation in the Old Testament. One must bear it in mind, for in the New Testament another Son of the same Father appears who is very different from this unruly people and who puts right what this people did wrong. In contrast, the one who is called Father in the Old Testament does not need to be replaced by any other God. It should be noted that in none of the passages adduced is it ever questioned that he is the Father of his people or that the people has a right to call upon him as such. Israel *is* his son. Yahweh disciplines it, but as a father does his son (Dt. 8:5). Even as he does it — we should recall Proverbs 3:12 in this connection — he loves it as a father who wants the best for his son. The painful contrast visible in the Old Testament is the contrast between the children and their Father, not a contrast in God himself. In the words of James 1:17, God is the Father of unchangeable light. This is how he gave himself to be known and experienced by Israel as the Lord of its history (Ps. 105 – 107). The unfaithful people may and must always seek him, the faithful One, continually thanking and praising him by whose mercy it lives, continually praying to him out of the depths [Ps. 130:1]. In this regard the people of Christ can only join the people of Israel. For apart from the one obedient Son who came in place of the disobedient, this people too is a people of children who are not worthy of their Father but can as such live only by his mercy.

Father! In all that we have said thus far we have not yet said one final thing about the subject intended and denoted by this vocative in the thought and speech of Christians — a final thing that is not just an extension and completion of the line followed thus far, but which forms the decisive meaning and sustaining ground of all that we have previously had to emphasize in developing the vocative. This last thing is no more and no less than the first thing which we have tacitly presupposed thus far, the starting point of the whole line that we have followed. We have been dealing as yet only with the predicates of the subject upon whom Christians call, namely, God the Father. We have been dealing with his being as the personal Creator and Ruler of everything and all things and therefore as the free origin and giver of all good things, as the one who has mercy. But what about the fatherly subject who bears and guarantees all these predicates, this whole being of God as Father? Who and what is God the Father himself who is not only *called* the personal Creator and Ruler, the origin and source of all good — perhaps because it occurs to Christians to regard him as such — but who *is* these things as the one true and real God in his distinctive nature? Abstracted from the true God, the predicates might point in very different directions from those in which Christians are looking when they call him Father. Have there not been people who in all seriousness and with profound credibility have even extolled and invoked war as the Father, Lord, and Benefactor of all things and all men? Abstracted from their Subject, all the predicates could be understood and expounded in ways very different from those that seem self-evident to Christians: the Creator according to the

model of the creature, the Ruler as the symbol of the self-glory of the in-
habitant of his house, his benefits as the best possible fulfilment of human
wishes and desires, his mercy perhaps as a mythological reflection of the
sympathy man feels for himself. Abstracted from their Subject, the predicates in themselves and as such might have no meaning at all, might simply
point to a void where there is no God, the Father with his qualities and
functions, so that it is pointless to look this way and to cry "Father." Even
when we accept the divine predicates contained in it, the Christian vocative
"Father" might still be for us an ambivalent and perhaps even a totally
futile enterprise, a "striving after wind" [Eccl. 1:14, etc.], unless we are
clear on to what extent the one we call upon according to Christian knowledge *is* God the Father in reality and truth.

Now the decision regarding the nature and existence of the Subject upon
whom Christians call as Father cannot be their own affair — the affair of
their own courage or concern — their own problem. This decision lies behind
them: not as one they had to make, nor as one which they had to win
through either casual resolution or more or less severe intellectual and moral
battles and traumas, nor as a commitment that might later be reconsidered,
that would indeed have to be reconsidered like all the human decisions we
make. Rather, it is a decision that has been made irrevocably at a very
different place, but also one that they may recognize and acknowledge as
a decision that was validly made for them. It is from this decision that they
come as Christians. They are Christians as their lives repeat this decision,
as each day they are obedient to it afresh. To be really obedient, to become
so again and again, and to remain so — this and this alone can be their own
affair, the affair of their own courage and concern. When they become and
are really obedient, then they find themselves confronted directly by the
reality and truth of God the Father: directly, that is, in such a way that
they could make themselves the theme of questioning and discussion rather
than they can the nature and existence of this Subject. They affirm these
in the venture of invocation — which they do not venture arbitrarily on their
own reckoning and at their own risk but simply in the commanded obedience. They have a Lord whom they follow by making this venture and who
in ordering them to do so guarantees and accepts responsibility for the
reality and truth of him whom he invites and summons them to invoke as
God the Father. Jesus Christ is the Lord whom they obey, in whose work
and word the decision is made and manifested concerning the nature and
existence of the subject, God the Father, who confronts them with this
Subject in such a way that they may recognize him and cannot but acknowledge him in his nature and existence. They come from the decision
which is taken in him with divine authority concerning the nature and
existence of the Subject, God the Father, when, without fear of looking in
the wrong directions or even in the void, they venture to cry, "Abba, Father."

What does it mean when, in the stereotyped greetings of Paul's letters, with
their wish (or better, perhaps, their promise) "grace be to you and peace," there is
regularly added to the phrase "from God our Father," which gives precision,

adds fullness, and appends an interpretation to the concept of the God in whose name the apostle speaks, the further phrase "and the Lord Jesus Christ"? Is this meant to describe God as our Father and also as the Father of the Lord Jesus Christ? In itself this is not impossible. He *is* (2 Cor. 1:3; Col. 1:3) "the Father of our Lord Jesus Christ," and he is expressly called this in the liturgical introductions to Paul's Epistles, which usually follow the greetings. On this view, the phrase as used in the greetings would be explaining how far we are in a position to speak of God as our Father, namely, because he is the Father of the Lord Jesus Christ. If it is more likely, however, that we have here a new statement and not just a repetition of one already made in the greetings, then the second genitive, introduced in the greeting by a καί (and), is not just giving us more information on whose father God is. It is instead a second indication from whom the desired or promised grace and peace will come and are to be expected. They come from God our Father, and that means, concretely, from the Lord Jesus Christ. Naturally this does not mean, as Zinzendorf would sometimes have it,[3] that Jesus Christ is really the God who is known and invoked as Father, but rather that it is Jesus Christ—of one essence with the Father and the perfect Executor and Revealer of his will—who as the Lord of his community guarantees Christians that God is their Father, making it possible for them to recognize him as such, and permitting and commanding them to call upon him as such. Thus the being in relation to God which is promised them—their being as those to whom his grace is addressed and who may thus have peace with him—is in its unity the work and gift of God the Father, their Father, and also the work and gift of him who discloses and guarantees to them the existence and fatherly goodness of God, who unites them to this God and claims them for him, namely, the Lord Jesus Christ. The grace and peace that they are promised as Christians, because Jesus Christ is their only Mediator and Revealer, are to be understood and described, concretely speaking, as his work and his grace.

But how does it come about that through Jesus Christ people are set in the relation to God in which the problem of his nature and existence is no longer a problem for them, God himself being directly present as their Father in a self-demonstration of his nature and existence that can neither be overlooked nor refuted? To this question we have given the primary answer that it comes about, that the confrontation of these people with the reality and truth of God as their Father takes place, as Jesus Christ enables, invites, and summons them to invoke him as such. Obedient to him as their Lord, they come to be and are set in that unproblematical relationship to God the Father. As they call upon him as such according to the permission, command, and order of Jesus Christ, God the Father in his nature and existence comes before them unmistakably and irrefutably. But how does Jesus Christ give them this order, and in what form do they receive him? We might ask as at baptism: What is the foundation, posited by Jesus Christ himself, of the invocation in whose obedient performance the one invoked is so directly present to those who invoke him? The answer in relation to

[3]Barth had in view N. L. von Zinzendorf's *Ein Gemein-Rede vom Vater-Amte des Sohnes* . . . , esp. pp. 3f. For extracts, see the German text, *Gesamtausgabe, Das christliche Leben*, p. 98, n. 16.

baptism was that Jesus Christ founded baptism and instituted it as the order, binding on the community, of the beginning of all Christian life, simply by letting himself be baptized by John in the Jordan. So now the simple answer is that he founded calling on God the Father—and made it binding on his people—by doing it first himself, and in so doing giving a prior example of what he demanded of them, or rather, demanding it of them by himself doing it. He took them up into the movement of his own prayer. His making of this movement was an integral part of his history as the Mediator between God and man. Hence, life in relationship to him, in his discipleship, in obedience to him as the Lord, will always consist in union with this work of his, in fulfilling this movement of his after him and with him. If the history of Jesus Christ is not a past phenomenon, if he rose from the dead as the subject of this history which happened then and there, and if in the power of the Holy Spirit he is here and now the living Lord of his community, of Christians, then he not only was but is here and today the man who exists in that movement to the Father, calling upon the Father in the place and at the head of all men. From the fact that he was and is this, there thus arises for all who recognize and acknowledge him as their Lord the obligatory command—the first of all commands—that they do as he does and join with him in calling upon God the Father.

The background of the demand in Matthew 6:9, "Pray then like this," is the fact, stressed in all the Gospels, that Jesus himself prayed as any other person does to God, and prayed to him as his Father. According to the important note in Luke 3:21, he prayed when he had himself baptized in the Jordan as one of the crowd that rushed there. According to Mark 1:35, he prayed when he moved on from a narrower sphere in Capernaum to preach more widely throughout Galilee. According to Luke 6:12, he prayed before calling the twelve. According to Matthew 14:23—an interesting point—he prayed between feeding the five thousand (Jesus and the world) and the perilous crossing of the lake by the disciples (Jesus and his community). According to Luke 9:18, he prayed directly before asking, "Who do the people say that I am?" According to Luke 9:29, he prayed in the act of transfiguration on the mountain. According to Matthew 26:36ff., he prayed as he entered on the way of the passion in Gethsemane. The author of Hebrews obviously saw in the prayers of Jesus, especially in Gethsemane, the action in his life that was decisive for his character as the new and true high priest: "In the days of his flesh, Jesus offered up prayers and supplications . . . to him who was able to save him from death" (Heb. 5:7). And always, when not just the fact of praying is noted but something is told us about the content of his prayers, "Father" is the address with which he turns to God. Thus at another decisive hour, when the seventy whom he had provisionally sent out came back (Mt. 11:25f.; Lk. 10:21), he prayed: "I thank thee, Father, Lord of heaven and earth, that thou hast hidden these things [the power of the imminent kingdom triumphant in him, the Son] from the wise and understanding and revealed them to babes; yea, Father, for such was thy gracious will." Again, in the prayer in Gethsemane, "Father" in Luke 22:42, "My Father" in Matthew 26:39, 42, and "Abba, Father" in Mark 14:36—perhaps according to a tradition to which Paul reached back in Galatians 4:6 and Romans 8:15. Again, in Luke 23:34: "Father, forgive them; for they know not what they do," and then in Luke 23:46: "Father, into thy hands I commit my spirit." Again, in John's Gospel at 11:41, before the raising of Lazarus: "Father, I thank thee that thou hast heard me," and at 12:27f., as he enters upon the passion: "And what shall I say? Father, save me from this hour? No, for this purpose I have come to this hour. Father, glorify thy name." Again and especially in the so-called high priestly prayer in John 17: "Father . . . glorify thy Son that the Son may glorify thee" (vv. 1, 5); "Holy Father, keep them in thy name" (v. 11); "Father, I desire that they also, whom thou hast given me, may be with me where I am" (v. 24); "O righteous Father, the world has not known thee, but I have known thee; and these know that thou hast sent me" (v. 25). From all these passages we learn not merely that Jesus prayed according to the depiction of his history in the Gospels but also that he prayed "like this" (οὕτως). He went before his disciples in obedience to his own command and thus made it obligatory for them. One might say that the command in Matthew 6:9 ("pray then like this") stands in the same relation to the prayers of Jesus as does the baptismal command of Matthew 28:19 to his baptism in the Jordan.

This imperative of Jesus Christ is thus the basis of the vocative "Father" in the thought and speech of Christians and hence also of their knowledge of the nature and existence of this God, whom there can be no question of their denying or exchanging for some other god. But now we must press on a little further. This imperative rings out for its part with the force of an indicative. Jesus has a right to call upon God as Father, and to command other men to do the same, because in distinction from all others he knows God as Father on his own, directly, without any need for guidance or instruction. He knows him thus because originally, properly, and by nature God is his Father. Thus the imperative that we others may and should call upon God as Father is not the requirement of a general morality or religion that suggests itself to all men. It is the command of Jesus Christ in his self-proclamation, the command of the covenant between God and us men fulfilled in him and in him alone. For the fact that God is our Father is not a general truth known and accessible to everyone. It can be accessible and known to everyone only through him in whom it is originally, properly, and directly truth, in whom the fulfilment of the covenant took place: *my* father, and for that reason, on those grounds, included within it, *your* Father and *our* Father. The fulfilment of the covenant that took place in him means that God and this one man — this one in place of all others — belong together as Father and Son, that they are indeed one to the extent that reciprocally they perfectly know and confirm and love one another. This Son perfectly executes the will of his Father, and this Father perfectly brings to light the work of his Son. This is what did not happen, and could not happen, prior to Christ's coming in the father-son relation between Yahweh and Israel. Now as this one who in the place of all others is united and one with God as his father, as the one Word of the unity and union of God and man as Father and Son, Jesus Christ, in anticipation and promise of what all others are to be called, addresses certain people called Christians as his brothers and sisters, manifests God to them as their Father too, calls upon them to call upon God as Father, and confronts them inescapably with this reality and truth. Thus our freedom to call upon God as Father is grounded absolutely in the way in which Jesus Christ called upon him, and still does so, when he turns to him. Not out of the depths of some capability of our nature, not in the exercise of such a capability, but in the power of the grace displayed and effective in Jesus Christ, in the power of the fellowship which God in the freedom of his love has set up between himself and us, within the new order of being instituted in him, that imperative rings out, and the vocative "Father" becomes possible, necessary, and actual in human thought and speech as the basic act of human obedience. In ourselves we have no freedom for it. But the one who called and calls upon God as Father because he was and is his Father, he, the firstborn among many brethren (Rom. 8:29), gives what he demands of us, freeing us for it.

E. Lohmeyer (*Das Vater-Unser*, 1947[2]) was right when he said that calling God Father, or the reality and truth indicated by it, "is the fact that underlies the whole life and faith of primitive Christianity . . . the one miracle which draws people out of all nations and men and draws them as children to their Father" (p. 25). Already in the Old Testament as an interpretation of the name of Yahweh, calling God Father had intimated the turning from the present age to the consummation (p. 27). According to the New Testament authors, however, it is obviously not at all self-evident that God should be called and objectively should be the Father. We have noted already that in the Synoptics the term is used for God only in sayings of the Lord — as though it were Jesus' privilege to call him Father. He alone can speak not only of *his* Father but also sometimes of *your* Father. He says "our Father" only in the address of the prayer which he commanded his disciples to pray (Mt. 6:9), and the "our" is not even there in Luke's version (11:2). Only in supreme and fearful astonishment can it be legitimately repeated when we pray the Lord's Prayer. That it denotes a miracle should also be remembered in relation to the repetition of "from God our Father" in the greetings in the apostolic letters. How can we indeed address God as Father and even as our Father? The importance of this question as the basis of our hesitation, and at the same time the secret of the true answer given in the apostolic greetings in the phrase "and our Lord Jesus Christ," may be seen in Matthew 11:27 — 29: "All things have been delivered to me by my Father; and no one knows the Son except the Father, and no one knows the Father except the Son and any one to whom the Son chooses to reveal him." On this basis the call goes out, "Come to me, all who labor and are heavy-laden"; on this basis, "Take my yoke upon you, and learn from me"; on this basis, "Pray then like this." This note is particularly basic in the message of the Fourth Gospel. Here too the word "Father" occurs only in Jesus' sayings, with three exceptions which simply confirm the rule: John 5:18, where the Jews complain because Jesus says that God is his Father; John 13:3, where the evangelist notes that Jesus knew the Father had given all things into his hands; and John 14:8, where Philip says to him, "Lord, show us the Father." Even more strictly than in the Synoptics there is here an avoidance even in the sayings of Jesus of any reference to "your" Father or "our" Father until we come to the Easter story, which at 20:17 contains the highly significant saying, deliberately not introduced earlier: "Go to my brethren and say to them, I am ascending to *my* Father and *your* Father, to *my* God and *your* God." The decisive point in all this is that throughout John's Gospel he who is called Father is described as the Father of the Son, that is, of Jesus (Mt. 11:27f.), the one who has sent *him* into the world, to whom *he* returns, whose work *he* has come to do, whom *he* and he alone reveals to men. The glory of the incarnate Word (Jn. 1:14) is that which he, the only begotten, shares with the Father (1:18). He, the Son, is in his Father as his Father is in him (10:38; 14:10). He always was and is in the bosom of the Father (1:18). He knows this Father as this Father knows him (10:15). He and this Father are not identical but one (ἕν, 10:30). Thus he who sees him sees the Father (14:9). Only he who sees him! Not to know him is not to know the Father (8:19;

16:3). "No one comes to the Father, but by me" (14:6). The reserve, or, better, the caution with which the New Testament uses the term "Father" for God should be noted. According to the New Testament, there is without question a way, an access (προσαγωγή, Eph. 2:18) that has been opened up for all men to God the Father. A freedom has been granted to all men to invoke God as their Father. To all men there is addressed, and all men may grasp, the promise of a life that is determined, oriented, and characterized by calling upon God in this way. Nevertheless (Mt. 7:14), the gate is narrow, and the way hard, that leads to this life. "I am the door" (Jn. 10:9). "I am the way" (Jn. 14:6). God is originally and properly Father as the Father of the one Jesus Christ. Thus it is "by me" (Jn. 14:6) or "by him" (Eph. 2:18) that God is "your" or "our" Father for other men, even for Christians. His brethren have it from him (Jn. 20:17) that his Father is also their Father and his God their God. The house with many rooms (Jn. 14:2) is the house of his Father. It is in his right to invoke God as Father that he gives a share to his people, to those chosen by him (Jn. 15:16), to those who believe in his name (Jn. 1:12). "Apart from me you can do nothing" (15:5); you do not have this right. As the evangelical and christological indicative shines forth and gives light: he knows the Father, he loves him, he is in him, he is one with him, he reveals him — so the evangelical imperative is issued and comes into force: "Pray then like this."

We still have to answer a final question. What is the meaning of the indicative in which this imperative is grounded, and with it the Christian's obedient invocation of God as Father? In what sense does he who sees Jesus see the Father? In what sense does Jesus reveal God as "his" Father and therefore as "our" or "the" Father? In what sense does he open up access to him? Certainly not by merely proclaiming a thesis to the effect that God is Father! We search the New Testament in vain for any such thesis. It would be no more than a fairly obvious thing that not a few people might arrive at on their own with no need for the proclamation of Jesus. It is hard to see how such a thesis, no matter how precisely it might be stated and explained or with what emotional force it might be presented, could ever have the power to establish that evangelical imperative. There is here only one answer that is appropriate to the weight of the indicative and then also to the imperative based upon it. The existence, the person and work, the history, of Jesus Christ in its totality, the whole direction and imprint of his word and work and passion, is, in Luther's words, "a mirror of the fatherly heart of God," the basis of the knowledge of the deity of God as fatherhood. What else is the history of Jesus Christ from beginning to end but the history of his perfectly obedient submission to the will of God, and therefore the history of the doing of this will? As this, it is obviously a reflection of the will and aim and purpose of God, and he who acts in it is in his action (Col. 1:15) the image of God himself. God wills what takes place in that history. He who wills what takes place in it is God. But what does take place? What is the work of Jesus Christ which corresponds to the will of God and therefore to God himself, which mirrors his will and therefore himself? In very general terms, Jesus in this work shares intensively and effectively in the reality of the world, in the being of man and therefore in the history of man. This is a free participation; it is required only by his obedience to God. It is a transcendent participation which he himself chose and willed step by step. But it takes place as he accepts solidarity with the world and the human race, as he identifies himself with it, as he makes himself responsible for it in unconditional and total self-giving. Again, it is not a blind participation but a percipient and knowledgeable one, for he sees plainly the sinister depths of world occurrence and the perversion and lostness of mankind. It is not for this reason, however, a resigned, skeptical, or pessimistic participation, but one that looks and hopes for ultimate and even penultimate solutions and liberations. Nor is it just contemplative or waiting or passive. It goes to work. It intervenes. It commits and exposes itself. It helps, and since it does so totally, it saves. It is the participation of the one who loves the world and people in their nature and even their degenerate nature. This participation is the work which God would have Jesus do and which Jesus, serving him, does. God? Yes, God. The will which Jesus affirms, and to which he subjects himself in service in the act of his participation in the world and mankind, is the absolutely transcendent will of another and greater. He himself shares in the being of this greater. The nature and existence of this greater are manifested in his history. Thus his own participation in the world and mankind is simply the reflection, the corresponding image, of the participation of this greater in them. He, Jesus, in his participation in the world and mankind, acts as he who is one in nature and existence with this greater. Thus he and his history are the perfect exhibition, or, as John's Gospel would say, glorification, of the nature and existence of this greater. As Jesus has pity on the world and mankind, he shows that the greater, whose will he does, is merciful. This greater, whose mercy to his creation and mankind Jesus puts into effect, is his Father. For Jesus shows himself to be his faithful and obedient Son as he exercises mercy. In doing this he also shows that the one to whom he is faithful and obedient is his Father — his Father as the Father of mercies (2 Cor. 1:3); the Father of all to whom his mercy, powerful and manifest in what Jesus does as his Son, is addressed; the Father of all those to whom he is manifest in the work of Jesus as his Father, who in the history of Jesus find access to him, may and will recognize and invoke as their Father, or *our* Father.[4] This is the meaning of the evangelical and christological indicative that serves as a strong foundation for the evangelical imperative: "Pray then like this."

The confession of Jesus Christ in which all tongues will join (Phil. 2:11) is not just "He is Kyrios," but "He is Kyrios to the glory of God the Father." Thus the name that is given him — because he humbled himself (v. 8) — is called (v. 10) the name that is above every other name, for at it every knee shall bow, in heaven and on earth and under the earth, since all true invocation of God throughout his creation has its possibility, basis, and prototype in his work. The true deity of his being — precisely ἐν μορφῇ θεοῦ ὑπάρχων, not in denial or loss but in supreme authentication of his true deity he took human form, μορφὴν δούλου (λαβών) (vv. 6f.) — consists in this, that his being is one of service, the service which wins and gathers

[4]The last three sentences underwent extensive revision in the TS. For the original MS version, see *Gesamtausgabe, Das christliche Leben*, p. 108, n. 22.

all creation in the invocation of God. It is not in an abstract being but in this function that Jesus Christ is Kyrios, very God. To be sure, when all opposing forces and powers, including death as the last enemy, are vanquished, then he will not only hand over the kingdom that has been set up in and through him, but he will also subject himself to God and the Father (1 Cor. 15:24f.) in keeping with his commencement in obedience (Phil. 2:8). He is what he is and does what he does, ruling as the Kyrios, not in his own favor or to his own glory, but that God may be all in all (1 Cor. 15:28). John's Gospel speaks similarly. Jesus does not seek his own glory (Jn. 8:50). This comes to him from the Father; to him, the incarnate Word, the Son who has been sent into the world by the Father (1:14). He would lose it (8:54) if he were to seek and have it as his own, if he were to seize and enjoy equality with God as a prey (Phil. 2:6). The Father is greater than he is (μείζων, Jn. 14:28). Hence his divine glory (4:34) is to find his food in not doing his own will (5:30; 6:38) but in doing as his own the will of the Father that sent him, completing in his own work the work of the Father, and not doing this according to his own judgment but in uninterrupted attention to the Father's own work (5:19, 30). "My Father is working still, and I am working" (5:17). What takes place as the will and work of the Son is thus the will and work of the Father, so that the one may be seen and known in the other, and the Father may be seen and known in Jesus. But what is the will and work of Jesus and therefore of the Father? The answer is plain: "God so loved the world that he gave his only Son" (3:16). He did not send him into the world to condemn the world but that the world might be saved through him (3:17) — "to seek and to save the lost" (Lk. 19:10). The will of him who sent Jesus is "that I should lose nothing of all that he has given me, but raise it up at the last day" (Jn. 6:39). Paul speaks to the same effect: "Who gave himself for our sins to deliver us from the present evil age, according to the will of our God and Father" (Gal. 1:4). In this light it is understandable that in the striking combination of "God our Father and the Lord Jesus Christ" and "the Father of mercies" we should have an interpretation of the first "Father" by the second as well as the second by the first. Jesus Christ is our Lord in his saving intervention for us, in the mercy in whose active fulfilment he gives himself to be one of us. He is Lord, then, to the glory of God the Father (Phil. 2:11), of his Father, or, in the words of John 14:28, of the greater who has sent him and to whom he is obedient. If he brings glory to the Father thereby — the glory or honor (Jn. 1:14) which he himself receives and has from the Father, the glory of his lordship in showing mercy — then the God whose faithful Son he is, is Father in being merciful, in being the eternal ground and guarantee of all the being distinct from himself, and as such the love, the free and omnipotent mercy, in whose fulfilment and manifestation Jesus acts as the Son and shows himself to be such. He is then, as Paul adds, "the God of all comfort," the God who is and acts and speaks in all-embracing consolation and admonition, and as such *our* Father just as Jesus Christ is *our* Lord. The disciples of Jesus, Christians, are commanded to call upon God as this Father of theirs. We shall have to describe their invocation of this Father of theirs as the obedience which is demanded of them.

2. THE CHILDREN

We have been occupied thus far with the question of the God invoked by Christians, that is, of their Father. With the same seriousness we must now turn to the opposite and corresponding problem of the subject at work in this invocation. Now it is true that, according to Philippians 2:11, the vocative "Father" will finally, as the goal of the rule and work of Jesus

Christ, be the word of all men and indeed of all creation ringing out in the harmony of universal invocation. On this side of the eschaton, however, it is only one note among many other invocations and exclamations that are hardly in harmony with it but call for notice just as loudly — or even more so. Here and now, in anticipation of the future universal praise of God, it is the affair of only a certain number of people, even a limited minority, to call God "Father." To live in this prophetic minority, and in this situation to call upon God as Father, is the destiny of Christians. It is to them that Jesus says: "Pray then like this."

The transmission of the Lord's Prayer counts on there being a number of people of this kind. The Father who is invoked is called "our Father" in Matthew 6:9 (though not in Lk. 11:2). The same first person plural may be seen in the last three petitions in both versions. Prayer is made for our daily bread, for the forgiveness of our sins, for our protection against temptation. To begin with, a special, qualified, but numerically limited number of people are commanded to call upon God as their Father. It is presupposed that there are many others who, not knowing the command, or disobeying it if they do, do not yet call upon him, or do so no longer.

Hence those who call upon God as Father do so as exceptions and even in a situation of conflict in which they do not as yet, or any longer, have many or most of the rest of the people on their side, but perhaps explicitly or inexplicitly have them ranged against them. We shall have to return to their existence in this situation. For the moment what concerns us is the obviously decisive question of whether and how there can be this invocation of God by certain people, of whether and how the existence of people who are free and able to invoke him is even possible or can become actual. In answering this basic question we unavoidably have to begin at once with the insight with which we reached our goal in the first subsection. But first we must consider the total import of this question.

"Father" is clearly an address which, whether used in a literal or a transferred sense, already presupposes among men great closeness to the one who is thus addressed. It has a familiar and intimate character. Not everyone may use it in relationship to someone else. Its use demands a permission and freedom which cannot be taken for granted but is very special. It has to be grounded in a particular right. How much more so is this true in relation to God! Those who say "Father" to God clearly think that they may regard themselves as God's children. How can they do that? How can they do it in view of the distance, indeed, the abyss of the infinite qualitative distinction in which God is God and they are humans, he the Creator and they his creatures, he in heaven and they on earth [cf. Eccl. 5:1]? In the light of this, how can they be his children? How can they call on him, then, as their Father? Even if this paradox can be eliminated by some synthesis, for example, by a general concept of divine sonship, even if on these grounds people might be able to establish a theoretical right to call upon God as Father, how can they ever come to claim this right in practice? It is a right that has been long since and irredeemably abandoned and lost.

Their fitness to call upon God as his true children would have to show itself in their regarding and treating all that is theirs as his property, and in their seeking their own honor in confessing him in word and work, in orienting themselves to him, in serving his will and work with all their powers. They would have to love him as the one who has first loved them [1 Jn. 4:19]. Those who might show and prove themselves to be God's children by doing this would be able to address him with uplifted heads as their Father. But what Christian could think of himself as a child of God in this sense? What Christian could boast of being such? How he would have to stand out from his background as a child of God in this sense! What light would have to shine forth from him! What promise would have to be sounded forth in his existence to the broadest circles around him! In fact, Christians are not particularly faithful people in their relation to God and therefore they are not particularly eminent people, nor do they awaken particular regard in their relation to their contemporaries. If they are the children of God, it is certainly not because they have shown themselves to be such, or can boast of showing themselves to be such, before God and man. They precisely recognize and confess that they have not now shown themselves, and do not show themselves, in any way worthy to be called God's children, to be God's children, or to be able to call upon God as Father. They precisely would be the very last people to dream of an ontological divine sonship on man's part. They precisely know that in no sense can they claim as their own right the freedom to invoke God as their Father. They precisely confess with the publican in the temple: "God, be merciful to me a sinner" (Lk. 18:13), and therefore with the prodigal son: "Father, I am no longer worthy to be called your son" (Lk. 15:19). They will cry "Father" without thinking at all that they are qualified to do so.

They *do* cry "Father" even though they cannot think that they are qualified to do so, even though they are not in fact so qualified. They do it in defiance of all that says they cannot and should not do it. They do it also with no doubts. They are not afraid that, caught in an arbitrary and empty illusion, they are crying into the void. They are not afraid of being presumptuous or of infringing upon the one whom they invoke. Yet even if they cry "Father" with assurance, they do not suffer from any illusions that they have by nature, or have won, or can win, the possibility of claiming to be God's children. The joy of calling upon Him as Father, and the certainty of being heard and answered by him, stands or falls with the absence of illusions of this kind. Any residue of such illusions will entail only a corresponding disturbance of the clarity of their knowledge of their situation and a reduction of their courage to do what is commanded in this situation. The more such illusions gain the upper hand, the more surely will their ability to do what is commanded be called into question, and the more sharply will they be threatened by the possibility of losing this ability altogether.

The freedom of the children of God to do what they are commanded to do is purely and simply the work and gift of the grace that is addressed to them and recognized by them. Because it is grace, the freedom cannot be one that is inherited or won. On any other basis and with any other origin it would be a pretended and false freedom, a secret and even an open non-freedom. Grace is the presence, event, and revelation of what man cannot think or do or reach or attain or grasp, but of what is, in virtue of its coming from God, the most simple, true, and real of all things for those to whom it is addressed and who recognize it. Grace is the factual overcoming of the distinction between God and man, Creator and creature, heaven and earth — something that cannot be grasped in any theory or brought about by any technique of human practice. Grace is the goodness of God which, without any cooperation or merit on man's part, discloses and yet also covers his corruption and guilt, judging him but also setting him up. Grace is God's sovereign intervention with man on his own behalf, and therefore his merciful intervention on man's behalf. The work and gift of this grace of his is the freedom of the children of God — their freedom to call upon him as Father.

It may be noted in retrospect that if Christians know and confess that they have no worthiness of their own to be called, to become, and to be God's children, and especially if there is no such thing as an ontological divine sonship on man's part, then this precisely is their recognition and confession of the grace of God and of the distinctive freedom which they are given. They do not know and confess this, then, on the basis of a specific critical self-understanding, of a power of metaphysical discernment, let alone of a morose skepticism. All this has nothing whatever to do with the self-judgment of the publican in the temple or that of the prodigal son. From these, relapses into optimistic illusion are not only not impossible but are only too probable in virtue of the automatic dialectic of all human thinking. It would be itself a remnant of optimistic illusion (perhaps the most dangerous) if men were to be of the opinion that negatively at least they know themselves and can be clear about their limits. Always the sharpest self-criticism and the most arrogant self-certainty are not only neighboring but all too easily exchangeable possibilities. Only in the freedom of the children of God as the work and gift of his grace can man be free from moral and metaphysical error regarding his own possibilities. Only in this freedom can he no longer imagine that he can claim the right of calling upon God as his Father, and therefore the right of sonship in relation to God, as a right which is his a priori, or which he has either won or can still win. It is as God elects and moves to intervene both on his own behalf and on man's that in this free and fatherly togetherness of God with men they acquire the right of invoking him as Father. This right is true and authentic, cannot be questioned, and is absolutely unshakable. By this positive thing, this true right, all supposed, invented, and illusory right is completely put in the shade and chased from the field. Their knowledge and confession that there can be no other right is thus in some sense the reverse side of their knowledge and confession of the true right given to them by God. Hence it is not a resigned or troubled but a triumphant and cheerful knowledge and confession. In the true freedom grounded in the grace of God they have no room or use for the counterfeit of a freedom originating in an intrinsic or achieved human worthiness. They have chosen the better part — the only good one — and so they can have nothing to do with any other nor come back to any other under the pressure of human, only too human, dialectic.

Men become and are God's children, then, by God's grace, which is his possibility and not theirs, by the goodness of the Father. It is not originally intrinsic to them, nor is it accessible to their own grasping and disposing. Rather, it is freely intended for them and addressed and promised to them, as this grace and goodness becomes a present event in their life and thought, in action and suffering, so that they acquire thereby the genuine freedom to cry "Father."

"See what love the Father has given us, that we should be called children of God; and so we are" (1 Jn. 3:1). This is what distinguishes Christians, as we continue to read (vv. 1, 2). It is the reason why the world does not know them as they are, for the world does not know the Father who turns to them in this love. "We are God's children now; it does not yet appear what we shall be," that is, how we ourselves and others will perceive us one day, at the end of all the ways of God. Being God's children is our true being, even though here and now it is wrapped in obscurity. We should note here the double ἐσμέν and its basis. The statement could not be more positive: "We *are* the children of God." But this does not come from ourselves. We may rightly compare John 1:13 here. The children of God are children of men like all others, but as the children of God they are not born in the same way as they and all others are as the children of men. They are born directly of God, independently of what they are on the basis of their human origin. "He brought us forth by the word of truth" (Jas. 1:18). In 1 John 3:1 the basis of the divine sonship of these men is described as a calling or naming. It is thus — note the ἴδετε — a wholly astonishing gift of love of him who elected himself to be their Father and who in this way elected, acknowledged, and addressed them as his children. 1 John 3:1 is not dealing, of course, with the point that on these grounds they for their part can and may and should address him as Father. In this regard, then, Galatians 4:6f. is all the more impressive: "And because you are sons [after he sent his Son, v. 4], God has sent the Spirit of his Son into our hearts, crying, 'Abba, Father!' " and thus confirming that we are God's children. We find a variation and extension of the same thought in Romans 8:14f.: those who are impelled (empowered, freed, and led) by the Spirit of God are the children of God, not in virtue of their own spirit rising up in and from them, but in virtue of God's Spirit coming upon them as the Spirit of sonship. Moved and driven by him they cry, "Abba! Father!" In Galatians 4:6 they really hear the Spirit make this cry. He does it, but as he does we are awakened by him and so it is the cry of our own hearts and lips. We could not make it of ourselves but he confirms and testifies and reveals (συμμαρτυρεῖ) to us, to our spirits, that we are the children of God (ὅτι ἐσμὲν τέκηα θεοῦ, Rom. 8:16). Our being named God's children (1 Jn. 3:1), our being born as such (Jn. 1:13; Jas. 1:18) by God, or by the sending of his Spirit as the Spirit of sonship (Gal. 4:6; Rom. 8:16), is obviously described as the secret of the existence of the sons or children of men who are also children of God and who have, therefore, a right, freedom, and power to call upon God as their Father. In another context, looking at his own calling to be an apostle, Paul described the same mystery in a brief sentence when he said: "By the grace of God I am what I am" (1 Cor. 15:10).

But what is this grace by which men are freed, entitled, and empowered to invoke God as their Father and in which they must see themselves as his children and act as such? What is this new and strange and very simple thing which herewith becomes a present event in the lives of men, overcoming the distance, establishing familiarity and intimacy between God and them? What is this pure goodness of God that appears so unexpectedly? What is this intervention of God with them on his own behalf and consequently on their behalf too? In short, what is the free being of God with them which has in fact taken place? How does it come about and what does it mean that God calls them his children, that they are born of him as such, that they are endowed with his Spirit, that they are thus required and, indeed, in the deepest sense are "authorized" to call upon him as Father? In all this we have not been describing a magical miracle or an experience of timeless mysticism. Nor have we been referring to a mere point of faith with neither basis, object, nor content. Nor have we been telling a wonderful anthropological story. We have been speaking about what happens to man in the history of the covenant that God made with him and brought to its goal for him: a covenant which God did not just establish between himself and man but in which man was called and impelled to play his own free and active part. The history of this covenant, however, is the history of Jesus Christ which embraces and integrates into itself that of every other man. The grace of God appears and works and speaks in this history. It is concretely described (2 Cor. 13:13) as "the grace of our Lord Jesus Christ." In this concrete form it is the life and rule of divine love, the naming and birth of the children of God, the imparting and communicating to them of the Spirit of God, the Holy Spirit. In the illuminating and awakening of men to an active recognition of the history of Jesus Christ which controls and determines their own history, people become the children of God, recognizing that his birth, his ministry in word and work, and his death, since he rose again and lives, *all* took place for *them*, so that their own history is anticipated in this history, is enclosed by it, is oriented to it, and has its *telos* in it. To the extent that their faith is faith in Jesus Christ — I believe in Jesus Christ, the only-begotten Son of God the Father, our Lord — to that extent but only to that extent, we can and must say with Galatians 3:26 that they become and are the children of God through faith (διὰ πίστεως).

What does not take place in any human history without him takes place in the history of Jesus Christ. What all other men in and of themselves are not, he is, not for himself alone, but for them, in their place, and on their behalf: Son, *the* Son of God as his Father and therefore as their Father too. He, then, is the fulfilment of the covenant between God and man. Concretely, God's grace is *his* grace. He is the Son of Man who lives and acts as the Son of God, and may be known as such, by being the executor of God's love in childlike obedience and service, in childlike trust, in the doing of his will, in unrestricted self-giving, and by glorifying him as his Father in this way. As man, he loves God in exact reflection, in full conformity to the love with which God loves him and in him the world. He displays himself actively as the Lord by not remaining in debt to God as his servant. He is thus the Son of Man who has merited and enjoys the unreserved good pleasure of God his Father. To say this of any other man is impossible. In comparison with his acts, all other men are in arrears, at fault, in opposition and contradiction. As man he does not just do something quantitatively greater than they do, but something qualitatively better. But he does this very different thing as and because, like them in all things, he is totally different from them. He is God's Son of Man in childlike obedience, child-like trust, and full self-giving to him. The nature of the Father is from the very first, a priori, and antecedently his own. To be Son is his nature and presupposition, the starting point of his work. He lives and acts and loves in conformity with the life and action and love of God. God's divine form of being is the form of his own being. The self-giving in which God him-self — without ceasing to be God but being supremely God — became and is man, this man, is that which is achieved and manifested in his self-giving to God as a human act. As this Son of Man — one with God his Father, one with his work and nature in his own work and being — as this Son of Man is *the* Son of God, the covenant of God with man is more than fulfilled by the act in which God reconciles and makes peace in his history. For the divine sonship of man ceases to be an illusory ideal and postulate and becomes a reality, the valid promise which is spoken to every human history.

In Jesus Christ, then, reconciliation has been made between the whole world and God. Peace has been definitively established between God and man. In this and beyond this, however, there goes forth in him who as true Son of God was and is true Son of Man, who as true Son of Man showed and proved himself to be true Son of God, the promise that is again directed to all men — the promise that as they look and cling to him, they too may become and be true children of God. In him they have all acquired a Brother, who even though he was and is this in great distinction, still was and is so — what a promise this is! — as the Son of God who for their sake became and was and is the Son of Man. Their Brother, who did what he did and was what he was, not for himself alone but also for them! He did it and was it in their place. And in their place, on their behalf, he lives, risen from the dead, as the one who he was and who did what he did. His person and work are not just of yesterday. They are the great reality and truth of today. Divine sonship, and with it — notwithstanding all that speaks to the contrary — the freedom to call upon God as Father, became and was in him a present event for all men of all times and places. There is no one who in him may not find himself justified before God, sanctified for him, called to the being and work of his children, named, born, and endowed as his child. There is no one who is not in him a recipient of God's grace, caught up already in the realization of that new and most simple thing, set in intimacy with God, enjoying the pure goodness of God, governed already by the fact of God's intervention for his own cause and therefore for ours too, placed in that free being together of God with man and man with God, sharing already the Spirit of sonship [Rom. 8:15], fully authorized and en-titled and empowered to call upon God as Father. In him! Not outside him! Not without him! We do not forget that what is at issue here is the incon-ceivable and uncontrollable grace of God and its gift. Therefore in him, in this strict but glorious, this exclusive but in its very exclusiveness supremely inclusive, "outside us"! Our divine sonship, and with it the freedom to make use of it, is in no sense to be sought in ourselves but in him, and it is in him that it will always be found. It is the divine sonship of the disobedient who are granted it only in him, in him to whom it was and is originally proper in virtue of his being and work, but proper to the glory of the Father and therefore in the service of his love. In him it is to be, and may and should be, both grasped in faith and practiced without pride and yet also with no false humility. In him, in Christ, the existence of special creatures called Christians may and should become possible and actual: the existence of people who know who and what he is, and on this basis who and what they themselves very definitely are not, but again on this basis who and what they are to become. Christian existence is the existence of people who have no option but to cling, yet also wish to cling, simply to what he is for them, to what they already are in him, to what they may continually become from him and through him and to him. They are the children of God who are allowed and commanded to call upon God as their Father.

Jesus is the Son through whom God has now spoken to us with the dawn of the end-time, through whom he made the worlds and whom he then made the heir of all things. He, the reflection of his glory and the express image of his nature (Heb. 1:2f.), has as the pioneer of their salvation (ἀρχηγὸς τῆς σωτηρίας αὐτῶν) brought many sons to glory. For he was not ashamed (Heb. 2:10f.) to call them brethren but bowed to the necessity of being exposed, like them and with them, to suffering and temptation. To what end? In order to be merciful to them, in God's service expiating the sins of the people as a faithful high priest. On what basis? Because he as the Sanctifier and they who are sanctified by him *all* (πάντες — in this he is originally together with them) derive and descend from One (ἐξ ἑνός) and have in him one and the same Father. It will be seen that his and their divine sonship is here a presupposition. From it there follows his brotherhood with them and the ruthless actualization of it to achieve the goal of salvation. Since he is their Brother and intervenes for them as such, they are his brethren and therefore the children of God. This is the implication. It is made explicit in Romans 8:29: God has fashioned his elect into a being in the likeness of the image of his Son, and from what follows we see that, as copies of this original, they are to be his sons. Then the goal of the divine will and election is stated, namely, that he, the Son, as the firstborn among many brethren (Rom. 8:29), may be the one he is, the Head of his body with its many members, to use another Pauline phrase [Eph. 1:22f.; 4:15f.; 5:23; Col. 1:18; 2:19], the *totus Christus* (Augustine). Thus the plan which God had and which he followed in his dealings with certain elect people is to create for himself many other children on the basis of the presupposition of the being and work of that one. Those who are impelled by the Spirit of God, those with whom God first reaches this goal, are thus his children (Rom. 8:14). As we have noted already, his Spirit is the Spirit of sonship (υἱοθεσία, Rom. 8:15). In the older text, Galatians 4:4f., Paul said the same thing in reverse. When the fullness of the time came, the fulfilment of all time and history in which their meaning became a manifest event in the approach of the kingdom of God, God sent (ἐξαπέστειλεν) his Son, born of a woman, subject to the law, an Israelite. Why? In order that we might receive sonship (υἱοθεσία). The meaning according to what follows is that in sending his Son, God promised and imparted sonship to us. Verse 6 tells us that since you are sons on the basis of God's sending his Son, God sent (again ἐξαπέστειλεν) the Spirit of his Son into our hearts crying, "Abba, Father." The unconditional priority of the sonship of Jesus Christ over all other sonship, the authorization of all other sonship by his, is just as plain in Romans 8 as it is in Galatians 4. The freedom to recognize, affirm, grasp, and practice their sonship is thus for all others (Gal. 3:26) a matter of their faith in Jesus Christ, the One in whom it is originally actualized. It is as they look to him, trust in him, and obey him that sonship can be theirs too. Similarly, we read in John 1:12 that those who receive the incarnate Logos that has come into the world as the true light are those to whom he himself gives the power (ἐξουσία) to become the children of God. This receiving is believing in his name. It is also possible, though by no means certain, that the beatitude in Matthew 5:9 points in the same direction when it says that peacemakers (εἰρηνοποιοί) shall be called the children of God. Peace is not just the opposite of quarreling, strife, and warfare between people in the community and people in the world. In the apostolic greetings it is not for nothing associated with grace, and it obviously describes the fruit of grace. The term is fairly frequently employed in close proximity to, or even as an equivalent of, the salvation which has come irresistibly with the appearance of the Messiah, the reconciliation of the world with God enacted in Jesus Christ. Thus peace in Luke 2:14 is declared as the earthly counterpart of the glory of God in the highest. Peace is also the word with which the risen Jesus greets his own (Lk. 24:36; Jn. 20:19ff.). He leaves them or gives them this peace which he established. On the basis of what he says to them, they have this peace in him (Jn. 16:33). If there are people whom the New Testament can call peacemakers as the recipients and bearers and bringers and makers of this peace, this is hardly possible except as they belong to him in whom this peace was originally achieved and revealed, and who is called our peace in person in Ephesians 2:14. If this one is the original of God—though Matthew 5:9f. does not say this—then those who belong to him and serve him as peacemakers can also be called children of God and can be called blessed as such.

The impossible thing that men should become and be God's children is thus possible and actual. The subject of the commended invocation of God, and therefore all real obedience, is constituted. It will now be our task to make some statements elucidating the question of the existence and the mode of existence of this subject, of these particular people, of Christians as those who are commanded to call upon God as their Father.

1. We begin with what is in practice a very necessary reminder. If they are not to cease to be what they are, then the grace by which they are what they are cannot and will not cease to be grace, the mystery and miracle of the free kindness of God, of the inconceivable and uncontrollable fact that he is their Father and they are his children, and that they have, therefore, the freedom to call upon him as Father. Their gratitude for this kindness, and also their desire to receive it afresh, can never break off or end. For if they were to turn their eyes away from this gift to themselves, they would always have to recognize and confess that they are not called to this invocation of God nor qualified for it. In fact, they can always venture to make use of it only on the basis of the fact that, as their liberation, it takes place afresh each day, like the food given to the Israelites in the wilderness [Ex. 16:1ff.; Num. 11:4ff.]. Stored up grace—grace as a natural state or merit or capital—would not be the power in which they became the children of God or in which they could be so again today as yesterday, or become

so again tomorrow as today. Only as the grace of the living God does it have this power. As a fish can breathe only in water and not on dry land, so Christians can live only as they drink from the fresh spring of free grace which is not natural, which cannot be won, but in which it pleases the Father continually to love his people and to call them his children. That they have God as their Father and may be his children is not an ongoing history in the same way as the relationship between people is, for it can be an ongoing history only in pure miracles. Its continuation, duration, and conclusion are, of course, guaranteed, but not in such a way that they can grasp and control the guarantee. Why not? Because they are children of God only in Jesus Christ and in faith in him: in him as the original Son of God who became the Son of Man and their Brother. They are justified, sanctified, and called in him; judged and blessed, killed and made alive in him. But Jesus Christ is their Lord; they are not his lords. It would be a fateful confusion of grace and nature, or grace and merit, if they thought they could treat him as their possession. They are simply his possession, and they can take comfort only in being this. His new presence, action, and declaration in their lives, their own new recognition of his work and his word, their new obedience, new trust in him, new sharing in his history, and, to make this possible, the new presence and power of the Spirit — all these are in the strict sense necessary each day and each hour if they are to have and retain aright, or rather, if they are constantly to acquire, their divine sonship and their concomitant freedom to call upon God as Father. They are the children of God by faith in Jesus Christ. But faith is a new act each day and hour, at war each day and hour with newly insurgent unbelief. Thus Christians, in Luther's words, have never become but are always becoming. Even their standing — there can never be any question of a sitting or lying in some static Christianity — can never take place except between two steps in their journey or pilgrimage, not to speak of their riding between death and the devil.

Here again we recall 1 John 3:2. They are the children of God insofar as, but also just as surely as, they believe in Jesus Christ. They are it then in their life which is hidden with him in God, that is, which is now manifest only to God (Col. 3:3). They are it as they cling to the promise which is given them in Jesus Christ, to their naming as God's children as this has taken place in him, to their birth as such which has been enacted in him. "It does not yet appear [it is not visible or perceptible] what we shall be [in the fulfilment of the promise]." "When Christ who is our life appears, then you also will appear with him in [the promised] glory" (Col. 3:4). Until then Christians walk only in faith (in him) and not in sight (not seeing or grasping directly how far their own divine sonship is reality and truth in his, 2 Cor. 5:7). In this respect they have various places to lodge but no abiding city (μένουσα πόλις, Heb. 13:14). They can only pass through the various lodging places. They have not yet attained, they are not yet perfect, but grasped by Christ Jesus (this is the continuity of their existence) and not looking at what lies behind, they press on to the goal that is set for them by the fact that he is their life, that they are in him and he in them (Phil. 3:12ff.). Everything seems to speak against the possibility of their following this path, of their even taking the smallest step on it, not merely at the beginning of their faith (as they confessed him in baptism), but on to its last hour. At every moment they can only look upward and ahead. Nor can they do even this in their own strength; they can do it only as it is given them to do. Again and again they do in fact take steps on the assigned and commanded path. It is a miracle that they can do this, that they have the freedom for it. For they do not have this freedom, nor can they take it, in and of themselves. They can take those steps, therefore, only as there takes place for them, and becomes their own, an unforeseen and incomprehensible liberation.

2. In connection with the first statement, we must say further that those who through God's grace (because Jesus Christ became and is their Brother) have the freedom to call upon God as their Father will never once, when they make use of this freedom, encounter God except as those who are inept, inexperienced, unskilled, and immature, as children in this sense too — little children who are totally unprepared for it. The invocation "Our Father," and all the Christian life and ethos implicit in this invocation, can never at any stage or in any form be anything but the work of beginners. Even at the most advanced stage and in the ripest form it can never be anything better, for in this field what is supposedly better can only be worse, indeed, it can only be evil. What Christians do becomes a self-contradiction when it takes the form of a trained and mastered routine, of a learned and practiced art. They may and can be masters and even virtuosos in many things, but never in what makes them Christians, God's children. As masters and virtuosos they would not live by God's grace. They might invoke it loudly and sincerely, but they would live by what they themselves can make of grace in their dealings with it. There could not be any more crooked switch, nor could any worse consequences threaten. If they will not be children, they cannot be the children of God; they cannot have the freedom of the children of God. All human errors and aberrations can be compensated for and made good, but not the inordinate desire of one who in calling upon God wants to meet him, and thinks he can meet him, in more imposing fashion than as a newly registered pupil.

From this standpoint, the art of liturgical worship, ordered and shaped by historical models and aesthetic ideals, although it has again come to be highly rated today, is an enterprise that is by no means free from suspicion. The same applies to a systematically constructed theory and practice of individual spiritual formation along the lines of the *Exercises* of Ignatius as these are still followed today both in and beyond Roman Catholic circles. The good that there might be in such attempts — and who is so bold as to rule out at once the possibility of good? — can perhaps be claimed as good from the Christian standpoint only in spite of their character as techniques, not because of it. Perspicacious friends of Christian liturgy and mysticism (including the so-called "little" Theresa of Lisieux) have not usually concealed this either from themselves or others. Spiritual life — we shall take up this concept again in the third subsection — begins at the very point where spiritual skill ends.

In invocation of God the Father everything depends on whether or not it is done in sheer need (not self-won competence), in sheer readiness to learn (not schooled erudition), and in sheer helplessness (not the application of a technique of self-help). This can be the work only of very weak and very little and very poor children, of those who in their littleness, weakness, and poverty can only get up and run with empty hands to their Father, appealing to him. Nor should we forget to add that it can be the work only of naughty children of God who have willfully run away again from their Father's house, found themselves among swine in the far country, turned their thoughts back home, and then — if they could — returned to their Father. What might sound a most intolerant statement must not be suppressed in this connection. Christians who regard themselves as big and strong and rich and even dear and good children of God, Christians who refuse to sit with their Master at the table of publicans and sinners, are *not* Christians at all, have still to become so, and need not be surprised if heaven is gray above them and their calling upon God sounds hollow and finds no hearing. The glory, splendor, truth, and power of divine sonship, and of the freedom to invoke God as Father, and therefore the use of this freedom — the Christian ethos in big and little things alike — depends at every time and in every situation on whether or not Christians come before God as *beginners*, as people who cannot make anything very imposing out of their faith in Jesus Christ, who even with this faith of theirs — and how else could it be if it is faith in Jesus Christ? — venture to draw near to his presence only with the prayer: "Help my unbelief" (Mk. 9:24). Mark well that this has nothing whatever to do with Christian defeatism. It describes Christians on their best side and not their worst, in their strength and not their weakness (2 Cor. 12:10). For as these people who are inept, inexperienced, unskilled, and immature, as these newborn babes [1 Pet. 2:2], they *are* dear children of the dear Father. They may call upon him, they can do so, and he hears and answers them. Secretly, but in truth, they are big and strong and rich, the righteous, the saints, those whom he has called. With such people Jesus Christ associated himself. Such he called as his disciples. For such he died. In such, when he has found them on earth (Lk. 15:7), there is joy in heaven. Such can and may and do become his witnesses. Such alone and no others! Such alone know what they are doing when they do not pray dutiful and smooth and more or less beautiful prayers, but with Paul, and especially with Jesus in Gethsemane, they *cry* to God their Father [Rom. 8:15; Gal. 4:6; Mk. 14:32ff. and par.]. Only the eyes of the blind can be opened, only the ears of the deaf can be unstopped, only the lame can be told to take up their bed and walk [Mt. 11:5, etc.; Mk. 2:11 and par.; Jn. 5:8]. Only for prisoners is there liberation (Isa. 61:1; Lk. 4:18), only for the hungry and thirsty is there the promise of being filled [Mt. 5:6 and par.], only to those who take a low place can the call come: "Friend, go up higher" (Lk. 14:10). To Christians who will not call upon God as those who are blind, deaf, lame, prisoners, hungry, and thirsty, and who will not take the lowest place, those acts of salvation cannot apply and will not happen. They are for Christians as *beginners*, but only for them. This is the second thing that needs to be said about the children of God as the subject of calling upon God the Father.

The main saying we have in mind here is the one in Matthew 11:25f. and Luke 10:21: "I thank thee, Father, Lord of heaven and earth, that thou hast hidden these things from the wise and understanding and revealed them to babes; yea, Father, for such was thy gracious will." The placing of the saying in the composition of both Gospels is very emphatic, although in different ways. In Matthew 11 it serves to explain the puzzling fact that the success of the proclamation of Jesus was not universal, as is obvious in the cities by the Sea of Galilee in spite of the mighty acts performed there. This was not because there were no wise and understanding people, but because he whom Jesus called his Father or the Father — a higher economy is at work here — had no interest in nor use for those who were already learned and instructed, for those who from the very first knew better. "These things" (ταῦτα) — his relationship to Jesus and that of Jesus to him, the dawning change of the times — he willed to reveal exclusively to babes (νήπιοι), who are obviously not to be construed as stupid or muddleheaded people. Rather, as we learn from the next verses, they are those who "labor and are heavy-laden," the sorrowful, the humble (because humbled), the hungry and thirsty of the first beatitudes (Mt. 5:3ff.). It is they whom Jesus calls, himself gentle and lowly in heart (πραΰς καὶ ταπεινός). It is they who, ordained for him by the Father and on the basis of the refreshment (ἀνάπαυσις) they are given, are summoned to go his way with him, to take upon themselves his yoke and his burden. In so doing they will show themselves to be his predestined brethren and therefore the predestined children of God. In Luke 10 the same saying occurs in a context that is governed by references to the disciples of Jesus, to their failures and also their relative successes (10:17–20). Here, in particular, they are the babes to whom are revealed the things that must be withheld from many of the wise and understanding, and which even many prophets and kings of the old covenant (as the continuation in v. 24 has it) did not get to see. In the sphere of the fulfilment of the covenant the decisive people are not the tested masters but the unproved pupils. In both forms of the tradition, and obviously in the saying that underlies them, the emphasis is on the fact that Jesus does not regret or bewail the described course of events; rather, he extols the Father, who is solemnly enough addressed here as Lord of heaven and earth, because things have had to turn out thus according to his arrangement and disposition. In this respect the Son confesses that he is one with the Father. Both records emphasize that there was a particular time or hour when this song of praise was uttered. Nor is there any other saying of Jesus which, as in Luke, is given additional emphasis by the observation that Jesus "rejoiced in the Holy Spirit" when he called upon God in this way. This distinction of babes must have been a central and not just an incidental matter in the tradition. For the wholly new thing that has come in Jesus is open only to those people who are an adequate match, who are open to it, because they have nothing behind them, because they are not stopped or blocked up against it by any intellectual, moral, aesthetic, or religious a priori that they have brought with them, because they are empty pages. This is plainly the point of the story about the child that Jesus set in the midst of his disputing disciples (Mk. 9:36 and par.); of the sayings about becoming like little children (Mt. 18:3) and not entering the kingdom of God except by receiving it as a little child (Mk. 10:15; Lk. 18:17); of the Johannine sayings about the unattainable birth from above (Jn. 3:3) or from God (Jn. 1:13); of the statement in 1 Peter 2:2 about newborn babes (ἀρτιγέννητα βρέφη). And perhaps it is the point of the saying in Matthew 11:16ff., in close connection with the cry of jubilation, about the children of wisdom playing on the streets, who justify the work of wisdom by their understanding, and truly honor it as its children. The sharp critics of the Baptist and Jesus, on the other hand, whose heads and lips are so full of correct things, regard the former as a fanatic and the latter as a carefree man of the world. There also belongs here what Paul says in 1 Corinthians 1–3 about the wisdom of God, which inevitably in the word of the cross seems folly to the cosmos, but which shows itself to be God's wisdom to the Corinthians both in relation to Paul's own very unassuming coming among them and also in the recollection of their own calling from a people consisting of the inconspicuous, foolish, weak, and humble. "Let no one deceive himself. If any one among you thinks that he is wise . . . let him become a fool that he may become wise" (1 Cor. 3:18). Obviously, he is not to become stupid or muddleheaded! The fools of Paul are no more this than are the babes or children of the Gospels. What distinguishes them from others is the ability to accept the radical new beginning which is made with men, apart from any enterprise of their own, in the gospel of the Father and the Son, in the Word of the cross. What distinguishes them is the willingness to begin at this new beginning. Note that it is not to the outside children of the world, to unbelieving Jews, proud Gentiles, idealists, materialists, and atheists, but to *Christians* that all these things are said and applied; it is they who obviously need to experience the call to begin again at this beginning and to take the place which they precisely are assigned as the children of God.

3. A final thesis that points in a rather different direction is that the subject of calling upon God the Father is not one child of God in the singular but the children of God in the plural. Each Christian, of course, can render personal obedience only on his own responsibility. But what he does in obedience he does not do as a private person. As the fellow man belongs constitutively to the nature of man, so does the brother to the child of God, the fellow Christian to the Christian. The brothers or fellow Christians, as we should add at once, for Christians could not be who they are without many others, not just one other. "*Our* Father" is the commanded vocative. In obedience, the Christian can call only upon *our* Father as God even when he finds himself in the greatest solitude. This "our" says first that God is not just Father in general, not just the Father of certain people and beings, but *your* Father and *mine*, and therefore *our* Father: the Father of each individual who may invoke him thus. It then tells us that as he is the Father of our one Lord Jesus Christ, he is the common Father of all who believe and of all who will come to believe him, so that they are all brothers and sisters as his children. To the vertical line of the relationship between God and man in which the one God encounters many as Father and will be invoked by them as such, there corresponds the horizontal line on which the many who encounter the one God and Father may and should call upon him. Cutting across all the other relations and unions that have arisen and persist both naturally and historically, and standing out against all these unions and relations, there arises here the community or people that is held together by the fact that it has the freedom, and no choice but to use this given freedom, to call God *our* Father. The community is a people of free persons liberated to call upon their common Father. As the community of the one Lord, it is not a monolith or collective in which the individual can be no more than a functioning organ, one among many moved and moving wheels in a mechanism. It is a *people* in which, as all these freed and free persons have a common Father, they are related, responsible, and united

to one another. It is not a heap of individual existences which, brought together by social need, binds itself by common agreement for a common purpose. It is the plurality of people who, individually, in virtue of the gathering, upbuilding, and enlightening unity of the Father who reveals the Son and the Son who reveals the Father, and in virtue of the awakening and illuminating Spirit of God the Father and the Son, are constituted a unity, a totality, by which each individual stands or falls, and in which each individual is in the closest possible relation to the other. The children of God who are liberated for invocation of God as their Father exist in responsibility to him and therefore to his people and therefore to each of its many members. None of them, then, can be indifferent to the fact, let alone find it disturbing or painful, or be harassed and confused by it, that he must be a Christian among other Christians, that he should see his equals in other Christians, that he should honor them and love them, and that he should call upon the Father together and in concert with them. This does not mean, of course, that he can think that he need not take the situation seriously, as though there were not demanded from each, as if it depended on him alone, supreme attention to the form in which the common command comes specifically to him. He cannot take the chance that the brethren will make up for his failures. He cannot think that he is excused because apart from himself there are others who seem to be doing a good job, or more of a good job than a bad one. Nor, if his fellows seem to be doing more of a bad job than a good one, can he think that he is released from any responsibility for these others who are at fault. In all circumstances he must be ready for the venture and the burden that the "our Father," as the prayer required of the community, is for a while and to some degree to be prayed by each alone as though he were himself the community. Nor again must he cease to take note how others are doing the same, how they are crying the same thing in their own way, so that he may again do it together with them. Temporary separations may be necessary in order that new and better future fellowship may be possible — but only for this reason. Like the divine sonship of the individual and his freedom to call upon the Father, the existence of the community as the people of the children of God — and therefore their common brotherhood — must always have a new reality and truth, and therefore must always be sought and discovered and practiced anew. Not everyone can or may act with anyone else as a brother, or, when he does, may or can do so in the same way. Many must wait for others before they can cry "our Father" together. In this regard one must remember that only God knows for certain who his people are [2 Tim. 2:19]. None of us can finally say which others are or are not children of God and therefore brothers and sisters. Supposed brethren may turn out to be false brethren, while on the other hand, dead brethren may become alive again and the lost may be found (Lk. 15:32). Thus supposed brethren are not immediately recognizable as such, let alone known and valued brethren. Divine sonship always includes human and Christian brotherhood with all the problems entailed. The idea that one is quite alone in invoking God the Father — Kierkegaard came suspiciously close to this idea — is one that the child of

God will simply forbid himself, no matter how things may seem to be around him. "I believe in . . . the *communion* of saints," the existence of the people of God as a people of brethren, even though I do not see these brethren, or see them only dimly. I am still ready to see them. Reluctantly perhaps or resolutely, not with mistrust but with a willingness to trust, I am prepared to stretch out my hands to them, to become and to act at one with them, or at one with them afresh, in calling upon the Father.

The New Testament is more restrained in its use of the lofty concept of "brother" than later times, especially our own. It does not loosely employ the term "child of God" for each and every person. In its vocabulary the children of God, and therefore the brethren, are those who are united by faith in Jesus Christ as the incarnate Son of God and therefore the firstborn among many brethren [Rom. 8:29]. They are those who meet and know one another in confessing him. In the Old Testament, also, a brother is a fellow Israelite, a fellow member of the covenant people (Ex. 2:11, etc.). As Zinzendorf puts it in his hymn "Marter Jesu," it is here — not everywhere or nowhere — that we all, as a community, join hands. Similarly, when the New Testament speaks of the body, it almost always has in view those who find themselves together as members of the community. "You have one teacher, and you are all brethren" (Mt. 23:8) — the "all" obviously being those who are taught by him, the company of his pupils. Again, the weak person, as a brother for whom Christ died, must not be confused by the strong who wants to practice his higher understanding in matters of idol meats (1 Cor. 8:11; Rom. 14:15). This weak person is, in the words of Romans 14:1, one who is weak *in faith*, and who is to be supported as such. He is not just any fellow man, although Christ undoubtedly died for all men, but a fellow Christian, a member of the people united by faith in Christ. So too is the brother who, if he sins, must first be accused before two witnesses (Mt. 18:15). So too is the brother in whose eye one would rather see a mote than the beam in one's own eye (Mt. 7:3). In the Epistles Christians, not all people, are the brethren who are called "dear brethren" because God loves them. It is they who are exhorted to practice love of the brethren (1 Thess. 4:9; Rom. 12:10; etc.). It is in relation to them that we are told with surprising sternness (1 Jn. 4:20f.): "If any one says, 'I love God,' and hates his brother, he is a liar; for he who does not love his brother whom he has seen, cannot love God whom he has not seen." All this has nothing whatever to do with a narrow indifference to others, but a great deal to do with the obvious emphasis of the New Testament on the inner unity and concord of the brethren, which is to be achieved, sustained, restored, and deepened. Why does the community need this? Not for its own sake, but, again in the words of Zinzendorf ("Herz und Herz vereint zusammen"), "so that the world may know that we are thy disciples." Love, and unity and concord in love, is the presupposition of the community's ministry of witness to others. For the sake of their essential service (of which we shall have to speak again and again) and to do justice to their outward cause, Christians have to be inwardly among themselves a gathered, closed, and concentrated people, not a centrifugal people disintegrating in all kinds of peculiarities. They must be a people made up of those whose unity among themselves already speaks for their one Lord and their one God and Father, a people of brothers and sisters who are inseparably bound together for all their individual freedom and distinctiveness. The apparent exclusiveness with which the New Testament, when it speaks of the children of God, of brothers, brotherhood, and brotherly love, refers only to members of the community, is, then, only the reverse side of the comprehensiveness with which (Rom. 8:21) it regards the manifestation of the glorious freedom of the children of God as the hope of all humanity and indeed of the whole of sighing creation. Only this narrow place can offer a vista of the wider sphere which includes those who are still outside, who are not yet the children of God, who are not yet brethren, but who one day may become and be so.

In elucidation, one may at this point, in spite of all the differences, recall that in our own time the efforts to achieve an ecumenical gathering and reuniting of separated Christians and churches have been decisively set in motion by concern for the task of external mission.

3. INVOCATION

The Christian life, the life that is to be lived in faith in Jesus Christ, in the knowledge of the reconciliation of the world to God that has taken place in him, is event, history, and action. That God is our Father and we are children of God is true as we respond to the Father's work and word by calling upon him as Father. This response is what concerns us here in the context of ethics.

In very general terms invocation is the movement in which the children bring themselves to the attention of their Father and cry to him in recollection, clearly reminding themselves that he is their Father and they are his children. He himself, of course, does not need to be reminded who he is and who they are. "Can a woman forget her sucking child, that she should have no compassion on the son of her womb? Even these may forget, yet I will not forget you" (Isa. 49:15). "Before they call I will answer" (Isa. 65:24). They, however, need to be reminded who he is and who they are. In this matter they continually need to be shocked and wakened afresh out of forgetfulness. Because their remembering can be meaningful, strong, and fruitful only when it is not just an emotional or intellectual matter but becomes their own free and resolute act, they are called upon to call upon their Father. To call upon him is to take up their position by him, to take him at his word that he is our Father and we are his children, and to confess this. What God the Father wills with and for us to his own glory and our salvation is more than a solid but stationary relation or a firm but passive connection. He is the living Father of his living children. What he wills with and for these children is, therefore, history, intercourse, and living dealings between himself and them, between them and himself. They too have to enter into these dealings on their side. They have to actualize the partnership in this history. They have to express in word and deed his fatherhood and their sonship. This is why he calls upon them and commands them to call upon him. He wills that their whole life become invocation of this kind. To be obedient to this command, to call upon him as Father, is to rise up as the prodigal son did, to take the way to the Father as his child, to speak intimately to him, to claim a hearing from him. Invocation, then, aims at the renewal, or rather, the dynamic actualization, of what has become a static, stagnant, and frozen relationship with him. On his side, of course, the relationship never ceased to be dynamically actual. He never stopped working and speaking as the Father of his children. On the side of his children, however, there was and always will be the dangerous possibility or, even worse, the evil reality of halting, resting, and rusting—a state in which the Father becomes for them what in and of himself he is not, a God seated on a distant throne, an alien and sinister God, a God in relation to whom, now that the relation is a distant one, they are not at home but abroad in a far country. Invoking God the Father is the enterprise that follows his word and summons to come back out of an atmosphere of unnatural cold and aloofness to one of natural warmth and intimacy. It is the attempt in relation to him who acts to meet him actively, not just to keep on waiting slackly for whatever develops; the attempt in relation to him who speaks to give an answer to what he says, not just to keep on being silent. In this way they attempt to overcome and leave behind the strange and perverse and totally unfruitful distance from him. This movement of the children to the Father is, in very general terms, the commanded invocation.

The children of God, however, are human, and it is as humans that they have to make this movement to him, their Father. "As humans" means specifically as beings who owe him thanks and can and may and should thank him. As human *creatures* (like and with all other creatures) they owe and may give him thanks that they are and are not, and that as those they are they may be within the limits of their nature and time. As *human* creatures they owe and may give him thanks that among all other creatures they are destined not merely to honor him as the plants and animals and elements do, but in their human fashion, with its limits but also its privileges, to recognize and love and invoke him, thanking him moreover that in the sending and act and revelation of his Son he has also made them his children and will address them as such, thanking him decisively that he has given it to them among all other men to receive his address, and thus to recognize and confess him as their Father and themselves as his children. None of these things is self-evidently theirs, neither their existence and being as God's human creatures, the work and word of grace done and spoken for them in Jesus Christ, nor above all the gift of his life-giving Spirit. Thus to call upon God as a work of obedience on the part of the children of God means especially to thank God and to thank him again and again—from this angle already invocation is a never-ending action—for all that he was and is and will be and all that he did and does and will do for them as his human children. To give thanks is to acknowledge as such a gift that someone else has freely given. The children of God know that they live only by the freely given gift of their Father, which consists of the fullness of his being and work for them and in them. The first motive of their movement to him, which as a basic note decides and determines all that follows, is that they owe him the boundless acknowledgment of his free gift, and knowing both him and themselves they have at least the will and desire to discharge something of this debt of thanks.

The children of God, however, are free; they have been freed for responsible decision and action. In this connection this means that if their thanksgiving is serious, then as acknowledgment of the freely given gift of their Father, it must also entail the honoring, extolling, lauding, and praising of their Father as the Giver of this gift.

Note that in the vocabulary of the Old Testament Psalms the words "thanksgiving" and "praise" are obviously used in such a way as usually to constitute a couple, "thanksgiving" necessarily merging into "praise" and "praise" being simply an enhanced form of "thanksgiving." As both terms describe the invocation that is owed to the being and action of the God of Israel, "thanksgiving" usually precedes "praise." Hence the giving of thanks, offering the sacrifice of thanksgiving to God (Ps. 50:14, 23; 107:22; 116:17), is, as it were, the initial act of serious and proper worship. It is with thanksgiving that we go through the gates of this God (Ps. 100:4) into his temple, and there we show him the honor that is his due by extolling, lauding, and praising him.

It is in keeping with this that in the New Testament εὐχαριστεῖν, thanks for the being and well-being of the communities as known to the apostle, forms the normal introduction to Paul's Epistles. It is in connection with this that he then moves on to positive and critical things that he has to say to them. If he omitted thanksgiving in the introduction to Galatians, replacing it (1:6) by an expression of astonishment at the confusion that had so quickly arisen there, this denotes the special character of the letter in terms of its purpose. Once in the older letters (2 Cor. 1:3) and then in Ephesians 1:3 and 1 Peter 1:3, praise of God (εὐλογητὸς ὁ θεός) is expressed in place of thanksgiving, the thanks now taking second place to the objective act of God in which it has its basis. To praise God is specifically to confess and to make visible and audible the fact that God is worthy (ἄξιος εἶ, Rev. 4:11, etc.) to be venerated and invoked as God. There may be seen here no abstract separation of the two concepts, but rather a relative distinction between them, as in the Psalter.

Praising God shows that thanks for his benefits cannot be concealed or unexpressed, but presses outward for publicity and confession, so that with the invocation of God there always has to be in some way the declaration of God as well. Thanks is not just the acknowledgment of received and expected gifts; it must also be an honoring of God for his own sake. It is thanks for God's benefits; it becomes thanks for his beneficence; it finally becomes thanks for the existence of God as the Benefactor and his acknowledgment as such. Overwhelmed by the greatness of the benefits shown him and the majesty of the beneficence in which they are shown him, man forsakes his neutrality, reserve, and even aversion to the Benefactor himself and as such. As such, in relative independence of his benefits and beneficence toward man, he stands now before him as the Benefactor himself. He evokes astonishment, and claims his service: he in his own dominion, righteousness, holiness, wisdom, and patience; he in his self-revelation which shines through and above all his works and working; he in his own glory.

In a less happy moment Melanchthon (*Loci communes*, 1521) emphasized the benefits of Christ instead of Christ himself as the incarnate Logos of the eternal Father. Various movements in modern Protestant theology have praised him for this. But it has had the result that in Protestantism praise of the divine Benefactor has become a very feeble matter, relevant at most only in poetry.

In the authentically required turn from God's benefits to his beneficence and finally to himself as the Benefactor, thanksgiving becomes praise. One might even say that the test of the free humanity of the children of God is whether or not this turn takes place in their calling upon the Father. We shall have to come back to this in the first three petitions of the Lord's Prayer with their most impressive "thy," the point here being that in thanksgiving honor is given to the Father himself for his own sake. We are forced to conclude that only in this turn to unselfish praise of God does invocation of the Father become what it is, the work of people who are free because they are freed by God for God.

Even so — and here we come to the decisive matter — these people are still humans in all their limited humanity. They are true children of God, for God has elected and loved them, but as he is unlike them, so they are very unlike him. What is common to him and them is neither a nature that embraces and determines him and them, nor an act common to him and them, but simply the free will and the free work of his grace, goodness, and mercy, a participation in his being and life which is freely granted to them, but which, even as it is granted to them, remains his and is never theirs. What is common to him and them, to his being and work and theirs, can never arise except through his gift and in their reception and use of what he wills to give them. In the freedom of his love, which is proper to him and him alone, he creates what is common to him and them, freeing them so that they are free to turn to him. They do not have this freedom; they can neither give it to themselves nor take it for themselves. All they have to do is receive from him and use what is received from him. As they do this, as they invoke and thank and praise him, they are unable — these are the limits of their humanity — to deal on equal terms with him, let alone to precede or anticipate him with something of their own that they bring and have to offer him. He is in heaven and they are on earth [Eccl. 5:1]. He is of infinite wealth, they are in total poverty. He can do all things and they of themselves can do nothing. He goes before and they can only follow. He speaks, and it is for them simply to listen and answer. Above all, he is the faithful and righteous and holy Lord who founds and upholds and fulfills the covenant between him and them, whereas they are his most unfaithful partners, who continually wander off and become entangled in contradiction and conflict against him, and therewith against their fellows, and thus against themselves. They are all too foolish and slothful and capricious recipients and enjoyers of the freedom he has given them. Inevitably, then, the use they make of it will always be misuse by which the fellowship that he has created between him and them is totally and irreparably called into question. Even their invocation, thanksgiving, and praise will always take place within the painful limits of their humanity. This means, however, that even as they call upon him they are always referred absolutely to him and his further gifts. Their thanksgiving and praise can be only that of those who have total need of him and his further free gifts. Even more, it can be genuine thanksgiving and praise only in unreserved acceptance of this neediness of theirs, only as crying to God for his further free gifts, only as petition. Like the strange thanksgiving of the Pharisee in the temple

(Lk. 18:11), or the lip service of the people of Jerusalem (Isa. 29:13), it could be offered in complete misunderstanding of the situation between him and them, in a serious overestimation of what they are before him and a serious underestimation of what he is for them. That they have found grace before him, the grace to call upon him, they will show by always wanting, genuinely wanting, the grace that they constantly need. But the giving of this grace can be only his affair, so they can only pray and sigh and beseech him for it. As they do this, as they act in accordance with the situation between him and them, they thank and praise him in truth. It is no accident, then, that the invocation of God the Father which Jesus taught his disciples in the Lord's Prayer takes the form of pure petition. The invocation of God consists of prayer. It does not detract from the thanks and praise that are due and must be offered to God, but gives definitive honor to their character as thanks and praise, when invocation is multiple petition presented to God with empty outstretched hands. Only thus is their invocation totally serious as the movement of men in their humanity turning to God in his deity. In this light one can see precisely why invocation is commanded by God and must be performed in obedience to him. His grace to men is as such a strict direction to seek grace and to cry for it.

This, then, is a sketch of the invocation of God for and to which his children are liberated and invited and summoned, and which must become an event in the lives of Christians as thanksgiving, praise, and prayer, and therefore as the primal and basic form of the whole Christian ethos. Before we proceed, we must pause a moment to recall how extraordinary it is that this event should take place. Only with great surprise, profound amazement, and even consternation and fright can one speak of the fact that there may and should be this calling upon God by Christians as his children. We stand before the mystery of the covenant — in its way no less a mystery than that of the incarnation and resurrection of the Lord — when we reckon with it that this is so. Something very special has to have taken place, and to keep on taking place, when certain people may not only be called the children of God but are this, and as such are qualified, entitled, able, and willing to call upon God as their Father, when in this calling, in their thanks and praise and prayer, the Christian ethos is actualized and maintained and continued and developed. This is not only not self-evident; it is totally inconceivable. We can count on it only as on a fact of unique order that the existence of such people and their action is possible, not once alone, but in the continuity of their lives. It would be an odd Christian who thought a person could be a Christian in the same way as a Marxist or an anthroposophist or an adherent of this or that philosophy or one who thinks salvation can be sought and found for the whole world on the holy Berge Caux (the center of Moral Rearmament). What has to take place, and to keep on taking place, if people are to be Christians, is a special movement and act of God in which he gives to the Word of his grace — the Word of the reconciliation of the world to him accomplished in Jesus Christ — the specific power to reach these specific people among the many to whom it goes out and is directed, so that they open themselves up to it in freedom, awake to the knowledge that he is their Father and they are his children, and can live in this knowledge. In virtue of this special movement and act of God, as they acquire and have the freedom to follow it with their human understanding, mind, and will, people become Christians. That is, they become those who desire and are resolved to take it literally that he is their Father and they are his children, so that no matter who or what else they may be, they have the right and ability and also the will to call upon him. In virtue of this movement and act of God, it can come about that they do in fact begin to call upon him, and continue to do so.

The highly astonishing event that has to take place, and must continue to take place if there is to be invocation of God the Father by humans as his children, is that of the fruitful meeting and the living fellowship of the Holy Spirit with them and with their spirits: their experience, perception, contemplation, and resolve. The Holy Spirit is God himself in his living, his eternally living unity as Father and Son, in his unity with himself as the origin and the issue of this origin. As the bond of peace [Eph. 4:3; cf. Augustine, e.g., *De trin*. XV,vi] he is in God, and as the revelation of God he is in the created world: God himself in his uniting power and in his power to enlighten and quicken the creature in its relation to him, to free it and set it in motion toward him, toward a being in peace with him. In particular, he is God himself in his own free power to open himself to certain people and to open certain people for himself, to join himself directly to them and them to him. In the Holy Spirit God presents and attests himself to the not at all holy spirits of these people in such a way that within the limits of their spirits, and despite the very painful nature of these limits, they are summoned and raised up for experience, perception, and understanding, for free and freely active acceptance of what he was and is and will be for the world, of what he — the Father through the Son, the Son in service of the Father and to the Father's glory — has done and does and will do for all men, and therefore for them too. In the Holy Spirit God has dealings with these people in such a way that he cannot continue to act onesidedly; he awakens and impels and enables them to receive him in return and makes their dealings with him the controlling element in their lives. In the Holy Spirit God comes together with these people in such a way that for all the ongoing distinction there arises fellowship, a common life, between him and them and them and him. In Johannine terms, God in the Holy Spirit makes himself the Paraclete [Jn. 14:16, 26; 15:26; 16:7], that is, their advocate at the forum of his judgment, but also their advocate at the forum of their conscience, the supreme and victorious advocate. Pentecost, the sending, outpouring, and giving of the Holy Spirit, baptism with the Holy Spirit — God himself in this mode of his being and work — this is the special movement and act in which certain people — not all — become Christians and as such are free to call upon him as their Father, obedient to him not once alone but again and again, in the continuity of their human existence on the basis of this special movement and act of God.

The free Spirit who frees them for this is *holy* because, as Paul says often in

Romans and 1 Corinthians, he is the Spirit of God, the liberating power of his work and word; because God himself is (Jn. 4:24) πνεῦμα, this free and liberating Spirit. We say exactly the same thing when we say that he is *holy* because he is the Spirit of God's Son (Gal. 4:6), the Spirit of Jesus Christ (Rom. 8:29; Phil. 1:19), the Spirit of the Kyrios (2 Cor. 3:17); because Jesus Christ in his work as the Kyrios is himself Spirit, life-giving Spirit (1 Cor. 15:45); because the liberating power of God is his power. As he is holy, the Spirit of the Father and the Son, he is the Spirit of truth (Jn. 14:17; 15:26; 16:13), and the power by which he liberates and quickens those people is the power of truth; indeed, he is himself the truth: the Spirit is the truth (τὸ πνεῦμά ἐστιν ἡ ἀλήθεια, 1 Jn. 5:7). Thus the other great statement can be made: The truth will make you free (ἡ ἀλήθεια ἐλευθερώσει ὑμᾶς, Jn. 8:32). It is as this Spirit that Christians have received him (Gal. 3:2, 14; 1 Cor. 2:12; Rom. 8:15). It is of this Spirit that they are born anew, from above (Jn. 3:7f.). It is as such that he dwells in them (1 Cor. 3:16; Rom. 8:11; Jas. 4:5) and may even fill them (Acts 2:4, etc.). It is as such that he moves and impels them (Gal. 5:18; Rom. 8:14), though only, of course, as a deposit (ἀρραβών, 2 Cor. 1:22; 5:5; Eph. 1:14) or firstfruits (ἀπαρχή, Rom. 8:23), given to them as the presence of the future and the pledge of the totality that they are promised and for which they wait, yet still the Spirit who leads them on to this totality, to all the truth (Jn. 16:13). Setting them on the way to it, he makes them free already here and now to be, even if provisionally, true worshipers of the Father as the Father desires them to be, that is, those who worship him in spirit and in truth (ἐν πνεύματι καὶ ἀληθείᾳ), in the Spirit and also in knowledge of the truth. In this way the impossible becomes possible and actual: my spirit prays (τὸ πνεῦμά μου προσεύχεται, 1 Cor. 14:14), better not in such a way that my mind (νοῦς) stops and becomes idle as among the Corinthian Christians, who spoke in tongues, yet still unhampered by the limits of the mind. For this takes place when the fellowship of the Holy Spirit (κοινωνία τοῦ ἁγίου πνεύματος, 2 Cor. 13:13) becomes an event. He, this Spirit of truth who is himself truth, God himself, the Kyrios, himself comes to help us in our weakness. We often do not know how to pray as we ought. When put under scrutiny, our Christian prayers often reduce themselves to the pitiful request (attributed by Voltaire to a Swiss captain; see *Voltaire's Correspondence*, ed. T. Besterman, LXXI, Geneva, 1962, p. 247): "God, if you exist, save my soul, if I have one," although in such a petition we are perhaps comfortingly close to Jesus' question on the cross: "My God, my God, why hast thou forsaken me?" (Mk. 15:34). When we do not know how to pray, however, the Spirit intercedes for us (obviously in union with what Jesus Christ is doing for us at the right hand of God, Rom. 8:34), with his own better sighing, which we can never express, that is, adequately imitate in any form of the activity of the human spirit. The Lord who searches the hearts, however, knows the adequate meaning of the Spirit when he cries "Abba, Father" (Gal. 4:6) or causes us to make that cry (Rom. 8:15). Since the Spirit is his Spirit and he himself is the Spirit, how can he fail to recognize his own voice in the cry and to acknowledge the intercession of the Spirit to be valid and effective for the weak spirits of his weak saints (Rom. 8:26f.)? The result, then, is the same as in the Magnificat: "My spirit (τὸ πνεῦμά μου) rejoices in God my Savior" (Lk. 1:47). This is the mystery of the invocation of God the Father by men as his children. This, then, is the mystery of the central and basic act of Christian obedience which controls and determines everything: the mystery of the Christian life.

We shall close this subsection with three elucidations, each of which points in a rather different direction.

1. In direct connection with what we have just said about the mystery of invocation and the Christian life as this is disclosed in the work of the Holy Spirit, we advance first the thesis that the Christian life is a spiritual one, that is, a life which in its distinctiveness is from first to last conditioned and determined by that special movement and act of God in the work of the Holy Spirit. It is a life which as calling upon God the Father will always consist very simply — we shall have to give this special prominence later on — in the prayer for the Holy Spirit (see Lk. 11:13).

In modern usage the term "spiritual" has wrongly been put in embarrassing proximity to the word "religious." It should be related to this word only indirectly and not very firmly. What has been forgotten is that, among Christians at least, the word "spiritual" can denote only a new definition of the human spirit, of the whole of this spirit, by the Holy Spirit, so that it cannot refer to a variation or modification of human spiritual activity as such. *Geistlich* and *geistig*, which, unfortunately, like *Geschichte* and *Historie*, can be distinguished linguistically only in German, denote two different things. *Geistig* denotes the capacity for orientation to something transcendent, and it thus implies a religious life in some sense and to some degree. But in the use of this capacity, what is *geistig* is not necessarily *geistlich*. The *geistlich* has contacts with it. It operates in its sphere. It uses its possibilities. It determines, controls, and penetrates it. Yet it has and retains its own individuality, distinctiveness, and movement in relation to the religious life as well as the scientific, moral, political, and aesthetic life. It has no special affinity to the religious life. It will be specially critical of it. More than likely it will have to be in particularly sharp controversy with this element in the life of the human spirit. This element needs sanctification no less, and indeed more, than all the other elements. At best it can only serve the spiritual (*geistlich*) life of man, and often it will not do so. Christians can be, but do not have to be, particularly religious people. Similarly, particularly religious people can become and be Christians, but if they do they are not Christians in their quality as specially religious people. They are fortunate if their being such does not prevent them from becoming and being Christians! Invocation of God the Father by his children, the spiritual Christian life, commences and continues as a human life within the whole life of the spirit and religion, to which it is always referred and with which it is always linked. Nevertheless, it will always represent and be a new and unique thing. Religiosity does not need to call upon a fatherly God. Hence it does not need any special movement and act of God. It does not need any baptism, sending, outpouring, and gift of the Spirit. It may work itself out in this way and take this form. But the spiritual life lives in invocation of God the Father and would be null and void without this special movement and act of this God, without the work of the Holy Spirit.

We are only sketching here the basic features of the spiritual and Christian life in invocation of God the Father as this transcends the life of the human spirit or the religious life.

Christians are people who, not of themselves, but moved by the Holy Spirit who is freely given them, find themselves in direct confrontation with God even though they are not like him but totally unlike. The spiritual life is life in awareness of the immediate presence of God that this entails. These people are only creatures. Indeed they are creatures who completely refuse and contradict and resist God. In the forefront, painful though it be, they have to do with themselves, with their creaturely nature, with their physical and intellectual distinctiveness and power and weakness, with their life and death in this nature. Yet properly, finally, and decisively they do not have to do with themselves, not even with their sin and guilt, but primarily with God as their only Lord and Judge. Again, they live ineluctably, just as they are, a life of fellow humanity in solidarity with their neighbors near and far. Yet they need not fear any man, for no man has the right or power, for good or ill, in his worth or lack of it, to intervene between them and God. Again, they live in the world, sharing its needs, pressed by its problems and riddles, tempted on all sides, inwardly as well as outwardly, by dominant powers and forces in all their glittering ambivalence. But none of the great and little darknesses that surround and frighten them can alter in the least the fact that first and last they may live before God and with him. Again, they live and are in the community. They would not be Christians if they did not, if they did not want to belong to God's people. They have and respect their fathers and brethren in Christ. They listen to their witness. They know they share responsibility for the discharge of the task of the community, for its continued discharge. But they find that its witness refers them directly to the one Mediator between God and man [1 Tim. 2:5] beside whom there is no other, and by him directly to God himself. All along the line, then, they are permitted and commanded to call him their Father. To this freedom the Holy Spirit frees them. In this freedom they live their spiritual life.

It is in the history, work, and word of the one Mediator Jesus Christ that, in spite of everything that might interpose itself and come between, they find themselves directly confronted with God and thereby set in that freedom. In him everything that might separate them from God or prevent them from running to him as their Father is relativized, put in its place, and robbed of the power to separate. The difference between Christians and other folk is that Christians may believe in Christ, love him, hope in him, cling to him, and call upon God in his name. For them God is God, not in the mists of some transcendence, not on the basis of their own opinion, thought, or speculation, not in the form of an image projected by them, but in Jesus Christ. They are thus protected from the hubris in which they might want to be equal to him, or like him, or at least a match for him, from a merely supposed, because usurped immediacy in which he would in truth be absent and they would certainly not be sheltered from all the threats to their freedom. But to cling to Jesus Christ, and therefore to live to and before and with God, unafraid of all the threats, as children of the Father because brothers and sisters of his Son — this is not a matter of their own reason and power. Apart from the Holy Spirit, no one can or will call Jesus Christ the Lord (1 Cor. 12:3), and therefore no one can or will call upon God as Father and therefore in truth. That Christians can and will do this, because they may, is their spiritual life.

This life is one that is always related to the Father and the Son. It is referred to the Holy Spirit, not just partially but totally. It cannot be grounded in itself or sustain and renew itself in its own power. It is cast back on him, from whom it derives and by whom alone it is also guaranteed. Christians live spiritually as and to the extent that they live *ec*-centrically. What are they in and of themselves but poor, weak, and foolish sinners who have fallen victim to death? They can only look beyond themselves, clinging to God himself, and to God only in Jesus Christ, and this only as they are freed to do so, and continually freed to do so, by the Holy Spirit. This is, of course, their plight — the plight of Christians alone. Who would live like that? say others to whom it seems as yet to be permitted or even commanded to rotate more or less sublimely around themselves. If Christians can no longer do this, or at any rate no longer should be able to do so as Christians, this is the plight in which they are called blessed. For in it they are truly exalted. Their plight is that of being left no other possibility than that of exercising their royal right as children of God to call upon God their Father. An evil and unhappy plight would be that of relying on all their own wealth and power and wit as whose possessors their only boast before God can be that of calling upon him as those who have nothing about which to boast. Christians are people from whom every basis for "confidence in the flesh" (Phil. 3:3) has been taken away. They know that here and here alone lies strong power and inexhaustible might. Their only option is to look to "Jacob's God and salvation" (P. Gerhardt: "Du meine Seele, singe"), to thank him and to praise him, to expect and request both great and little things only from him. This life in this happy plight is their spiritual life.

This spiritual life in invocation, which is related and referred entirely to God in Jesus Christ, can and may really be lived by them, and lived by them as an ongoing life in time. Spiritual life is not just a matter of a single moment, or a number of exalted moments, in the life of these people; it is a matter of their life-history. Certainly it is constantly threatened, each day afresh in evil ways, by interruption and even cessation, the end. Certainly they have in themselves no security against this threat. Certainly the worst intensification of the threat would be for them to try to secure themselves against it. The eternity of the gracious will of their Father, the once-for-all act of love performed by his Son their Brother, and the promise and fellowship of the Holy Spirit, which are just as valid and effective today as yesterday and tomorrow, ensure the continuity of the Christian life, the perseverance of the saints. Like the disciples in Gethsemane, even the best Christians, let alone the rest, can be guilty of sleeping, drawing back, stumbling, regressing, and erring in the activating and fashioning of the spiritual life. But "he who keeps Israel will neither slumber nor sleep" (Ps. 121:4). That his Spirit blows where he wills (Jn. 3:8) means that he blows in the dark valleys as well as on the bright mountains. He blows also in the holes where Christians constantly find themselves. And he takes good care that when they have fallen asleep — their spiritual life, grounded in him and sustained by him, goes on — they will always be awakened again by him, they will again call upon him whom they have forgotten but who has not forgotten them, and after the many nights they will begin new days of better, if not the best, activating and fashioning of the spiritual life. New and fresh each morning is the grace and the great faithfulness of the Lord

(J. Zwick: "All Morgen ist ganz frisch und neu"). Their life as Christians has no guarantee but this. But it does have this guarantee, and with this guarantee it has continuity and they constantly have the freedom of the children of God to call upon God as the one he is, as their Father. Thus for all its questionability and frailty, their life-history becomes the history of their spiritual life.

2. The freedom of Christians to call upon God as their Father, their living spiritual life in this freedom, and their life as a whole in its activation and development, is, of course, a very personal matter; but it is not a private matter. It is not a matter of the private salvation and bliss of the individual Christian, for the individual Christian can call upon God only as *our* Father. He can do so only as one among many brethren. Similarly, the brotherly fellowship of Christians, the Christian community, is not an organization for the common cultivation of the very private concerns of its individual members. Their invocation of God is as such a supremely social matter, publicly social, not to say political and even cosmic.

To be sure, we must always speak of Christians as specific people whom God in his free grace has empowered for this required invocation, and who are thus distinct from others. We must always speak of *their* specific destiny, of the Holy Spirit sent into *their* hearts, of *their* faith in Jesus Christ, of *their* knowledge and confession, of *them* as the people of the children of God existing amid all other peoples, and therefore of *their* invocation of God the Father. This has to be so, and we do not go back on it. God's revelation of grace in the history of Jesus Christ is not a general light which rests everywhere on the whole world and on all men, which reaches all men equally. Where it shines it is a very special event in which some participate but many do not. In Luther's words, it is a "moving shower" that comes and goes. The same applies to the receiving, grasping, and seizing of the reality and truth of his history, since the Holy Spirit who awakens men to the knowledge of the work and word of Jesus Christ is the working power of the free God. It applies also to the realization of a possibility that is not offered to each and all but to this one and that. God's Word goes forth and is heard where and how he himself wills. We hear the blowing of the wind, but who knows whence it comes or whither it goes. "So it is with everyone who is born of the Spirit" (Jn. 3:8). As election is the living ground of Israel, so it is the living ground of the community of Jesus Christ. This means, however, that children are a special people as God's children. And as they call upon God the Father, they are, with all the implied ethos, on a special way which cannot be confused or exchanged with any other. They are not humanity as a whole. They are not a ruling majority within it. Even from the standpoint of their external and apparent constitution, and even more so from that of their inward and real constitution, they are a fairly fragile and not very impressive minority. For their own eyes as well as those of others, the fact that as a minority they exist representatively for the whole is one that is deeply hidden.

Even in the glorious age of David and Solomon, what had Old Testament

Jerusalem to speak of compared to the world-cities on the banks of the Nile and the Euphrates with their religions and cultures? Within Jerusalem and Samaria, what were the seven thousand who would not bow the knee to Baal [1 K. 19:18; cf. Rom. 11:4] nor listen to the false prophets of Yahweh? The big battalions were always on the other side. And in New Testament days, those who wanted to belong to them would do better not to become Christians. Christians were and are a "little flock" (Lk. 12:32). Only a few, not many, even find the narrow way that leads to life (Mt. 7:14), let alone tread it, let alone tread it to the end. "For not all have faith" (οὐ γὰρ πάντων ἡ πίστις, 2 Thess. 3:2). Not many, only a few are chosen (Mt. 20:16; [22:14]). Especially in the second half of the Gospel of John is it noticeable that Jesus seems to be positively concerned only with the small number of his disciples. The "Jews" and the "world" now stand at a distance as the alien setting in which the disciples find themselves. It is for *them* that he, the shepherd of his flock, lays down his life (Jn. 10:15). *They*, the disciples, are to believe in the light while they have it, thus becoming children of the light (12:36). *Them* he has loved and loves to the end (13:1). *They* receive from him the new commandment that they should love one another (13:34, etc.). *They* are invited to pray in his name (14:13). To *them* and not to the world he manifests himself (14:22). To *them* he gives his peace (14:27). *Them* he calls his friends (15:15), and for *them* he has chosen (15:16). *They* are now sad but will rejoice when they see him again (16:22). *They* can take comfort because he has overcome the world (16:33). *They* are the ones his Father has given him out of the world (17:6). For *them* and not for the world he prays (17:9). He wills that *they* be where he is (17:25). For it is *they* who have recognized that the Father has sent him. Not knowing the Father (17:25), the world does not know *them*, his children (1 Jn. 3:1), but hates them (Jn. 15:18; 17:14; 1 Jn. 3:13), showing thereby that it lies in the power of the evil one (1 Jn. 5:19). Hence they for their part cannot love the world and what is in it (1 Jn. 2:15). They have reason to be fearful in it (Jn. 16:33). They can live in it only as aliens and exiles (πάροικοι καὶ παρεπίδημοι, 1 Pet. 2:11), only in the diaspora (Jas. 1:1; 1 Pet. 1:1). Hence Abraham, the father of all believers (Rom. 4:1ff.), is a paradigmatic figure not least of all because he went to a foreign country and lived there only in tents (Heb. 11:9), because God gave him not even a foot's length of property there (Acts 7:5), and because all he could find there was his grave (Acts 7:16). The kingdom of the King in which Christians dwell is not of this world (ἐκ τοῦ κόσμου τούτου, Jn. 18:36). All this should be noted and heeded and taken seriously.

A Christian is always "a lonely bird on the housetop" (Ps. 102:8). As may be seen from the wider context of the psalm, this bird is finally and basically a contented one. Yet it is still a lonely bird. The song it has to sing is not an old familiar and popular one, but a rather strange one in whose refrain no great choirs can be expected to join. Christianity as a whole is a kind of "forlorn hope," finally and basically exalted, yet still a forlorn hope, with few or no chances to become some day the triumphant membership of a so-called world religion.

At this point, however, a terrible misunderstanding threatens. Invocation of God the Father, the spiritual life of Christians and the Christian community, the Christian ethos shaped thereby, is not an end in itself. It is not a wonderful glass-bead game played for its own sake by a company of initiates in a quiet valley with no outward contacts. It is not a self-propelled theoretical/practical alternation between misery and redemption, sin and grace, darkness and light, death and life, the devil and God, and, from the standpoint of the human subject, remorse and comfort, anxiety and joy, unbelief and faith. Christians, as is plainly emphasized in John's Gospel (17:11), are in the world even though they are out of it. Jesus does not pray that they should be taken out of the world (17:15). Their invocation of God the Father, then, does not take place on an "island of the blessed" but precisely there where all other men live under the same conditions with all their other undertakings. Are they to be there in vain as superior spectators, as indolent know-alls, even as a laughing third party? Jesus Christ himself did not come into the world to live for himself there in an alien, unknown, and superior glory. Even in his resurrection and ascension he did not retreat into separation from the world. On the contrary, it was for the world and not himself that he acted and that he still acts, seated at the right hand of the Father as God's plenipotentiary to all. God's gracious and mighty Yes was spoken to all in him, when as God's eternal Word he was made flesh and manifested in his glory.

We may simply note here that it is precisely John's Gospel, which so strongly isolates Jesus and his disciples, that in both the first and second halves speaks in even stronger tones about the universality of his sending. "Power over all flesh" is given to him (Jn. 17:2). He came as and because God loved the world (3:16); he came to save the world (3:17; 12:47); he came to give it life (8:26); he came to draw all people to himself—in his exaltation on the cross—and to the Father (12:32); he came that the world might believe in him (17:21) and know him (14:31; 17:23): "I have other sheep that are not of this fold; I must bring them also. . . . There shall be one flock, one shepherd" (10:16). In his father's house "are many rooms" (14:2).

That precisely as the King of Israel and Lord of his elect community he is the Savior of the world is decisive also for the strange special existence of Christians as his brethren and therefore as God's children. Their calling, awakening, and quickening to be such is not an empowering for the satisfaction of some special interest or the actualizing of some special knowledge, work, or happiness that will then be their private affair or the common affair merely of these special people, this special group. Not for their own gratification or glory are they the separated minority they are. They are this minority to discharge the ministry in which they are placed when they are called God's children, begotten by him through the Holy Spirit, and liberated for faith, knowledge, and obedience. They are it for the fulfilment of the mission that is laid upon them, for the giving of witness to the work of God revealed to them, to the covenant, the reconciliation, the peace which he has set up between himself and the world in Jesus Christ. The world needs this witness, and its content has to do with the world's salvation. Christians are ordained, engaged, empowered, and separated to declare this witness in its midst. They owe it to their Lord, the world, and not least their own existence to do this. Their existence as such has the significance of a necessary function. It has a publicly social character, but whether the public and society note, acknowledge, and value this makes no difference.

In the nexus of human history as a whole, Christians in their special nature are not outsize figures, not prodigies. They are certainly not miracle workers or world-renewers. They are indispensable ordinary little people with the task of doing here or there, in this way or that, what is entrusted to them and demanded of them, namely, passing on the news of the mystery and miracle of the renewal of all things which has taken place in Jesus Christ and which in the last time of ours is moving toward its definitive manifestation.

In Matthew 5:13 they are called the salt of the earth which must not lose its savor, its particularity. In Matthew 5:15 they are called a lighted lamp which there would be no sense in putting under a bushel. Along the same lines, and more beautifully, Matthew 5:14 calls them a city set on a hill that cannot possibly be hid. They are appointed to bear fruits (Jn. 15:8, 16). In the very strong expression in John 17:10, Jesus has already glorified himself in them. They are the messengers that he sends before himself (Lk. 9:52). "As thou didst send me into the world, so I have sent them into the world" (Jn. 17:18; cf. 20:21): into the world, to the men of the world, to proclaim to them his own coming. The simple point of their sending and therefore of their existence is that they should be witnesses (Jn. 15:27), his witnesses (Acts 1:8; 22:15), witnesses — as is often emphasized in Acts (1:22, etc.) — of his resurrection, of his life and work, which is present and not past. No more than that, but also no less! They cannot be what he is. They cannot do what he does. But as those who know him they can and may and should show others who he is and what he does. They have to make known the good news of God concerning his Son (Rom. 1:1ff.), which as such is the good news of God's grace (Acts 20:24), in places where it is not known, or only half-known, or not correctly known. They have to proclaim the kingdom of God (Acts 20:25; 28:23, 31). That they may and should and can do this is the point of their special existence as God's children. They are powerfully set aside for this by their Father in his Son through the Holy Spirit. In Romans 1:14, Paul called himself a debtor to the whole of the Gentile world. Not just subsequently or occasionally, but precisely in what they are and have, originally and essentially, Christians are debtors to all non-Christians.

All this has incisive significance for the proper understanding and practice of the invocation of God the Father in which their existence as his children finds its vital nerve.

For one thing, in their being in the world, on earth and under heaven, in the freedom given them for this work, they are very different from their fellow men and all other creatures, for they are directly determined by the one who gives them this freedom and will give it to them again. Yet they too are his creatures, people like all the rest. They too exist in the depths of all creaturely human being. Not on the heights with God, but out of these clearly recognizable depths they call upon him, upon him who is who he is in heaven, in the heights of his own unapproachable place, in the distance which he alone can overcome from his side. They are in the world. Yet they are not so in vain. They are significant and important for the world as world. As they thank and praise God and pray to him, in contrast to all religious hubris and moral heaven-storming; in contrast also to all wild dissipation and indolent negligence, they realize the only legitimate possibility in relation to the world; in contrast to all optimistic and pessimistic illusions they fulfill the truth of being of the world and man in relation to him who is God as Creator and Lord of the world and man. What his children do when they call upon him as Father is precisely what a true child of the world ought to do, whether he knows it or not as they know it.

Again, in spite of their likeness to all others, their difference from them cannot be altered, nor can their existence as that minority of aliens, exiles, and pilgrims. In the affliction and distress that unavoidably hangs over them, they call upon God as their only reliable strength and stay, as the one who has made himself responsible for them with their separation and commission, as the one who will stand by them, who will not abandon them or leave them uncared for in any solitude, as the one to whom they owe their freedom for joyful, defiant, and peaceful endurance and perseverance in this situation, as the one whom they cannot thank and praise enough as the Giver of this gift, as the one whom they must continually seek afresh in unwearying prayer. To call upon him is to seek refuge with him to whose right of possession and power of disposal even the alien world around them is subject, without whom even the obviously much bigger battalions of the rest of people, the clever and foolish and dull and sharp opponents of his children, cannot take a single step or do even the smallest thing. His children call upon him as the one with whom they know that, even in their well-founded anxiety, they are better sheltered than by the best guarantees that all men put together could offer them, than by all the forms of security which they themselves constantly demand and snatch at in their folly. That they call upon him means that they commit their ways to him along with all that might hurt their hearts upon these ways [cf. P. Gerhardt: "Befiehl du deine Wege und was dein Herze kränkt"].

Finally, and above all, God's children are not what they are either in vain or for their own sake. Here in the world among all others they are freed and determined for service of their Father and attestation of his work and word. Not simply out of personal need, but as messengers in his service they call upon him. They do this in the weakness in which they exist in this function of theirs — a weakness of which they are well enough aware. They are referred to the fact that they have to accept their commission, since without it they would not be what they are, and therefore to the fact that it will constantly be confirmed and renewed — something that they cannot give or take for themselves, something that can only come to them, something that they owe to him. The wonderful freedom which, in giving them their task, he imparts to them for its execution, calls for new and wonderful liberations by the one Liberator. When they call upon him, this means that they ask that he should not fail to be their Liberator even though they notoriously fail again and again in his service, even though they so obviously let him down. They ask that he himself should take up the cause which has been entrusted to them and which they have served so unfaithfully and with such serious incompetence. When they call upon him, this means that they want to be comforted and reassured by him, that in his service they need not and should not venture anything on their own that is not pure obedience to him, but that when something is commanded as pure obedience to him, then, without anxiously wondering what they can or cannot do, or what might be the success or failure of their action, they may venture it without fear and trembling. They thank him because he wills to have them and to use them as witnesses of his work and word. They praise him for the eternal meaning that their existence acquires and has therewith. They pray to him that he who alone can give it meaning will do so today, tomorrow, and the day after.

From this final point our path must now take an important turn. As God's witnesses to all other men in the world, Christians are God's children and may and should invoke God as their Father. It follows that in their hearts and on their lips the vocative "Father" must have a significance that transcends and bursts through the limits of their own sonship as this is known and grasped in their faith in Jesus Christ. What does "*Our* Father" mean when the *we* who utter this cry are not, as God's children, a private club with a sacred private end, but the people and community of his witnesses to all other men? In this situation "Our Father" means more than: thou, who as the Father of Jesus Christ art our Father, the Father of each of those who believe in him. It also means more than: thou who art our Father, the Father of those who by thy Holy Spirit are united in common knowledge and common confession of Jesus Christ. These people cannot cry "Our Father" without including those with whom they do not live as yet in this union of knowledge and confession because Jesus Christ is still a stranger to them. They cannot cry it in separation from the overwhelming host of half-believers, heretics, the superstitious, and unbelievers all around them. They would not be taking seriously their ministry as witnesses of the reconciliation of the world with God accomplished in Jesus Christ; they would not be taking seriously their own divine sonship, nor taking God at his word when he says he is their Father, if they were to regard exclusively as their own Father the one whom they may know as Father in Jesus Christ, if they were to call upon him merely as such. Apart from and in spite of what they deserve, by Jesus Christ and through his Spirit they have been taken up into *his* invocation of God as *his* Father. They have been liberated and empowered to follow him and join with him as his brethren in calling upon God as *their* Father too. As they make use of their freely given freedom to do this, they necessarily have to accept and make the same movement as that in which he associated them with himself. As his "My Father" opened up to include them, so their "Our Father" must open up to include those to whom he, being sent by his Father into the world, has sent them as witnesses of his sending. They would not be the "we" to whom he has granted this inestimable privilege, but to whom he has also given this task, if they could be content with the "corner happiness" [cf. H. Sudermann's play of this title] of knowing and invoking God as *their* Father. When the "Our Father" goes forth from their hearts and is spoken by their lips, it has to be extended and opened up. It has to become a bold anticipation of the invocation to which in Jesus Christ — they have to attest this all — not they alone but these others are also ordained. In their name, then, and not just in their own, they will cry "Our Father," as the provisional representatives and vicars of the rest; as those who now do for them what they themselves may and should do but do not yet do because they are not yet liberated and empowered and willing to do it, although they will not finally fail to do it when the lordship of Jesus Christ over all creation is manifested, and with it the reconciliation of the world to God that has taken place in him. For the moment, without being asked or commanded by them, and without expecting any thanks from them, Christians can only do it for them and not with them. But they cannot possibly cease to do it for them if they do not wish to be incredible to themselves, and utterly useless and unserviceable, as those who are called to be witnesses of Jesus Christ and therewith the children of God. With what sincerity and joy could they turn to others, what power could the message of Jesus Christ have on their lips, if in those who are not yet their brethren they did not recognize and acknowledge their future brethren and therefore did not want to join company with them in their dealings with God? In the hearts and on the lips of Christians as God's children "Our Father" has to mean: thou whom we may now know and fear and love as our Father in Jesus Christ, but also: thou who art the Father of us all in Jesus Christ; thou who art the Father of those who do not yet know him thy Son, who know thee as his and therefore as their Father, and themselves as thy children; thou the Father of those who, far from calling upon thee with us, do not show themselves at the moment to be our brethren but perhaps even our opponents and enemies as they resist and contest what we are doing. Thou our Father, but theirs too, because they too are thine elect and beloved children in thy Son, because he died and rose again from the dead for them too, because he lives for them too, seated at thy right hand as their Lord without asking whether they acknowledge him as such. It should be clear enough that the "Our Father" of the children of God corresponds only in this anticipatory extension to their task as witnesses of God's work and word to those from whom it is as yet concealed. Again, it is only in anticipatory extension that this can be the act of their faith in Jesus Christ in obedience to the impulsion of the Holy Spirit. Again, in this extension it does not become thinner or fainter or weaker in its narrower and more obvious sense, or in its personal meaning and intention: thou the God who is believed, known, and loved by us in particular as Father. In this extension it becomes all the more intensive and joyful, for it is freed from the shadow of the suspicion of sacred egoism and given wings by its connection with the great hope of God's consummated act of revelation. Finally, in this extension the very odd thing that a few Christians do (whether they are few or many makes little difference), namely, their invocation of God the Father, acquires the character of a serving function in the life of human society, of a contribution to world history that is indispensable as an antidote. In all quietness and concealment, expecting no recognition or thanks but also fearing no disappointment or futility, they do what is not just in their own interest but very much in the general and public interest. Where here or there a Christian or the Christian community calls upon God as Father in even the most unassuming form, in the smallest sphere and in all modesty, there takes place representatively what ought to be the work of all and what will finally have to be the work of all. There takes place that which is commensurate with the enacted fulfilment of the covenant between God and man, with the accomplished reconciliation of the world to God which is still to be universally manifested, with that which "inwardly" holds the world together as in its present form it rushes on to its end. As Christians persist in their extended "Our Father," in secret but very real dignity they are like the watchmen on the walls of sleeping Jerusalem, who to the glory of God, and the salvation of all who dwell within the walls, cannot keep silent day or night (Isa. 62:6). Their prayer when they cry "Our Father" is a prophetic prayer.

3. As we have described it thus far, the invocation of God by his children in which the spiritual life and also the witnessing ministry of Christians in the world have their basis, root, and norm, and which is the nerve of their whole Christian existence, is an integral part of the history of the covenant between God and men. It is an integral part of the dealings which God in Jesus Christ, beyond what he has done and does for all men in him, and on the basis of what he wills to do with all, has opened and continues to open with these specific people in the specific movement and act of the Holy Spirit. The invocation of God by Christians is the subjective, or, as one might simply say, the human factor and element in this history and these dealings. We remember that it is due only to the free grace of God that as there can be dealings with God at all, so there can be the special dealings between God and these men, the history of their encounter, the concrete intercourse and exchange between them, a living relation in which not only God acts but these specific people may and should be truly active as well. The grace of God is the liberation of these specific people for free, spontaneous, and responsible cooperation in this history. In his free grace God purges himself from the base suspicion that he is an unchangeable, untouchable, and immutable deity whose divine nature condemns him to be the only one at work. By God's free grace these people are not marionettes who move only at his will. They are given the status of subjects who are able and willing to act, able and willing to do what is appropriate to them in dealing with him, able and willing to call upon him as the Father of Jesus Christ and therefore as their Father and also as the Father of all men. In his free grace he orders them to do what he has freed them to do, namely, to call upon him as Father. By God's free grace, what they do when they obey his command, their "Abba, Father," becomes the basic act of the Christian ethos.

Our description of this basic act of the Christian ethos would have a serious gap which would call everything into question if we did not engage in a specific discussion of what it means that the invocation of God as their Father, as a free and responsible human action, belongs inseparably, as a kind of lower pole, to the objective or, more accurately, the divinely subjective element in the dealings. As God begins these dealings with his children as the brethren of his Son, he makes himself their partner and them his partners. The divinely subjective element in these dealings, which not only corresponds to the humanly subjective element of their invocation but is indissolubly related and united with it, consists of the hearing which God grants to those who call upon him. We cannot speak of the human action — and this is what gives it its force and dignity — without immediately thinking of its continuation on the other side, on God's side. As God frees his children to take sides with him, so when they are obedient to what he commands he for his part is active on their side as their Father. He does not fail to hear them. He does not merely hear them. He hears and answers. In general terms this undoubtedly means that in perfect freedom, yet consistently with his grace and occasioned by their invocation, he again does something, something new, namely, that which corresponds to their invocation, to their thanksgiving, praise, and prayer. This is the upper pole, the divinely subjective element in the dealings, intercourse, and exchange, without which the humanly subjective element that may also be at work, the invocation of the Father by his children, the Christian ethos, could not be understood nor evaluated in terms of its seriousness and joy, nor indeed, in the strict sense, have any meaning.

It is not true, then, that the point of calling upon God is to be found only in the kind of alleviation, uplift, and purification that a person might achieve on his own when engaging in a lofty monologue as though he were speaking with God as another. It is in this way, as the supreme and most intimate act of self-help, that Schleiermacher and others understand prayer. Let us not enter into the question of how effective this self-help is in the form of a monologue of this kind. The fatal thing about this teaching is its presupposition. It can speak only poetically and not properly of an invocation of God by man, and it cannot speak at all of a corresponding hearing on God's side, for this kind of reciprocity between God and man, this kind of codetermination of a divine action by a human action — might it not involve an attempt by man to control God? — is thought to be totally out of keeping with the sovereign nature of God and the absolute dependence upon him of all the reality that is distinct from him. Over against this presupposition it must be stated that the God who is known as "our Father" in Jesus Christ is not this supreme being who is self-enclosed, who cannot be codetermined from outside, who is condemned to work alone. He is a God who in overflowing grace has chosen and is free to have authentic and not just apparent dealings, intercourse, and exchange with his children. He is their free Father, not in a lofty isolation in which he would be the prisoner of his own majesty, but in his history with them as his free children whom he himself has freed. He does not just speak to them. He wills that he also be spoken to, that they also speak to him. He does not just work on and for them. As the Founder and the perfect Lord of this concursus (cf. *CD* III,3 § 49,2), he wills their work as well. He for his part will not work without them. He will work only in connection with their work. Thus he is not so omnipotent or, rather, so impotent, that as they call upon him, liberated and commanded to do so by him, he will not and cannot hear them, letting a new action be occasioned by them, causing his own work and rule and control to correspond to their invocation. His sovereignty is not an abstract and absolute sovereignty but the relative and concrete sovereignty of his free and real and effective grace to people in Jesus Christ and of his real and effective Holy Spirit who truly liberates them. It is very proper for him, then, to let his action be codetermined by his children who have been freed for obedience to him. As he wills and does this, his free hearing and answering of their invocation gives to it a significance and range that totally surpass and put in the shade the very dubious self-help they might try to derive from it.

"He fulfils the desire of all who fear him, he also hears their cry, and saves them" (Ps. 145:19). Note that the positive concern of the self-help theory, the inner uplift that goes with prayer, is not abandoned, but is given its proper due as itself God's answer rather than the work of human self-help: "On the day I called thee, thou didst answer me, my strength of soul thou didst increase" (Ps. 138:3). From this there follows what is said about the word "Amen" in the last question of the Heidelberg Catechism. This little word, we read, signifies that the thing is true and certain. For my prayer is much more surely heard by God than I feel in my heart that I desire it of him.

The humanly subjective element in the dealings between God and man has always been beset by very difficult problems. As regards the divinely subjective factor, the hearing granted by God the Father to the children that call upon him, there are no problems. When God's children invoke him as Father, this is in no sense a venture, a mere gesture, a shot in the dark, an experiment, or a gamble. They do this as those who have a part in the history in which God is their partner and they are his partners, in which they are liberated for this action and summoned to it, in which there is also given to them the promise of his corresponding action and therefore of his hearing. The dealings he has opened up with them and into which they enter when they call upon him as their Father can take no other course than to show that he for his part, in both word and deed, is in fact their Father.

Their invocation, however, is already determined by their expectation of this continuation on his side. They cannot invoke God on the presupposition of the fiction that he might perhaps be that impotent omnipotent God, that prisoner of his own sovereignty, who as such would not consent to let his divine action be codetermined by their human action. In such a case their invocation might well be a venture that would be just as well or better left alone. In calling upon God as the Father of Jesus Christ, however, they have learned to know him as their own Father in a very different way, namely, as the God who lets himself be spoken to, who comes afresh in his free grace to those who, moved by his free grace, come to him, who gives when his children ask obediently, who satisfies their seeking by letting them find, who accepts their knocking and opens to them (Mt. 7:7). The seriousness, the joy, indeed the meaning of their action depends on their calling upon him as this God with the self-evident certainty that they do not just seem to do, or do in vain, that which they do as he has freed and commanded them to do it. They can do it only with the unconditional expectation that their calling upon him does not fade away in the void and is not just heard but is also answered. They will not suffer from the delusion that God is in their hands or in their power, that with their action they can control him and his action, that they do not always have to pray that their invocation will be answered, as is done throughout the Psalter. It is his free grace alone — the grace they always need — that he wills to conduct those dealings, that intercourse and exchange with them, in such a way that he makes them his partners and himself their partner, that he forges so close a link between their invocation and his answering, their action and his. He willed this and did it when he brought them to know himself as Father and called them his children. In so doing he blocked the way back to the fiction that they were dealing with a self-enclosed deity that worked alone. He forbade and made impossible a type of prayer which on that presupposition was merely trifling, experimental, and full of doubt, like the prayer of the "double-minded man" of James 1:5ff. How can they take God literally as their Father, and take themselves seriously as his children, if they are not unconditionally certain that their prayer is heard? Invocation apart from the unconditional expectation of God's answer would be blasphemy. Such invocation is out of the question. Better no prayer at all than prayer with no awareness of this solid relation. The only prayer that can be unanswered is prayer that is uncertain of an answer, so that it is not calling upon the true God. In this regard we consider again that true calling on the true God is in its origin the action of those who in Jesus Christ may know themselves to be God's children. It is participation in *his* calling upon *his* Father. "We pray as it were by His mouth" (Calvin, Geneva Catechism, 1542). Except on this ground Christians can neither begin nor continue. But when they pray on this ground, in a weak and feeble but still an authentic echo of *his* calling upon *his* Father, this cannot be done in uncertainty, hesitation, or doubt — for the Holy Spirit, who is no skeptic (Luther), does not let them talk to themselves — but only with the confidence that the Father, who *is* the Father and they *are* his children, will hear and answer, corresponding to their action with his.

This confidence of Christians toward God has nothing whatever to do with human presumption. If it had — and in and of themselves they have no protection against it — they would be quickly enough rebuffed and put to shame and put back in their proper place by being forced to see that even when they call upon God and he hears them, he still very definitely keeps the reins in his own hands. As they call upon him with confidence, they do not gain the mastery over him or acquire control over his gift or his giving, let alone himself as the Giver. As they invoke him as their partner, they stand and act in his *service*. This is decisive too in relation to his answering, of which they may and should be certain. Their invocation of the Father, being promised and in all circumstances granted a hearing, acquires the character of a codetermination of the divine action, but this implies no limitation of the divine sovereignty. It means that God's sovereignty is not like that of a tyrant. In his exercise of it he does not disregard the service of his children but pays it free and — what is in his judgment — proper regard. Yet in fact he never lets the reins slip from his fingers. His divine hearing is that he makes use of their service. However, he, and not they, decides how and to what extent he does so. He certainly corresponds to their invocation. But he does it according to his own good pleasure and purpose, to his own glory, and therefore in their own best interests too. Their most serious invocation takes place within the limits of their human knowledge, will, judgment, and desire. Yet he does not despise it in this inadequacy. He lets himself be touched and moved by it. His divine hearing always consists of the fact that in corresponding to it, he understands it infinitely better than they understand themselves and therefore gives place to their invocation in an infinitely better sense than that in which even at best they can perform it. He hears it in his power (Eph. 3:20) to do everything in far higher measure than that of their own asking and thinking. He does not hear them on account of the cleverness or strength but in the foolishness and utter weakness of their invocation. As he hears them, he breaks down and crosses and extends their limits. He hears them superabundantly, that is, in such a way that they later recognize the invocation that proceeded from their hearts and minds and mouths only with the greatest astonishment at the gracious transformation with which he corresponds to it and manifestly comes to meet it. He hears them — and for this they for their part are superabundantly grateful — in such a way that he is to them the Greater, the Lord. It is as such that he corresponds to their invocation. Yet he does correspond to it; he hears and answers it. He does so truly and fully as the God and Father upon whom they call.

He hears their thanksgiving; it is not lost in the void. In all its imperfection it is not offered to him in vain. He graciously accepts it as "eucharist," as acknowledgment of his grace — even though they, his human children, hardly sense, let alone know, what they are really saying when they give thanks that he is good and "his steadfast love endures for ever" [Ps. 106:1; 107:1; 118:1ff.; 136:1ff.]; even though in fact they rarely enough thank him and never do so with anything like sufficient seriousness. He notes and accepts their thanks because they offer it to him as the brethren of his Son, as acknowledgment of his grace conferred on them in him, in concert with his perfect thanksgiving. He lets himself be moved by their giving of thanks because, as he hears it, their weak and dissonant voices are sustained by the one strong voice of the one by whose eucharist the inadequacy of theirs is covered and glorified in advance.

He also hears the praise they offer to him, whether it be loud or soft, joyful or forced, well considered or shoddy. In all its forms it needs his hearing. It also receives it. Their praise reaches and pleases him. Since it is often enough interrupted by their self-satisfaction, defiance, and forgetfulness, and is rarely enough undertaken and executed with any consistency, there is seldom the crescendo from treasuring and admiring God's gifts, by way of astonished veneration of the wonderful ways and modes of his giving, to the unselfish and wholly unpragmatic worship of the Giver for his own sake — the crescendo which constitutes the essence of this aspect of the invocation of God by his children. It is by no means self-evident that he should be pleased by their praise, that he who does not need it should seriously let himself be honored by their far too slender and often also far too bulky praise. Yet it does in fact reach and please him. In his service he has a use for even the most stupid and clumsy praise offered by his people and all its members. For again he accepts it as the praise of those who are his children as the brethren of his Son. He accepts it as praise of the almightiness of his mercy shown in that one, both to them and to his whole creation. In their doubtful praise he hears *his* voice, his "I thank thee, Father, Lord of heaven and earth" (Mt. 11:25 and par.). In this context their praise, for all its poverty, is praise that is heard. In all seriousness it secures and enjoys the divine good pleasure.

He hears also and especially the petitions, great and small, reasonable and unreasonable, that are brought before him and to which the thanksgiving and praise of his children always lead again. "No little tear is too small before Him" (P. Gerhardt). No little hands, stretched out or folded before him, are too dirty to achieve something with him; they do in fact achieve something with him. Here, above all, the total weakness of those who call upon him is manifest. What would they be with all their prayers if he to whom they bring them did not have better knowledge — the very best — concerning what they really mean and want and desire? They ask for this and that. Inevitably they do so according to their own estimate and opinion of what they and others need, of what is good for them and the church and the world, of what, according to their own thinking and program, God ought to be doing to be a Supporter, Helper, and Savior for themselves, for those around them, and for the race as a whole. They may and should pray, and God will hear them. No request by any child of God is not fulfilled by God his Father. Fulfilled! According to the meaning and intention with which it is brought before him, the petition might be largely and even mostly an empty, shortsighted, arbitrary, unreasonable, and even perverted and dangerous one. Already as a request it needs fulfilment, that is, correction, amendment, and transformation by the one to whom it is directed and before whom it is brought. In the great and little matters with which his children approach him, he and he alone knows what is really and properly and fundamentally necessary, what is helpful and fruitful, what will truly be to his own glory and their salvation. There is no reason, of course, why what they intend and desire should not be very close to this. There is no reason why the divine hearing of their human prayer, as sometimes happens, should not be more or less congruent with it without any notable correction. There is no reason why the request cannot be fairly literally fulfilled. Nevertheless, it would be wholly inappropriate and impossible for the children of God to expect and demand that the glory of the hearing should consist in the congruence of the divine fulfilling with the limited form of the asking, or even to accept as a hearing only a divine fulfilment that conforms to their own thought and intention. The rule is instead that they must accept already a fulfilment, that is, a transformation, of the prayer itself. God's hearing begins when he receives the prayer as he himself has transformed it. He will correspond to it the more surely and the more gloriously in this corrected and amended form. Somewhere along the line of their human asking — perhaps at a point which to them seems very distant because it is not foreseen and determined by them but by God their Father — they certainly may and should expect that it will be heard and that God's action will thus correspond to theirs. In all circumstances they can be sure of an answer. In all circumstances it will come to them in the form determined by their Father. In regard to their praying as God's children as well as their thanksgiving and praise, the firmness of the connection and sequence of human invocation and divine hearing is unshakably guaranteed by the fact that Jesus does not command them to pray in their own name but in his name, in the name of God's Son, their Brother, Jesus Christ (Jn. 14:13f.; 16:23f.), that in him they have access to the Father, that they are adopted into fellowship with his praying. They cannot and will not pray in vain for that for which he has already prayed to the Father; for in their voices with all their false notes the Father hears his pure voice. As those who may and can and should pray together with him, they too pray with no doubt concerning God's free and gracious but also powerful and dependable hearing.

Having reached the end of this first train of thought, which we ventured in relation to the invocation, "Our Father in heaven," we are now in a position to attempt a brief summary in relation to the problem which here concerns us, namely, that of the Christian life and its distinctive ethos. In terms of the norm which may be seen in the invocation and extracted from it, one may say positively that from the Christian standpoint we may describe as good and permitted and commanded — as authentic and right as a work of the freedom for which Jesus Christ has freed his own [cf. Gal. 5:1] and for which they are free in the power of his Holy Spirit — the human action which in great and little things alike, both inwardly and outwardly, takes place in the required responsibility of the children of God to their Father and therefore in the course of their calling upon him. The Christian community as such is obedient, and so are Christians as its members, when explicitly or implicitly, directly or indirectly, their thought and speech and action finds itself in this movement; or, to speak in greater detail, when it presents itself as a form of the thanksgiving which they owe and are willing to render to God, as a form of the praise of his gift, his giving, and himself as the free Giver, and as a form of the prayer which, in every respect, it is always necessary that they address to him; or, as one can and must also say, when it is some kind of activation and development of the spiritual life that they may live in the service of God, namely, for the attesting of his work and word to the rest of the world, and in this way to their own salvation; or, as one may finally and very definitely say, when the invocation of God the Father which sustains and determines their thought and speech and action takes place with the unconditional certainty of a hearing on the part of their Father, a free hearing, yet in all circumstances a gracious hearing that will never in any circumstances be withheld. On the other hand, from the Christian standpoint derived from that invocation, everything is evil, bad, and forbidden which implies a silencing of the invocation, a halting of thanksgiving, praise, and prayer, a denial of the spiritual life that is opened up for the children of God, an omission of the ministry of witness which constitutes its point or, finally, everything that implies a lack of trust in the hearing which has been infallibly promised. Already, then, by a proper understanding of that invocation the distinction may be made which it is the task of Christian ethics to illumine, namely, the distinction between what the Christian community and those who have entered it in baptism are to do and what they are not to do, between the ways they are to choose and the ways they are to avoid.

§77

ZEAL FOR THE HONOR OF GOD

Christians are people who know about the self-declaration of God, whose beginning has already taken place and whose consummation is still to come. As such they suffer because he is so well known and yet also so unknown to the world, the church, and, above all, themselves. They pray that he will bring his self-declaration to its goal with the manifestation of his light that destroys all darkness. Meanwhile, in accordance with this prayer they have a zeal for the primacy of the validity of his Word in the world, in the church, and above all in their own hearts and lives.

1. THE GREAT PASSION

Christians are people with a definite passion. In no circumstances, then, can they be cowards, blind-worms, bored, boring, or commonplace. They are not, of course, "angry young men" who seek a reputation by plunging from one emotion and convulsion into the next and indulging outwardly in one eruption after another. Formally, their passion may indeed be a burning one. Sometimes it can and must break out openly and come to very loud expression. Nevertheless, for long periods it may also be a quiet one, deeply concealed, not under a forced and artificial and merely apparent composure, but under one that is true and genuine and self-evident. An inner calm that is still there even when their passion erupts will constitute a necessary complement of their passion and an important criterion of its Christian character. Yet they cannot be without this passion. They are not allowed to be ashamed of it. In no case may they extinguish it.

A passion is a person's suffering from an unfulfilled desire which seeks fulfilment, the fulfilment in which it can transform itself and become delight and joy instead of pain. Christians by definition are people who suffer from such an unfulfilled desire that seeks fulfilment. There are different kinds of passions, great and small, unconquerable and conquerable, transitory and permanent, harmless and dangerous. Let us say at once that the Christian passion is a great, unconquerable, permanent, and even dangerous passion. A small, conquerable, transitory, and harmless passion would not be the one by which Christians are moved. We must also say that, strictly speaking, only the special passion of *Christians* as a great, unconquerable, permanent, and dangerous passion is here at issue.

The passion of Christians, as may be seen already in the way we have characterized it, is a very definite and special passion. To anticipate, we may state that it is connected with their election and calling to active knowledge and attestation of the work and word of God, or, in the language of

111

the preceding section, to their standing and pathway as the children of God the Father. As people like all others, of course, they live in different contexts. They are children of the world even though they are more than this. This means — and it would be pure imagination to think otherwise — that they are not determined by that special passion alone, but in all kinds of variations by very different ones as well. There also exists in them, with no little force, the general, hardly definable, yet not on that account any less urgent, yearning for life, the craving for food and drink and sleep, the desire for love and hate and hate-love, the urge to have dealings with interesting and eminent people, the longing to be acknowledged and valued by such people, the hankering for pleasure, power, possessions, and position. There are animal desires and spiritual desires; there are political, social, aesthetic, technical, and scholarly desires. All these are unfulfilled desires that cry out for fulfilment and for the pleasure expected with it. Passions exist, then, in many other forms than that peculiar to Christians as such. Simply to speak of them as evil or base or of little worth makes no sense. No matter how they present themselves or work themselves out, they are all connected with the human creatureliness which God elected and willed and which is thus in origin and nature good. No Christians have no other passions — perhaps not a few other passions — than that which is peculiar to them as Christians. The Christian passion of all Christians is surrounded by a more or less light or dark cloud of other passions. The Christian passion of all Christians is exposed to remarkable permutations that can happen to them as well as to others. Since they have to admit the force of other passions along with their special Christian passion, the fire of Christian passion with its special craving has to be kindled again primarily and especially in direct encounter with these others and not just in what they find out about such passions from those around them. In this context we shall be content simply to describe and understand these passions in relation to the Christian one with no disparaging assessment. Even what we said about the superior greatness, unconquerability, permanence, and danger of the Christian passion was not meant to exalt this passion and dismiss all others as of little or no worth. It was simply meant to emphasize the distinctiveness of the Christian passion. About this we have to speak. The passion that Christians have has a motive that other passions — known to Christians perhaps better than to others — do not have. It thus has an object and character alien to others. It is in this peculiarity that it moves Christians, who are, of course, moved by all kinds of other passions too. We shall have to speak about this peculiarity and uniqueness in the present section. We have it in view in the title "Zeal for the Honor of God."

The first petition of the Lord's Prayer will lead us now to the goal of a further development of Christian ethics under this theme. It runs: "Hallowed be thy name." This is the first material element in the invocation with which the children of God may and should approach their Father. Invocation in this form too is undoubtedly thanksgiving and praise, but it is decisively petition: asking for something that only God can do and give and that is thus to be expected only, but very definitely, from him. To this petition, as to the address "Our Father," there belongs — as both presupposition and consequence — a human attitude and mode of action that ineluctably comes on those who seriously bring the petition before God: something which characterizes their whole being, life, and action in such a way that it necessarily has to be that of children of God calling upon their Father. We had this in mind when we spoke in the introduction about the distinctive Christian passion. Its concern is for the honor of God. This is at issue in the first petition: God's hallowing of his name. The person who seriously prays for this obviously suffers from the unfulfilled desire that in a way that has not yet happened to the world, the church, or himself, in a way that is proper but that only God can bring about with his own action, work, and gifts, God's name should be sanctified, secured against all slander, and validated; that the honor which is due God's work and word, and therefore himself as God, should be manifested by himself, who alone can do it, in all its greatness and glory. The Christian thinks and speaks and acts with this desire when he seriously prays the first petition. He is filled, impelled, guided, and ruled by this hot desire. If he were not, how could he pray the first petition seriously? To describe this passion we use the biblical term "zeal": zeal for the honor of God.

It might be asked whether the biblical term "desire," which we had to use in connection with passion, would not be nearer the mark. The human attitude implied in the first petition certainly has to do with a desire. Nevertheless, it is better not to make this a leading concept because in the New Testament the word ἐπιθυμία has with few exceptions the pejorative sense which is normally (though incorrectly) associated with passion. The passion at issue here can appear in many dubious forms. But it is a necessary, praiseworthy, and noble passion, a holy passion. The word "desire" tends to conceal this.

The situation differs somewhat in relation to the term "delight." In the Old Testament especially this is often used very positively for the correct attitude of man to God, as in Psalm 37:4: "Take delight in the Lord." Thus it calls for consideration. Nevertheless — and this is why we reject it — we do not catch in it the note of suffering desire for what is not yet present, nor do we see in it the active and warring element which is expressed by "passion."

We choose the word "zeal" because this term clearly speaks of a passion (we cannot be zealous without suffering), because it has a predominantly positive sense in both the Old Testament and the New Testament, and finally and especially because in the Old Testament it denotes a divine attitude accompanying and preceding the human: the passion with which God acts and makes himself known in displaying his grace and judgment. Paul also speaks of a "zeal of God" (2 Cor. 11:2), and Hebrews (10:27) refers to a consuming fire of zeal which is obviously that of God. Originally, Yahweh is a zealous God (Ex. 20:5; 34:14). He is zealous that Israel should accept and venerate him alone as God over against all the gods of other peoples. Faithful to his election, he is zealous for his land as its Protector (Joel 2:18) and for his people (Isa. 26:11) and Jerusalem (Zec. 1:14) as the Lord of the covenant. The zeal of the Lord of hosts will bring it about that a remnant shall escape out of Jerusalem (Isa. 37:32; 2 K. 19:31). Again, his zeal will bring in the prince of peace of the end-time (Isa. 9:7). His zeal threatens the peoples (Ezk. 36:5), and it threatens his own people because of their apostasy (Ezk. 5:13; 16:38ff.; 23:25), and finally, the whole earth (Zeph. 1:18; 3:8). In all these contexts he is zealous — at this point we are obviously close to the content of the first petition of the Lord's Prayer — for his holy name (Ezk. 39:25). He wraps himself in this zeal as in a mantle (Isa. 59:17). His sacred right to it and the saving nature of his exercise of it are never even remotely in question.

The zeal of man for the honor of God's name is not so simple a matter. This zeal can be inappropriate, as may be seen in no less a man than Joshua (Num. 11:28ff.). Paul also speaks not merely about the evil zeal of the false Jewish Christian teachers in Galatia (Gal. 4:17) but also about the unenlightened zeal for God (Rom. 10:2) in which he sees the Jews trapped when they so completely overlook the judicial divine decision that has been taken in Jesus Christ. He himself had been a man with a perverted zeal for God (Acts 22:3), so zealous for the traditions inherited from the fathers (Gal. 1:14) that he had become a zealous persecutor of the community (Phil. 3:6). Later he had to confess his personal guilt in this regard. In many of Paul's lists of vices, "zeal" is used in a warning sense to denote a trivial human jealousy. Zeal in this lower, not the higher, meaning is plainly at issue when 1 Corinthians 13:4 tells us that as love does not boast or puff itself up, so it is not jealous. In contrast is the zeal of Elijah, which is like that of God himself, when he complains: "I have been very zealous for the Lord, the God of hosts; for the people of Israel have forsaken thy covenant, thrown down thy altars, and slain thy prophets with the sword" (1 K. 19:10). With this may be compared Psalm 119:139: "My zeal consumes me, because my foes forget thy words"; Psalm 69:9 (the saying quoted at Jn. 2:17 in the account of the cleansing of the temple): "For zeal for thy house has consumed me [eaten me up], and the insults of those who insult thee have fallen on me." If that is not passion! Paul too speaks clearly in Galatians 4:18: "For a good purpose it is always good to be zealous (ζηλοῦσθαι)." He expressly commanded his communities (1 Cor. 12:31) not merely to desire but to be zealous for the best gifts. He told his disciple (Tit. 2:14) not just to be active but to be zealous in good works. He duly praised the Corinthians (2 Cor. 7:7) for their zeal for him and his apostolic work, and he confessed to them that he for his part was zealous for them with the zeal of God (2 Cor. 11:2). Paul if anyone — the whole of Galatians shows this as well as other passages — had a real zeal for God, not just as a Pharisee but even more so when he became and remained an apostle of Jesus Christ. The Fourth Evangelist was also right when he discerned a consuming zeal at work in that which moved Jesus himself in the incident in the temple. And what do we see but zeal when at Pentecost (Acts 2:2ff.) the tongues appeared from heaven with the rushing of the wind and came to rest on the disciples with the result that all the Jews of the Diaspora in Jerusalem heard them speak understandably in their own languages? It does not seem to be any accident that these tongues are called tongues of fire. What those first witnesses said had something impressive about it like consuming fire, so that those who heard Peter were, in another expression, "cut to the heart" (Acts 2:37). Note that they were cut to the heart, not given a blow on the head! The fire was not the kind that the same disciples (Lk. 9:54) had once wanted to be brought down from heaven to consume the village of the inhospitable Samaritans. Yet the fire that fell from heaven at Pentecost seems already to have been a consuming fire. Somewhere behind the story stands the story of the announcement of one who comes after the Baptist and who in distinction from him will baptize with the Spirit and fire (Mt. 3:11). There also stands especially the saying of Jesus recorded at Luke 12:49: "I came to cast fire upon the earth; and would that it were already kindled!" When will it be kindled? Obviously it will be kindled properly, definitively, and comprehensively only when God does what is prayed for in the first petition, when he finally takes things in hand himself and brings about completely the hallowing of his name, which took place already in the history of Jesus Christ and which began to be manifested in the world in his resurrection from the dead. In the meantime the fire may and should and will burn provisionally—this brings us to the zeal required of Christians—in the hearts and lives and words and works of disciples, of the Christian community, thanks to the Holy Spirit, who is given to them as a first installment and firstfruits.

Has there ever been a great Christian who has not in his own way had a fiery zeal for God after the manner of Elijah, whose Christian faith and love and hope have not had the definite character of the passion to which we here refer, even though it has been surrounded, of course, by all kinds of dubious things, even though it has often enough been to the shocked astonishment of those close to him and very seldom to the delight of the wider circle of his contemporaries? Not all have openly confessed with Zinzendorf that God and he alone was his only passion (C. R. v. Zinzendorf: "Mir ward Vergebung reich zu teil"). But what great Christian has not had it? And can one even be a little Christian, like the rest, without this sacred fire of Pentecost? Is not one of the things that distinguishes a good sermon from a bad one the fact that the sacred fire of Pentecost, zeal for the honor of God, which, one hopes, will not be confused with emotional and rhetorical enthusiasm, burns in (or at least among the ashes of) the former, whereas in the latter there is plenty of wood or even straw that *could* burn but does not? There is also, of course, a resting of the Christian life in God of which we shall have to speak in connection with the third petition. And why should not this gain the upper hand a little, for example, in old age? But a person to whom zeal for God's honor is alien can be no real Christian. And the one who has lost it can no longer be a Christian. Such a person obviously cannot yet or can no longer pray the first petition, "Hallowed be thy name" or can pray it only on the lips. And in such a case the praying of the second and third petitions will necessarily be a more than doubtful business also.

On the basis of these deliberations it will perhaps be in order if in this section, with its orientation to the first petition, we say categorically that from this standpoint there has to be in the Christian life a kind of necessary Christian passion: zeal for the honor of God.

2. THE KNOWN AND UNKNOWN GOD

In this subsection we shall speak about the situation from which Christians are freed and required to pray their Father for the hallowing of his name, so that they themselves are made zealous for his honor. This situation is characterized by the fact that God is both a known and yet also an unknown God to the world and his community, to men in general and Christians in particular, to all of us. He is the God who in his concealment is not absent but present, not veiled but manifest. God is not anonymous. He has a name. He has made himself a name. He has made it known as his holy name. He has already hallowed it. He has already invested it with honor, validity, radiance, and glory. This is one side of the situation. The other is that this known God is totally unknown. His intrinsically holy name is widely desecrated—and who of us does not have a hand in this? In this ambiguous, divided, and ambivalent situation, Christians, not staying in this situation, cry to him: "Hallowed be thy name." What they mean is this: Father, do what thou alone canst do. See to it finally, perfectly, and definitively that thou and thy name are known—only known, and no longer in any place or to any person unknown. See to it that thy name is no longer desecrated but always and by everybody regarded as holy in the way that it is in fact holy as thy name that thou thyself hast sanctified. Dispel the fatal ambivalence of our situation: "O that thou wouldst rend the heavens and come down, that the mountains might quake at thy presence — as when fire kindles brushwood and the fire causes water to boil, to make thy name known to thy adversaries, and that the nations might tremble at thy presence" (Isa. 64:1f.). When they cry to God in this way, they for their part, in the sphere of their human insight and capacity, cannot fail to be zealous for the honor of God, for the making known and sanctifying of his name in the world, the church, and first and foremost in their own hearts and lives.

As indicated, there are three concentric circles in which God is known and unknown in different ways, in which his name is hallowed and honored as it should be, but also desecrated, disputed, and slandered. The world is the outer circle; the church — and it is better to speak of the church here rather than the more strictly theological community — is the middle circle; and the inner and outer personal life of the Christian is the inner circle. None of these circles is totally separate from the other two. They touch and overlap. Yet they do not simply coincide. To gain a comprehensive view, then, it will be best to look at each of them separately and in turn.

1. Moving this time from the outside to the inside, we begin with the world, God's creation in its totality.

It is as well to think in this regard of the world of nature as the totality of the material powers or powerful materials that are more or less known to us as phenomena and that at any rate surround, determine, and sustain or burden us on every hand, whether close by or at a distance. When we know and confess God as the almighty Creator of heaven and earth, how can we not believe? We may even sense that the glory of God is great there too, possibly and probably infinitely greater than in our human world. It may well be that the universe in its movements (besouled or not?) — from those of the heavenly bodies to those of the red and white blood corpuscles in our veins, not to speak of the infinitesimal units out of which everything is constructed — hallows the name of God infinitely more seriously than everything that comes into consideration as hallowing of this name among and by men. There can be no holding down the impression, which Paul expresses in his words about the sighing of creation in Romans 8:19ff., that even in the statics and dynamics of the world of the largest and smallest physical things, the honor of God may be surrounded by puzzling contradictions and countermovements, and that there may be needed for the decisive hallowing of his name not merely the appearance of a new humanity but also, in virtue of the appearing of the new humanity in the one new man, the coming of a new heaven and a new earth (Isa. 65:17; 66:22; Rev. 21:1). Let us frankly admit that the relationship between the glory which God undoubtedly has there too and that which perhaps he does not have there, between what "old" means there and "new" means there, is a mystery to us that we had better not try to unlock with any speculations of our own, no matter how well intentioned or profound they might be. If it is undoubtedly appropriate, even in relation to the world of nature, to pray "Hallowed be thy name," nevertheless the need to be zealous that arises in relation to the world of humanity and especially the church and the self certainly does not arise in relation to that of nature. In regard to what is new and different there, the only thing that is obviously in place is hope for what God alone can and will do, and therefore the petition, but not any corresponding human action.

While we do not forget the problem of the larger sphere, but also remember and respect the limits that are set for our consideration of it, we take the term "world" to refer specifically to creation as the world of the man who shapes the wider sphere and who is thus responsible to its Creator for the way it is. The world, then, is the world as this man can to a large extent see and grasp and control it. It is the human world. Man is the world. Its history is his history. The question of the honor of God that is put in it is put to him. It is he who must answer it with that petition but also with the corresponding thoughts and words and works of his human zeal for at least a partial hallowing of God's name. At this point speculation does not arise. At issue here is the question of the known and unknown God, of the honoring or desecrating of his name, in practical existential form. Here the petition "Hallowed be thy name" acquires its specific sense, and the zeal demanded of Christians in this matter acquires its clear place and occasion. We have in view the human world as such. The church and Christians also exist in it. In all its problems they have a passive or an active part, or at least they share responsibility. This world, then, comes under the theological aspect proper to them. But we shall be speaking of the inner circles later. The history of the church and the individual histories of Christians take place within world history. They are interwoven with it in many different ways. Though they are not determined by it or dependent on it, they are not apart from it and are highly distinctive in relation to it. World history is also—but not only—natural history. It is distinct from natural history as the history of the aspirations, enterprises, and accomplishments of people who are capable of such things. World history, then, includes world economics, culture, and power in all their forms, world views of many kinds in more or less sharp competition with one another, world religions, hot and cold world wars, and world peace in the most diverse ideals. World history is the totality of human thought, volition, speech, and action as it has taken place, and does and will take place, as production, profit, and trade, as games and sport, as work, as pleasure, and as pure amusement at different stages and in all kinds of forms, but always and everywhere with a striking final likeness or similarity. For the rest, world history occurs in large measure simply in the advertising and propaganda that we humans as children of the world engage in for ourselves and our various interests and undertakings with more or less skill, tact, taste, and force. World history is the history in greater or smaller spheres that is carried out, directed, impelled, or retarded, but always in some way endured, by the more or less conscious and outspoken children of the world—and Christians also are always children of the world of this kind.

We are probing into the relationship of this human (not Christian) world and world history to God; into the hallowing and honoring of his name that takes place or does not take place in it. One thing is sure, and this is what distinguishes the world from the two other circles, that of the church and that of the individual Christian: the relationship of the world to God cannot be one that is ordered to him principially and teleologically. To him it cannot be one that is essentially determined. So far as we can see, it is the world of the man who is still alien to the covenant of grace, who is not yet committed to it, who is not yet called to bear witness to it. Hence the relationship to God can only be one that is open and neutral. There is an elect and called community which for all its possible and actual deviations is related by order and structure to God and to the hallowing of his name. There are elect and called children of God who, as better or worse Christians, exist by definition in this relation. We may and must go further and say that man as such, whether he be child of the world or child of God, stands primarily and properly—and, as the good creature of God, necessarily, by order and structure—in relation to him, so that "his heart is restless until it rests in Him" (Augustine). But we cannot say of any of the worldly constructions or enterprises selected and undertaken by the children of the world, the children of the world who do not yet know and are not yet committed to Jesus Christ; we cannot say of any of the works of world history that they are necessarily, by order and structure, related to God and to the hallowing of his name. Essentially proper to the life of the world as world is that which no less essentially opposes the life of the church and Christians, namely, an unordered and undetermined relationship to God. "Unordered and undetermined" does not have to mean negative, but it also does not have to mean positive. Essential to the world as world is the ambivalence, neutrality, and indecisiveness of its relationship to God. This means that God is not simply unknown to it; he is indeed well known, and yet he is also unknown, as its being and actions show. His name is holy in its midst, and yet it is also seriously desecrated. This is not a negative relationship but something much worse, a perverted one. We shall have to speak of a relationship to God on the part of the church and Christians that is similarly ambivalent and perverted, although in a distinctive way. In regard to the worldly church and worldly Christians, we shall have to take this relationship even more seriously, for there it ought to be excluded by the order and structure of their life and thus represents a plunge from a great height. From the world as world—from the world of children of the world who are not yet called to be children of God—nothing different from that ambivalence and perversion is in the first instance to be expected. This does not excuse it. It becomes guilty by living in that ambivalence. By way of anticipation, however, we must say that the church and Christians become even more guilty by living in that ambivalence in which God is both known and unknown to them also.

The Edomites and Moabites, Egypt, Assyria, and Babylon all sinned. Unquestionably, however, the Old Testament takes the view that Israel and the Israelites sinned even more severely, since in distinction from all the rest they were God's chosen and called people.

Our first thesis is that God — we speak of the one true and living God who is the Father, Son, and Holy Spirit — is very well known in the world and world history, in the human, non-Christian world.

Should we say this because the Christian community and Christians as its members also have a share in the life of the world? Is he known in the world and its history thanks to the fact that their witness and proclamation, their existence as such, which is eloquent in its own way, takes place and plays a not inconsiderable role in the midst of all else that happens there? For all the required reserve and caution, we can and may and even must say this too. God is known in the world thanks also to the ministry of Christianity. The sum of obedience, love, and energy which through the centuries, in varying degrees of faithfulness, objectivity, and wisdom, Christianity has brought to the discharge of its task of putting on a candlestick the work and word of God in Jesus Christ in the midst of a world with other interests and concerns, has not simply vanished without a trace. What is called the spread of the gospel is within limits a fact that has changed the face of the world in a remarkable fashion and is thus with many others a sign that speaks very plainly. In this connection, it is appropriate today to think especially of modern missions to the heathen, but also in the last decades of the astonishingly intensive preceding activity of the various churches, and specifically of all the evangelistic enterprises of the modern age. In older periods as well, the church has seldom been really lazy or inactive. To the best of its knowledge and understanding, it has worked honestly to carry out its mission in narrower or broader circles, not to mention the quiet and concealed but extensively effective activity at various levels of the innumerable known and unknown Christians who constantly meet us in the history of the church. No matter what we may have in our hearts against Christianity and Christians, it would be shortsighted not to take note of this, ungrateful to deprecate it, and unbelieving to act as though, even if it took place in the strangest forms, it could all have happened without the approval, support, and blessing of God, and without God in some way being made known thereby in the world. Why should we not in this regard give God our maximum trust, even though we cannot give more than a minimum confidence to the reliability of Christians both old and new? With God there is indeed more mercy and more powerful support for the witness of his people than we often think. No matter what our attitude toward this witness may be, in all its poverty it can thus help to make God known in the world, even though this can as such be only his own work. We must not fail to see that in hidden and indirect form, and even in open and direct form, there is a kind of Christian influencing — permeation would be too strong a term — of the life of the world, of the culture valued and fostered by the children of the world, of the course and character of world history in its various detailed sections. Much if not all in the world would have had, and would still have, a very different course and appearance if Christianity as a whole and Christians in detail had not been and were not present in their own special way and with their own special contribution, if their own tiny weight had not been and were not also in the scales. Where that has happened and happens, they have had and have at least a ministering share in the fact that God makes himself known in the world, that he hallows his name in it, that he kindles the light of his free grace at least in some places and contexts within the being of the world, opposing its perversion and disturbing its ambivalence in relation to himself.

Nevertheless, when all that is duly thought and said, a certain disquiet remains. There is surely more to it than this. The statement that God is known and even well known to the world is too strong, and the resulting accusation that the world is guilty because God is also unknown to it is too serious for us to think that the statement and accusation have a sufficient basis and explanation in a simple reference to the Christian ministry of witness. It should be considered that the cause reflected in the life and acts and views of this group of people is God's cause. Have the church and Christians really been concerned about God? Is it really he whom they have made known in the world? If we simply had the Christian ministry of witness, God could be known to the world only in a very limited, opaque, and — who knows? — perhaps even a very perverted way. And the guilt of the world because God is unknown to it as well as known, the guilt of the ambivalence and perversion of its relationship to him, could seem to be at the very least greatly mitigated. We need not and must not abandon what has been said about the witness of the church and Christians, but we must look beyond it for a surer basis and explanation of the statement and accusation.

We obviously reach a deeper level when we recall that God already made himself known in his free grace, and already hallowed his name in a far more unequivocal way than anything Christianity has ever done or will do, when it pleased him to determine for himself and orient to himself the nature of man, his human essence, in its irreversibly good creation. If man would know himself in this nature and inalienable orientation of his, if he would be true to himself, he would find himself confronted with the one true God who, in creating him, has made himself known to man and therefore to the world, so that to man and to the world in the nature he has given them, he is objectively a very well known and not an unknown God.

We are referring to the objective knowledge of God as the Creator of human nature, not to man's corresponding knowledge of God. To know him man has to recognize him, that is, to honor and love him in the obedience which is due him as God. To recognize him he must first know himself and his orientation to him, taking himself seriously, being true to himself. But man is not true to himself, to his given nature; he does not know himself at all, and consequently he does not know God. It is in vain that God is well known to him in nature, that "what can be known about God is plain to them" (Rom. 1:19), that he is not far from any one of us (Acts

17:27). Yet all this does not alter in the least the objective knowledge of God in the world, the offer that is made to man in his own nature even if it is rejected by him. As the one who is recognized by God, every person has the chance to recognize God in return and therefore to know him. Man, not God, is at fault if a subjective knowledge of God on man's side does not correspond to God's objective knowledge.

God's name, then, is already holy in the world that he created good long before Christianity begins to pray for its hallowing or to be zealous for the honor of God. Is not his name holy in every blade of grass and every snowflake? Apart from us and even in spite of us, it is holy in every breath we draw, in every thought we think, in every effort of man, undertaken and executed well or badly, with praiseworthy or suspicious or plainly wicked intentions, to subdue the earth to himself both in practice and in theory (Gen. 1:28). Man's subjective ignorance of God, about which we shall have to speak later, and which is a burden peculiar to himself, does not alter in the least the objective fact that he and the world confront the one true God, being constantly known by him in defiance of their own defiance. Whether it knows it and is grateful or not, the world lives by the objective fact that it is his world, that he is constantly open to it. It would long since have perished in and of itself if God had willed to repay like with like, unfaithfulness with unfaithfulness, if he had willed to turn away his face from it as it has done from him. In its basis and constitution it is held together and sustained by the perfection with which he loves his enemies, causing his sun to shine on the good and the bad and his rain to fall on the just and the unjust (Mt. 5:44f.)—which includes causing the educated and the uneducated de jure and de facto to see and note his wisdom, the constant and inconstant to see his sustaining patience, and those who know him and those who do not know him to see his openness for them. Upheld and guided by him on the most diverse paths both long and short, with or without their own understanding, with or against their own will, and to their salvation, people cannot and will not all escape him. Incontestably, he is at the heart of world events and world affairs. In all the secularity of his world as it is marked by man's subjective refusal, victoriously contradicting its contradiction, he is already as its Creator the God who is objectively well known to it. What Christianity can and may and should and does do to make him known in the world can never do more than follow what he himself does, and it will always be highly debatable. What God already does himself as Creator in this regard is never in all its concealment a subject of debate.

Should it not also be noted that the concealment in which he does it, which is due to man's blindness, is in fact broken and becomes transparent, if not everywhere, at least in places? When we meet outspoken children of the world, and read expressly secular literature, do we not sometimes at least, quite unexpectedly and to our shame, get the impression that God the Creator does not contradict the contradiction of his creature for nothing? In spite of all the worldliness and unfaithfulness and ignorance of people, does not God in fact see to it that the knowledge of God is not ineffective, that people *must* — in the sense in which Kutter wrote about Social

Democrats at the beginning of the century in his book *Sie Müssen* (Zurich, 1904) —
that they *must* know about God and therefore know what they do not want to know
or in fact seem to know? *Must* they not simply because the objective knowledge of
God seems to be stronger than all their unfaithfulness and ignorance, because his
openness for the world seems to be stronger than its being closed against him? Will
not this objective knowledge be at least as strong in places as that mediated to the
world through the witness of Christianity? These impressions should not be gener-
alized and systematized along the lines of natural theology, but when they lay hold
of us with serious force, they cannot be denied. Worth noting is the saying of Jesus
(Lk. 16:8): The children of this world are in their generation, in relation to the place
from which they come, wiser (φρονιμώτεροι) than the children of light in relation
to their light as the much better place from which they may come. It is also worth
noting that Jesus obviously in his addresses — and perhaps this is the authentic
commentary on that saying — found very worldly (profane) processes and relations
apt and worthy for use as parables of the kingdom of heaven.

With regard to this objective knowledge of God in the world, we must
now raise and answer the question of the guilt in which the world implicates
itself because the God who is well known to it is also unknown. The world
undoubtedly makes itself guilty by evading the witness of the church and
Christians. But in this connection it might regard itself as at least in large
part excused because of the dubious nature of this witness. But what valid
excuse is there when man, in dealing with God as unknown, obviously does
not know himself in his given nature with its orientation to God, when he
is not true to himself, when he sets himself in opposition to himself, when
he could and should know God but does not in fact know him? He may
blame the church and Christians but he cannot blame God his Creator for
this palpable fault. The world is at fault for existing in the ambivalence of
objective knowledge and subjective ignorance. It and not God is the ground
of its structural perversion. God does not withdraw his objective knowledge.
He holds and upholds the world by causing it constantly to see and note his
wisdom, patience, and peace. The brightening of the darkness which is
plain to see at times also speaks for God but not for the world. It speaks
against the world, accusing it instead of excusing it. The world and not
God is responsible if, desecrating his name, it is in the power of the evil
one (1 Jn. 5:19).

Is the statement cogent and valid that God is known to the world? The
reference to the fact that he is present and known to it as its Creator,
especially as the Creator of man whose nature is determined for God and
oriented to him, is correct and important and cannot be refuted. Yet, like
the reference to the perceptible witness of Christianity in the world, it has
an unmistakable weakness. With it the decisive word has not yet been said
in this matter. If the statement is to stand validly, then this reference, like
the first one, must be grounded, supported, and strengthened by a very
different one. Here we cannot take the course that is usually taken in what
is called natural theology. It cannot be claimed that as we can count on the
perfect objective knowledge of God the Creator as a fact, so we can count
on an approximately corresponding subjective knowledge of God that is

proper to the world and mankind. It cannot be claimed that as God himself as Creator hallows his name, so it is hallowed to some degree by the world, by man as a child of the world. On this side, even though we cannot deny the possibility of occasional and highly astonishing exceptions to the rule, we have to admit that the knowledge of God the Creator is concealed, wrapped in the great darkness which is due to man's unfaithfulness and lack of perception, to his contradiction against himself. On this side God the Creator is as unknown to the world as he is well known to it on his side. His name is just as surely desecrated by the world and man as God himself constantly hallows it to the world and man. Certainly God in his openness is not idle or ineffective as its Creator. Certainly the world owes its preservation and permanence to the contradiction of its own contradiction, to God's faithfulness in spite of its own faithfulness, which he has posited and upholds with his objective knowledge. Certainly there are breaks here and there in what is usually his hidden knowledge, so that he may be sensed and conjectured if not recognized and known. On the whole and at root, however, the knowledge of God as Creator is a hidden one which is not definitely apprehensible and which cannot be unequivocally established in its law and continuity. We cannot count on it. No sure appeal can be made to it of the kind that all natural theology regards as possible, necessary, and salutary. To the objective knowledge of God as Creator there does not correspond with any reliability or continuity a subjective recognition and knowledge on the world's part. There is no faithful person who knows himself as God's creature and who thus knows God as his Creator as he is known by God [1 Cor. 13:12]. Even Christians do not know him thus. Here the knowledge of God as Creator, perfect though it is in itself, has a limit. This is the weakness of the second reference, which does not allow us to think that it offers an adequate basis and explanation for the statement that God is known to the world. What it points to—and from this an exculpation of man and the world might be deduced—is a knowledge of God in which the knowing subject has no necessary, self-evident, and unconditional part. Strictly it points only to an offer, a very pressing one, but one which, de facto if not de jure, can obviously be rejected.

As we search for a knowledge of God in the world that is unequivocally achieved both objectively on God's side and subjectively on man's, as we look for a point where his name might be clearly and distinctly hallowed on *both* sides in and for the world, we can think only of the one Jesus Christ. In him the knowledge of God in the world does not lack either the definiteness of the objective element, as in the case of its attestation by the church and Christians, or that of the subjective element, as in the case of the hidden glory of God in his creation. In him the circle closes which elsewhere is disturbingly open on the one side or the other. In him we do not have either the seeing human eye without the purity of the divine light nor the purity of the divine light without the seeing human eye. What takes place on God's side is more than an offer. What takes place on man's is more than an attempt. We have to do neither with man problematized by God nor God problematized by man. Man is known by God and knows

God. God's own glory as Creator is accompanied by his glorification by his creature. God's good pleasure in his man, his grace toward him, and man's joy in his God, his gratitude to him, are not two things but one. The true God attested by the creaturely nature of man, the God who as God is the God of man, coincides with the true man attested by Christianity, the man who as man is the man of God. The being with and in each other of this true God of man and this true man of God is the event of the history of Jesus Christ — the history of his birth as the incarnation of the eternal Word, of his life, his death, and his resurrection from the dead. It was and is the event of the perfect becoming and being known of God in the world on both the one side and the other. At this point God's name is perfectly hallowed both by himself and the world.

We look back for a moment. What we said positively about the witness of Christianity and that of God's creation does not have to be erased [MS: denied] or withdrawn in the light of the perfect knowledge of God on both sides in Jesus Christ. On the contrary, from this clear point or closed circle the first two references acquire and have a relative justification. The weakness of both was to point to only one element of the knowledge of God in the world and to seem to have nothing to say about the other. Is it really God who is made known by the witness of Christianity? Is he really known to man through the witness of creation? In both cases it is an open question whether we have a true knowledge of God in the world. But in the light of the perfect knowledge of God on both sides in Jesus Christ, it is obvious that in their own ways the first two references both have meaning and content, not independently nor absolutely, but as and to the extent that with them the reference to that perfect knowledge of God is also indirectly intended and purposed. The reference to the perfect knowledge of God in Jesus Christ sustains them and gives them their limit but also, within this limit, their incontestable justification. Not in and of themselves, but in the reflection of that one light they also shine in their own way. "In thy light we see light" (Ps. 36:9). It was for the sake of the one Jesus Christ and with reference to him that God created the world and created man in orientation to himself to be a witness of the knowledge of God both to himself and the world. As Christianity is determined for the service of the one Jesus Christ, and as he makes use of this service, God establishes it also as his witness, making himself through it the God who is well known to the world. We cannot dissolve this relationship. If these two lights did not shine in the one light, they would not shine at all, and they would not be lights. They have the force of revelation only to the extent that they are granted it by the act of revelation of the one true God of man in his unity with the one true man of God. The relationship obviously cannot be reversed. It would be nonsensical to understand the history of Jesus Christ as a supreme achievement and form either of the Christian kerygma or of human nature. God is also known in the witness of Christianity and his good creation when these are ordered to and dependent on the one knowledge of God in Jesus Christ, which is perfect on both sides and which is on that account decisive, comprehensive, and sovereignly effective.

In the history of Jesus Christ, at this one point in the world and its history, God has made himself known. He is indeed — and this is what we cannot say on the basis of the other two attestations — the God who is finally, totally, and definitively well known. Because Jesus Christ rose from the dead, because and as he is himself present on all sides as the living Son of God and Son of Man, God is and always will be the God who is known anew to the world. The true man who lived and lives here as the man of God and therefore in direct unity with God as the God of man, did not and does not live for himself, but as the "first-born of all creation" (Col. 1:15), as the last Adam who in order is the first (1 Cor. 15:45), he lived and lives for all men in the place of all. All people, therefore, are elected, justified, sanctified, and called in him. In his knowledge of God a decision is made concerning theirs. Their knowledge of God is enclosed in his. In him they too are men of God, and they are infallibly and irrevocably confronted with the God of man as their God too. Hence none among them has any reason or right to exist without the knowledge of God. In relationship to him, the world of humans must be defined as the world in which God has made himself known once and for all to all mankind and is thus once and for all well known to all men. Now that God has made himself known within the world in Jesus Christ, ignorance of God has been fundamentally outdated. It has become a brute fact devoid of meaning or basis. It can only be noted as such. In and with the history of Jesus Christ and its manifestation in his resurrection from the dead, we can say something that could not be said merely in the light of the witness of Christianity and God's creation, namely, that the last shred of any exculpation or self-vindication has been completely stripped away from man. In relation to Jesus Christ, ignorance of God can be recorded and defined only as an excluded and absurd possibility. In relation to him there can also be no question whatever of vacillation between knowledge of God and ignorance of God. In Christ every person can only be lifted up totally to the knowledge of God and not left at all in ignorance of God. We can only be looking past him if we say anything different.

It was on the presupposition of this comprehensive, sovereign, and universally valid decision taken in Jesus Christ that the apostles, according to what we learn from the New Testament about their highly astonishing thinking, went out into the world and approached the people of the world. They did not do this on the assumption that these people might still have a chance, in face of what they had to say to them, to appeal in a legitimate and normal way to their ignorance of God and to entrench themselves behind it. They did it on the assumption that in Jesus Christ, whom they proclaimed, any such chance had been taken away from them — on the assumption, then, that God was in truth known to them. Otherwise, how could they have made the uninhibited but extremely important use of the word θεός, which they did according to all the New Testament records? They did not attack ignorance. In faith in Jesus Christ, whom they proclaimed, they appealed to the knowledge of God. In the great ignorance of God which they ran up against in the world they saw only the brute fact of the world's monstrous lie. They could approach it only as such. In the light of their knowledge of the living Jesus Christ by faith, they could regard it only as meaningless and nonsensical in face of the phenomenon of the name of God which was hallowed in Jesus Christ but desecrated and not hallowed in the world. Read John 1: the life which was in him was the light of men (v. 4). This light shines in the darkness, and the darkness has not overcome it (v. 5). He was the true light which lightens every man, and he has come into the world as such (v. 9). He thus came to his own, to those who belonged to him from the very first (v. 11), as the One who in the beginning was with God and was God (v. 1). Was it not something impossible and intolerable, something inexplicable and inexcusable, something which can be recorded as a fact only with horror, that in face of all this it had to be said: "His own received him not" (v. 11), that the name of God which is truly hallowed in the world is in fact desecrated and not hallowed in the world, that God who is known in the world is in fact not known in it. This line of thinking was not adopted by speculative minds but simply by people who had seen the glory of the Word that was made flesh and dwelt among them (v. 14). The impetus of the apostolic message and also, to anticipate, the intensity of the petition "Hallowed be thy name," and of the zeal for the glory of God that is inseparable from it, are completely incomprehensible if we do not see that in face of the impossible, intolerable, inexplicable, and inexcusable, because long since outdated ignorance of God which it met in the world, New Testament thinking could only be the deeply estranged, and even horrified, but also the a priori victorious thinking that it was. As such—"Thanks be to God, who gives us the victory through Jesus Christ our Lord" (1 Cor. 15:57)—it hurled itself against the ignorance of God that darkened the world as against the great lie, confident that in Jesus Christ God was in truth not unknown but well known to the world that was reconciled to him in Jesus Christ.

But now we must turn the page and speak about the ignorance of God that is so characteristic of the world, and about the desecration of the name of God that takes place so widely in it.

We must do this only after overcoming a certain hesitation and with the exercise of the corresponding restraint. In no case should it be forgotten (1) that from the center of the Christian faith the knowledge of God in the world is much more interesting and important than the fact that God is also unknown to it. In no case should the second statement (2) become a favorite theme of Christian thought and speech. It is a dubious sign when Christians turn with pleasure to such negative theses, especially this one. In no case must this statement (3) have a stronger emphasis than what has to be thought and said about the ignorance of God and the desecration of his name in the life of the church and Christians themselves, as though the Old Testament and the New Testament did not focus more sharply on the ignorance of God among his own people and its members than on the ignorance of God in the world. And in no case should the ignorance of God in the world be viewed (4) as a specific problem of the world today, the "modern" world.

At these four points we part company with a whole trend in Christian and even theological thought and utterance that has most unfortunately prevailed for some decades. Enough of the sorry futility and futile sorrow which constantly assures us that in this century—as though the nineteenth and sixteenth centuries and the Middle Ages were golden ages in this regard—we have to do with a world which is alienated from God in a distinctively radical and refined way, having become totally secular, autonomous, adult, and profane! Enough of the impenitence that will not even inquire into the serious ignorance of God in Christianity itself but at most will only chide it for being so insensitive, old-fashioned, and clumsy in dealing with the children of the world who today have supposedly become so terribly ungodly! Enough of the critical pyschological and sociological analyses of the age with which it is hoped to understand and reach the children of the world, but with which they are not in truth understood or reached, because the problem of their ignorance of God certainly cannot be exposed in this way, and all the delight and love lavished on the problem can only detract from the joy in the knowledge of God with which alone the children of the world can be effectively and victoriously met! And enough especially of thinking and speaking with an order of priorities that is wrong because in the light of the center of Christian faith it is impossible; it is an order according to which people are, even if only temporarily, more strongly stimulated and claimed by the undeniable ignorance of God in the world than by the knowledge of God in the world, as though the former were not from the very outset of a far lower rank than the latter! All this has nothing whatever to do either with the petition "Hallowed be thy name" or with an intelligent zeal for the honor of God.

This disavowal must not prevent us from looking with appropriate seriousness at the obvious ignorance of God in the world. Like the devil, demons, sin, or, in short, the nothingness to whose kingdom it belongs, this ignorance has no final power, significance, or dignity of its own. When it lays claim to such, and seems to have it with its display of might and cunning (Luther), we should remember at once that it has lost this and has been destroyed in Jesus Christ. It lives only by what it negates. In all its forms it exists only in reaction against the superior knowledge of God which is first in the field. It is to be taken seriously within its limits, but only within them. We may not speak of an absolute, independent, and exclusive ignorance of God in the world. The devil would like to be sovereign Lord of the world, but he is not. The ambivalence with which God is well known in the world and yet still most suspiciously unknown is bad enough. Not a reigning darkness but this ambivalence, the shocking survival of darkness even when it is overcome by light, is the situation which gives rise to the petition "Hallowed be thy name." It is against this that the required, intelligent zeal for God is directed.

We shall now try to present the most notable forms of the ignorance of God which painfully enough competes with his knowledge in the world. Since they all overlap and supplement one another, we cannot separate them. But we can distinguish them, for the ignorance takes on more of one character here and more of another there. Even if in all of them we have the one absurd possibility of the negation of what cannot basically or meaningfully be negated, even if the ignorance is equally perverted, dangerous, and powerless against the opposing knowledge of God, a more exact scrutiny allows and bids us to differentiate the worth or worthlessness of the various forms. Within the badness proper to all of them we can think and speak of the bad, the worse, and the worst.

The most primitive form of the ignorance of God in the world is intellectual godlessness, the theoretical atheism that consists very simply, grossly, and trivially in the denial of the statement "There is a God." Not all theoretical atheism is practical atheism, just as not all theoretical knowledge of God is practical knowledge. In this context, however, we shall look at the theoretical denial of God as the most noticeable representative of the ignorance of God in the world. This denial is no modern discovery. There was atheism already in the supposedly so pious Middle Ages and even in antiquity, with its supposed delight in myths. Psalm 14:1 and Psalm 53:1 speak of the fools who say in their hearts, "There is no God." Even the basing of the denial on the idea of an absolutely self-positing world in which there would be no room for God, even if there were one, is by no means new. Nor is the hypothesis that the maintaining of the negated statement is a psychologically or sociologically explicable fiction. Nor is the fervor of an individual or social anthropomonistic mysticism and morality as the positive complement of the atheistic denial. In all its aspects and for all its variations in detail, atheism is a unified phenomenon. Its primitive character is what makes it interesting in its own way. In this form (1) it expresses so naively, directly, and consistently the great ignorance of God in the world and the great desecration of his name, which in other forms are not declared so crudely but for that very reason so much the more intolerably. Whereas the world at other points will largely not accept its alienation from God, in atheism, as the word itself proclaims, it confesses that God is alien to it, indeed, that he does not exist. Previously, it had not said this; here it does. It even says it scornfully. To give it cogency, it invents world-views that exclude God's being from the start and theories that describe God as the product of more or less well-intentioned and benevolent but also dangerous illusions. Atheism is interesting in its primitive form (2) because it shows that while the world to whom God is unknown would like to deny him, it cannot in fact do so. It cannot frame its negative statement in such a way as to bring out the seriousness of its intention. That there is no God may perhaps apply to the deity of philosophy, or to a deity that might be regarded as the common denominator of the gods of the different religions, or to a deity that demonstrates its existence by having a place in a world-view of human construction, or even perhaps to the "God" who is in one way or another poorly proclaimed and understood in some Christian tradition or theology. The atheistic negation applies to a "God" who, if he exists, must do so in the same way as the data of other human experience or the contents of other human reflection exist for people. The true and living God, however, is not a "datum" of ours. He is his own "datum." Only thus, only as he is his own "datum" and reveals himself, is he there for men. He is the one whom the world does not know [1 Jn. 3:1]. This is why the atheistic negation — which negates only a God who, if he exists, has to be a "datum" of ours — does not touch him. That he is not the true and living God, the world, not knowing him, not only cannot prove but cannot even maintain with any meaning. The most interesting thing of all about the primitive nature of theoretical atheism (3) is, however, its belligerent character. It constantly breaks out in polemics. If God were absolutely unknown to the world, if the world were as ungodly as it is supposed to be according to its atheistic confession, why does it need such a confession? Why does it have to try to deny God throughout the centuries? To what end is the stubborn stupidity of atheistic movements old and new? The fact that in this form of its ignorance the world has to fight God so excitedly, instead of being happy and content with various kinds of anthropomonistic mysticism and morality, tells us plainly that in some way, and not just superficially, it finds itself unsettled, pressured, and threatened by the objective knowledge of God, so that it has to wrestle and debate with him, with the God whom, since it does not know him, it cannot affect with its negation, but who, even as it denies that there is a God, is in fact present for it as the true, living, self-existing, and self-revealing God, actually unsettling, pressuring, and threatening it in lofty supremacy over it. The world simply cannot be absolutely godless, as it would like to be. The ambivalence of its opposition to God betrays itself in the violence with which it asserts it. It thinks it should deny him. In a foolish way that misses the point, it actually does deny him. But in practice it unwittingly and unwillingly has to confess him. Theoretical atheism is, of course, a frightful profanation of the name of God. Yet we may quietly say that the particular way in which it profanes God's name is not the most frightful. Indeed, since it is the most easily explicable, compared to others that we shall mention later, it is relatively the most innocuous. Connected with this is the fact that when the biblical prophets and apostles directed their criticism against the world outside Israel and the community — which they rarely did — they even more rarely concerned themselves with the possibility of its godlessness.

Godlessness appears in a worse form in religion than it does in theoretical atheism, for here it does not make open confession as it tries to do in atheism, but thinks it has sought and found a positive substitute for what is lacking. Among the religions we must differentiate between (1) the disguised ones, in which certain secular values (power, property, culture, progress, and the like) are shamefacedly, or even with antireligious protestations, distinguished, honored, and cultivated in religious fashion, and (2) those which are usually called religions because they consciously and explicitly take the form of faith in God and the worship and service of God. Nevertheless, we must look at the two forms together. The same applies to the relationship between the so-called higher, "ponderable" (H. Scholz, *Religionsphilosophie*, Berlin, 1822), spiritual, and "nobler" religions that have been thought through intellectually and morally, and the so-called primitive or naive religions that are cruder and crasser in invention and structure. The distinction seems to force itself on us. Yet it is a more than dubious one. What do we mean when we call a religion higher or primitive? No religion is genuinely "high," for every religion is in any case a work of the world to whom the true and living God is unknown. No religion is seriously primitive, for every religion is a work with which the world tries to deal with this God, and secure itself against him, in a much more thoughtful and effective way than by trying to deny him. The rise of religions, like that of the denial of God, may be traced to the fact that the world objectively finds itself confronted with the true and living God and adapts itself positively to its inability to escape his self-declaration, in which, of course, it does not know him. It meets this God who makes himself known by attempting in its own way to make itself acquainted with him, that is, by doing justice to him who is his own "datum" in the form of deities which are *its* "data," to which it for its part gives being and existence. The various religions are the various attempts of the world to make something out of the presence and revelation of God which is known to it but not recognized by it. In religion the world tries to domesticate the God who is known and yet also unknown and strange, to bring him into its own natural and intellectual sphere of vision and power. In religion, then, the world unwittingly and unwillingly confesses that God is known to it as well as unknown. Not recognizing him, however, it fashions for itself, in the form of what seems to it to be a suitable image, worship, and service of God, surrogates of his being and action, and of the human being and action demanded by him, believing that it can satisfy him with these surrogates and at the same time satisfy itself. It would be perverse to be incensed by atheism but to see in the religions paths or preliminary stages to the knowledge of God and of what he wills and does with man — to regard them, therefore, as suitable points of contact for the proclamation of the true and living God. It would also be perverse to give a positive rating to at least the so-called higher religions in this regard, in distinction from the so-called lower religions. In all religions, even the highest ones, or what are usually called the spiritual ones, we simply have surrogates in whose invention, use, and enjoyment the world thinks it can help to safeguard itself against, and to offer satisfaction to, the present God who is not known to it. They owe their origin to the great ambivalence that God is objectively known to the world as well as subjectively unknown. As surrogates they document the fact that he is unknown, not known. Because they do this positively, they do it in a much more illuminating, tempting, and dangerous fashion than any denial of God. In atheism the world defends itself against the threatening self-giving and self-declaration of God. In religion it tries to deal with him by establishing itself behind a wall of self-invented and self-made images of God, so that it may really be left to itself. This is why the angry protest of the biblical prophets is not directed against atheism but against the idolatry that characterizes the world around Israel, which may be seen in the religions of other peoples, and which is absolutely intolerable for Israel as the people of the true and living God.

There is, however, a desecration of the name of God which in comparison to that in atheism and that in the religions is even worse. This is the attempt of the world to exalt its own cause as God's or, conversely, to subject God's cause to its own, to make it serve it. In both forms one might call this an attempted "nostrification" of God. This attempt arises when the world, unavoidably confronted by God even though it does not know him, believes that he can be very useful and even indispensable to its own goals and aims and aspirations; so that, instead of denying him or coming to terms with him with a bit of religion, it takes the cleverer course of resolutely affirming him, affirming itself in and with him, affirming his deity as its own and its own as his. Now it may triumphantly dispense with both atheism and also the idolatry of religions. Now it integrates itself with God or God with itself. Now it equates God with itself or itself with God. It is not against God, as in atheism; it is not incidentally with him, as in the religions.

It is with him consistently and in fanatical earnestness and zeal. It thinks it can be an infinitely better, more effective, and more triumphant world if it is with him instead of being against him or only incidentally and partially with him. It even thinks that it can really be happy and certain about what it wills and does in politics, economics, law, and society, in work and leisure, in culture and education, in science and art, if it can understand and do everything in the radiance and dignity of the slogan: God wills it! God does it! It thinks its freedom of control is really ensured if God is the world-God and itself the God-world, if it may be secular in its piety and pious in its secularity. In every time and place there has been "nostrification" of this kind. When the world is really shrewd, as it is not in atheism or idolatry, it tries to help itself in this way over against God. Over against God! It is clear that this "nostrification" can be carried through only against the background and on the presupposition that God is objectively known to the world, that he is a problem for it with which it must wrestle wittingly and unwittingly, willingly and unwillingly. From this fact, however, one may not conclude that it knows him. If it did, it could not secularize him or deify itself any more than it could deny him or deal with him religiously. This third and most insolent and, if one will, most ingenious and eminent way of dealing with him points to what is, if anything, an even darker ignorance in which it moves in relation to him. How there can be a transition from this to the knowledge of God, it is difficult and even impossible to see.

There is one point, however, where the previously mentioned forms of the great ignorance of God and desecration of his name meet as at a kind of boiling point, where any appearance that they might be merely theoretical, principial, or programmatic vanishes, where all of them — as concrete, if finally unrealizable efforts — are eminently practical. The world or, better and more directly, man, who in virtue of his denial of God, his idolatry, and his foolish attempt to equate God with himself and himself with God, does not know God and in all these things desecrates his name — this man does not know his fellow man either. His ignorance of God culminates and manifests itself in his ignorance of his fellow man. He regards him as an object to whom he as subject may or may not be in relation according to his own free choice and disposal, whom he may pass by as he does so many other objects, or with whom, if this is out of the question, he may have dealings as it suits himself within the limits of what is possible for him. He does not know him as a fellow subject whom God has set unavoidably beside him, to whom he is unavoidably linked in his relation to God, so that apart from him he cannot himself be a subject, a person. He is not for him an indispensable, but in certain cases a dispensable, companion, associate, and fellow — not to mention brother. He can get along just as well without him as with him. By chance or caprice or free judgment he can just as well be to him a tyrant or slave as a free supporter, just as well a hater as an admirer, a foe as a friend, a corrupter as a helper. He can be one thing to one person and another to another, or now one thing, now another, to the same person. In relationship to his fellow man, also, he exists in total ambivalence. One may not say more than this. He cannot live without him nor can he be wholly against him. Some connections, links, and relations always exist in the world between man and man. This is another sign that whether the world knows and wills it or not, it is confronted by the true and living God who acts and is revealed in Jesus Christ as both true God and true man. It is another sign that the true and living God is not completely unknown to it. But as it is capable not only of atheism and idolatry but also of identifying God with itself and itself with God, thus betraying that it for its part does not know the God who is well known to it (for if it did, it would not be capable of all these things), so there is no necessary and solid relationship between man and man but only incidental, arbitrary, and temporary connections. This is a sign that man does not know man either (for if he did, here too no alternatives would arise). This second ignorance derives directly from the first. The first manifests itself in it. If man knew the true and living God who himself became man in the one Jesus Christ, who in divine faithfulness gave himself to all men, and united himself with them, then only faithfulness (and not a faithfulness which is constantly accompanied and shot through with unfaithfulness) would be possible between his fellow man and himself, himself and his fellow man. Recognizing themselves in the God who is true God and true man, man and fellow man can wish to live not without or against one another, but only with one another. If they can be and, in fact, always are so divided in their relationship to one another, if man can be important to man, a neighbor, friend, and helper, and yet at any moment indifferent, a stranger, enemy, and corrupter, if he can be and actually is to him more of a wolf than a person — all this is a manifestation of the ambivalence in the relationship to God. In it all there takes place a blaspheming of the name of God which is more dreadful, palpable, and unequivocal than anything the world may do in the form of atheism, accursed idolatry, or foolish self-deification. In it all, everything achieves full potency, concentration, and self-characterization, for everything now takes place as a practical, everyday event in world history, whether in big things, small things, or the smallest of things. Above all, it all takes place here as an expression of the world's stupendous ignorance of God even in face of his subjective as well as his objective self-declaration in Jesus Christ, so that not a vestige of rationality or excusability remains. If we wish to know what is the true and final point of the petition "Hallowed be thy name," and of the zeal of the honor of God that is demanded of us, when they are seen in this first relationship to the world, then we had better focus our attention on this one thing, on the evil fact that we humans, whose God in supreme mercy has taken up the cause of each person and all people in Jesus Christ, can be and are both everything and nothing to one another, both fellow men and wolves. Here in this chaotic contradiction the holy name of God is decisively and supremely desecrated in the world.

2. We must now speak of the knowledge and ignorance of God — of the hallowing and desecrating of his name — in the church. The church is also in the world. It does not merely have all the aspects of a worldly phenomenon; it is in fact — not exclusively but also — a worldly entity, unique, yet comparable with other worldly entities. At the same time it stands to the

rest of the world in an independent and distinctively critical and positive relationship. For it is not just one worldly entity among others. It also exists in a dimension in which the others do not. It is in the world as the people, the possession, and the sanctuary of God.

Here too we begin, as is proper, with what can be said in this sphere about the knowledge of God and therefore about the hallowing of his name. Being in the world, the church participates first in what is true of the world as such and as a whole. For it, too, God is well known by reason of the good nature of man by creation, of its hearing of its own witness, and, finally and especially, the divine self-declaration that is given in Jesus Christ both objectively by God and subjectively by man. But now we must immediately go on to emphasize the differences. God is known to the church in a way that is qualitatively as well as quantitatively quite different from the way in which he is known to the world. The completed self-declaration of God in Jesus Christ has not just happened for the church as it has for the world, as though its attitude toward it, even though it is directed to it, could still be an open question. The church has its origin in the completed self-declaration of God. As this took place in the world, it not only became true and actual that the whole world was confronted with it, but there arose within and across the other peoples of the world a people in which it took root, in which it was perceived and accepted. This people is the church. It is the people whose life is grounded in it. It is the people of Jesus Christ in the world, not separated from him as he is not separated from it. It lives as in it there sounds forth to the world God's Yes to man and also man's Yes to God, both spoken in Jesus Christ. It lives as this Yes is seen and takes shape. It lives from the very outset in and by the reception of this double Yes of Jesus Christ, in and by hearing his divine Yes and repeating his human Yes. As he lives, as he lives within it as its Lord and Head at the right hand of God, and as it lives with and by and under him, its only choice is to hear his divine Yes and repeat his human Yes. This is the basis and goal of its existence. This is its function in relationship to the rest of the world. It has the task of bearing witness to Jesus Christ: God as the God who in him has reconciled the world to himself and the world as the world which is reconciled to God in him, God as the God of man and man as the man of God. The church lives and has its being in virtue of this special origin and by having and discharging its special task. No other people has either this origin or this task. No other exists in this knowledge of God to which there is no alternative. Only the church, even in all its worldliness, lives and has its being in the necessary structure of this knowledge of God. For it there can be no question of the characteristic and distinctive ambivalence of the world with its knowledge of God and ignorance of God, with its hallowing of God's name and desecrating of his name. For it a positive attitude toward God's self-declaration is behind it and not still ahead of it. God's name is sanctified in it as it itself is sanctified. It is on this presupposition that it goes into the world and through the world. This is what distinguishes it from the world. "We know that we are of God"

(1 Jn. 5:19). As it lives by him and bears witness to him—and only so—it is faithful to the world to which it belongs but into which it is also sent.

If Israel was unfaithful to the covenant that Yahweh made with it, to the order of the covenant, and therefore to its task among the nations, so that its God could be alien to it and it to its God, this was not envisioned in its election and calling but was excluded by it, so that it cannot be seen and spoken of as a possibility but only as a terrible impossibility. This explains the horror with which the prophets and the prophetic histories all speak of the actual apostasy of Israel. Similarly, the point of presenting the two paths of Israel's future at the end of Deuteronomy [30:15ff.] and Joshua [23–24] can obviously only be to make it clear that the second way, the way of disobedience, is ruled out by the first, the way of obedience. The choice of the second can only be an abhorrent choice. No less plainly in the New Testament is the *ecclesia* addressed as what it is in terms of its origin, goal, and essence: the church of God (1 Cor. 1:2), brought forth by the word of truth (Jas. 1:18), not destined for wrath but for the actualizing of salvation (1 Thess. 5:9), God's temple in which "God's Spirit dwells" (1 Cor. 3:16), the body of Christ (1 Cor. 12:27), who loved it and gave himself for it (Eph. 5:25), who has sanctified it for himself (Jn. 17:19), to whom it is affianced (2 Cor. 11:2), a holy priesthood (1 Pet. 2:5), the pillar and ground of truth (1 Tim. 3:15). You *are* the children of light, of the day, and do not belong to the night, to the (TS: "in the") darkness (1 Thess. 5:5). You *are* washed, sanctified, justified by the name of our Lord Jesus Christ and the Spirit of our God (1 Cor. 6:11). You *have* the anointing of him who is holy and who knows all things (1 Jn. 2:20), and this anointing abides in you (2:27). You *are* the light of the world (Mt. 5:14). All these and many parallel sayings are stated and intended categorically and without either reservation or condition. Criticisms, reproaches, accusations, reprimands, and threats may be addressed to the same *ecclesia*, but these do not invalidate the statement, nor may they naturally be put alongside it; but as a description of what is not envisioned by it, their relationship to it is one of paradox, total alienation, and contradiction. The horror with which the authors of the New Testament speak of the backsliding of the community from what it really is and has been is no less than that of the Old Testament prophets when they refer to the falling away of Israel from the basis of its being in the covenant of Yahweh.

Deeply disturbing as the world's ignorance of God is, the fact that there can also be an ignorance of God on the part of the church is incomparably more sinister. That the God who is known to it in such a special way should also be unknown to it is alien to, and contradicts, the very nature, constitution, and structure of the church. It is incomprehensible and inconceivable in relation to its origin and goal. We can only describe it as unnatural that the prayer for the hallowing of God's name and zeal for his honor should be necessary and demanded not only in relation to the world, which is in the power of the evil one, but also—precisely, primarily, and especially— in relation to the church. Yet one cannot ignore, deny, or gloss over the fact that the fatal ambivalence of the knowledge and ignorance of God may in fact be seen at work here where it can only be excluded by God's election, calling, and commissioning, that it may be seen at work here in even sharper contours than in the world that surrounds the church. One cannot fail to see that the light which shines out from the church into the world is not a pure one but a miserably opaque and obscured one. It has not become utter darkness. Darkness does not reign alone even in the world. But here in distinction from the world one ought to see only light, the purest light. The twofold horror is that there is darkness too and that the light is thus broken, clouded, and obscured. The name of God is certainly hallowed here, but here too, in a doubly shocking way, it is also desecrated. There is no overlooking the fact that as the criticism of the Old Testament prophets is directed only marginally at the peoples around Israel and centrally at God's own chosen, called, and sanctified people, so the criticism of the New Testament apostles only marginally concerns the ungodliness, idolatry, and self-deification of the Greeks, Barbarians, and Romans of their day, but centrally concerns the lack of knowledge of God (1 Cor. 15:34) which in unheard of fashion occurs in the Christian community in deviation from its most proper being. It is only indirectly that the Bible as a whole speaks critically through the window to the street but always directly that it speaks critically inside, to those who are in the house, the special house of God.

There are two main forms in which the paradoxical ignorance of God appears in the church, or, more exactly, there are two false developments that are inwardly related and correspond outwardly even though they move in opposite directions. The one sinister motif in both is that the church neglects, abandons, and loses its nature and task as such, thus becoming unfaithful to itself and denying its being as the church. This happens when and to the extent that it deals with the living Lord, who makes it the living community and upholds it as such, as though he were not the Lord and not living; when and to the extent that it will no longer live solely and seriously and joyfully by his Word and in obedience to his Spirit; when and to the extent that it wants to be the church otherwise than in the discharge of its task and ministry; when and to the extent that it thus denies him in and with all these things. When this happens, when the church is involved in apostasy, there arises ignorance of God, desecration of his name, and darkness where there should be only light. Again this is not total darkness, just as darkness does not reign alone even in the world, because objectively the self-declaration of God, even though the world does not know him, is still victoriously at work in it. Especially in the church the darkness can never be total, for the church differs from the world in that it may live by and in the knowledge of God in his self-declaration. Even in its fall it cannot cease entirely to be the church, which will remain forever (Augsburg Confession, VII). No matter how high and solid the gates of the realm of the dead may be and pretend to be, they cannot overtop the height and solidity of the community of God (Mt. 16:18), not because this is in itself so insurpassably high and solid, but because God is the one to whom the community belongs. There can be no question of God repenting of the gifts and calling in which he has made and upholds the community and which is the meaning of what he promises it in detail (Rom. 11:29). In the church too—and especially in the church—the knowledge of God victoriously confronts the most frightful ignorance of God and the holiness of his name its worst desecration. Even in the sharpest prophetic sayings of the Old Testament there is no mention of any revocation of the covenant between Yahweh and Israel. Nothing more than ambivalence can arise in the church. Nevertheless, this does not mitigate its unfaithfulness to itself, that is, its falling from its Lord, the partial darkness that follows, and the incomprehensible contradiction in which it exists. The inconceivable thing is that even in the church Antichrist is at work as well as Christ, that it is at one and the same time both the true church and the false, that in the church too there is an ambivalent knowledge of God that constantly threatens to turn into ignorance of God. The half-light in which the church exists is dreadful when it is involved in denial of its Lord and in apostasy from him.

The one form of the denial and apostasy is the church in excess, the presumptuous church which exalts itself and puffs itself up.

At this point one is naturally inclined as a Protestant to think especially of the Roman church. There may be something in this. But one should keep in view that the Roman church is not just a church in excess, involved in apostasy only on this side. One should also keep in view that, even if in less striking and classical form, the church in excess, in apostasy on this side, may be very clearly seen in the non-Roman Christian world, not only on its right wing among the Eastern Orthodox, Anglicans, and Lutherans, but also on the left wing, even down to the Baptists, though only on the margin.

The church in excess is the church exceeding the limit within which alone it can be the church of Jesus Christ: the limit of the basic determination that the living one to whom it owes the origin and constitution of its life, who in relation to it — and to it specifically — is the freely acting and speaking *Lord*, that this one is its sovereign. The threat is that it will serve its own needs instead of him, that it will become its own means of life and glory. Insofar as the church here is primarily interested in itself, and in its Lord only for its own sake, one might call it, in relationship to him, the introverted church. In whose honor is so much pomp put forth, for whom is there such energetic and skillful propaganda? That he is the Lord — our Lord Jesus Christ — the church does not cease constantly to recite. It knows very well that only attesting him makes its own existence possible and can lend it strength and dignity. But it knows this only too well. It must bear witness to him as its Lord for its own sake, in order that it may use him as such, to differentiate it, to give it distinction, to declare and establish its claim over against the world. It can boast about itself only as it boasts about him. It becomes and is the church in excess by boasting about him in order to be able to boast about itself: about itself in the holiness he has given it, in the loftiness of the tradition, teaching, and order that derive from him, in the administration of the gifts that he has granted, in the power of decision and control that he has lent it, in the continuation of the incarnation of God that began in him, as his re-presentation. That he gives himself to it, the church takes to mean that he is in its hands. It will not be without reservation a creature of the Word (Luther), a church which simply and unequivocally serves him. Appealing to its institution and empowering through him, it wants to be the church that reigns in his name. He must act only on and with and through it. As to the world, so also to itself, he must speak only in the form of its own speech and action. It integrates his priestly, kingly, and prophetic office with its own. *It* speaks his truth; *it* extends or denies his grace; *it* proclaims his law. With his staff, scepter, and sword in its own hand, exercising his authority in the power of its own, *it* reigns: only in his place, it will assert again and again, yet still in his place, as his full representative. *It* has his Spirit. *It* expounds the Scripture that bears witness to him. In dealing thus with him, in leaping over the barrier between it and him, the church makes it hard to see how far he is over it, how far he is its Lord, as it does not cease to profess, how far he is the Lord whom it must hear and obey and to whom it is answerable, how far it has not exalted itself as his lord, how far it has not made the Word the creature of the church. Can it still be the church in this form? It is at least obscure how far it can be. Yet there is no reason to give up the church for lost when it falls in this direction. In fact, Jesus Christ is always and in all circumstances the Lord of the community. Undoubtedly, then, he remains in control even in the church in excess, even in the church that exalts itself. He can always assert himself as such. When the order of its relation to him is turned on its head, he can always restore it again both in detail and as a whole. He does in fact restore it more frequently and persistently than we can see or think. Even if in many fetters, Scripture as witness to him is open in the church. And who knows what can happen when it proclaims itself again in its own dynamic. The Holy Spirit, who in it also blows where he wills (Jn. 3:8), can at any time show himself in the church to be a freer Spirit than its own, to be the Spirit of God himself to its salvation. It would be doubting him to doubt the possibility of a renewal even of the church in excess, a renewal that does not come from itself, but comes all the more powerfully from him. But there can also be no doubt that in the church in excess (in all its forms) we have a false development in which the knowledge of God is inevitably obscured — how can it help being obscured when Jesus Christ is not recognized and respected as the Lord of the church? — and intolerable damage is done to the holiness of his name. How can God be confessed, and not instead profoundly unconfessed, when his Word is not free but bound (in conflict with 2 Tim. 2:9), when ostensibly to the greater glory of God it is bound to the church? Whenever the church is on the point of becoming in this sense the church of excess, there is every reason for the petition "Hallowed be thy name," and for zeal for the honor of God.

The other form of apostasy is the church in defect, the church which does not take itself seriously enough because it is only half sure of its cause, which takes up this cause only hesitantly and with reservations and compromises, which only in a timid and uncommitted way ventures to give itself to its task.

At this point Protestantism of every denomination has reason to think first of itself. It might well be, of course, that in this sphere there has been and is too much of the church in defect because the grapes that the church in excess really wants are too high up for it, because it has experienced too much weariness and too many disappointments on the various ways to Rome, which attract it also and on which it has often gone quite a stretch. However that may be, too great a sense of the church is not as a rule the evident fault of Protestantism, but a painfully small trust in the authority and power of him who has called, gathered, and sent out the church as his community is its fault, —a pitiably feeble courage when it should be resolutely facing the world with the task that has been set for it. Yet the Romans would be well advised not to rejoice too soon or too loudly on this side, as though this opposite error did not in any way concern them. It could be that the lack of trust and courage which characterizes the church in defect is the most fertile soil for the development of the church in excess, that the overblown sense of the church in the latter is simply a complementary reaction to the lack of genuine trust and courage that is more hidden here but still present. There is sin, then, within the walls as well as outside them, although again only on the margin.

The church in defect is the church that is unfaithful to its determination vis-à-vis the world, which has been given to it with its establishing and upholding as the church of Jesus Christ. It is unfaithful because it neglects and denies the second aspect, namely, that its Lord—he is its determination—is the *living* Lord: the Lord who by his resurrection from the dead is in his death superior to death, and therefore to the world as the world that is marked and ruled by death; the Lord who overcomes the world, since God reconciled it to himself in him, so that his people need fear no one and nothing in this world. The church in defect is not comforted as it may and should be in view of this victory. To be sure, it knows and recites the words: "The third day he rose again from the dead; he ascended into heaven, and sitteth on the right hand of God the Father Almighty." But it does not say this with total confidence, only with half confidence. It does not stand defiantly on it. Only occasionally and not fundamentally and consistently does it think and speak and act in the light of it. It is at any moment ready and able to think and speak and act apart from this presupposition.

To speak in terms of Matthew 14:25ff., it sees the Lord coming to it on the storm-tossed lake, but it is terrified of him as though it saw a ghost; and when he tells it to be of good cheer and not to be afraid, and when it—or a Peter in it— ventures to follow his invitation to hasten toward him, it again looks past him at the wind and waves, is afraid again, genuinely afraid, begins to sink, and happy it is if it can at least cry out, "Lord, save me!"

One might also call the church in defect the extroverted church. It is the church that certainly looks to Jesus Christ but not without the subsidiary thought that perhaps he is only an idea or *mythologoumenon* to whom it might be dangerous to cling. It wants to go to him, to celebrate Christmas, Easter, and Pentecost seriously, to be the Christian church, but it finds and feels itself burdened by the fact that it is also powerfully impressed and frightened by the world around it, by the autonomy and despotism of the world's doings, by its politics, economics, and science, by what is called "real life." The church in defect is the church which looks anxiously to its Lord but even more anxiously to everything else; which painfully compares itself to the world; which for this reason seeks possible points of contact from or to it; which is intent on bridges from the one place to the other. The favorite word of this church is the little word "and," not in the forceful sense of the New Testament καί, but in the weak sense of a mere hyphen, in such expressions as "revelation and reason," "church and culture," "gospel and state," "Bible and science," "theology and philosophy." The anxious purpose always is to give the first element in these expressions a small but guaranteed place alongside the second, or at best to achieve security for it in the protective sphere of the second. The church in defect — in what one might call its defective faith, its little faith [cf. Mt. 17:20] — is the church which, in order to have a joyful certainty of the reality of what it believes, thinks it has first to ask concerning the possibility of its faith. It is the church which for the sake of security wants to construct an ontology before beginning theology; which instead of expounding the Bible gives itself with deadly seriousness to the problem of hermeneutics (to love of love instead of love itself!); which instead of speaking the Word entrusted to it speaks constantly of the speech event; which constantly analyzes humanity instead of speaking simply and directly to it (because it knows what it wants and has to say). Supposedly to reach people where they are, this church is forever paying regard to them, adjusting itself to them, trying to win their attention and sympathy, attempting to be — or to appear to be — as pleasant as possible to them. It is the distracted and therefore the chattering church, the squinting and therefore the stuttering church. In connection, perhaps, with the fact that its interests are largely (or mainly) determined from outside, in distinction from the church of excess, it is a church that constantly breaks up afresh into every possible group and party and school and trend. Yet again there is no reason to give up the church that is gripped by apostasy in this sense, by secularization instead of sacralization. The church of little faith still lives as the church by the fact that Jesus Christ has risen again, has robbed death of its power, has overcome the world, and as its Head sits at the right hand of the Father. He can have mercy on this church too. He can cause to rise up in it once again the light of the knowledge that he long since had mercy on it also and especially, that there is no basis for the care and anxiety that underlies its error, the fear that, in relation to the world, it will get the worst of it, that it need not sink if instead of letting itself do so it goes cheerfully to him. Scripture, which bears witness to him the living Lord, can again become a summons to this church also in the power of his Spirit, telling it that it need not be afraid, that there is real comfort for it, that sure of its cause it can live in his service. Once again, it would be doubting him to doubt that every day and every moment there can be renewal of the doubting church by him. We have to realize, however, that without such renewal — in a doubting, distracted, and squinting church that halts between two opinions [cf. 1 K. 18:21] — if the Word of God is not taken with resolute seriousness, the darkness of the ignorance of God will arise and spread in his people and sanctuary, and the name of God will be irremediably desecrated from the human standpoint. On this side, also, there is thus an urgent need for the first petition of the Lord's Prayer and the zealous obedience corresponding to it.

We shall now try to have a brief look at the two false developments of the church together. In both, the mystery of the ignorance of God is the same as both basis and consequence. In both there is an apostasy of the church from its living Lord. Whether the fall be sought and found on the one side or the other, the corruption is the same. The saying about the mote in the brother's eye and the beam in one's own is apposite here (Mt. 7:3ff.). It is certainly not the pure church but precisely the church in defect that usually characterizes and accuses the church in excess with such suspicious clarity and force. It is certainly not the pure church but the church in excess that can win so suspiciously glorious a triumph over the heresy of the church in defect. The pure church is always there and speaks the Word where "the ruin of Joseph" (Amos 6:6) is seen and judged neither by some here and others there but by all of them in its unity as apostasy from the living Lord; and where it is also set in the light of the grace which he never refuses. Thus the Old Testament prophets describe it as both an act of arrogant confidence in the covenant and also as an act of cowardly forgetfulness of the covenant, the one provoking the other, but both taking place in the sphere of the covenant of grace. In the church the ambivalence of the lordship of Christ and Antichrist, and the ignorance of God which underlies and follows and manifests itself in it, neither can nor will be seriously called in question, let alone set aside, by any judgment issued from the one side or the other. The only promising thing is common submission to the verdict on both false developments in a common hope in the grace of the one Lord of the one church which is superior to both. The common hope will precede the common submission; the common submission will have its basis in the common hope.

A final note concerning this second point. We have intentionally here looked only at the obscuring of the knowledge of God and the desecrating of his name which have their basis in the false development of the church contrary to its true nature and structure. In so doing we have not forgotten — we can only state this now and not develop it — that as it is also in the world, being in its own way an element in the being of the world and its events, the church has to its good a full share in that general objective knowledge of God, but it also has to its ill a full share in that equally general subjective ignorance of God in the world and its bad, worse, and worst manifestations. Atheism is thus a phenomenon that is also found within the church, the only point being that as a theoretical denial of God it may be seen here at most only in the esoteric presuppositions of certain theologians, but all the more frequently it has the form of a practical denial of God. It may be that the latter rather than the former is in view when we are told what fools say in their hearts (Ps. 14:1 and par.). It need hardly be said how easily the lack of knowledge of God — not only in the church in excess but also in the church in defect, and in the one no less than the other — can also take, and constantly does take, the form of self-willed and arrogant religion and consequently of idolatry of the worst kind (from the Roman hyperdulia of various madonnas to that of "faith" in some recent products of Protestant theology). Thus the distinctive characteristic of the world, that of trying to equate itself with God and God with itself, has parallels that are only too exact on both sides of the apostate church. So too, unfortunately, does what we have called the point of convergence and culmination in the world's turning away from God, namely, the ambivalence of the relationship between man and fellow man. In the church also these can obviously exist both with one another and also without or against one another. The same unhappily applies to the relationship between those who are in the church and those who are outside. It is fatal enough that this is so, that all that is said about the ignorance of God in the world can be said with modifications about the ignorance of God in the church; that the church not only exists in the world but also in its own way exists far too much in the manner and style of the world. This is fatal enough for the hallowing of the name of God which is to be expected in and from it. Our present task, however, is to recognize the false developments that are peculiar to the church as the church. The church is faceless in these false developments in which it participates and yet does not act or express itself originally, but unfortunately merely does and leaves undone what the world around it does and leaves undone. This painful doing and leaving undone in concert with the world is to be understood, of course, in the light of its own typical false developments. Only as the church falls away from its living Lord does it happen — and happen necessarily, since this is the only option — that it equates itself with the world and accommodates itself to it. When it becomes the church in excess or defect, and secretly both, the original mistake takes place which carries all the rest with it. This original mistake is made when the doors and windows of the church, which ought always to be opened to the world from inside as the church sympathetically bears the burdens that afflict the world and in loyalty to its task tries to proclaim salvation to it, are instead pushed in from the outside. It is made when, as the church takes itself far too seriously or not seriously enough, and either way denies its Lord, the world seizes and takes over the church, the church being pleased to let itself be secularized. The original mistake is made when the church which should be calling the world to God lets itself be called by the world, cleaving to the world instead of God and thus being untrue to the world and on both sides to itself. If there is no overcoming of the ambivalence in which the church is the church by origin and nature and yet as the church in excess or defect is not the church, then there is no overcoming of the ambivalence in which it is unlike the world and yet like it in unfaithfulness to God, the world, and itself. How then can it serve by its witness to overcome the ambivalence in which God is known to the world and yet also unknown? What can an inwardly divided church say for the salvation of a world that suffers from its own division? How can the church that suffers from division help but share in suffering from the division which is peculiar to the world? The hallowing of God's name in the church? We can already say here that this means secondarily the freeing of the church from so much secularization, but it means primarily (Jer. 2:13) its return from leaky cisterns that do not hold the water to the source of living water which it has abandoned in these original false developments, the inevitable consequence being its succumbing to secularization.

3. We have now reached the innermost circle of our deliberations. As God is both known and unknown in both the world and the church, so he is also both known and unknown in the life of the individual Christian existing as a member of the church. The problem does not arise first or solely in this innermost circle, nor does it arise with greater seriousness here than in the other circles. The only truth in the opposite and rather fanatical view of the existentialists is that the very serious problem of the world and the church ceases to be a relatively distant but only apparently distant one and moves close to us and in some sense hits home at this point. As the problem of this or that specific person existing in both the world and the church, it now poses itself as his problem, which in a provoking way can and must mean that it is our problem or, more exactly, mine and yours. At the very latest it should be clear here, as it ought to have been already, that when we spoke of the antinomy and division prevailing in the world and the church, we were also speaking of ourselves and our own ambivalence and division. It must also be clear here that we are still speaking of the world and the church when we are speaking of ourselves. Our own problem, the personal problem of my life and yours, is, not with greater but with equal seriousness, their problem. Not first or solely this or that specific person existing in the world and also in the church, not first or solely we, I and you, but also this specific Christian person, and also I and you, exists in the division and therefore in the desecration of the name of God which consists of his being both well known to us and also completely unknown. The fatal contradiction of righteousness and sin by which the world and the church are ruled, which is significant, powerful, and dangerous both in those circles and also in this circle, and which is to be described most surely in this circle as a confession and an address, takes on here the scandalous form that I and you are at one and the same time both righteous and sinners.

We shall follow the same procedure here as in the first two points and consider first the positive but sharply contested definition of Christian existence: that I and you are righteous. God is well known to the individual Christian. He is so first and primarily because the Christian, I, you, and each of us, has a share in the being of the world and therefore in the objective knowledge of God which the world does not lack. The determination for God, for brotherhood with his Son, which is granted to human nature in and with its creation, is the unlost and unlosable determination of his existence too, no matter whether it be fulfilled or not in his life. The witness of the Christian community in the world is for him, as it is for all people, no matter whether it has reached him or not, or in what form, or with what result. Supremely and decisively, the same Jesus Christ, the Son of God who became Son of Man for him, died for him to reconcile him to God, lives as his Mediator, represents him before God and represents God to him, and all this before and irrespective of man's own attitudes toward him. No matter how much or how little of all this he is in a position to experience, affirm, make fruitful, or even notice, all of it, summed up in its essentiality in God's perfect self-declaration in Jesus Christ, is God's Yes spoken objectively to you and me and each of us; it is my and your and our objective righteousness before him, also our objective sanctification for him, also the objective word in which God calls you and me and us to himself in his service, God's objective making of himself known to us. All else flows from this and can only flow from it, having in it its presupposition and basis. The whole existence of each individual Christian can only be and is the history in which he is grasped by this objective reality, may then take a few steps beyond it, but then with good reason will quickly come back to it and again and again begin and advance from this point. From this objective reality, from this knowledge of God that is wholly superior to his own knowledge and ignorance, his own understanding and lack of understanding, his own acceptance and rejection; from this objective righteousness that belongs to him, he can become and be a Christian, and can become and be it again and again.

Nevertheless, the fact that like everyone else in the world he is confronted with God's objective self-declaration, even in its perfect form in Jesus Christ, does not decide the point that he becomes and is a Christian, a person who has the distinctively Christian knowledge of God and may to that extent be addressed as a righteous person.

This is, of course, the presupposition without which no one and on the basis of which anyone can and should and ought to be a Christian. On this basis alone he lives as a Christian and again and again becomes one. What makes a person a Christian, however, is something particular that happens precisely to him. He becomes a Christian through the Word of Jesus Christ that is spoken to him specifically in the power of the Holy Spirit. Without ceasing to take part in the being of the world, he is called by this Word, that is, awakened, enlightened, and liberated, to being as a member of the community of Jesus Christ. By this Word, spoken particularly and distinctively to him, he is separated from the rest of the world. Though he still belongs to it, he is set over against it as one who knows and bears witness to the objective self-declaration of God. As we must emphasize, it is a matter of his calling to being a member of the living community of the Lord Jesus Christ; of his membership in this people, the church that exists in its knowledge of God. If this community is engaged in any kind of apostasy from God, if it thus exists in the total darkness of ignorance of God, then membership in it, in a dead community, cannot make a person a Christian. But we have seen that in no case does the church exist only in such darkness. It exists also in the light of God's being known in it. No matter how badly, it is always the living community. We must now stress that a person becomes a Christian by being called to be a living member of this community which is not just dead but which is also the living community. This means that a person becomes a Christian by being called to be one who is not just surrounded and washed by the life that the community has from its Lord, as an island is by the sea, but who may share personally in this life, hearing and obeying the voice of his Lord in personal knowledge and responsibility in and with the community. Insofar as everything that is said about the living community of the living Lord, and its origin, constitution, and structure in him, applies to this or that individual who is called to being in it, that individual is, you are and I am, a Christian.

It thus follows that of each individual Christian one may say that he exists as such, as a living member of the living community of the living Lord Jesus Christ, in total and exclusive openness to God's self-declaration, in total and exclusive commitment to his work, in total and exclusive freedom for his will and service. He exists in a knowledge of God in which he has a fullness of possible realizations yet no material alternative, no way but that of continuing on the path that he entered at the beginning. For a Christian the basic decision concerning himself is not still ahead of him but already behind him. It has been taken once and for all in the double sense that God has made known to him his election and he has made his own choice accordingly. "By grace you have been saved through faith; and this is not your own doing, it is the gift of God" (Eph. 2:8). Yet the Christian, and the community too as he sought and received baptism from it, has also validated his calling as God's free act of grace for the whole of his future. There — not as the result of his understanding of the world and himself, but as the Word of God which he has received, the message of the turning and reconciling of the world (which embraces him too) in the crucifixion of Jesus Christ — there the Yes of God was and is spoken to him too in an unrestricted way that is eternally valid and binding. And there too his own answer was and is given, in which he for his part, hoping and praying that he may give it again and again as a hearer of God's Word, said Yes to God and his work in a way that is valid and binding for him. The Christian does not exist in a vacuum; he exists on the basis of this double decision. He exists in Christ. He always exists only because and as Christ exists for him and is his Head: for him who is a member of his body, one of his people. He exists in this way and this way alone, in the light and only in the light, not in the darkness too. This is the light of the closed circle of the promise that applies to him and the faith that clings to this promise. It is the light of the divine love and the responsive human love awakened by it. It is the light of the command that is given to him and the obedience to which he for his part is summoned and for which he is empowered, impelled by the Spirit and therefore walking in the Spirit [cf. Rom. 8:14; Gal. 5:16, 18, 25]. This is his total and exclusive knowledge of God, the completed hallowing of God's name in his life. By it, by this double decision, his path is determined. No way back is envisaged in it; it rules out any such way.

What the New Testament says about the community as such in this respect usually applies clearly to the individual Christian too, and vice versa; because most, if not all, of the statements that are made specifically about individual Christians, it seems, are intended to refer to the community as such and are to be understood accordingly. When a person hears and understands the Word of God, he thereby shows himself to be part of the good soil in the field of the world from which some measure of fruit is to be expected (Mt. 13:23). As another parable puts it, "every sound tree bears good fruit . . . and cannot bear evil fruit" (Mt. 7:17f.). Or as John 13:10 puts it, "He who has bathed does not need to wash . . . but is clean all over; and you are clean," "by the word which I have spoken to you" (Jn. 15:3). Or Matthew 6:22: "If your eye is sound, your whole body will be full of light." Or 1 Peter 2:4f.: Christians are those who have tasted the goodness of the Lord, "living stones" destined and fitted as such to be fitted to the living stone which men rejected but which is in God's sight chosen and precious, so that they contribute to the building of his "spiritual house." God in Jesus Christ has not said Yes and No to them but an unequivocal Yes, establishing and anointing and sealing them (2 Cor. 1:19ff.; Eph. 1:13). To this they themselves have said an unequivocal Yes. Thus their relationship to him is grounded not in their feeling or supposing or thinking but in their being. They *have* peace with him (Rom. 5:1). He has not merely laid his love before them as an offer or opportunity but poured it in their hearts by the Holy Spirit (Rom. 5:5). Even more strongly, he who cannot be made a liar by unbelief has by his own testimony given them the eternal life that has come into the world in his Son (1 Jn. 5:10f.). "You *were* washed, sanctified, justified in the name of the Lord Jesus Christ and in the Spirit of our God" (1 Cor. 6:11). You *have* "put on" Christ, the Galatian Christians are told (3:27) as they are reminded of the faith that has come to the world and to them (v. 25), and also of their baptism. The Corinthians are also told that they are to see themselves as people in whom *he* is (2 Cor. 13:5). What does all this mean? Christians are people to whom the irrevocable and irreversible thing that decides their whole existence has happened, namely, that the crucifixion of Jesus Christ has become a present event for them, not as they are taught about it and persuaded of its significance, not by any sacramental act, that is, baptism or the celebration of the Lord's Supper, but by the Holy Spirit in the power of his living Word. It is present as that which took place at Golgotha: the decisive moment of his history has become the decisive moment of their own history. The old man they were has been crucified with him and totally and definitively robbed of his power (Rom. 6:6; Gal. 2:19; 5:24). As those they were they are dead with him (Rom. 6:8; Col. 3:3). By their participation in his death, old things have perished to return no more; they have been destroyed and terminated (2 Cor. 5:17). This death is theirs, the death of their old being, as they have themselves been baptized; the community confirms this by baptizing them (Rom. 6:3; Col. 2:12): baptism is not a death but a solemn·burial as befits the dead. Primarily, of course, they are always to look back and refer to their baptism with the Holy Spirit, but secondarily to the confirmation of the death of the old man that is expressed in their baptism with water as their good confession which they have made with the community before many witnesses (1 Tim. 6:12). This is the double decision from which they come, the beginning of all the thinking, willing, and doing that follows, the root of their whole being from now on. It means (2 Cor. 4:14; Rom. 6:8) that the only future they have and can envisage as those who are made alive with him (Col. 2:13; Eph. 2:5) is one analogous to the resurrection of Jesus Christ, a life in a new form (καινότης ζωῆς, Rom. 6:4), a life for God (Rom. 6:11), a life in his service (Rom. 6:22). Their still mortal bodies are alive already through the Spirit dwelling in them (Rom. 8:11); their members, which were instruments of unrighteousness, are now instruments of righteousness (Rom. 6:13); they themselves who *were* the slaves of sin have now become free, that is, obedient from the heart (Rom. 6:17). "I live, and you will live also" (Jn. 14:19). As Jesus lives, life is their future too, this new life to the exclusion of any other life, which is not indeed called life (ζωή) in the New Testament, let alone understood as such. Risen with him (after having died with him), they have indeed only the one choice, namely, to "seek the things that are above." Christ is above and sits at the right hand of God. Their life is in him and with him; it is truly and certainly theirs, laid up for them, though still hid in God. When he will be (definitively and universally) manifested, then they, Christians, will be with him in glory with this new life of theirs. Their only choice can be to live this new life, which here and now is already theirs, by seeking it where it is, namely, in Christ [Col. 3:1ff.]. As John puts it, he who believes in the Son already has eternal life here and now (Jn. 3:36; 5:24; 6:40). It is impossible to see how there can be any way back, how there can be any other way than that of this seeking of their life in him, of faith in him. It is impossible to see how there can even be the thought of any alternative.

To the extent that we are Christians, or seriously wish to be such, this is our knowledge of God, yours and mine. This is the hallowing of God's name in the personal life of the individual Christian. It makes no sense to play down this positive statement, to take into account from the outset the possibility of restricting negative statements, to try systematically to bring these into harmony with it. Naturally, questions and objections arise almost involuntarily. Naturally, a host of opposing negative statements that speak about a dark ignorance of God even in the lives of Christians may also be found in the New Testament. It should be noted, however, that these do not limit the positive statement but oppose it, and not in such a way as to posit a mutual systematic relationship between them, but in such a way that they are set over against one another as mutually exclusive.

Fundamentally, then, we misunderstand what calls for consideration as the terrible ignorance of God and desecration of his name even in the lives of Christians if we refuse to accept the fact that what calls for consideration as the positive knowledge of God in this innermost circle is unquenched and unbroken by the objections and questions. Any limitation would at once entail a weakening there and consequently a minimizing of the whole problem. One thing must never in any circumstances he said about the darkness of the ignorance of God in the life of the individual Christian as in the world and the church, namely, that its irruption is right in some higher sense, that it can take place in the sphere of a pact and compromise between itself and light, that it can be made intelligible within the bracket of a dialectical synthesis that embraces both itself and light. It certainly belongs to the essence of this darkness — if one can speak of the essence of something that has no essence — that it would like to swagger abroad in a peaceful agreement with the light of the knowledge of God, in a coexistence that is validated in a concordat. It wants to be understood theologically in a dialectical synthesis with this light. It certainly cannot and will not overcome the light (Jn. 1:5). But its aim — this is the dishonoring of God's name in the life of the Christian as well as the world and the church — is the consolidation of the ambivalence and division. Its aim is the state of suspense in which God is indeed known to the individual Christian but might also be an unknown God in virtue of some valid law. Having secured for itself this place, it would then like at least to conceal its character as the darkness of human corruption, aberration, sin, and guilt. In this balance it would like to present itself as a higher necessity and thus claim exculpation, toleration, and acknowledgment for its reality. Only with this thrust toward balance, toward "both/and," will it then characterize itself as the darkness that is radically opposed to the light—the light that only as it reigns supreme is the light of the knowledge of God. For this reason he who believes in the light [cf. Jn. 12:36] cannot and must not abet this tendency by seeing and coordinating darkness with the light on the same plane as in some sense a necessary and legitimate rival.

If we take this view, we primarily misunderstand the knowledge of God in the life of the individual Christian. This is pure, full, and total light which will not have the darkness of the ignorance of God alongside it but completely excludes it. In face of it this darkness cannot have the character of a necessary opponent, nor can it expect from it the exculpation, toleration, and acknowledgment of its reality. For the Christian as a living member of the living community of the living Lord Jesus Christ, there is no freedom for darkness that he may practice as such. His freedom is his freedom for the light; beside this he has no other. If he believes in the light, he does not believe in the darkness. He does not believe in its necessity, in its possibility, in its legitimacy, in its potential intelligibility, in the higher basis and worth of its claim. If he were to believe in the darkness, he would not believe in the light. What he held to be the light in which he purported to believe would not be the light of the knowledge of God vouchsafed to him as a Christian. As a light necessarily and rightly limited and called into question by the darkness of ignorance of God, it would itself be darkness. If he believes in the light, he can only fight against the darkness, not as against a rival coordinated with the light, but on the presupposition that it stands in dreadful juxtaposition, his ignorance of God confronting his knowledge of God, not as something necessary or possible or in any sense justified, respectable, and intelligible, but only as the epitome of the impossible, the illegitimate, the worthless, and the unintelligible.

We come to the same result when we finally ask concerning the possibility of a concordat between the ignorance and the knowledge of God in the human life of the Christian as such. If there were such a concordat, this would mean that he would have to respect two principles and norms, that he would have to exist in two spheres, that he would have to serve two masters, a greater and a smaller, perhaps, or a primary and a secondary, or even, perhaps, an inner and an outer—but still two masters. He would fail to understand the darkness as well as the light if he did not see that both are masters claiming his service in one way or another. But can he serve two masters? According to the categorical saying in Matthew 6:24, he cannot. Nor can anyone. He deceives himself if he thinks he can. Which of the two masters, then, will he serve? The Christian is one in whose life this is not an open question. By the Word of God spoken to him and his own answer to it he has made his decision. Knowing God, he will serve him and love him and cleave to him. The other that wants to be his master, even if only in co- and subordination, even if only in a limited sphere of his life, yet is not but only claims to be, this other he will not serve but can and will only hate and despise. No matter how divided his life may in fact be, there can be in this life no concordat between his ignorance of God and his knowledge of God, no normalizing and stabilizing of the division. There can only be life-and-death conflict waged on the presupposition that one of the two masters is the true and legitimate one whereas the other merely raises a claim to be such but is in reality a totally illegitimate usurper. This conflict with the dragon (not with an equal opponent) is the life situation of the Christian. For him, then, it is completely impossible to hold and hold together light and darkness as two comparable possibilities or to bring them systematically under a common denominator. The Christian would have to misunderstand or lie to himself if he were to try to do this. Whether he wounds the dragon or is devoured by him is a separate question, but he can only be engaged in the conflict between what is absolutely and exclusively possible and what is absolutely and utterly impossible. Only in this conflict can he consider the problem which relates to him and has to be worked out by him.

These are the reasons why it makes no sense to try to make easier the astonishingly definite statements of the New Testament about the knowledge of God in the life of each Christian by bringing in various qualifications and restrictions and diminutions. To do so is to make it impossible to understand the real situation of the Christian in and from which he may and should call to God, "Hallowed be thy name," and in which he is summoned to zeal for God as his Lord.

Having stated that light and darkness are not and cannot be coordinated in the life of the Christian any more than they can be in the world and the church, we can now describe darkness in its absolute strangeness as such. We have not questioned its distinctive reality, but indirectly affirmed it. Ignorance of God does exist in the life of each individual Christian. It is an absurd element in his history but it cannot be overlooked or denied. If it cannot be comprehended or explained, it has to be recognized as a brute fact, like the phenomenon of the dragon spewing out fire and smoke at the entrance to its den. In the words of the old Bern liturgy, we have to confess that "from our youth up even to the present hour we have sinned greatly with evil thoughts, words, and works, as thou, O God, dost know us to be guilty, and as we cannot adequately perceive." We — not poor heathen, unbelievers, and ungodly — but we Christians, and not just a wild section of us that has gone astray, not just others but all of us, each without exception in his own place and manner, and this from the very beginning and throughout the further course of our existence, so that the whole congregation has every reason to confess it. Evil thoughts, words, and works, thought and said and done in sharp contrast to our unequivocal knowledge of God, but obviously in no less unequivocal ignorance of him. At one and the same time both sinners and righteous. At one and the same time: not thought, said, and done after we have in some way laid aside and lost our knowledge of God, in some way releasing ourselves from it and getting rid of it. This does not happen. What makes a Christian a Christian — his calling by the

Holy Spirit and his answer to this at baptism — stands as firm as the creative Word of God which makes the world the world and the church the church, so that no indifference or revolt on the world's part can alter the fact that by the resurrection of Jesus Christ from the dead it is the world that in him is reconciled to God, and no apostasy on the part of the church to the right hand or the left can alter the fact that it is the people he has chosen and called. The great scandal in the life of the Christian is that in opposition to his knowledge of God he thinks evil thoughts, says evil words, and does evil deeds, so that he lives in plain ignorance of God and has no choice but that of confessing, along with his confession of faith in God the Father, Son, and Holy Spirit, that this evil is his sin and therefore his open guilt: not a regrettable weakness, not a sickness that has unfortunately overtaken him, not an ineluctable fate that has come upon him, but responsibly committed sin in which he has neither thought, spoken, or acted, nor does think, speak, or act, innocently, in which he has dealt with God, and does deal with him, as an unknown God, in which he has become a debtor and becomes a debtor afresh each day, to the known God. Thus the division and contradiction, the ambivalence of the knowledge and ignorance of God, of the existence of the Christian as both righteous and sinner, the hallowing and desecrating of God's name in his life, his being in the light and also in the darkness — this is the great scandal in this innermost circle too. It is no more than the great scandal, no more than the incoordinable factor, no more than darkness mighty in his life! As in the church and the world, so here there is no more than this triumph of the *simul*, of the stupid and blasphemous "and." But there is this triumph here, as in the church and the world. And here too it could hardly be more painful and intolerable. As we concede this triumph, we Christians make ourselves guilty of blasphemy against God. In face of this triumph, we are summoned here again to the petition "Hallowed be thy name" and also to the corresponding zeal.

What the New Testament describes and bemoans as the sin, transgression, and failure of Christians, beginning with the disciples and members of the apostolic communities, is in all its strangeness and inconceivability the choosing, willing, and actualizing of inner and outer attitudes, ways, and concrete expressions, some spiritual and some physical, which are not possible for them on the basis of what makes them Christians, that is, God's decision and theirs, which can only be impossible, but which are nevertheless chosen, willed, and actualized by them. Everywhere the New Testament reckons with it that this takes place in crying and intolerable contradiction to the grace of God which has been addressed to them and gratefully received by them. To be sure, not all of them think, speak, and do all the things that arise on this fatal path. Not all the disciples betrayed Jesus as Judas did. Not all of them denied him in plain words as did Peter. Not all of them were constantly "murmuring" as many were said to do in John 6:61. Not all Christians did what Ananias and Sapphira did in Acts 5:1ff., or the man who committed incest at Corinth in 1 Corinthians 5:1, or Alexander the coppersmith in 2 Timothy 4:14. Not all loved the present world as Demas basely did in 2 Timothy 4:10. The fact that there is a list of vices in almost all the New Testament Epistles, as also in Mark 7:21f. and Matthew 15:19, is naturally worth noting alongside the positive statements in these writings. It certainly does not mean that we are to picture the congregations in

Corinth, Rome, and so forth, as regular dens of robbers and knaves, or even as examples of the Karamazov family. Nevertheless, the list of vices is unrolled before the whole church. All the disciples involuntarily put the question "Lord, is it I?" (Mt. 26:22) as though each of them was or could have been Judas. All the disciples slept when they should have been awake (Mt. 26:36ff.), even Peter, even the sons of Zebedee. All of them later left Jesus and fled (Mt. 26:56). Not without reason, Jesus put to all of them the question "Will you also go away?" (Jn. 6:67). The warning of Romans 6, surprising though it is in view of Romans 3–5, applies to all Christians. Starting from the crucifixion of Jesus Christ and their own baptism, they are not to persist in sin, or to want to sin, because they find comfort and joy in the supremacy of grace. With a reference to himself, and therefore in a way that is most exemplary, Paul astonishingly states and describes in the well-known passage Romans 7:7ff. the terrible contradiction between the law of God and the law in his members, the will that is good and the acts that are bad. The clear presupposition of the exhortation to Christians that is so palpable in every New Testament context is that all of them, though they are not all renegades and scoundrels of this or that kind, though they are not all thieves, whoremongers, haters of parents, pederasts, and so forth, nevertheless all of them are viewed and addressed as people who vacillate between consistency and inconsistency in their election and calling, practicing the fatal "freedom" of either continuing on the way from the crucifixion of Jesus Christ and their baptism or of interrupting it in some refined or coarse manner (and often enough the latter), walking according to the flesh instead of the Spirit (Rom. 8:4), continuing in the flesh what was begun in the Spirit (Gal. 3:3). This vacillation or neutrality in which Christians can be and are one thing or the other, thinking, speaking, and doing one thing or the other, is the monstrosity which is envisioned, expounded, and tackled in the vigorous inner Christian polemic of the New Testament. This is the evil in the evil, the sin in the sin, which is charged precisely against Christians. This is the corrupt mode of existence from which they have to be called back in apostolic exhortation, now by admonition and now by threat, because it is wholly unsuitable and forbidden and completely inexcusable. What James 3:5ff. says specifically about the tongue, about the speech of the Christians addressed, can in context be related to the whole of their Christian life. Being one of vacillation, beyond the power of any to tame, the tongue is a "restless evil (ἀκατάστατον κακόν), full of deadly poison." With it they praise the Lord and Father and they also curse men made after the likeness of God. Praising and cursing come from the same mouth. Οὐ χρή, it ought not to be, my brethren, ταῦτα οὕτως γίνεσθαι, that things are so. "Does a spring pour forth from the same opening fresh water and brackish?" Unhappily, this is what does in fact happen. One recalls what the same letter (1:6ff.) says about the man who prays but doubts and is thus like a wave of the sea that is driven and tossed by the wind; as an ἀνὴρ δίψυχος, unstable (ἀκατάστατος again) in all his ways, he cannot really expect to receive anything from the Lord. Nor should one forget that in the same letter (1:23f.) the one who is a hearer of the word but not a doer is like a man who looks at his face in the mirror and goes away and immediately forgets what he looks like. All New Testament exhortation has this instability in view. Why else would its tenor be an unmistakably urgent appeal that Christians should watch, stand, remain, persevere, and persist in what has made them Christians and in that in which alone they can be Christians? They are plainly seen to be standing with one foot on this impregnably firm foundation but with the other, partly under threat and partly in mortal danger already, on marshy ground or the edge of an abyss that runs through the whole of Christian existence, not yet beyond the reach of a loud shout or a firm handclasp, but already by human judgment on the verge of being lost. "My brethren, this ought not to be so." Yet it is unmistakable that, in fact, in the darkness of the inconceivable ignorance of God even on the part of Christians, things are so not only in the world and the church, but also in the personal inner and outer lives of individual Christians.

In conclusion, without claiming to cover all the ground but in summary fashion, let us take a more specific look at our own lives. In what we may refer to as taking place also among us Christians, we shall not be dealing merely with the trivial contradiction between our theory and our practice, but with the phenomenon of the fatal split in the whole of our lives. And as in the case of the lists of vices in the New Testament, what may be mentioned by way of example will not apply to all of us with the same directness: "Pious man, do not apply everything to yourself," namely, if this or that does not really fit.

Thus we Christians are astonishingly in a position not only to know but to live fundamentally with a clear understanding that we brought nothing into this world and can take nothing out (1 Tim. 6:7), that there is no greater deceiver, no one less worthy of our respect, than King Mammon — and yet when it is a matter of mine and thine, of prizes and awards to be received and given, of saving accounts and checking accounts, as though we could in fact serve two masters (Mt. 6:24 and par.), by day and night we are more zealous and worried and cunning and stiff-necked than many children of the world are in maintaining and, where possible, increasing our possessions.

We have a profound sense that we, like all people, are always in the wrong before God, but we also have a profound feeling that, compared to us, people in general are terribly in the wrong, whereas we ourselves are strongly in the right and have the duty as well as the power to proclaim and defend this.

We are confessing members of the Christian community, and as such we are brothers among brothers and sisters among sisters (heart united with heart, as Zinzendorf puts it in his hymn), but is it not a fact that we find it strangely hard to live in real unity of spirit with our fellow Christians, and are we not strangely tempted to accept as our real brothers and sisters only a few open and congenial people or a little circle of such?

We see clearly the need to handle weak, confused, and curious fellow men in the church and the world with special patience and solicitude, to "receive" them as Romans 14:1 puts it, to bear with them (Rom. 15:1); and yet we do not bear with them, we are quickly at odds with them again, we take their strangeness amiss as though we had to do with bad healthy people instead of poor sick people.

We believe in peace, perhaps even world peace, and preach it, and yet do not Christian fighters for peace of all schools compete with non-Christians for the honor of being the most difficult of all God's creatures?

It is written on our hearts that we and others need not and should not be plagued by anxiety about tomorrow [cf. Mt. 6:34], and yet, with the claim that our very special situation makes it necessary, we suddenly regard it as both permitted and commanded.

Nothing is more certain to us than that the world and its lust is passing away [1 Jn. 2:17], yet so long as the world has not passed away we are neither slothful nor inept in ensuring our own share in its lust, whether secretly or in some Christian modification.

Conversely, we really live in the joy of the Lord, which we know to be our strength (Neh. 8:10, etc.), and we speak about the great joy of Advent and Christmas and Easter and Pentecost, and yet when we have to suffer our reverses and endure our depressions and put up with our more or less justified feelings of irritation, we have the odd freedom to react if possible with even greater pessimism, distress, and peevishness than do other people who have not heard Paul's "Rejoice" [Phil. 4:4] as we have.

We believe in the primacy and power of faith, with reference, one hopes, to its pioneer and perfecter (Heb. 12:2), and yet every moment we think it appropriate to think and to take up positions according to the rules of some self-invented or acquired psychology, politics, aesthetics, or morality unaffected by theological considerations.

Who it is that lives and rules and speaks the Word as the only person of serious and final interest at the center of all being and occurrence is not really concealed from me as a Christian, and yet it is more than natural for me to see another person, namely, my own, at this center, to cause all others either secretly or openly to circle around it, to measure them strictly by my own experiences with them, by my own impressions of them, by what they mean for me either in good things or in bad.

It stands indelibly before our eyes that our freedom can be genuine freedom only in obedience to God, but look, we suddenly seem to be glad of it in the form of our own caprice.

Conversely, it stands no less indelibly before our eyes that the obedience we owe to God can be achieved only in the freedom of the Spirit and of our hearts, but look, we can suddenly imagine that to be obedient to God we must bow before the Gessler hat (cf. F. Schiller's *Wilhelm Tell*, Act 1, Scene 3; Act 3, Scene 3, etc.) of this or that human standard, ancient or modern.

We live by forgiveness, and suddenly it turns out that deep down (which is our deepest depth?) we would still rather live by certain fine achievements and accomplishments that we think need no forgiveness, and we find excuse after excuse if we do not succeed in producing any.

We pray and we know what we are doing, for we know that without prayer we cannot seriously work, and that no serious prayer is not definitely heard by God, but how does it come about that prayer can suddenly become a mere habit for us, or even a burdensome law, which in a pinch we can omit because we are so busy with other things? And how does it come about that we can suddenly dare to think that we can complain about supposedly unanswered prayers?

"The fear of the *Lord* is the beginning of wisdom" (Ps. 111:10). What Christian would not confess this from his heart? But again, what Christian does not manage at the next opportunity, this confession notwithstanding, to regard his own opinions, insights, and intentions as the beginning of all wisdom?

This is how the Christian looks, at once righteous and sinner, from a few among many possible angles. This is the ambivalence, vacillation, and division in our personal Christian lives. This is our notorious knowledge of God accompanying our equally notorious ignorance of God. We fill up the measure of our desecration of the name of God if we will not at least openly admit this.

3. HALLOWED BE THY NAME!

From the division or the ambivalence in which the same one, true, and living God is both known and unknown to the world, to the church, and to us Christians, there arises, piercing it directly from below as an underwater volcano pushes through the surface of the calm or ruffled sea, the petition addressed to God our Father: "Hallowed be thy name." The content and meaning of this first petition of the Lord's Prayer is, briefly, as follows. In it the one who first and truly bears the pain of our division, the one who is humbled and wounded by it but who is yet wholly superior to it, namely, God, is called upon to take to himself this disorder and distress, not adjusting the evil *simul* of light and darkness, the division, for there is nothing to adjust, but rather destroying and totally removing it from the world by an act that only he can perform and a word that only he can speak. He is asked to make an end, a total and definitive end, of the twilight in which the world, the church, and we Christians exist in relationship to him. He is asked to cause the sun to rise, the night to pass away completely, and the day to dawn. The radically new thing at the heart of the sphere of the known and unknown God which we have traversed thus far is that suddenly this petition, which does not simply take place in it but looks and reaches beyond it, is uttered and ascends directly above; that "Abba, Father" (Rom. 8:15; Gal. 4:6) in the hearts and on the lips of his children acquires the specific content that the Father will set aside and put an end to the "and" which so iniquitously controls and characterizes this whole sphere. Put out everywhere, in all these three circles, the darkness of ignorance of thyself! Let there shine wholly, unequivocally, and exclusively the light of thy countenance and therefore of the knowledge of thyself! This is the first petition of the Lord's Prayer.

It is the church, and within it Christians, who, provisionally representing in the name of the world those who do not yet participate, call upon God with this request. They do not do it out of their own need and impulse. If they did, they would no more do it than others do. They do it in the responsibility laid upon them by their special knowledge. They do not do it, however, according to their own invention, assessment, or judgment, but as they are bidden to do it by their Lord. We recall that invocation of God is as such, and in its specific content, an act of obedience. It is not conceivable that the people of God and its members should not be horrified by the dishonor that is done to God in that *simul* relation; that they should not fear the judgment that must follow this dishonoring. The intolerability of the division cannot be concealed from them. They cannot fail to see that adjustments and compromises cannot be the way to overcome it. We are referring to the living community of the living Lord Jesus Christ and its living members. As a dead community it would know nothing of this disquiet, and its dead members would show themselves to be dead precisely by the fact that the great "and" and *simul* would not seem to be monstrous to them but normal, congenial, and respectable. The church, however, does not exist only in apostasy and as a dead church. Christians do not exist only in contradiction of what makes them Christians and therefore as dead Christians. To the extent that both as a whole and in detail a living remnant [cf. Isa. 1:9, 7:3; 10:20ff.; 11:11ff.; etc.] has been preserved and is present, unrest in relation to the ambivalent neutrality and suspicious openness of the situation, consciousness of the intolerability of the whole theory and practice of halting between two opinions [cf. 1 K. 18:21], will not go fast asleep but will remain awake and continually awaken again. The wakeful church and its wakeful members pray "Hallowed be thy name" even though all around them, uttered even by themselves sometimes in their waking dreams, there continues the apathetic and monotonous murmur: "At one and the same time both righteous and sinner, world without end. Amen." No, the living community and its living members cannot say Amen to this.

The petition clearly presupposes that even though God is unknown to those who make it, he is not just unknown but also very well known. They know about his name, and knowing about it, they pray that it might be hallowed.

Luther's explanation in the Large Catechism begins (probably with reference to the concept of the name of God) by saying that the petition is rather obscure and is not expressed in the way we speak. Elucidation is indeed necessary. Name undoubtedly signifies the linguistic designation of a thing or person by the corresponding term. Older exposition of the petition, like that of the third commandment [Ex. 20:7; Dt. 5:11], has thus had a tendency to understand the hallowing of the name of God predominantly as respect for all the terms that denote him in contrast to their misuse in curses, oaths, conjurations, jests, and the like. An attempt has also been made to understand the first petition in direct connection and even in union with the preceding invocation, and especially with the name of Father, which seems to be so important there. In regard to the concept of the name, we are in fact not merely permitted but commanded to think of this term and indeed of the other terms that designate God linguistically, and in relation to their hallowing we must protect them against all kinds of linguistic disorders perpetrated by too much ungodliness on the one side and too much piety on the other. But we must not stop there. The concept "name" (*shem*, ὄνομα), while intended as a term to denote this or that god, has in biblical usage a dimension and dynamic that it has lost in our modern Western languages. In this usage no one and nothing is named accidentally or arbitrarily. No one and nothing might just as well bear some other name. A person is what and how he is called; a person is called what and how he is. The name is not just appended to the one who bears it. It is his external self-outworking and self-expression in relation to all other beings. One might say, then, that the name is the being itself as it acts and expresses and declares itself toward others. All this applies in a preeminent sense to God. "The name of God is God Himself" (A. Calov): it is God himself in his self-declaration outwards, God in his work and word. Thus the terms used for his name deserve the respect that is owed, not to the terms as such, but to him. This is why these terms should not be misused or spoken uselessly. This is why it is a fearful thing when God's name is denied, blasphemed, or dishonored. What is done to it is done directly to God himself. This is why it can be said of God's name that it is great and lofty, that it comes and is manifest, that it is near to man, that it dwells in a place, that it remains and abides [cf. Ps. 76:1; Jer. 10:6; Ezk. 36:23; Mal. 1:11; Ps. 148:13; Isa. 30:27; Dt. 12:11; 14:23; 16:11]. This is why God wills positively—we are putting all this in biblical terms—that one should think upon his name, recognize it, fear it, trust in it, wait for it, believe in it, love it, hope in it, call upon it, confess it, be glad in it, indeed, rejoice in it, thank it, praise it, extol it, and proclaim it in the world [cf. Ps. 119:55; 1 K. 8:43; Isa. 52:6; Dt. 28:58; Neh. 1:11; Ps. 86:11; 33:21; Isa. 50:10; Jn. 1:12; Ps. 5:11; 69:36; 119:132; Mt. 12:21 (Isa. 42:4 LXX); Gen. 4:26; Ps. 75:1; 1 K. 8:33, 35; Ps. 89:12, 16; 106:47; Neh. 9:5; Ps. 9:2; 30:4; 44:8; Ex. 9:16; Ps. 45:17]. This is why great things can and may and should be done in the name of the Lord [cf. 1 Sam. 17:45; Ps. 20:7; 44:5]. All these things are understandable and make good sense because God himself, "in the totality and singularity of His being" (E. Lohmeyer, *Das Vater-Unser*, Göttingen, 1962[5], p. 50), is his name in his outward works, in the act of his self-presentation and self-attestation in the world. He is really his name to the extent that in all his incomprehensibility and majesty he may be grasped in human thought, may be heard in human sounds, may be put in human ideas, and may be received or rejected, affirmed or denied, by human hearts. Lohmeyer has called God's name the "threshold" in the sense of the place of transition from God's being to his revelation, from his unity to the multiplicity of created things and beings, from his holiness to the world. It is odd that Lohmeyer can then make the further statement that the name of God (as though there were a way back) is also the threshold from the revealed God to the hidden God. From all that the Bible says about the name of God as such, the reverse sequence is the only possible one: from the hidden God to the revealed God. And since God himself is at issue in his name, would it not be better to speak, not impersonally of a threshold but personally of a step—the great crossing over that God makes to what is outside himself when he makes for himself a name, or when he wills to be and is himself also in his name?

God has his name when, without ceasing to be God in and for himself, he willed to be, became, and is God not only in and for himself but also in and for the reality distinct from himself. He has his name when he made himself known, makes himself known, and will again and again make himself known. In the light of this self-declaration, the question of an unknown and hidden God may arise de facto, but there can be no question of such a God de jure except *per nefas*, that is, to the extent that his name has not yet been proclaimed among us or to the extent that we will not yet recognize and confess it, love and praise it, trust and hope in it. He can be to us a hidden God only if his name is still or again denied, blasphemed, and dishonored by us, only as the God before whose self-declaration, before whose approaching step, before whose coming, before whose outward word and work, before whose dwelling in our midst, we run away, to whom we oppose the resistance of our indifference, aversion, and hatred.

When Jesus teaches his disciples to pray "Hallowed be thy name," no matter what their ignorance of God may be, he does not speak to this but to their knowledge of God. How could they pray for the hallowing of God's name as he requires if they did not know him, and know him in such a way that they could and might call upon him as one who is present with them? How could they make this prayer if he were an absent God? How could this request come into their hearts and onto their lips, how could the hallowing of God's name be impressed upon them, if they did not in some measure want to love and praise it, no matter what their attitude to it might be in other respects? In this regard Jesus takes them seriously by empowering, leading, and summoning them to pray this prayer. In so doing he charges them (and us) to see themselves not only in the darkness but also in the light. We can and must say that the invitation and command to the church and Christians to pray thus is already the gospel. When a person is required to pray thus, even though to his hurt he still exists in the counterpoise of light and darkness, there is addressed and accredited to him the freedom to break out of it, to decide gratefully for the light and against the darkness. As he prays thus, the balance is at least disturbed, and the worthless peace of "and" and *simul* is already challenged. This is the special situation of the church and its members as they make this prayer at the behest of Jesus. The fact that they are in the world, and that they may and should make this prayer representatively for it, casts a light on those who do not as yet pray with them; for there, with promise for them too, a step is made toward the name of God that corresponds to its own coming, dwelling, and abiding. Along with all else that takes place in this prayer, this takes place too. Nor is it a little thing. Ventured at the behest of Jesus, the petition "Hallowed be thy name" is itself as such a pledge that the painful vacillation between the knowledge and the ignorance of God in the world, the church, and ourselves is not at any rate a law of brass that cannot be broken.

It should also be noted that we have here a petition to God that he himself should sanctify his name and thus do in the matter what he alone can do. If this prayer is part of man's invocation of God, it does, of course, entail necessarily that there should be the corresponding willing, acting, and doing on man's part. We shall have to turn our attention to this aspect in the fourth subsection. Naturally one will also find in the petition the implicit request—and this should be noted in its exposition—that God would motivate us to perform the corresponding deeds. Nevertheless, the decisive and central point in it is not that with God's help there should be our human action and the zeal for God's honor, which is, of course, required of us. If God does what is asked, sanctifying his name, this is more and other than enabling us to sanctify it within the limits of our own possibilities. It is true that this ought to happen, that it cannot happen unless God motivates us thereto, and that we pray that he will do this. But we miss the point of the prayer if we expound it as though this were its real content. If we cannot pray it without being aware of the admonition under which the one who prays it is put, and puts himself, nevertheless it is not a thinly disguised admonition to the one who prays, but a pure petition that looks beyond all present and future human zeal, volition, ability, and achievement to a work whose subject God alone can be and which will be that of his own volition, ability, and achievement.

Reformation exegesis, which follows St. Augustine here (*De sermone Domini in monte, CCSL,* **XXXV,** 109), is very good but misleading in this regard. Thus Luther in the Small Catechism explains that God's name is indeed holy in itself, but in this prayer we ask that it may become holy among us too, which takes place when the Word of God is purely and simply taught and we live holy lives as God's children in accordance with it: "Help us to do this, dear Father in heaven." Similarly, in the Larger Catechism he says that it is a matter of God's name being holy in our use of it, which happens when both our life and teaching is godly and Christian. According to Luther, we pray for what God commands in the third commandment, namely, that we should laud and praise and honor him with both words and works. The Heidelberg Catechism looks in the same direction in Question 122: "Hallowed be thy name, that is, seriously grant to us that we may sanctify, laud, and praise thee in all thy works. Grant also that we may so direct all our lives and thoughts and words and works that thy name may not be blasphemed on our account but honored and praised." None of this is wrong. All of it is indeed very estimable. The only problem is that it obscures the character of the petition as a prayer for an act that cannot be ours, not even with the help of the Holy Spirit, but which can and will be only God's own act. Attention is thus focused on the ethical implications of the prayer before the prayer itself is elucidated. Lohmeyer (p. 53) is right when he points out that what is at issue in the petition is not a form and content of human life, not a task which is daily and hourly put to it, which is constantly present and never completed, but a once-for-all event that will be — why else should we pray for it? — a once-for-all act of God. We shall see that the petitions which follow in the Lord's Prayer also have this in view. The first petition, then, prays that God himself will hallow his name in this act as his sovereign work.

To understand this, however, we must first step back a little. An act of *sanctifying* — a highly extraordinary one, of course — is the object of this petition. Sanctifying — perhaps Luther found this a little obscure as well — is, in the language of the Bible, very generally an action in which someone or something is lifted out of the secularity of the surrounding world and his or its own previous existence, dedicated to the service of God (often cultically), and made worthy and suitable for this purpose. Sanctification means the separation, claiming, commandeering, and preparation of a person, place, or object with a view to this higher purpose destined for them.

We have here a highly extraordinary sanctifying primarily because what normally happens to a creaturely person, locality, or object is to happen here to the name of God. Other sanctifications take place with a view to the service of God. But now he himself, his name, is to be sanctified. How can this be necessary? Well, it is a matter of God's name. In relation to a naked, absolute, and hidden God, the concept of sanctification would obviously be meaningless. The name of God, however, is God concretely, God in his step outwards, God in his work and word, God in his self-declaration, God as he is known in the world. The world is the place where other factors also declare themselves and where *per nefas*, but de facto, we have to reckon not only with the light of knowledge of God but also the darkness of ignorance of God. In the world (and, as we have seen, in the church and the personal lives of Christians as well) the knowledge or name of God has become problematical. In Luther's words, God in his self-declaration is in himself holy: the one, true, and living God who as such is worthy to claim the sanctification of his creatures for his service and mighty to bring this about. Yet since his name is his self-declaration in the *world*, in it he is hemmed about by the question whether he really is the one he declares himself to be. This question can be and is answered both in the affirmative and also in the negative. Hence his name is here thrust into the world's vacillation and darkness and does in fact need to be sanctified. That is to say, things cannot be left as they are. God's name cannot be denied, blasphemed, and desecrated by such questioning. The knowledge of God grounded in his self-declaration cannot be made problematic or subjected to opposition. His self-declaration cannot and will not be given a negative answer. There cannot be a powerful ignorance of God too. The name of God cries out to be sanctified, to be known and confessed as such, to be known and not unknown as his name. It cries out among all other names for the differentiation, distinction, and honor that is its due. Hence the first petition of the Lord's Prayer prays that this due honor may be paid it, or, as one might simply say, that the light, instead of being overpowered by the darkness, should shine forth in the darkness [cf. Jn. 1:5]. How can there be any other sanctifying — that of creatures for the service of God — if first God himself is not lifted out of secularity, if he is not removed from the desecration that has come upon him in the world, the church, and the lives of Christians, if his name is not first and foremost exalted in the world which is his and in which he himself has proclaimed it, if his confession as the one he is is not validated?

A further point — and this again makes the sanctification at issue in this petition a highly extraordinary one — is that God is *himself* asked to sanctify his name, to validate it. More accurately, he is himself asked to sanctify himself (since it is his name), to take into his own hands the matter of his outward differentiation, distinction, and honor, to bring about the triumph of the knowledge of himself over all the darkness of ignorance of himself. It is no mere question, then, of a sanctifying of his name that will be done by those who know and confess him, which will be a work of the church and Christians. A demand addressed to the church and to us that we should do what we can in the matter makes good sense, of course, in its own place and manner. Even here we shall see that this is in fact commanded and that we must obey this command. But what we can do in the matter will just be done, and when we have done it, or done something of it, we are always forced to confess that we are unprofitable servants who have simply done what is their duty to do (Lk. 17:10). Here, however, we have to do with something that can hardly be mentioned in the same breath with our very dubious fulfilment of our duty, namely, the basis of the command and of obedience to it. At this basis of the command, what is at issue is the sanctifying of the name of God which is not our work but God's, so that we can only pray that it take place. "Hallowed be thy name," then, is not a kind of pious wish of human longing mounting up to heaven — the wish that in the course of an historical process which is perhaps already in motion it will somehow come about that the sanctification of the name of God will go ahead in the world, the church, and Christians, that the light of the knowledge of God will shine forth more brightly than hitherto in the darkness of ignorance of God. How do we know whether there is any such gradual historical process of the sanctifying of God's name, so that the process merely needs to be speeded up? And even if there is such a process, would not all possible or conceivable progress in its further course still manifest in an even more painful way the continuing division and therefore an incomplete sanctification? No, the prayer here, the appeal of the children to the Father in heaven whom they have previously invoked, is not that our little bit of sanctifying action, nor the automatic progress of a sanctifying process that has already begun, but that God himself should provide a remedy for the wrong relationship between his work and word on the one side and that which opposes him and dishonors his name in the world, the church, and ourselves. We can only *pray* that he should do this. Here, then, prayer is made, not out of human caprice, but at the behest of Jesus when he taught his community and its members to pray in this way.

What takes place in the hallowing of God's name, when what is meant is the action whose subject can only be God himself, so that it cannot be expected from any other? Not from any man, no matter how earnest he may be in his obedience to the command that he for his part should also sanctify this name! Not from any mechanism of an historical development that is perhaps moving toward the sanctifying of this name! Not even from God, except as prayer is made that he himself will do it! There cannot be meant a mere shift in the relationship between light and darkness, a mere expansion and increase in the knowledge of God and a corresponding decrease in the ignorance of God in the world, the church, and ourselves. This we should certainly not despise, but it might also be the work of humans or of an historical process favorable to God's cause. In our longing for such, there is no necessary reason to appeal to God himself. We do not have to pray that it will happen. Such a shift, even if brought about by God himself, would not overcome but would simply reduce, or even perhaps conceal, the division or ambivalence of the situation between God and man, which in the second subsection we learned to see as the true desecration of his name. In such a case, even at best the contradicting and opposing of God's self-declaration would simply be pushed in a hole in the wall and solidly plugged in there, like the spider in J. Gotthelf's story (*Die schwarze Spinne*, 1842). From there it could still be a threat, and might even break out again (possibly only after hundreds of years, but still fairly soon) and spread abroad death and destruction. The pendulum could still swing between Yes and No [cf. Peter Abelard's *Sic et Non*], which is as such an open offense against God. A mere shift in power relations would not in any sense satisfy the honor that is God's due. This cannot be satisfied so long as there is only a partial and provisional superiority of light to the darkness that opposes it, so long as there is only an increase in the knowledge of God and a decrease in the ignorance of God. It cannot be satisfied so long as the iniquitous "and" and *simul* are still there to determine the situation. In such a case it is only with rhetorical exaggeration and deception that one can say that

God's name is now hallowed. The advance of Christianity in the form of success in missions abroad and evangelism at home may well take place. This or that noteworthy reform might well be achieved in the life of the church and its development over against the world. A serious turning might perhaps take place in our own lives. All these things are good. They are even perhaps great things and events. But they are not the sanctifying of God's name by God himself, the hallowing for which prayer is made in the Lord's Prayer. They cannot be this so long as the devil, though humbled, can still be cheerful and sure of his cause in his relations with the good Lord, as Goethe has depicted him with such mastery in the Prologue to his *Faust*. No, "Hallowed be thy name," as a prayer for God's own act to establish his holiness, means, in the words of G. Arnold's hymn, that "God the Lord should crush, break, and destroy all the power of darkness, subject it to judgment, make us certain of victory, lift us from the dust of sins, cast out the serpent's brood, let us find freedom, freedom in the Father's house." What we pray for is the work and word of God, which does not merely limit and weaken the enemy but extirpates it, which does not merely give power and propulsion to his purpose but radically and definitively fulfills it. What we pray for is the hallowing of his name not just in a partial and decisive but in a total and definitive action, whose force does not leave a little opposition and contradiction, but none at all, depriving all ambivalence, balance, and neutrality of its point. What we pray for is that the name, self-declaration, and knowledge of God may win the field as the only truth of all the reality distinct from himself. The sanctifying of God's name, undertaken and accomplished by God himself as we ask of him in the first petition, is the glorifying of his name.

Πάτερ, δόξασόν σου τὸ ὄνομα (Jn. 12:28) is (Lohmeyer, p. 45) an exact translation and interpretation of ἁγιασθήτω τὸ ὄνομά σου (Mt. 6:9; Lk. 11:2). Δοξάζειν, which Luther finely renders as "verklaeren," "to transfigure," means to overcome all misunderstanding and obscurity concerning someone and to set forth and display his true being openly and clearly — the rare μεγαλύνειν is in the offing — to make him known distinctly and unmistakably as the one he really is. In the New Testament the verb is with few exceptions used in both the active and passive with reference to God. It is a peculiarity of John's Gospel that always in it, though not in it alone, δοξάζειν can also denote an action of God, Father or Son.

When John 1:14 says that the community in whose name the evangelist speaks has seen the δόξα of the incarnate Logos of God tabernacling among it, this means that it has seen something that the world does not know but *it* does, namely, who and what Jesus really was. What is said is the same as what the Synoptists say in narrative form in the story of the so-called Transfiguration [Mk. 9:2ff. and par.]. In Johannine terms, it is the Father's business to glorify the Son, to give him glory, and the Son's business to give the Father glory, to glorify him. We also read in Acts 3:13 that "the God of Abraham and of Isaac and of Jacob . . . glorified his servant Jesus."

The same applies to the glorifying of the name of God which is mentioned explicitly only at John 12:28 [cf. Rev. 15:4 (Mal. 1:11 LXX)]. Here in answer to the prayer of Jesus the voice from heaven cries: "I have glorified it, and I will glorify it again." Who else could intervene and speak effectively for God, for the incomparable meaning and content of his name, for the dignity of his self-declaration in contrast to all others? Who else could glorify God's name but God himself? But in glorifying his name God sanctifies it, setting forth his self-declaration in its as yet concealed because unknown particularity, displaying himself as him who alone is holy and his truth as the truth alongside which there is not a second and coordinated truth, which cannot be limited or rivaled by any other truth, which does not merely limit or rival any other truth. In sanctifying and therefore glorifying his name, God has completely eliminated any competing truth and any ambivalent relation between his own truth and all truth that might supposedly compete with it. We are reminded here of the trisagion of Isaiah 6:3: "Holy, holy, holy is the Lord of hosts, the whole earth is full of his glory"; also of passages like Psalm 83:18: "Then shall they know that thou alone . . . art the Most High over all the earth"; also Psalm 148:13: "Let them praise the name of the Lord, for his name alone is exalted, his glory is above earth and heaven"; also Isaiah 42:8 (cf. 48:11): "I am the Lord, that is my name; my glory I give to no other, nor my praise to graven images"; and especially Zechariah 14:9: "And the Lord will become king over all the earth; on that day the Lord will be one and his name one." This—the completed and definitive expansion which needs no extension, the display of this exclusive knowledge of God—is the secret of the name of God which is to be manifested in his glorification, the clarifying and expounding of his true divine being in his revelation as God's own act. This—the final appearing of his name in its distinctive perfection—is its sanctifying accomplished by God himself. That it may take place, that God will end all the division and ambiguity of our present situation, that he will leave no trace of the ambivalence, vacillation, and balance, that God will become all in all (both people and things) (1 Cor. 15:28)—this is what we pray for in the first petition.

So much by way of exposition and paraphrase of the direct wording of the petition. We have not understood it, however, if we do not face and answer correctly two questions that unavoidably arise out of our findings thus far.

The first is simply this. How do those who pray thus—the Christian community and its members, we ourselves—how do we come to know what we have learned to be the object of the first petition of the Lord's Prayer? How has there come into our circle of vision the glorifying of the name of God as his own act in which he removes the division in the relationship between him and us (the world, the church, and ourselves personally), so that there can no longer be any ignorance of God, any darkness, any *simul* of light and darkness, but "they shall all know me, from the least of them to the greatest" (Jer. 31:34)? How can the accomplishment of this glorious change in our whole situation be even prayed for if it is not in some way before our eyes; the far side of all the balance and twilight in which, in great desecration of the name of God, we still exist in relationship to him; the possibility, indeed, the expected reality of the overcoming and removing of all the vacillation, the irrevocable rising of the sun and breaking of the day; God himself as the agent of this radical change? To what extent are we in a position to expect all these things and therefore to know all these things, though naturally at a great height and distance, so that we can only pray that they might happen, that God might cause them to happen? This is the first question that we have to face. If we cannot answer it, then obviously we have not understood the petition that now concerns us and will thus pray it without understanding.

Only one answer can be given. We began our exposition of the petition by stating that it is possible and conceivable only in the hearts and on the lips of people to whom, while God is also largely unknown, he is not just unknown, since in some way he is also well known. We have also to reckon with this objective knowledge of God among those who are outside Christianity, but in this outermost circle there does not, or does not yet, correspond to it a subjective knowledge of God, the thanksgiving and praise that are his due. The distinctive thing about Christians is that even though among them there is still much ignorance of God, nevertheless it is given to them to know God as he is revealed to the whole world and all people in Jesus Christ. The Christian world knows him as the one who has acted and spoken in the history of Jesus Christ. It knows this work and word of God as it happened once and for all but is still present in the power of his Holy Spirit. As God comes before its eyes as the one true and living God, it knows something that is not known by the surrounding world of those who do not believe in Jesus Christ and do not know the God who acts and speaks in him, namely, what the sanctifying or glorifying of God is as the work of his own sovereign act. No more than other people or groups of people does it know this from any other source. It does not know it as the product of a better philosophy accessible to it, for the sanctifying of God's name by God himself, far from being an idea that can be reached by reflection or speculation, is a once-for-all event brought about by God. It does not know it in the light of any achievement in church history old or new. It certainly does not know it in the form of higher or deeper experiences of individual Christians, even the greatest, for such experiences take place in the sphere of division, vacillation, and obscurity, so that they neither were nor are the overcoming and removing of this sphere as such, and they cannot therefore be equated with that for which the first petition asks. To know certain concepts of Christian philosophy or certain high points of Christian life in church history or individual biography is not by a long way to know the total and final sanctifying of the name of God whose subject is God himself. The living community and its living members know this as in the knowledge of their faith they look beyond themselves and all their achievements to him who is the basis of their being and their Head and Lord, being begotten of his living Word and finding their only nourishment in this living Word. In his history, as God's work, there took place the total and final sanctifying of his name. This was not just perhaps a particularly strong and notable strengthening and increasing of the light of the knowledge of God and a happy change in its relation to the darkness of ignorance of God. Quite the contrary: "The Son of God, Jesus Christ . . . was not Yes and No; but in him it is always Yes . . . that is why we utter the Amen through him, to the glory of God" (2 Cor. 1:19f.). "Morning radiance of eternity, Light from uncreated light" (C. A. P. Knorr von Rosenroth), and therefore a morning without evening, was what dawned there, dispersing the darkness, removing any relation of light to it, establishing the sole sovereignty of light, of the knowledge of God, and with it a new era, a new form of the world without division, obscurity, or vacillation. As John 1:14 puts it, "We have beheld his glory." Not a particularly noble and successful warrior but the perfect victor in the battle, the Lord of glory (1 Cor. 2:8), the one who banished conflict as such out of the world, is the one whom the New Testament witnesses perceived in Jesus of Nazareth, in the unique, definitive, and completed divine act of his life and death. "Peace I leave with you; my peace I give to you" (Jn. 14:27). Wherever his work and his living Word are preached and received in the power of the Holy Spirit, wherever they find faith, or rather awaken it, there his coming, his appearing, the dawn of his day is also perceived. Coming from Good Friday and Easter Day, the Christian world knows what it is talking about when it prays God for the hallowing of his name. It is praying for the taking place of the unique and definitive divine act which it knows to have taken place already in Jesus Christ. This is undoubtedly how the answer to our first question must be formulated.

But with this answer there inevitably arises the second question, which is much harder to answer. Christianity knows what it is praying for when it has before it the establishment of the sole sovereignty of light as this has been effected and has taken place in Jesus Christ so as to need no supplementation. To what extent, then, can this also be future? To what extent can and must it be the object of the prayer that it may happen? What is the point of "Hallowed be thy name" when it is perfectly hallowed already in Jesus Christ? In other words, how does it stand with us who are obviously in the middle between the "is" and the "will be"? How does it stand with our "present" as we understood and described it in our first subsection, namely, as that of the absurd vacillation between the knowledge and ignorance of God which dominates and characterizes the situation of the world, the church, and our own personal lives?

The fundamental presupposition in answering this second and more difficult question has to be that none of the three statements that make this question a question must be in any way weakened. (1) We must not reduce in any way the answer to the first question. In the history of Jesus Christ as the New Testament bears witness to it we really do have the already effected and completed victory of light over darkness in the unique and definitive act whereby God himself hallows his name. This was and is already the end of all God's ways, the eschaton. Hence it does not need to be continued or repeated. In it, in the person of him in whom God himself came down to act, the world is already fully reconciled to God, the church is already the pure bride and holy body of his incarnate Son, and every Christian is God's dear child, elected, justified, sanctified, and called by him. (2) Nor must we reduce in any way the statement implied in the first petition of the Lord's Prayer (and not in it alone), namely, that the act of the sanctifying of God's name by God himself, which has taken place once and definitively in the history of Jesus Christ, and which is the origin of the living Christian community and all its living members (for without its revelation and recognition they would not know what they were praying for), is also their future, so that it must always be indeed the object of their prayer. (3) Nor must we reduce in any way what must always be said about the present out of whose confusion and distress Christianity prays as it does in the first petition. There must be no holding back in recognizing the evil of the balance between knowledge of God and ignorance of God which darkens our present because it does despite to God and desecrates his name. There must be no carelessness in relation to the world, the church, and not least of all, ourselves. Any reduction at any one of these points will falsify in advance the answer we give to the second question.

We shall begin with the third point. Looking at the present condition of the world, the church, and our own Christian lives, we neither can nor should view and understand it in any other way than as that of the confusion and distress of the division which desecrates God's name and which consists in the fact that the one, true, and living God is both known *and* (*simul*) unknown, that we live in the twilight between light and darkness, in vacillation between the law of righteousness and that of sin [cf. Rom. 9:31; 7:23, 25]. Why do we protest against the scandal? Why do we suffer under the distress of this contradiction? Why should we not perhaps recognize the ambiguity and see and understand the present more comfortably? Should not the division be construed, perhaps, as a dialectical determination which unavoidably characterizes the meaning and course of all things, the two-sidedness, vacillation, and swing of the pendulum of all events in the world, the church, and ourselves as the natural play of thesis and antithesis, of darkness and light, of harmony and disharmony, which like everything natural may be painful in part but must be finally accepted with humor? In this ultimately synthetic view, might not the "and" and the *simul* appear to be, not only not an objectionable, but in the long run the aptest, wisest, and soundest solution? Why should there not be a profoundly Christian view of the contradiction, namely, that we must bear it worthily and militantly in its painfulness, and yet, because it is what makes life interesting and exciting, we must also come to terms with it and even acquiesce in it? Could it not be a legitimate and comforting consideration that everything is right already in itself, in the immanent course of its existence? In face of the present as it is controlled and characterized by the contradiction, is it really true that there finally remains for us only the profound sighing of an unrest that cannot be allayed; only a No of protest; only an appeal to God himself; only a call for his intervention which will not tolerate the contradiction any longer, which will remove it, which will dispel the mist and twilight, which will render impossible all neutrality and vacillation and every *simul*; only the petition "Hallowed [or glorified] be thy name"; only the cry that God will arise in might and scatter his enemies (Ps. 68:1)? Is there no other possibility? For one convincing reason there is not. If as the living community of Jesus Christ and its living members we cannot escape a final profound disquiet in face of the fact of the juxtaposition of light and darkness which dominates our present, this is because the total and final sanctifying of the name of God and the removal of the juxtaposition has already been revealed to us by the Word—the "Peace be with you" of him who is risen from the dead [Lk. 24:36; Jn. 20:19, 21, 26] — as something that has taken place already in the work of Jesus Christ. This sanctifying of the name of God that has already taken place perfectly in Jesus Christ as God's free act stands in our way, forbidding us to come to terms and be content with the desecration of God's name in our present, as without this veto we would want to do and might do, and as the world which does not know him succeeds thus far in doing. No matter what satisfying points might be made concerning the present state and course of things under the sign of the desecration of the name of God, in face of the cross of Jesus Christ, and as we hear the Word of the cross through him, the risen Lord, they all become flat and hollow, idle chatter that can no longer appease us. For he who died on the cross so hallowed the name of God in his death as the crowning of his life, so confessed God, the one, true, and living God, the God who is divine in his almighty compassion, that all ignorance of God is not only censured and attacked and condemned but also disarmed, destroyed, and done away in his person, and with it the whole juxtaposition of light and darkness, every possibility of regarding their simultaneity and balance as necessary and justifiable and tolerable, and even normal in virtue of some "and" and *simul*. The person who sees and hears him can never be resigned to the present state and course of things, whether mournfully or cheerfully, whether tragically or with some kind of humor. He can only suffer it finally as a disorder that cannot be excused, an evil that cannot be alleviated. He can accept no solution that leads to a recognition of the ambivalence of light and darkness that has been destroyed once and for all in the history of Jesus Christ. Aware of what happened then, he is now forced up against the wall, where he can only bewail with sorrow the present state and course of things in the world, the church, and ourselves, even after the perfect sanctifying of the name of God which took place then, even after Jesus Christ in whom this took place. The basic assertion in answering our question is that what took place then is full of critical dynamic, preventing any easy pacification among those who perceive it, and constituting an irrefutable veto of the compromise of an ambivalence of light and darkness, not only at that time, but on into our present too. What took place then did not take place only in the past. It took place in its own time for every time, for our time, as the unappeasable disquiet into which it plunges us demonstrates. It took place then in the power to raise an unmistakable protest against the dishonoring of the name of God in our present, to characterize it as a scandal which we cannot condone, as a distress which cannot be reinterpreted in any other way. It took place then, and it takes away from us today the possibility of coming to terms and being content with the twilight and balance in which we exist. It took place then, and it forces us today up against the wall where we can only bewail the present and pray that what took place then, the same perfect sanctifying of the name of God by God's own act, may become and remain the future of our present. It took place then in the history of Jesus Christ, and it becomes today not only the prohibition of the same Jesus Christ against our acquiescence in the

desecration of the name of God but also his command: "*Pray* then like this:
. . . Hallowed be thy name."

Our final statement has already brought us into the circle of a broader
assertion which is needed to answer our question. The total and final sanctifying of the name of God that has taken place in the history of Jesus Christ
with validity and power for all times and therefore for our present too, does
not have for us only the critical significance of taking from us all possibility
of being content with the ambivalence that controls and characterizes our
present. It certainly takes this from us, but in so doing it also reveals to us
a new thing, permitting and commanding us to look up and see beyond this
determination of our present to its conquest and removal. "Look up, and
raise your heads, because your redemption is drawing near" (Lk. 21:28). It
would not be what it is if it simply opened our eyes to the intolerable nature
of our present situation, if it simply forbade and prevented the conclusion
of an easy and arbitrary peace with it, if it simply put us at the foot of a
wailing wall where, enlightened unequivocally and hopelessly as to the disorder and evil of this situation of ours, and set in a position where we could
not regard it as acceptable, we could only be silent and let our hands sink.
It would not be the event it is — the event in which God glorified his name
once and for all and not just transitorily — if, even while it signified judgment on our present and consequently on ourselves, it did not also set us
up within this present, orienting us to the once-for-all manifested glory of
God as also the future of this present of ours and therefore the goal of our
existence. It would not be the once-for-all event it is if it allowed us today
to look at it only in retrospect, as though it were the event of a past golden
age that is now unfortunately far beyond us (cf. Hesiod, *Opera et dies*,
109-126), our own past being hopelessly compromised in contrast to it.
No, in the same present in which, startled by that event, we find ourselves
unequivocally accused of desecrating the name of God, it permits and commands us to look for what has taken place in it, that is, to see in the perfect
sanctifying of the name of God that has taken place in Jesus Christ not only
our yesterday but also our tomorrow, not only our whence but also our
whither, to find in him in whom God then acted once and for all the Alpha
and the Omega, the beginning *and* the end (Rev. 1:8; 22:13). He is today
the one he once was yesterday and will be some day — tomorrow. Alive and
present in our present, he is the one who came and will also come again.
If we today really come from him, then necessarily we also go to him.
Grateful that we may know him, we longingly strain to know him again
and afresh: to know him in whose history God himself has glorified his
name. "I *have* glorified it, and I will glorify it *again*" (Jn. 12:28).

The point and meaning of the petition "Hallowed be thy name," and
especially the implied and, at a first glance, very surprising relationship of
perfect and future, is now no longer wholly concealed from us. Answering
the second question, then, is no longer totally impossible.

It is clear that we pray in the midst of our present in which God's name
is not hallowed but is desecrated in the world and even in the church and
our own lives as Christians by the division which dominates all things. But

now we are not abandoned to the scandal and evil of this division nor thrown back on our own resources. We are not directed either to sink into a hopeless silence or assault the clouded and covered heavens with hysterical cries of protest and distress and appeals for help. Jesus Christ lived once, but not only once. As the one who lived once, he also lives today, even in this confused present of ours. As he forbids us to come to terms with our confusion, he also does not leave us stuck in our impasse in relation to it, but shows us the way out by ordering us to turn to God with the request that he himself will take in hand the sanctifying of his name.

It is also clear that he commands us with the authority and credibility of the one in whose history it has already happened that the request has been fulfilled in all its range by God's own act. It was then his own petition: "Father, glorify thy name," and the answer came from heaven: "I *have* glorified it" [Jn. 12:28]. What was to happen was done then in the history of Jesus Christ, and it was done perfectly and definitively. If God had not done it then, Jesus Christ would not be among us today as the living One; for as the one in whose history God did it once, God has made him alive from the dead as him who lives for all time. His command to us that we should make his petition our own would be an empty one if God had not done it, not just because we would not then know what we were praying for, but also because he would then have no authority or power of command over us. We can make this petition only as we come from the one in whom it is already fulfilled.

It is clear finally that the petition that we are commanded to make by him who has the power to command it looks beyond the division of the present in which it is made. With the promise, "I will glorify it again," it looks ahead to its future fulfilment. We are directed to this as we are commanded to pray thus. Future fulfilment means the fulfilment that has the division of our present behind it; fulfilment in its absolute elimination from the world, the church, and ourselves in the same sense in which this has already happened in Jesus Christ; fulfilment in which the whole picture that we had to sketch of the known and unknown God is absolutely wiped out and erased and done away; fulfilment in the fact that God will be all in all (both all people and all things) [1 Cor. 15:28], his name being given the honor that is its due. This is not a different, second, or better fulfilment than that which has already taken place in Jesus Christ. What took place in his history was God's perfect and definitive act of sanctifying his name, which needs no supplementation and certainly cannot be surpassed. The saying from the throne on high, "Behold, I make all things new" (Rev. 21:5), was and is pronounced once and for all. There are, however, two times — a once and a then, a yesterday and a tomorrow — of this one perfect act of God. Our time, our present in division, is the time between these two times of the one act, of the one Word of God spoken in this act. What has still to come for us in terms of the then, the tomorrow that is still future, is the revelation of what took place in the history of Jesus Christ validly, efficaciously, redemptively, and correctively for the world, the church, and each individual. In the division of the present the universal range of what took place once is still hidden from us to the extent that, while we may believe in the Word of God spoken in the resurrection of Jesus Christ from the dead, we cannot see it as yet, either in the world, the church, or above all our own hearts and lives. What we see in these is the misty landscape, the luminous darkness, in which God is both known and unknown. In our time between the times the veil has not yet fallen, so that the already enacted fulfilment in Jesus Christ of the petition "Hallowed be thy name" is still concealed from us today regarding its saving and corrective significance and range in destroying and annihilating all contradiction and resistance and therefore the whole ambivalence of light and darkness. It is still before our eyes in the person of Jesus Christ, who was made alive again from the dead, but only in his person and not yet in the world, nor the church, nor above all our own hearts and lives. Nevertheless, the hallowing of God's name already accomplished in Jesus Christ presses toward the manifestation that will not just lift or pierce the veil here and there but remove it altogether. Hence we are both permitted and commanded to look and wait and move toward the same act and word of God from which we come; more than that, to pray to God that it may be the event of our future, not in greater perfection, but in the revelation of the comprehensive force and significance that are proper to it. The petition "Hallowed be thy name" relates to this last thing. Like the petitions that follow, it prays that the one who came and was manifested once, yesterday, as the First, the πρῶτος, will come and be manifested again then, tomorrow (the morning with no evening), as the Last, the ἔσχατος [cf. Rev. 1:17; 2:8; 22:13]: as the Victor over the division of the present which he already is and as which we may already view him by faith, but then to be seen and looked upon and touched by all and in all (1 Jn. 1:1) as he was by his first disciples at the commencement of his parousia on Easter Day. Along these lines we say with Luther: "Help us in this, dear Father in heaven."

4. THE PRECEDENCE OF THE WORD OF GOD

The order to ask God to hallow his name implies a command to do something ourselves in the matter. How could the prayer be truly prayed in its strict christological and eschatological meaning and content if those who pray it in the present were not summoned to a corresponding use of their freedom as the brethren of Jesus Christ and children of the Father whom they here invoke, if they were not caught up into being and action along the lines of the petition? The law of prayer is the law of action. Calling upon God with this petition is itself an act of their obedience, of their free answer to the command accepted by them. They are forbidden to come to terms and be content with the ambivalent state and course of things, with the twilight and vacillation of simultaneous knowledge and ignorance of God. They are told to turn to God with longing for the great and final day or, rather, for the first true, because lasting and eternal, day, the sabbath day of the light of God which abolishes all the division of the present. Yet their calling upon God with this request obviously would not be an act of obedience — they would obviously be praying it without knowing what they were praying for, or believing that their prayer would be answered — if they did not turn toward the day for whose coming they pray with some movement of their own, if their thoughts and words and works were not drawn into this forward movement toward the day, if their lives were unaffected by the petition, if they were not directed toward its content and goal, if they were not shaped and stamped by looking to this coming day, to Jesus Christ in his future. If it is true that we can only fold our hands when we pray "Hallowed be thy name," that we can expect the answer to it only from God, that we can commend it to him alone, this cannot mean that, this time with profound Christian piety, we may be content to rest quietly in a waiting room in face of the division of the present, intent on the great act for whose occurrence we pray, and leaving the world, the church, and ourselves to the state and course of the great twilight and vacillation. Those who really press and involve God with this petition in the expectation that he will answer it, as people who are seriously and fundamentally disquieted and startled, press and involve themselves too in their own place and manner as people and within the limits of their own human capabilities and possibilities. They declare, and within their limits take on responsibility, that in the matter about which they pray to God something will be done correspondingly by them. In the title of this section we have described as zeal for the honor of God the attitude and conduct of those who pray the first petition of the Lord's Prayer. In our opening remarks we have also called it the great invincible and lasting, if also dangerous, passion of the Christian. The command implied in the order to pray this first petition demands this zeal for God's honor from us. Thus it does not demand an occasional, tepid, and sluggish movement in which we grow tired, are constantly pausing, or even stop altogether. It demands a movement analogous to that which we ask and expect from God. When we call upon God — we recall that he arises in his might and will scatter his enemies and avenge his honor ("As smoke vanishes in the air, as wax melts in heat, destroy their hosts") — when we call upon God in this way, then, without wishing to compare ourselves to God or to replace him, we cannot possibly refrain from rising up ourselves with zeal and burning passion and going toward him and living to him. What we are commanded in and with the order to pray the first petition is that we should rise up in this way.

We have seen that according to the Reformation understanding of the first petition, its goal and fulfilment was that with God's help it might come about that he would be honored and extolled as God through our works and words, through our lives and through our teaching. In the light of the understanding we have now reached, this was not a wrong exposition of the prayer but a truncated one. As a petition it does not look merely to the present and future will and action of men. It looks beyond all present and future human possibilities to the goal of time in the manifestation of Jesus Christ on and through the clouds, in the revelation of the universal significance, power, and scope of the glorifying of God's name that has aleady taken place in his person and history. Calvin was close to this perhaps when he wrote in the Geneva Catechism (1545) that while God's honor can neither increase

nor decrease, we desire that his glory be exalted in everything and in all things
. . . that it be manifested as is its due. Our petition is directed to something that
God should do, that all his works should appear glorious as they are, so that he
should be glorified in every way. We need not decide whether these statements are
meant to be or can be understood eschatologically. Calvin certainly does not give
them a christological basis. But be that as it may, we have now reached the point
where we can seriously adopt what the Reformers had in view in this matter,
namely, the active participation of Christians in the hallowing of the name of God
for which they pray to him. It is undoubtedly true that we have our own part to
play in this matter. That this is so, that the attitude and action of zeal for God's
honor is demanded from Christians, is perhaps fully clear only against the background of the christological and eschatological understanding of the petition that we
have now reached.

The christological and eschatological context in which we must now
speak directly about the ethical relevance of the first petition does, of course,
make some delimitation and clarification necessary. Our part — what is required of us — what we have to contribute and do in the matter, can indeed
only be ours. As already indicated, it can be done only in our human place
and our human manner, only within the limits of our human capabilities
and possibilities. It can be done in obedience to God's command only when
it stays within these limits, so that, taking place in due modesty and honesty,
it is a zeal that is pleasing to God, that is, that corresponds and is analogous
to his divine act. Active participation in the hallowing of God's name is
thus an idea and concept that we are not to reject, but to adopt and validate,
yet which we are to use only after careful consideration and elucidation if
it is to be appropriate to the matter in hand.

The active participation of Christians in the sanctifying of God's name
has been presented and depicted as though what God posited and empowered them for, and required of them, were a zeal for his honor equal to his
own; as though they for their part had to think and speak and act in a
divine way, with divine absoluteness, self-assurance, and authority; as though
they had to be the doers of at least a part of the divine work; as though
they had to share responsibility with God for its occurrence, its success, and
also its consequences. But if there were really given to them the freedom
for such divine being and action, if such divine being and action, a zeal
equal to God's zeal, were really ascribed to them, if their portion could
really be a life in absolute love, purity, integrity, and the like, and therefore
in divine sovereignty, clarity, and perfection, why should they be able to
do only a portion of God's work? What need would there be of another
portion of this work that is enjoined upon God himself? Would not God
become superfluous and, as it were, unemployed if these people were really
at work in his own style and as the achievers of all kinds of absolutes? The
result of such ideas of human participation in the glorifying of God's name
has in fact always been that sooner or later no place is left for God alongside
Christians who live and work in this divine manner. Christians working on
their portion in this divine manner are all that remain. The glorifying of
God's name becomes in fact the glorifying of their own human name. God

may still be mentioned, but he has quietly become irrelevant. Their own wonderful attitudes and acts are at the center of the picture. When the Christian sees himself as the doer of divine acts, in what sense can he still regard it as suitable, necessary, or even possible to pray "Hallowed be *thy* name"? We must be careful lest the goal and end of the way that begins by ascribing to Christians a zeal equal to God's might not be first a secret and then an openly expressed atheism. Warned by this perspective, we do better to renounce at once this idea of the participation of men in what God does. What God commands of us when he bids us pray for the hallowing of his name is certainly not that we should want to act or be like him. Rather, this is forbidden us by his command. We are to play our part but not to try to play his.

The same warning arises out of a consideration of the eschatological character of the petition "Hallowed be thy name." While this petition carries with it the command to play our part in the matter and the need to obey this command, it cannot be the affair of those who pray it to accomplish with their own deeds the act of God for which they pray, to answer themselves the sigh "Amen. Come, Lord Jesus" (Rev. 22:20), and thereby to make it pointless, by following it up with Christlike words and actions. Christians must have forgotten that they are *praying* what they are praying, that they can play their part in word and deed only along the lines of this prayer that looks toward the coming of the Lord, if they regard themselves as subjects who have authority and power to bring in with their own deeds that for which they pray. If we want to take the hallowing of God's name into our own hands, speaking and acting in a divine manner in God's place, then, quite apart from the fact that this is an impossible enterprise fore-doomed to failure, it would in fact result in a further desecration of the name of God. We should also do best to avoid the commonly heard expression that we are to hasten the dawning of the great day by what we can and should do as we move toward it. Prayer may be made that his coming will be soon (ἔρχομοι ταχύ, Rev. 22:20), though astonishingly there is not a single prayer to this effect in Revelation. In no case, however, does it lie within our competence or skill, nor can it be the purpose and point of what we are commanded to do and what we do in obedience to the command, to try to make God hurry up, to stir him up to greater zeal—as though he needed stirring—by active zeal on our part. Those who try to do too much here will in fact do too little, and in their wholly inappropriate identification with God they will not do what they are commanded to do in obedience to him.

Leaps toward the goal that is before us, or even giant steps toward it, absolute attitudes and acts or attempts to achieve such, are not, then, the thing that is required of us and that we have to achieve in correspondence with the first petition of the Lord's Prayer. Since we cannot act as gods, what is required is from the very first a limited action both qualitatively and quantitatively. It is simply our existence in movement, as we pray the first petition, in the everyday affairs of our personal lives and the life of the church and the world. It is our obedience precisely at the point where, coming from the sanctifying of God's name that has already taken place in Jesus Christ, and moving toward its future revelation again in him, we find ourselves as Christians here and now, in the problematic present between the times. It is a matter of the steps that we have to take hour by hour, not accidentally or arbitrarily, but rather, as we pray for the hallowing of God's name, in the manner that corresponds to this petition and the sure and certain answer to it. It is possible and even probable that in the lives of all Christians there will at least be times when great steps, Sunday steps as it were, are at issue and are necessary. Very rarely, there might even be a giant Christmas or Easter step or what is thought to be such. Such steps can be taken only with a certain resolute spring and swing. But they can never be divine steps, and they neither can nor should try to be such. As a rule, the steps will only be little ones, or apparently little ones, made with no particular elevation on the way in our present. But what do great and little mean in this context? Measured by whether it is analogous or not to the hallowing of God's name for which we pray, a supposedly great step might be a fairly small one. Measured by the same criterion, a supposedly little step might really be a very big one. We may simple say, then, that it is a matter of steps that, when we pray the first petition and thus come from Jesus Christ and go to him, we are freed and required to take as people: as people of our time in what is (even in the most extraordinary case) the fairly small sphere and framework of the opportunities we are offered and the possibilities we are given, and in the fairly narrow view of our situation and problems that we usually have, yet still, be that as it may, as the people we now are, as God's children and not as gods.

The limitation of the action required of us does not alter in the slightest the urgency with which it is required. As the people we are, we exist between the times and therefore in the sphere of the great ambivalence of light and darkness that desecrates the name of God. As God's children, as Christians, we also know from what point the world, the church, and we ourselves are coming and to what future the world, the church, and we ourselves are going. This cannot be an idle knowledge. The church and we ourselves as its member are commanded to pray for the future glorifying of God's name. This cannot be in question. As we accept and follow this command, we are set under the power of the living Word of Jesus Christ, always as the people we are, always in the great or small but restricted context of our human existence, yet as God's children. Still in the sphere of that evil ambivalence, we are already put in the very different sphere of the Holy Spirit who awakens, enlightens, comforts, and impels us. Christians are people who, irrespective of the limits of their humanity, are in no way deified but are certainly touched by God; they are no longer left on their own but within their narrower or broader context liberated, called, and set in motion in a specific direction. They are so by God. This is not a motive whose goodness or significance can be debated, which can be obeyed with more or less seriousness, which can even be evaded. It means the irruption into human life of an offer, indeed, a command of incomparable and inescapable urgency and force, of ultimate and total seriousness. It relates only to the possibly great, possibly and usually small, but at any rate human steps in which we never move out of the sphere of ambivalence and can never leave, and ought not to desire to leave, the sphere that is there allotted to us. But the command relates to these human steps of ours, to their form and direction, with all the weight that is proper to it as the command of God. In each of these little steps the great God, as surely as he has loved and loves and will love us again, is supremely interested. What is demanded of us is that we should not take these human steps of ours in disobedience but in obedience to God's command, that we should not evade the living Word of Jesus Christ, the awakening, enlightening, comforting, and impelling of the Holy Spirit, but give these free course and let them do their work in our lives. What is categorically demanded of us Christians is that we should take these steps of ours in all modesty as our responsibility in face of the coming glorifying of God's name by God himself, in face of the sole sovereignty of his light which he will establish — that they should be steps on the way to this goal, distinguished from the steps of other people by the fact that even though they are done here and now in the midst of others, they are done already with a view to this future act of God, and they thus bear witness to this act. Our steps should do this by being, as little human acts, not like the great acts of the great God, yet still, for all the unbridgeable gulf between them, not just unlike but similar. To take these steps which resemble God's own sanctifying of his name, to do so in great humility but also with great resoluteness, this is what is commanded and required of us and what is to be done by us as Christians who are ordered to pray the first petition of the Lord's Prayer: no more than this, but also — the command of God is clear and urgent — no less.

What is demanded of us Christians is no more and no less than zeal for the honor of God. As in awareness of what took place on the day of Jesus Christ, we pray for the dawning of the day of his final manifestation; the twilight that holds sway in the world, the church, and above all ourselves, the regime of vacillation under which we exist, can no longer be tolerable to us but is wholly intolerable. Those who look back to the first revelation of the hallowing of God's name that took place in Jesus Christ, and who also look forward to its second and final revelation, cannot come to terms and be satisfied with the status quo. It would be a sign of threatening spiritual death if a person were to begin to regard it as natural that knowledge and ignorance of God, righteousness and transgression, truth and falsehood, light and darkness should alternate and be evenly balanced in the world, the church, and his own life. In the eyes of the living community and its living members this can be only a or *the* great scandal and never a reality that must be respected, not even in the sense that although they pray "Hallowed be thy name," while the answer to the prayer is still ahead, they acknowledge, tolerate, and leave intact the twilight and vacillation as a state which for the moment is to be accepted as natural and even perhaps necessary and normal. This would be an unbelieving confirmation of the dualism that dishonors the name of God, and it would not be made any better by the mere prayer that this dualism may be overcome, however sincere and earnest that prayer might ostensibly be. For the prayer is not at all sincere and earnest if those who pray it look only to the act of God that sets aside the dualism but in the meantime accept and confirm it by the kind of steps they take. This would obviously be a knavish interim and not just an interim that has the knave "behind it" [hinter ihm" punning on "interim," a proverbial saying]. Necessarily, those who pray for the future sanctifying of God's name cannot accept its present desecration. Necessarily, the movement of their lives will have to correspond to the petition, will have to follow it, in all its humanity. We have seen that it will not do this as the Icarus flight of an enterprise in which it is a matter of taking God's place and acting as he does. But it will be a humble and resolute striding on earth and in time along a way that corresponds in its direction to the act of God which has already taken place in Jesus Christ, but which in its manifestation has still to come and is thus an object of Christian prayer and hope. Beginning to tread this way is demanded, necessary, and unavoidable if we are not to give the lie to our prayer. Just as we cannot by our actions banish from the world the insulting of God that still takes place under the regime of vacillation, so our actions cannot be neutral in relation to this, as though we ourselves were not directly challenged by the ongoing insulting of God. Rebellion and resistance against the regime of vacillation are necessary. It is the command of the hour, of every hour. This command is issued to us Christians in the time between the times, and we have to obey it. Zeal for the honor of God means holy and resolute marching off in that direction. It means revolt. The overthrow of the regime cannot be an affair of our action. That God himself will overthrow it is what we pray for. But to rise up in rebellion against the regime — this is what we want to emphasize — is something that is humanly possible, that we can do. It is the action that is commanded of us on our allotted path.

For all the dissimilarities, this may be compared with the resistance movements, which were not pointless or futile because they obviously could not topple the totalitarian power against which they were directed, but could only question it in practice at various points, bring to light its limits, strengthen nonconformity over against it, issue an impressive warning against collaboration, and keep alive the hope of liberation, which was expected and would come from elsewhere. In the same way, it was not without point or in vain that the Huguenot woman scratched the word "Résistez" on the windowpane of her lonely prison. The angels read this inscription and its message. This was enough, for they undoubtedly carried it further in their own distinctive way. The zeal for the glory of God which is to be put into effect by us Christians can only be an element in this kind of provisional and very relative and modest resistance which often enough will be confirmed and valued only by the angels, though this should be a great comfort to us. What is certain is that we cannot possibly fail to offer it, but must offer it with courage.

Obviously the steps we take in this zeal for God's honor, in this revolt and resistance against the regime of vacillation that insults ourselves as well as God, will always be unlike the act of God in Jesus Christ on which we look back and to which we look forward. One reason for this is that the overthrow of the power against which we offer our little bit of resistance was and is and will be God's work, not ours. Another reason is that, strictly speaking, we can engage only in continual beginnings of resistance, in continually new steps in the allotted direction. A final reason is that even in its best forms our resistance, within its limits, will on good grounds never be more than a very feeble and not a perfect work. Nevertheless, undertaken in obedience and ventured with humility and resoluteness, it will not just be unlike God's act but also like it, running parallel to it on our level, a modest but clear analogue to the extent that it is directed against the abomination that has already been defeated and removed in God's completed act in Jesus Christ and which will be visibly shown before the eyes of all to be a shattered power in the manifestation of Jesus Christ as the goal of our path. It is to this action of resistance against the desecration of God's name that we are summoned—this action which even in its humanity is similar, parallel, and analogous to the act of God himself. It is to this ministry of witness that we are called as Christians. Obedient to this call, and therefore zealous for God's honor, we certainly shall not be like God, but we must not be wanting in fellowship with him.

The title of this last subsection is an attempt carefully but definitely to point to what is at issue in the obedience that is to be rendered in agreement with the first petition of the Lord's Prayer, in the orientation of human action to the hallowing of God's name by God himself as this has already taken place and is still to be manifested, in resistance against the regime of vacillation, twilight, and ambivalence that characterizes our present, in the great or little steps we Christians are required to take in this direction. To sum it all up in a single concept, Christians have to consider, to put into effect, and to confirm the precedence of the Word of God in what they will and choose and do. As they do that, the zeal for God's honor which is demanded of them will properly demonstrate, express, and certify itself. As they do it, their action will look and move toward the act of God for whose enactment they pray with certainty that this prayer is heard. It will be similar, parallel, and analogous to this act. It will be the ministry of witness with which they are charged. They will be obedient when and to the extent that they give the Word of God the precedence that is its due in what they will and choose and do. They would be disobedient if and to the extent that they wanted to, and actually did, deny it this precedence in practice. Christian life, seen and understood in connection with the first petition of the Lord's Prayer, is a life in this order, in this super- and sub-ordination. As it respects and follows this, within the limits which it cannot transcend as human life, and still under the regime of vacillation, it is a special life, different from ordinary human life, yet in its distinctiveness an example and promise for ordinary human life. We shall now consider what the precedence of the Word of God means for the Christian life as the rule and criterion originating in the first petition.

In this context we specifically understand by the Word of God the Word of the living Jesus Christ, in which God in the power of his Holy Spirit has made himself known, and continually makes himself known, to the world, the church, and Christians as members of the church. Christians are people whom this Word has reached in such a way that they have had to confess it, certifying this confession by having themselves baptized. They have heard and received and understood it. They have accepted it in faith, each according to the measure of his faith [cf. Rom. 12:3]. It has been inscribed on the consciousness and conscience of each in his own way. Thus the one, true, and living God is not just unknown to them but also known. Unfortunately, it is still true that he is still largely unknown, that ambivalence also reigns in their lives. This must be expressly remembered. Nevertheless, it would make no sense if Christians, when addressed concerning God's Word, were to act as if they did not know what was meant by it. They are to be addressed on the basis that they have heard it, that they have even begun in due form to answer it, that God is known to them, that his light is not alien in the darkness which surrounds and indeed fills them. To them the saying in Micah 6:8 applies in its full sense: "He has showed you, O man, what is good and what the Lord requires of you."

As the Word of God is spoken to them, they are also told unmistakably that to this factor which has come into their lives and been inscribed on their consciousness there belongs the precedence over all other possible factors. There are in their lives many other factors that speak more or less powerfully and demand to be heard and obeyed. Among them are some that certainly deserve to be acknowledged and respected as such: vocational tasks, fixed obligations to others, special responsibilities, perhaps, in church, state, or society. There are also others that under special conditions and with specific reservations are to be taken seriously: the natural instincts of self-preservation and self-development, the particular love and gratitude that binds them to certain people, well-considered convictions and practical principles. There may be others also that are undoubtedly factors in their lives but do not deserve to be so, and it would be better if they were not: impulses of inner life, inclinations and habits in outer life, outside influences to which they have unwittingly become subject. Whether these factors are positive or negative, however, we shall here group them all together and simply say that in the lives of Christians precedence over all of them is due the Word of God which they have heard. It would be unrealistic to say that they are not factors over against God's Word, that all of them individually and corporately have been erased and set aside as insignificant by God's Word. This would mean that Christians would have ceased to be human. There is no person in whose life other factors are not at work and do not speak, whether de jure, de facto, or both. God's Word no more swallows up man than eschatology does history. The Word of God does, however, bring order into a man's life: super- and sub-ordination. It does this by putting itself at the head of all the active and speaking factors in his life. It would not be God's Word if it allowed some other factor to take this place or to be at the head with it. It cannot be regarded and treated as simply one factor among others. In relation to all the others, even the most significant, there belongs to it, no matter what may be the result, the first place — precedence, priority, primacy: apparently as the first among equals, but in reality as the first among unequals; effectively the first in its dissimilarity from all the other forces that lay claim to man. No matter what may be the worth, importance, or urgency of other forces as they legitimately or illegitimately speak, in the lives of Christians the Word of God is to be heard first, and only after it has been heard is the voice of the other factors to be heard too.

Why this order? The Word of God, which the Christian has heard and may, it is to be hoped, hear again, is among all the factors that determine his life the only one that works and speaks unequivocally. In making God known, already in the present it points radically, unbrokenly, and definitively beyond the regime of vacillation and ambivalence that characterizes the present. It points beyond the evil "and" and *simul*. It points beyond the whole world of balance and compromise, which is untenable and intolerable even in its best and most unavoidable forms. As the Word of Jesus Christ, as the message of the act whereby God perfectly sanctified his name in the crucifixion, as the Word of him who is risen from the dead, it is also the firmly established and intrinsically clear promise of the morning without evening, the truth without contradiction, righteousness without resistance, peace without end. As God speaks his Word, he makes himself known to those who receive and accept it as the one who has overcome the division in his creation in which we exist and who will manifest this defeated division, and therefore his own glory, before the eyes of all. In the lives of those who recognize it, this gives his Word a distinction, a majesty, a dignity, which marks it off and differentiates it absolutely from all other factors in their lives when it comes among these factors and close to them, no matter how estimable or worthy or significant or positive these factors may be, no matter how seriously they must be taken. None of these other factors has the character of a promise pointing beyond the sphere of ambivalence. They are all equivocal, and they speak equivocally. Among all the other forces that move people, there is none that does not have a negative side as well as what may be a very positive side. All the other possible or effective factors in their lives are dialectical and speak dialectically. They can point upward here today and downward there tomorrow. They are all complementary. Even at best they presuppose their opposite. Though they may not include it within themselves, they certainly produce it. They make it unavoidable. At the least, then, they confirm the division of light and darkness. They may deepen and sharpen it. They may give fresh nourishment to the incipient demand for agreement, compromise, and armistice, and therefore to the validity of the law of this aeon. They cannot arrest the desecration of God's name; they can only continue it in some way. They will do this unless their usurped sovereignty is taken from them; unless they cannot claim, either together or individually, the primacy in human life that ultimately and decisively determines what is willed and chosen; unless they are brought under the direction and control of a very different and superior factor; unless they work themselves out and express themselves only under the direction and control of this factor. This other factor is the Word of God, which unequivocally opposes the regime of vacillation and unequivocally points beyond it. It is the Word of God as the Word of the hallowing of God's name in the act that is past in Jesus Christ and still future in the manifestation of this act. In the power of its distinction, this Word, when received by us, sets itself irresistibly at the head of all the factors that determine our lives. Hence the order. For all those who want to be obedient to God in accordance with the petition for the hallowing of his name, it is surely obvious and self-evident that they must adapt and subject themselves to this order, that what they choose and will and do must take place within the framework of this order.

"The *precedence* of the Word of God" — note that this is a fairly restrained expression to denote the order of the Christian life. One might ask whether it is not too restrained when one considers that what is at issue here is the new life that we may and should live on the basis of the cross of Christ, in fellowship with him the risen Lord, in movement toward the fulfilment of his manifestation, not a life according to the flesh but according to the Spirit [Rom. 8:4]. Should we not have spoken, not just of the precedence, but rather of the *lordship* of God's Word over all other factors in life, not just of their direction and control by God's Word, but of their *subjection* to its lordship? The phrase "precedence of God's Word" is perhaps a little weak, yet it is appropriate — this is why we chose it — when our task is that of trying to understand and characterize zeal for God's honor very plainly as an action which may be ascribed to us people, which is humanly possible, which is practicable on the assumption, of course, that we are living members of the living community and hearers of the Word of God. Would we not be guilty of doing something that is unfortunately all too frequent in the language of the church, namely, filling our mouths with grandiose speech, saying too little in too big words, if we were to tell Christians that they had to establish that lordship and practice that subjection in their own lives? Would this not be asking for something ethically attainable, something they could and would practice? To allow and give the Word of God the precedence over other constitutive factors in their lives — that is something that *can* take place. It *can* be done. Here the Holy Spirit can enlighten, command, and help. Presupposing that the Word of God is also a factor in our lives, even though at first it seems to be only one among others, we can attain and put to work the simple insight that this factor so differentiates itself from all others that it does not just stand in line with them but, stepping out, belongs at their head, so that no matter how it may be with the other factors that also act and speak, in the choosing and willing of our steps, of our thoughts and words and works, we have always in all circumstances to give it the priority and consult it first. Whether we do that, and with what steadfastness and strength we do it, are separate questions. But we *can* do it. Nothing superhuman is being asked when we are told — when we are all told — that if we are to be obedient we *must* do it, that it is disobedience not to do so.

In what follows we are presupposing that the other, equivocal factors will always be present in the life of the Christian, will always be at work and speak too, will always claim him in their own ways. In hearing God's

Word, he is also God's creature, a natural and spiritual being, existing in his own place in the narrower and wider spheres of human society, concerned very intensively about his self-preservation and self-development, a worker, a fighter, also in many respects a more or less involved spectator in what others do, and sometimes simply wanting pleasure. Both inwardly and outwardly he too is exposed to all kinds of hindrances and attractions. The Christian too is engaged in the struggle for existence in the broadest sense, and he has to endure a particular part of the pain of the creaturely world and especially of humanity, and all this in the perverted way which is peculiar to man as the creature of God but which constantly resists the grace of God, and therefore he is a rather strange saint. Again, there can be no question of trying to ignore or eliminate these other factors. We would not be human if they did not claim us. We live as human beings as we wrestle with their claims day by day and hour by hour, now regarding this one, now that, as the most urgent and important, and choosing, willing, deciding, and acting accordingly. The question is whether our way of dealing with them is accidental, arbitrary, or at least self-willed, or whether it is necessary because commanded. We Christians also live in the struggle with these other factors. From the highest and noblest of them to the lowest and most dubious, they are at work in us, they speak to us, and we have to pay heed to them in one way or another. Because they are all so equivocal, this might mean that in our choosing, willing, deciding, and acting, in our thoughts and words and works, we Christians continue — not very comfortably, but conveniently, since we see no other option beyond this state and course of things — to affirm the regime of ambiguity and vacillation which is as such the great desecration of the name of God. This side of the coming of the eschaton and the appearing of the eschaton, and within the limits of our humanity, there can be change, not total, only by way of intimation, yet still change when we do not refrain from doing what we can, but do it, and when we do not do what we can refrain from doing; when we grant to the unequivocal Word of God, which speaks of God's perfect act, the position that is its due at the head of all the factors that claim us, when we resolve at all costs to hear its claim first and only then, as determined by this claim, the claims of the other factors. If we then have to choose between these, taking some more seriously and some less, this will not take place in a vacuum. It will not take place simply according to our own contingent impressions, feelings, and inclinations, or no less abstractly according to what may be our well-considered and even clever and right, yet still self-willed, evaluation, but according to the standard and under the direction of the claim of the factor that is superior to all of them, and along the lines indicated by this claim. Along these lines they too should be heard and considered, and they should partly determine what we choose, will, decide, and do, but only along these lines and as authorities that only partly determine and do not guide and control us. I live and think also as a man who in soul is constructed and talented thus and thus: as Homo sapiens, Homo faber, Homo ludens, as father, businessman, teacher, as patriot with obligations here or there, as thinker oriented more idealistically or more positivistically, as a man with this or that political or aesthetic gift, and simply as a sexual being with all that that implies. So be it. Yet I live, think, and act as, above all things, I hear the Word of God. For us Christians, who pray the first petition of the Lord's Prayer, our thoughts and words and works cannot result merely in a sanctioning of the status quo of our being in the world of ambivalence, in the recurrence of all things, on the roundabout of the "and" and *simul* which are so insulting to God, of the knowledge and the ignorance of God. They will in fact lead to this, however, if we leave their guidance and control to the other factors, or to one of them, even the most worthy and important. Where the Word which speaks of God's perfect act of sanctifying his name and its future manifestation is not just heard but is also given its due primacy over all other factors, there will necessarily be acts that repudiate the status quo, the law of the recurrence of all things. In these acts of repudiation is actualized the Christian's wrestling with the other factors that partially determine his life. The result of this wrestling will be that he will pay heed to their claims but accept them as only partially determinative along the lines indicated by the primacy of the Word of God. This will mean, however, that in handling them under the control of God's Word there will arise within the world of ambivalence certain emphases on the knowledge of God over against the ignorance of God, and these will necessarily take the concrete form of preferences for one of the other factors over one or all of the rest. In testimony to the untenability of the balance, or, positively, to the superiority of the knowledge over the ignorance of God, of the light over the darkness, and therefore as an act of repudiation of the regime of vacillation, greater weight will be given to one of the factors over one or all of the others (ambivalent as they all are in themselves). The claim of this one factor will be respected and the claims of the others at least temporarily set aside in its favor. The possibilities it offers will be chosen, willed, and actualized, while the other possibilities will not be chosen, willed, and actualized for the time being. In this hour and this situation this action must be seen as important and performed; others at the moment must be set aside as less important or not important at all, and they must at least wait, even if they are not discarded altogether. This must not be done, of course, according to my own whim or ever so deep intuition ("I feel it" [the characteristic phrase of Zinzendorf]). Nor must it be done according to some intrinsic value or importance of this or that possibility. Nor must it be done according to its a priori precedence over others. It must be done as and because it acquires this precedence under the guidance and control of the Word of God, which is above all human possibilities; as and because the Christian, as he prefers it to all others and seizes it, has to resist in practice the regime of vacillation and bear witness to the superiority of light over darkness, here in the present in which this may not be seen and indicated but has to be believed and then attested by the one who knows it in faith. The steps that the Christian takes in obedience are movements testifying to the victory of God, which has already taken place but has yet to be manifested.

These are all interim steps. They can have no more than provisional and relative significance and range. We recall that if all is not to be lost, the Christian himself must not in any circumstances ascribe definitive and absolute significance and range to them. He cannot be, and should not try to be, a Christian Hercules. He can neither repeat nor anticipate God's victory. He can serve only as its mirror. His decision to give God's Word priority over all the other factors that partly determine his life, his good resolve to hear and respect these others only along the lines indicated by the first factor, will never be securely and once and for all behind him no matter how great may be his willingness and readiness. Nor especially will be the certainty of his confirming it on the path that he has entered and in the obedient preferring now of this possibility and now of that. His decision and resolve and confirmation can only be a matter of ever new hours and situations. When, following the direction of God's Word, he ventures to emphasize and prefer some human possibilities over others, displaying in them, as in a mirror, the superiority of light over darkness and thus bidding defiance to the regime of vacillation, he can never create and introduce facts that speak unequivocally, since there is no unequivocal human possibility. Even the most powerful emphases, for example, the emphasis on love as against the impulse of self-preservation, or the emphasis on convictions and principles as against personal inclinations or the conventions of the world around, or the emphasis on social interests and obligations as against private ones — all these emphases are still made in the sphere of ambivalence and can never leap out of it, and so they are always open to misunderstanding. Far from the sanctifying of God's name becoming his own act, he cannot even manifest it; at best he can only bear witness to it. Regarding the power of his witness, he is always thrown back on its verification by God himself, on the testimony of the Holy Spirit hastening to help him. He will finally offer resistance to the regime of vacillation but he will not overthrow it, nor can he emerge as victor and triumph with any of the steps that he takes. Even when he has done all that he has been told to do [Lk. 17:10], he will still at best be far behind in his duty. He will have cause for the greatest modesty, and he will have new cause every day in relation to even the wisest and bravest steps that he takes. He will have the most solid of all reasons to understand what he does, his zeal for the honor of God, only as the necessary annex to his prayer, "Hallowed be thy name."

One thing, however, he will never have cause or reason to do, namely, to refrain from action like the lazy servant of Matthew 25:24ff., either on the ground that too much is asked of him in view of his powers, insights, and prospects of success, or later with the request to be excused because he has done enough and is too tired to do more. If the annex of action is missing, then the first petition (and with it the whole of the Lord's Prayer) becomes no more than idle chatter in his heart and on his lips, and he would do best to stop praying it altogether. The problem of the desecration of God's name in the world, the church, and his own personal life is an actual one every day. No less actual is the command and permission to pray to God that he himself will hallow it. The word "actual" comes from act. It demands an active disposition. The intolerableness of the status quo of vacillation between light and darkness, between the knowledge and the ignorance of God, in which the Christian exists, and the petition that is placed in his heart and on his lips for the hallowing of God's name, are together the demand for the disposition which has now been generally described, that in which he will modestly but resolutely give God's Word the precedence over the claims and promises of all the other possibilities that present themselves, and in which, under the guidance and control of God's Word, he will choose and actualize those possibilities that best serve to testify to the superiority of light over darkness, most effectively contest the regime of vacillation, and most clearly make known the promise of morning without evening. There is demanded of him with great passion this zealous action for the honor of God. Be it noted that so long as he lives he is always caught up in some zeal and some action. The question is not whether he will do something but whether he will do that which corresponds to this demand, whether he will do what he does in zeal for the honor of God. In doing it he will not be asked concerning the great or little strength that he brings to the task, nor concerning the urgency of the other motives that impel him, nor concerning the greater or lesser endowment with which he comes to the task, preferring this one and rejecting others, nor concerning the power of the witness he may accord to his action, nor concerning the success that he might expect from it. He will be asked only whether he is willing and ready to embark on this action. And this question, to his salvation, can never in any place, time, or situation leave him completely at ease.

We conclude with a discussion of the beginnings which the Christian finds he is required to make in the interim, because he is still in the kingdom of division and twilight but already also a hearer of the Word of the sanctifying of the name of God that has been achieved and is yet to be manifested. Assuming that he is a person for whom this requirement is too strong to be avoided, and assuming that in the sense of the first petition he seriously wants to be a Christian who must simply and soberly resist the great ambivalence in which the world, the church, and he himself exist, giving the Word of God the precedence over all the other factors and motives that also determine his life, what beginnings will he have to venture on this basis? In what acts and conduct will he have to be zealous for the honor of God on these assumptions? As we have established in the second subsection, he exists simultaneously in three circles, as a child of the world among children of the world, as one of the members of the Christian church, and also in the relative isolation of his personal Christian life: all in inseparable unity but also in individual particularity. The general answer that must be given here will be most clearly perceptible if we try to give it with reference to each of these three circles in particular.

1. It is advisable to begin this time with the innermost circle: the personal life of the individual Christian. This is not because the question of what each Christian must be and do for the salvation of his soul is more

important than the question of what he must be and do in the church and the world, or as though the latter question could be replaced or rendered superfluous. What he is for himself he is also as a living member of the church. And what he is as a living member of the church he can be only in and for the world. In all three circles he is a person from whom zeal for the honor of God is required. Nevertheless, what this may mean for himself, for his personal being and action, is not just a special question but the one that is nearest to hand, so that as a rule it needs to be answered first. It is a test question for the obedient character of his whole enterprise to the extent that in the church and the world he can be obedient, and can behave and act obediently, only in the same sense and measure as he is first obedient in the sphere of his own inner and outer life. What he is and does here is important, not apart from, but precisely in relation to, what he is and does there, in the church and the world. It is precisely in that relationship that the question of what he is and does here in the narrowest circle acquires and has its relatively independent significance and commends itself for consideration before the other two questions. Summoned to commence action corresponding to the first petition, the Christian first encounters — himself.

There was once the danger of an ethics too strongly oriented and even restricted to the Christian individual. In view not only of the strong piety that still exists in the churches, but also of the incisive influence of Kierkegaard in theology, one can hardly say that his ethical individualism has been eliminated. Yet modern discussion has had the result that it is no longer a danger and need not be suspected as such. Indeed, another danger is perhaps just as great today as the pietistic one. This arises out of the widespread tendency to omit, to leave aside as not too important, the question of what the Christian is commanded to do and to do in his personal life, and to turn instead to what he is to be and to do outside, in the church and the world, in answer to the problems that await him there. This procedure usually avenges itself. What we are or are not in the innermost circle, what we do or fail to do there, what we do rightly or wrongly, will always be ultimately decisive for what we are and do in the outer circles. Faithfulness or unfaithfulness, seriousness or lack of seriousness in the one will sooner or later bring about the same in the others. If, then, we are not to end up in blind alleys there, we do well to weigh our steps and place them cautiously here at the starting point. If we do end up in blind alleys there, we are well advised to turn around and redirect our steps there from a better starting point here. In no circumstances may one let drop the personal question or deal with it only distantly and superficially.

As we have seen, the Christian — each Christian in his own way — exists in the intolerable contradiction of Yes and No. This is for him the contradiction between his election and calling, on the basis of which he has no alternative but the free and unconditional obedience of the children of God, and the absolutely inexplicable and inexcusable being, action, and conduct of a person who deals with God as with one unknown to him — at one and the same time *(simul)* both righteous and sinner. Because as a Christian he knows the nature of the contradiction, this means that he himself shares some responsibility for the desecration of the name of God which marks our whole present. It is in relation to his personal situation first that he is given the freedom, but also the command, to pray "Hallowed be thy name," and with this he is summoned to the action, the zeal for God's honor, which corresponds to that prayer. The question is: What kind of action can and must this be in the innermost circle? What can and must be meant by zeal for God's honor in this specific situation of his? We have seen very generally that he will have to grant and allow to the Word of God, the Word of the hallowing of God's name that God himself has already accomplished and has yet to manifest, the precedence that is its due over all other factors and motives; that he will have to think and speak and act in the order prescribed thereby. He will have to keep to the same order in what he does and does not do in the church and the world as well. First, however, we shall try to outline what life in this order involves in his personal existence as it is entangled in that absurd contradiction.

Two extreme answers to this question must be ruled out in advance. The first is that the Christian can never in any circumstances, whether in intention or result, think and speak and act as though God were unknown to him. He can indeed deal with God as though he did not know God. He can achieve insolent, indolent, and untruthful thoughts and words and acts in which he obviously seems to have forgotten that God is his Father and he his child. By sinning he can show palpably that he exists in that contradiction, that God is in fact unknown to him. He not only can do this; he does it every day and every hour. In so doing, he incurs some personal guilt for the regime of the balance of light and darkness, so that he cannot just perceive and bewail and condemn it outside in the church and the world. He can fall, and he does so again and again. But he cannot do more, or even try to do more. He cannot fall into the abyss. He can love darkness rather than light [Jn. 3:19]; he cannot decide for darkness. He can have dealings with the devil; he cannot validly sell out to him. He can go astray; he cannot simply be lost. He can become a Judas; he cannot cease to be an apostle. He cannot reverse his election and calling, which are not his own work but God's. He cannot make himself again a man to whom God's Word has not been spoken. Even though he acts contrary to it a thousand times, he cannot alter the fact that the precedence of the Word over all the other factors in his life pertains to him and that he knows very well it does. He cannot break away at least from the goad that pricks him or the hand stretched out to him from there. A Christian is a person who is grasped and held by God and cannot escape his claim. He can undertake and do many things against God but not against the fact that God knows him and is also and always well known to him.

The other extreme to be ruled out is sainthood: the Christian cannot be a saint, a person who, again in intention and result, can be determined only by his knowledge of God. He can think about God with what may be great seriousness. Even when he goes astray, he is never just bad. He is also capable of good thoughts and words and works. Time and again, and sometimes with considerable force, he can turn away from darkness to the light. At this point or that he can even be a resolute and not unsuccessful fighter for the light and against darkness. He is certainly not just a sinner. Primarily and supremely on the basis of his election and calling, he is also righteous. It may well be — there are plenty of good Christians of whom this is true — that his life as a whole, at least when seen from a particular angle and by close and well-disposed observers, shows more bright than dark features. Nevertheless, no Christian has demonstrated and presented himself in a life that simply follows a consistent course from his election and calling, simply as a victorious fighter against sin, death, and the devil, simply in attestation of his knowledge of God, simply as a figure of light. Indeed, the most remarkable Christian personalities are as a rule the very ones whose image is marred by the heaviest shadows and the deepest problems of character, habits, and decisions. And who among us less interesting Christians does not display some obvious weakness or distortion, some small error or confusion, that calls into question the better things that might be reported of him? If the Christian cannot fall into the abyss with his acts, good care is taken that he also cannot mount to heaven, but that he confirms in his own way the regime of twilight and balance. Necessarily, the sanctifying of the name of God has to be God's own work over against that of the best or the good Christian. The Christian prays for this sanctifying, but he cannot expect its achievement from what he himself does; he cannot even make it his own task.

What the Christian can and may and must do is never determined merely by his ignorance of God on the one side or his knowledge of God on the other. It will never be an action that is either pure light or pure darkness. Even at worst it will not be demonic, and even at best it will not be angelic. As human action, it will take place somewhere between these extremes. It is here that God's Word reaches and touches and frees and claims the Christian. It is here that God discloses himself to him as the one who has already achieved the sanctifying of his name and will universally and definitively manifest it with his glory. It is here that he permits and commands man to call upon him, "Hallowed be thy name." It is here that he also demands of him the action corresponding to this petition. It is here that he demands that the Christian be obedient to his Word, that he give it precedence, that he place all that he wishes, wills, and does under its direction and control. It is here — within the lower and upper limits denoted by those extremes — that he has to go his way and take his steps, totally resolute yet totally modest, totally fearless yet totally without illusions, totally courageous yet totally humble. It is here that with his hidden or open action or refraining from action he has to bear witness to the gospel before the face of God and man and also before the eyes of angels and demons. In answering the question of what we must think and speak and do according to the first petition of the Lord's Prayer precisely in the relative loneliness of our Christian lives, not everything, but a great deal at least is gained when it is clear to us that in all cases we have to move in the place between those extremes and in respect for the law that is posited by the borders of this place.

It would not be good, however, to spend too much time recollecting this rule as such. The Christian's action in the unity of courage and humility, commanded in the limits of his place, cannot be regarded as an end in itself. This might be merely a variation of Stoic ethics. As a hearer of the Word of God, the Christian has to accept a certain responsibility within the limits of his place and under the law posited thereby. He knows, indeed, he has been told, that the dualism which rules this place and his whole situation, and which is reflected plainly enough in the two-sidedness of what is a good and necessary rule (things being as they are), cannot seriously and finally be the norm, but can be only a provisional norm that is valid only *per nefas*. The Word of God reaches and touches and frees and claims him on the assumption that he still exists in the sphere of dualism. Yet it does not confirm or sanction, but radically challenges that assumption. To him who first in his personal action and refraining from action shows palpably enough that he exists under the regime of vacillation, twilight, and ambiguity, it reveals as the great new factor the glorifying of God's name that has been accomplished and will be demonstrated, and with it the true starting point and goal of the Christian life. To him who is subject to the law of this regime it already proclaims this gospel. It places his present, the present of one who bears some personal guilt for the strength of this regime, under the promise that in this present, in which he has no lasting city (Heb. 13:14), he comes from Jesus Christ and goes to him as the morning without evening, the light without shadow. It thus commands him — not in an empty, formal, or moralistic way — to live with that courage and in that humility, to collect his thoughts and words and works modestly but resolutely in the petition "Hallowed be thy name," and in accordance with this petition modestly but resolutely to orient himself to the act of God from which he comes and to which he may go. To him, who has not deserved this, there is granted and ascribed, as he is summoned to this petition and the corresponding action, the trust and honor of personal responsibility for making perceptible this gospel of God through the dedication and service of his life, of being instituted as a witness to it. He, this man, as he displays in the fulfilment of his thoughts, words, and works the true beginning and the true end of his way, has to be a witness to the beginning and end of all ways. He is chosen and called to do this. This is why he is kept from falling too far or rising up too far. This is why his action cannot be demonic and may not be or try to be angelic. As one who is chosen and called, he has to accept and carry responsibility that the gospel of him who is the Alpha and the Omega [Rev. 1:8; 21:6; 22:13], of the hallowing of God's name that has already taken place in Jesus Christ and will in the future be manifested in him, will not be hidden but declared in the present that is still overshadowed by that dualism as already a radical challenge to it.

It is not the case, then, that the Christian in his sphere, with both its lower and upper limits, can take his ease when he considers that he can neither rise up too far nor sink down too far. If he does, he fails to see why he is assigned to this place midway between demons and angels: that precisely here as man he is addressed by God and summoned to set out and make himself God's witness on the way, pursuing this way, not as one who reveals, but certainly as one who bears witness to the unequivocal Alpha and Omega. In this midway place there is for him no resting, let alone settling down and making himself at home. In this midway place he can only be on the road as a pilgrim. He would have to neglect the honorable task with which he has been entrusted if he were to delay and tarry here. Indeed, to do so would at once mean his acknowledgment of the status quo, of the regime of vacillation, twilight, and ambivalence, of the "not only . . . but also," which he is nominated to resist. He would then be obviously recognizing and agreeing that this is how things must be just now, that they must be accepted until God's future intervention, that he is both righteous *and* a sinner, belonging to the light in his knowledge of God and to the darkness in his ignorance of God. Resting and reposing in his inner division, he would confess this as a waiting room which has been built and set up for a period, as a possible and even perhaps a not wholly uncomfortable shelter. In this respect, however, the Christian cannot come to terms and agree with the God who speaks to him, and therefore he cannot do so with himself. He can never be happy under that regime which is so strong even and precisely in his own thoughts, words, and works. He can never be reconciled to the sense of malaise it causes him, as though this were just an annoying sickness but one he could put up with. The ground beneath his feet is on fire here. He can only hurry, move, and run. The unrest that the Word of God has brought into his life will never leave him so long as he has this life. It will never release him from brave wrestling with that regime, whose fall and end he hopes and prays that God will bring about even in his own lifetime. None of the movements he makes in this struggle can be anything other than a small or great movement of resistance: an attempt to check his own all too powerful tendency — the tendency of his soft-living flesh — to compromise, to make a concordat, to conclude an indolent peace; or, more positively, an attempt willingly and readily, not shamefacedly but in all humility and modesty, with uplifted head to move toward the manifestation for which he hopes and prays. With purely provisional and relative, yet still with definite, steps, he will venture to contradict the contradiction in which he finds himself entangled, to speak here and now a clear and impatient practical No to his own toleration of the contradiction, to speak a No grounded in the great Yes of the gospel accepted by him, or, again positively, to set up against it a sign of the hope that lives in him. The Christian would be no true man, or would know himself poorly in his humanity if, apart from all that he sees outside himself, he did not see the whole stream of his own human thought and feeling, desire and will, flowing down strongly to the ocean wastes of compromise between light and darkness. But the Word of God, which has made him a witness to the light without shadow, wants from him the big but not impossible thing that precisely as a person, no matter what may be the result, he should not flow with the stream, but that following the lead of the Word and accepting its discipline, he should continually swim against it. He can have peace with himself only as he finds peace with God. He can find peace with God only as, contrary to himself and his tendency to make peace between light and darkness, he acknowledges that the One who speaks his Word to him is in

the right and he himself, hoping in God, is in himself in the wrong. Any
human thought that is thought in this movement, any human word that is
spoken in it, any human deed, however small, that is done in it, will be
well thought and spoken and done, fulfilling the task or witnessing to the
gospel that is laid upon the Christian and being accepted as well-pleasing
to God. If there burns in him the great and lasting, if dangerous, passion
of zeal for the honor of God, he will find himself in this movement which
is neither demonic nor angelic but truly human. Very provisionally and
relatively, at first occupied with himself—for it is he who is reached, touched,
freed, and claimed by God's Word—then enlightened to choose and will
aright, and in this sense concerned only about his soul, he will think the
thoughts and speak the words and do the significant or insignificant deeds
of hope that point in this direction, and he will thus venture that resistance,
suppressing as far as possible thoughts of another kind, leaving unspoken
as far as possible words of another kind, leaving undone deeds of another
kind. How could he be a Christian if this passion, even though deeply
buried under all manner of ashes, did not burn in him? Seriously to want
to be a Christian means giving this passion free rein. It means doing so first
in this innermost circle, in the encounter with oneself, in the inwardness of
one's own moral, intellectual, and social existence. It means zeal for the
honor of God in the form in which it is in fact primarily and most urgently
demanded.

2. Yet we cannot stop here. This cannot be the end of the organization
or reorganization of the resistance which to God's honor is to be modestly
but resolutely offered in the life of the individual Christian. The Christian
is in the church. He is not just in it externally, accidentally, or incidentally.
He is not in it merely in the sense that he might first be a more or less good
Christian by his personal choice and calling and on his own responsibility
as a lonely hearer of God's Word, and only later, perhaps optionally and
only at his own pleasure, he might take into account his membership in the
church. If he were not in the church, he would not be in Christ. He is
elected and called, not to the being and action of a private person with a
Christian interest, but to be a living member of the living community of
the living Lord Jesus Christ. It is by the Word which gathers and builds up
this community and calls it to service that he is made personally responsible.
The church's witness to the act of sanctifying his name which God has
performed and will reveal is the witness with which he is most urgently
commissioned. It is as one of this people, standing for all and for the cause
of all in his own person, that he may and should pray, "Hallowed be thy
name," and that even though he is still subject to the regime of division
which desecrates God's name, he is already required to make that movement
of hope and resistance and therefore, zealous for God's honor, to live a
Christian life.

J

It would be most inappropriate to obscure or even deny that the saying *Hic
Rhodus, hic salta* (cf. Aesop's Fables, 33) also applies very seriously to this central
sphere which we are now considering. Here again, without either reservation or limit,

the reference is to the existence of the Christian. It was an historically understandable and not unjustifiable reaction, but it led to a distortion of the whole complex of problems, when in the steps of Kierkegaard — and even further back, Pascal — an existential character was ascribed to Christian being and action only in the innermost circle of the encounter of the Christian with himself, or it was recognized again only with reference to the Christian relation to the world, a leap being made over the middle circle to the outermost of the three. Certainly the Christian, when he is commanded to get going in accordance with the first petition, will first of all encounter himself in his personal situation — this is why we dealt with this first. Certainly he will encounter himself again in his quality as a child and citizen of the world. Nevertheless, these two do not exclude but include his being and thinking and speaking and acting in the church as well, not just peripherally but centrally, not just technically but materially, not just as a spectator but with total involvement. Hence the question how and in what sense he has to do this must be asked here with the same emphasis. Since the problem of the church always presents itself no matter how we deal with it, a failure to recognize this will have fatal consequences on two sides.

First, in allowing the Christian to set himself at a distance from the church, this failure evokes a type of criticism of it which, even though its reproaches and complaints may be very largely correct, will necessarily be sterile because those who make it have either never accepted or have thrown off with a sharp jerk the burden of personal responsibility for what the church is or is not, for what it does or refrains from doing, for what it does well or badly. Thus they now speak about the church and against it, perhaps with sharp cuts and dazzling light, yet externally, without serious engagement, without having made its cause their own, in an inward or outward detachment. They speak as though it were a matter for other folks, the pastors, or boards, or the mass of perdition of much scolded churchly Christians, they themselves being isolated and playing no practical part. Not every leap out of a boat is like Tell's (cf. Schiller's *Wilhelm Tell*, Act 4, Scene 1). An inner or outer leap out of the church is surely no leap at all. Again, the failure creates a vacuum in the middle circle that no amount of witty and supposedly prophetic and reforming criticism of the church can fill. It plainly evokes a correct longing for the church which sooner or later will result in a strong susceptibility to a conception in which what is missed will express itself all the more strongly, uncontrolled because of that failure. Was it not a fact that an existentialism that bitterly and arrogantly bypassed the problem of the church opened up more than once some very interesting ways to Rome? Might not Roman Catholicism — there are other affinities as well — show itself one day to be in greater measure the almost naturally necessary complement of this kind of existentialism? Be that as it may, fruitful consideration of the whole complex which now concerns us will always have to start with the fact that in the church, as in his own life and the world, the Christian is totally involved. In this middle circle too he is fully responsible both in what he is and in what he does.

As a member of the church, the Christian comes up at once against the dominating picture of the same division and contradiction that he knows only too well from his own life. As in his own life, so in the church he also comes up against the powerful tendency to accept this fact, to come to terms with the great Yes and No, to acquiesce in the regime of vacillation. Not that the church does not feel this to be a problem and try to deal with it. Do we not find even in the peaceful periods of church history a secret and perhaps even an open concern for better preaching? Are there not powerful and exciting enough attempts to break free in the periods of church conflict? The fact is discussed; it is obviously open to discussion; this or that view or attitude may be taken in relation to it; it causes pain, but no less obviously it may be accepted as insoluble (perhaps with the help of a theory of necessary tensions). If there have always been in the history of the people of God — and there are so in its present — some unsettled and unsettling prophets, there have been even more assured and reassuring priests, and between them an even greater number of those who are alternately assured and a little unsettled. A decision that is normative for the whole church and all its members has never been taken, and it does not seem as though it will be taken. Is not a churchman by definition a person of compromise? The first petition of the Lord's Prayer is prayed hundreds and thousands of times, but when and where in the church's exposition and explanation of it has its trumpet blast been really heard and unmistakably accepted and passed on? How remarkable it is that precisely in the church the regime of vacillation can present itself as so tolerable that it can find formal justification in the strange *theologoumenon* of the coincidence of opposites *(complexio oppositorum)* (cf. E. Hoffmann, "Die Vorgeschichte der Cusanischen Coincidentia Oppositorum," *Schriften des Nikolaus von Cues in deutscher Übersetzung, 2, Philosophische Bibliothek* 217, Leipzig [1938], pp. 31-35, esp. pp. 31f. and n. 38; E. Przywara, *Katholische Krise*, Düsseldorf [1967], esp. p. 250, no. 2). This is the situation in which the Christian, over and above what he has to do about himself, must accept responsibility for actualizing his zeal for God's honor as a member of the church: every Christian as such and not just the one who bears office or who has charismatic gifts. In face of this situation, the Christian cannot break solidarity with other Christians. He cannot make a separate peace with God or wage a separate war for his honor. He stands or falls with the cause of the church. The church's situation under that regime and the question of its tolerableness or intolerableness is his situation. We recall that in a way that is structurally essential, and in terms of its unique basis in Jesus Christ, this situation is that of its full knowledge of the one, true, and living God, not just an objective knowledge but in contrast to the world a subjective knowledge as well, which in common answer to the call and commission of its living Lord is proclaimed to angels and the world. Yet in a way that is clearly possible and actual in its terrible ignorance of the same God, it is also the situation of its apostasy in ever new forms, of its constant unfaithfulness to its Head and therefore to itself. It thus exists here as though he were not its Lord, as the church in excess, in self-glorification, and it also exists there as though he were not its living Lord, as the church in defect, as the disorganized and defeatist church. Either way it exists as the church that is all too similar to the world to which it owes its message of God's holy name. Where does the Christian belong in this church? Where has he to come in with his action? How has he to put into practice in it his zeal for God's honor, always presupposing that he is putting it into practice first and supremely in his own life?

Here too we must rule out two extremes in advance. It would definitely not be zeal for God's honor that would cause a Christian to regard and treat the church simply as Babylon [cf. Rev. 14:8; 17:5; 18:2, 10], as the harlot church (*ecclesia meretrix*; cf. Rev. 17:1ff.), as the church which has lost the knowledge of God, which contradicts its own confession, and which has thus become the synagogue of Satan [cf. Rev. 2:9; 3:9]. Words of rebuke of this kind may have had good grounds, may have had to be spoken, and may still have to be spoken. In no case, however, can or may or should they either intend or pronounce a judgment on the being of the church. If in certain instances it might have proved (or still proves) necessary to renounce for the present this or that corrupt form of the church, in no case could or can such a step mean an absolute and definitive separation from it. Even in its most fatal developments and forms, the church can never fall so low that the basis of its being is shaken, that its living Lord, because it has become a dying and not a living church, ceases to hold his hand over it and to keep open the way to new resurrections—so low that it simply ceases to be the church. For this reason the Christian will also remain open and willing and ready in relation to it. To deny the confession, "I believe one, holy, catholic, and apostolic church," even though it might seem to be justifiable in view of the church's corruptions and misdeeds, would be identical to denying the confession of the main sentence in the third article: "I believe in the Holy Spirit"; and this would be impossible for the Christian in view of the indispensable clause that follows: "I believe in the remission of sins." With all that this involves, he would be running away from God himself if he were to run away from the church. He cannot even want to do either, let alone actually do them. What he may in faith in his Lord hold true in his own favor, namely, that he may go astray but can never perish, in faith in him who is also and primarily the Lord of the church, he must and will hold true in the church's favor as well. The gates of the Underworld will not close behind it [Mt. 16:18]; it will remain forever (Augsburg Confession).

The other extreme to be ruled out is that it is not compatible with the commanded zeal for God's honor for the Christian to persuade himself, or to let himself be persuaded, that he has dealings only with a holy, pure, and infallible church, that the church is never anything but full of the Holy Spirit and the knowledge of God, that he should bring only the fullest confidence, love, and respect to it, to its proclamation, to its ordinances and resolutions, to its attitudes toward the world, that because it is guaranteed and confirmed and covered by its Lord in all things, it must simply be affirmed and approved by its members. How can he overlook the spread of so much ignorance of God within it, the direct opposition of its Lord to it in many matters, the fact that in some measure it is also Babylon, the harlot church, the synagogue of Satan, the apostate church vacillating between excess and defect, between unteachable arrogance and anxiously fawning subtlety? Precisely as he does not abandon it, precisely as he loves and respects it, precisely as he refrains from looking for, or where possible trying to set up, an unassailable community somewhere outside it, precisely when he does not do something worse and regard himself as for the time being the only member of the one, holy, catholic church, precisely then the Christian will find himself summoned to criticism, as of himself, so also of the church, to the criticism that here too is careful distinction between its character as the holy church and the harlot church. The cause of the church and its task in the world can be served as little by blind adherents, supporters, and followers of the confession "I believe the church," by Christians who go along with the swing of the pendulum between excess and defect in the church's life and do not even notice the offense involved, as it can by what is said and done by disengaged outsiders who peevishly repudiate that confession. The church lives in its involved and, to that extent, its faithful members. But these will continually have to be faithful in the form of faithful suspicions, questions, and warnings, and often enough in the form of faithful protests against the state and course of things in the church, against the traditions it inherits and the novelties it ventures. The church, like the world, needs salt, not pepper. As a member of the church, the Christian owes it the debt of being salt in his own place and portion [cf. Mt. 5:13], of disturbing the equilibrium, of working against the ignorance of God within it, of serving the knowledge of God, and of thus being to it an element of unrest and hope.

What is it that he can and should do along these lines? With all other Christians, he can and may and should pray earnestly to God for the appearing of the one, pure, holy church, of the new Jerusalem, which is lit by the glory of God and therefore needs neither sun nor moon (Rev. 21:23), of the bride adorned for her husband [Rev. 21:2]. It is for this that he prays in the first petition of the Lord's Prayer. This church, unlike the tower of Babel [cf. Gen. 11:1ff.], will not rise up to heaven in the strength of human effort (be it ever so radically Christian). It will come down from God out of a new heaven and on to a new earth (Rev. 21:1f.). Nevertheless, as and because he hopes and waits for this, the Christian as a member of the church will not be able here and now to fold his hands. In this respect also, he will find himself making a move. He will not tarry, let alone settle down comfortably, in the defile between what the church is in terms of its Lord Jesus Christ and what it is in human terms. Here where it meets him in the community and therefore in the nexus within which he has his personal existence, the system of domesticated and pacified dualism is if anything even more sinister and intolerable than in the innermost sphere. Yet he can cling to the fact that in any event he lives in the community and has a share in the great "Forward" which is given to it and laid upon it. Here he can find comfort in his struggle with the division and with false attempts to bridge it in his own life. Here he can find support. If here he comes across the misery of the same situation between Yes and No and light and darkness, and if above all he comes across the same tendency to unite the two, upon the same apparently natural and therefore sanctified coexistence of the two, it might well be that this causes him even more pain and upsets him even more deeply than the twofold aspect of his own situation. This will not, of course, cause him to flee his own misery or to take it less seriously. But be that as it may, his movement in this middle circle will also have to be one of resistance, not, of course, against the church but *for* the church, a countermovement that is to be initiated and executed within the church for the sake of the church. This in any event is where the Christian will be found and will be active.

In this context this means that he will in any event be found among those for whom the issue in the sphere of the church, in its proclamation, pastoral care, and instruction, in the shaping of its liturgy, in its proper inner and outer order, in its evangelizing and mission, and finally in its theology, is simply but very definitely that of giving precedence to the Word of God and not to any tradition or ancient custom or modern fashion, not to the dogma and confession of the fathers, not to the claims of any contemporary (philosophical or nonphilosophical) movement, and certainly not to the wishes and demands that might be presented by political rulers or majorities. The church will never be without people of this kind in any time or situation. They may not always come forth as a group. It is to be hoped that they will not take the form of a party or school — of "-ians." But they will quietly and tenaciously take the position that the Word of God must be heard first in the church. This means that the church must hear first the word of witness given by the prophets and apostles and received by it at its very commencement, the word of those who saw and heard and touched [cf. 1 Jn. 1:1] the incarnate Word of God [cf. Jn. 1:14], the living Lord of the church. It must hear first the original declaration of his Holy Spirit. It must hear first, if not exclusively, Holy Scripture. There are undoubtedly other factors and motives that are important in and for the life of the church and that thus have to be taken into account. To deny their influence or to discriminate against them in advance would make no sense, for time and history are where the people of God is on the march among many other peoples. Yet it may and should be expected of God's people, and should continually be demanded, that each and all of the other factors and motives that move it should be secondary and subordinate to the one, to the Word of God which it heard at its commencement in the witness of the prophets and apostles. Only thus should the other factors and motives come into play in its thoughts and words and acts. The Christian's zeal for God's honor will not take the form of disregarding and rejecting these other influential factors and motives but rather of contending for the proper order, for the establishment of the head of the order, within which alone the others can achieve their proper rights and dignity. As the Christian contends for this in the community, here too he makes, in the service of the cause and commission of the community, the countermovement demanded of him. When the Word that may be perceived in Holy Scripture has the precedence, then for the time being one can no longer dream either the bad dream of a church that is merely unholy or the all too beautiful dream of one that is merely holy. At least for a time the swing of the pendulum between the church in excess and the church in defect is also halted. Provisionally, also, an end is put to satisfaction with a peace between the knowledge and the ignorance of God, between light and darkness. The spirit of Moses and Jeremiah, the spirit of Paul and John, no, the Holy Spirit of God will see to it that we are kept alert and watchful, so that for the sake of peace with God and true peace on earth, that peace cannot stand. Always and everywhere, when the church is at one again concerning the primacy of the Word of God heard from the beginning, there arises and endures a church which is not perfect, which is not divinely impregnable, but which along a narrow line is here and now the true church, open to the gospel of the great day of God, and therefore willing, empowered, and equipped to carry out its task of giving the world its witness to this gospel. In all circumstances the Christian as a member of the church belongs where there is unity again on this matter, where the movement that it promotes takes place, and where the true church tries to set out in the direction given. That the zeal for God's honor is also a dangerous passion, that the Christian must bring with him the courage to swim against the tide instead of with it, or at least to accept a good deal of loneliness, will perhaps be nowhere so clear and palpable as in the church, where he would so much like things to be different. Yet he cannot and he will not refuse to take this risk and pay this price. In all circumstances he belongs where the reformation of the church is underway or will again be underway. Reformation is not the restoration and conservation of the old and sacrosanct. Nor is it revolution. Fundamental crises are the last thing that the church needs or that is good for it. Reformation is provisional renewal, a modest transforming of the church in the light of its origin. The Christian is interested in this as a member of the church. When he prays the first petition of the Lord's Prayer, he has a part in fulfilling, as is always and everywhere commanded, the improvement that is to be ventured under the direction of the Word of God. Nor is this simply the passive part of a spectator. It is an active one according to the measure of knowledge and strength that he is given.

3. The Christian is finally a child and citizen of the world. That is to say, he exists also in the context and according to the customs and laws of a humanity to which the one true and living God is objectively present and known but not present and known according to its own free, conscious, and responsible knowledge. How he would have to deceive himself if he refused to accept the fact that he himself is also world, that he is at home in the world, that he too belongs very simply to the general public, the people, the "they" (cf. M. Heidegger's *Being and Time* [New York, 1962], pp. 163–68), that he does not have to declare his solidarity with it later but is in solidarity with it from the very first, that he is in line with it, and that he thinks and speaks and acts in the same way as it does, that he has a part, and not an inconsiderable part, in its distinctive ignorance of God and consequently in the desecration of God's name in its acts. When seen in the light and as a whole, is it not true that his Christianity in the first two spheres, which distinguishes him from others, is in fact only a fairly small portion of the field of his life which is ruled by a host of very definitely secular forces, both spiritual and unspiritual, to which he constantly gives access? Conversely, how he would have to deceive himself about the meaning of what distinguishes him from others, and what a sorry thing would

the first petition be in his heart and on his lips, if he could forget that his existence as a Christian and a member of the church can only be one of service to the *world* which is still without the knowledge of God! He is not a Christian and a member of God's people for his own sake or for that of the church but in order to be a light in the world [Mt. 5:14]. If here we call the world the outermost circle in which the Christian is ordered to obey the command of God, this cannot mean that the command has less urgency here, that the obedience he owes here is less important and even perhaps optional, or that zeal for God's honor might slacken in this field. A Christian concerned only about himself and the church and not also, in his personal and communal Christianity, strongly and totally concerned about the world too — the world that does not know God but is loved by him and reconciled with him in Jesus Christ — would be a contradiction in terms, no matter how laudable might be his work in the innermost circle. It is here in this outermost circle that his existence has its practical scope or has none at all.

This is an insight that has been discussed at large in the last decades, perhaps even a little too loudly and one-sidedly, so that it might serve to give added depth if we were to interpose at this point a warning. The action of Christians in this outermost circle presupposes the greatest concern that everything be in order in the other two. Christians who are disorderly in their personal lives, who think, speak, and act carelessly, who fail to resist the regime of vacillation in themselves, will not be people who can serve as credible witnesses to the world concerning God's coming day. No matter how bold and powerful their voices may be, they will have a hollow ring and at bottom will not be able to move the hearts of anybody. Conversion to humble but courageous action in the innermost circle is continually commanded of all Christians precisely with a view to their accreditation in the outermost circle. Similarly, a church that preaches and generally presents itself in comfortable recognition of that regime of vacillation, a church that triumphs here in excess and is despondent there in defect, a church whose reformation has come to a halt or has never even begun, cannot be an organ that is capable of inciting the world to take the decisions it really needs to take or of encouraging it to revolt against that regime. It may embrace the whole world with its missionary and evangelistic addresses, it may raise a rather imprudent claim to its public character, as in our own century, but with all this it accomplishes nothing if in its own sphere it is not engaged in sifting and clarifying what it wishes to make public in the form of its ministry. Zeal for the honor of God outside has promise only when it is first at work, as in John 2:17 [Ps. 69:9], as zeal for the honor of God's house. The purifying of the temple — in the forecourt but perhaps in the holiest of holies too — is necessary first if we are to do the purifying that is needed among all kinds of pagans. Only very little steps are appropriate in the outermost circle if one has to admit that one's rear is not covered in this respect. Those who are not ready to take these inner presuppositions seriously need not be surprised or upset if the finest Christian advance outwards does not seem to make much of an impression on the people resident there. It may be that their penitence sadly does not come about because our own readiness to repent leaves so much to be desired. Yet this should not weaken the insight that the existence of Christians and Christianity embraces the world in its radius. It should rather deepen and strengthen this insight, helping to put it into effect.

There outside — outside the more or less cultivated or untended garden

of the personal Christian life, outside the church gate, not only in all that
the Christian reads in the newspaper, hears on the radio, sees at the cinema,
and experiences on the street and at work, but also in all that he does
actively every day and every hour — there outside, the great division unquestionably confronts him for the first time with stunning and overwhelming force: in the modes of thought and speech, in the doings and activities
of the people who are supposedly or actually without belief, or have other
beliefs or superstitions, or are at any rate outside the church; in the contours
and colors that make the division so distinctive and impressive. Something
is probably wrong if the division does not perhaps for the first time truly
strike and agitate and depress the Christian there outside, if he does not
notice that in the existence of these people, however different they may be
from him, a mirror is held up to himself in which it would be as well for
him to recognize himself. The Christian who is truly and seriously shocked
by the folly and wickedness there outside would do best not to give too
much play at first to this shock but to ask himself whether, on an honest
view, what he can and must see within in himself and the church should
not fundamentally affect him just as painfully, and even much more so in
view of the advantages that he and other Christians have over those outside.
All the same, it is true that the phenomena of the great division that confront
him there outside are also very painful. We recall that the non-Christian
world also knows the one, true, and living God very well objectively. Is it
not the world of the man who by his creation is destined for God and in his
whole nature is oriented to him? Is it not the world in which the light of
knowledge has risen and, even if they do not see it, shines for all men — the
light of a knowledge that is actual as well as possible, subjective as well as
objective, man's as well as God's? If the Christian himself really believes in
Jesus Christ, how he must take this seriously and keep it before his eyes in
relation to all the dominant secularity that confronts him there outside!
Again, is it not the world in which — blurred though it may be in the existence of Christians — the light of the proclamation of Jesus Christ, and therefore of true God and true man, is already present and spreads a certain
brightness? The Christian cannot think only skeptical thoughts in this regard. We also think, however, of all that the world has always done in its
manifest ignorance of God, of all that it is still doing on continents and
islands: of its wonderful atheism, of its even more wonderful religious
enterprises, of its bold nostrification of God, and finally and supremely, in
concentrated opposition to its knowledge of God, of its crude and refined
inhumanities of all kinds. It is not inappropriate to be shocked at this division, and it is not surprising, even if out of place, that Christians under
the influence of this shock at the world should prefer to close the windows
and doors against those outside, to withdraw into a Christianity of the
individual or the church, and to be content with the problems that this in
itself poses. Above all, the Christian sees the world too using refined skills
to hold at a distance the painfulness of the contradiction in which it exists,
domesticating and thereby alleviating it, trying to bridge it with all kinds
of syntheses, to paint it over or drown it out, to come to terms and be

content with it in some way, and thereby to find some rest. The very worst thing that the Christian finds not only in himself and the church but also there outside in the world, namely, the *worldliness* of the world, is the self-evident way in which, without serious dispute, it accepts the desecrating of the name of God by the system and regime of balance, which finds its true triumph there outside and with the establishment and preservation of which man knows only too well how to comfort and justify and safeguard himself. It is to be hoped that the Christian will not make this a matter of special reproach but keep in mind his own self in which he constantly finds first the same system and regime. Yet it does meet him there outside as well. It typifies the whole manner of life of all the people who do not have the advantages vouchsafed to him. And since he himself — also a child and citizen of the world — is outside as well as inside, in its worldly form it is his problem too. He will thus pray the first petition in relation also to the state and course of things in the world. In so doing he will be set before the question what he must do accordingly as a Christian living in the world. What does obedience mean for him in relation to the fact that as a member of the people of God he also belongs to this far larger human people? What can the practical scope of Christian existence be in this outermost circle? What form can and should the witnessing ministry of the Christian take here?

Two extreme answers are to be ruled out here also. In view of the special complexity of the problem we shall have to enlarge upon them a little in this instance. The Christian might try to begin with the negative presupposition that there outside he has to do primarily and decisively with the world which, even though it is reconciled with God in Jesus Christ, is still resisting God in its great ignorance, so that the Christian has to contest it, to teach it better, to call it to order. What the ignorance of God is may not be wholly hidden from him in his own life and that of the church, but he still thinks he must regard as more relevant his otherness from the world on the ground of his knowledge of God, namely, the grace of his election and calling. He still thinks that he must bring to the attention of the world the gospel of God which it has not yet heard or has not heard properly. He thus understands himself as an alien in an alien environment. He understands Christianity as his special and superior point of view. He understands his task to be that of making this point of view clear to those outside, of representing it to them, of winning them over so that they leave their own point of view and accept his. In this regard two ways open up between which he may alternate and which sooner or later converge. The first way one might call that of principial monasticism. On this path the Christian wants to be a witness in the world by holding as far aloof from it as possible, or at least from its tendencies, habits, and forms of life (e.g., in matters of property or sex or the understanding and practice of individual human freedom). He wants to be as distant as he can so that in the language of the facts created by him in this distance and isolation he can stir the world to see a dimension alien to it, giving indirect visibility to the new and different thing that as a Christian he has to represent among it. [That as a witness

he may sometimes—obeying a special command in a special situation—
have a duty to take steps of withdrawal in this way is plain to see. The
question is, however, whether to become a witness he has to be a monk
principially and systematically, whether he can and may give his witness
this form in a general way.]¹ The other way that opens up on the same
presupposition is that of a principial crusade. On this path the Christian
displays his otherness, his point of view that differentiates him from the
world, and he thereby gives his witness, by passing over, either individually
or with others, perhaps in the ranks of a whole Christian front or party, to
militant acts: defensive acts upholding the intellectual, moral, and even
political positions which, according to his conviction, are grounded in his
knowledge of God and established in the Christian view of God and man;
and offensive acts contesting other positions which according to his conviction can be adopted and supported only in ignorance of God. Either way
the aim is to do injury to the worldliness of the world, to woo and win those
who are outside for the gospel of God, and thus to chase away the darkness
by the light. [Now certainly the Christian must sometimes be willing and
ready for big or little crusades of this kind. The question is again whether
his witness should have in principle and as a whole the character of such
defensive or offensive actions, whether he really can or should from the
very outset and all along the line oppose the world as a general or standard-
bearer or soldier in the service of the cause of God.]¹ The closely related
figures of the monk in principle and the crusader in principle are the one
extreme that is to be ruled out in answering our question. In relation to
both, we may say that for the sake of his witness the Christian will from
time to time have to make individual decisions of a monkish or crusading
type. Principially, however, he should not try to be either a monk or a
crusader. Neither isolation from the world nor a militant approach to it can
be a consistent law of his action in the world, for this must be the action
of a witness. These two forms of a legally antithetical orientation of action
are faulty because (1) they basically underrate the objective knowledge of
God that is at work in the world too, which Christians are aware of, in face
of which they cannot adopt a globally negative judgment on what the world
seeks and does, in face of which the world cannot be only alien to them
and to God and cannot, therefore, be seen and treated only with negative
criticism. They are also faulty because (2) they both overrate their own
value, competence, and power to confront the world as teachers, judges,
and conquerors who know better, as though this were permitted or even
possible in the light of their own worldliness. They are faulty (3) because
in both there is an obscuring of the positive content of the witness which
Christians owe to the world, as though the No of God to the world which
may be heard alongside the Yes could be an independent theme, as though
it were a matter of being primarily and decisively opponents of the world
acting in the name of God. Finally they are both faulty (4) because Christian
action in the world—in defiance of the prayer for the hallowing of God's

¹ These sentences were in the TS but were later excised.

name by God himself, and as though it could be more than an annex to this prayer — seems in them to want to deny its character as a purely human witness and in monastic or crusading garb to appear rather as a kind of divine action and revelation. In sum, these two paths are closed to Christians because they cannot take either the one or the other without losing the required humility and modesty.

In this matter also a second extreme is ruled out, which is the direct opposite of the first. The Christian might also proceed on the positive assumption that there outside he has to do primarily and decisively with the world which, although it still opposes God, is already reconciled to him in Jesus Christ, so that he may and must affirm the world as such. In view of its enacted reconciliation with God and the prospect of the future revelation of this reconciliation, he need not see himself as a stranger in a strange land but can understand himself as one who there outside is at home in his Father's house. Believing that the world belongs to God, he can confidently open himself to it and modestly join it and adapt himself to it. While not failing to see its corruption and need, he will try to overcome it, not from outside by holding aloof or fighting against it, but from inside. Belonging consciously and willingly to it [participating joyfully in its confession of God, also participating sadly in its ignorance of God and its attempt at neutrality and vacillation between light and darkness],[2] he will understand his task as a witness, and construe the parable of the leaven (Mt. 13:33), along the lines that as the divine is not alien to him, so is nothing human (cf. Terence, *Heautontimorumenos,* 77). His job, then, is to usher in a kind of Christian secularism or secular Christianity. What he means by this is thinking, speech, and action in the expectation that he can most fittingly serve the gospel of God among children and citizens of the world by the closest possible approximation and assimilation to their attitude and language and even their thought forms, and by the greatest possible cooperation with their efforts, so that in his own person he will set before them the fact of God's love and thus lead or at least direct them to the knowledge of this fact. In direct contrast to the ideals of the monk and the crusader, he has in view a practical symbiosis and cooperation with those who are outside, the goal and the hope being that he will invite and win them to a symbiosis and cooperation of their previously non-Christian existence with his own Christian existence.

The Christian who engages in this kind of action in the world can quote — not without some truth — some welcome sayings of Paul in support of his position: the admonition to Christians to rejoice with those who rejoice and weep with those who weep (Rom. 12:15); the exhortation to seek what is generally acknowledged to be true, honorable, just, and so forth (Phil. 4:8); the statement that Paul became as a Jew to the Jews, as one outside the law to those outside the law, as weak to the weak — "that I might by all means save some" (1 Cor. 9:20ff.); and perhaps the best known of all, the saying that "all things are yours" in 1 Corinthians 3:21f., the cosmos being expressly mentioned among the all things.

[2] These clauses were in the TS but were later excised.

Here again one cannot deny that in many circumstances and over broad areas the action and witness of Christians may and must take this form, so that recollection of this (liberal) possibility is very much in place even as a reaction against the dogmatism of the first extreme. Knowing that the world outside is not just darkness without light, Christians have the freedom — and in obedience are to a large extent under the obligation — to take seriously their solidarity with those outside and to take their place alongside them without making any claims.

Dietrich Bonhoeffer possibly had something of this in view in his last years when he made certain rather cryptic statements in his posthumously published *Widerstand und Ergebung* (ed. E. Bethge, Munich, 1951; E.T. *Letters and Papers from Prison* [1971]). Did he perhaps take this line only under extraordinary impressions and experiences? If so, one should not claim that it represents the true scope of his life's work.

Understood principially, raised to the level of a general example and therefore of a system, this answer is also to be rejected. At fault in it[3] is (1) the naiveté with which the Christian obviously assumes here that the opposition of the world to what God has done for it in Jesus Christ is not so bad that he cannot confidently range himself with it — accompanied by the naiveté of the idea that it lies somehow in his own power to overcome from within the opposition that still remains. At fault in it is (2) the fact that along these lines the Christian must constantly keep it quiet that he has to show the world something new, so that he is forced to play an unworthy game of hide and seek with a view to overcoming its resistance from within, and to run the risk that out of sheer zeal not to isolate himself from it he will withhold from it the very thing he is meant to attest to it. At fault in it is (3) an obscuring of the insight that if the positive content of the gospel as God's gospel is to be heard, the delimiting No must also be heard without which it has no form. At fault in it is (4) a forgetting of the fact that the annex to the prayer for the hallowing of God's name and the zeal for God's honor that is demanded of the Christian must consist in a special action which is distinctly differentiated (Rom. 12:2), even though in the greatest concealment, from that of those who do not pray this prayer or know this zeal. In sum, if the Christian's action along this line also is not to be lacking in humility and modesty, even more so it must not avoid, even if it must not seek, the courage that must characterize his obedience in the world, the necessary resolution, and a certain nonconformity in relation to those outside.

In obedience to God, the Christian will steer a middle course between these two extremes. In so doing, of course, he will not try to square the circle by uniting them in his own person, nor will he adopt a stiff attitude to right or left, making sure that he never thinks, acts, and speaks along

---

[3] In the typescript Barth advanced three faults: (1) its overrating of the world's openness; (2) its underrating of the new thing that takes place in the work of the Holy Spirit; and (3) its game of hide and seek in suggesting that Christian earnestness can achieve along these lines a Christian secularity or a secular Christianity.

monastic-crusading or liberal lines. He will instead maintain his freedom to take a few steps or even to go a good way along either path as need requires. He will not be afraid to take either view or to make compromises on either side. He will be ready to expose himself to the charge of fanaticism on the one side and libertinism on the other. While he will certainly not aim to challenge or provoke anyone, he cannot always avoid giving offense to one person or another. For all the secularity that he cannot peel off, his action in the world will be a spiritual one, since its concern will be neither with basic opposition to the world nor basic agreement with it, but only with ever new attention to the free and living Word of his Lord as the Head of the community that he has chosen and called and also as Lord of the world. Constantly this Word will call him back from every standpoint and lift him back out of every front or Christian clique. How can he defend this Word against the world or cause it to prevail in attack upon it? How can he conceal it from the world or fail to speak of it? How can he expect that with its help he himself should or can or will overcome the world from without or from within as though this were his affair? No matter whether he has now to negate the world or now to affirm it, whether he has now to be somewhat alien to it or now to be somewhat in conformity with it, with courage and humility he has to be a witness of this Word to the world.

To be a witness — this means that among all other men of the world he has to think and speak and act as himself a man of the world who in distinction from the rest has heard the Word and recognized the value that it has for him in this outermost circle of his existence too, the authority which it claims here, and the promise which it pronounces here. To give it validity and force in the power of the divine revealing, to help it to pierce and conquer and rule the world, this may under God be the growing fruit of his human action, but it cannot be its meaning and purpose. It would be better if precisely at this point Christians would confine themselves to speaking only about what may be said and done at the human level. What is to be expected of Christians is simply but undeniably this. In what they do or leave undone they can make themselves known to the world as understanding hearers of the Word and thus draw attention to the Word in their existence in the world. What is to be expected of them is that this Word will give their choosing and willing a specific character so that their lives will become a text accessible not only to their fellow Christians but also to their non-Christian fellows. So long as they do not have the vocabulary, grammar, and syntax, the latter may not understand it, but it is legible to them as written by a human hand. In the persons of Christians as hearers of God's Word, the Word itself is present to their non-Christian fellows also. In the way that Christians shape their lives as people of the world confronting the same problems as others, their life's task in the midst of others documents the Word, brings it to notice, and draws attention to it. They cannot do more than this and should not try. It may be that in time they will have to answer questions concerning the reason for the special character of their works, that they will have to comment to others on the text of their lives, that they will have to offer an introduction to the understanding of the text and therefore speak about it. But the first and proper thing that as men of the world they owe other men of the world, apart from their participation in the word of witness of the community, can only be the "behavior without words" which 1 Peter 3:1 commends to Christian wives, namely, the fact that as hearers of the Word they document and draw attention to its presence, following it in practice according to the measure of their faith [Rom. 12:3] and knowledge, and thus being doers of it in the midst of others [Jas. 1:22f.]. To make this witness of theirs fruitful and successful — the same applies to the word of witness of the Christian community — is God's affair, not theirs. Their affair is to be unassuming and resolute doers of the Word and in this way to be witnesses to it in the non-Christian world. They cannot escape this, for if they did they would not be hearers of the Word, and therefore they would not be Christians at all.

The thoughts and words and works of Christians, however, will be characteristic, they will be a legible if not immediately understandable text to the non-Christians around them, and they will thus be a witness given among them, only when they follow their invocation of God and in particular their prayer for the hallowing of God's name. As regards the form of their human action in accordance with this prayer, in this outermost circle, too, all that is at issue is the very great and very simple thing that as in their personal lives and their lives as members of the community, so in their lives as people of the world among other people of the world they have to let the Word of God be a "lamp to their feet" (Ps. 119:105), to give it the precedence over all the claims of all the interests and enterprises that to some extent motivate them, and of all the rules and obligations and customs that to some extent bind them. They cannot ignore or suppress these other claims. They must not act as though they could or should. But they will place them after and under God's Word. They will reject control by them. Doing this demands a good deal of them, but not too much of people who are called Christians. They have to do it. When they grant God's Word this place and function, their actions take on a distinct character. They become a readable text. Even in all their humanity they are a witness in and to the non-Christian world.

Obviously, Christian action in this sphere will have the nature of a movement of resistance: not to other people of the world with whom the Christian finds and knows himself to be in solidarity, nor against their interests as such, since these affect him too, but against the desecration of the name of God which pollutes this sphere and which is brought about by the mixture of light and darkness that rules it, against the system of the ambivalence of the knowledge and ignorance of the one true and living God. We are not presupposing that his action also and primarily in his personal life and his life as a member of the church will be Christian in the sense that he prays the first petition of the Lord's Prayer and repudiates that system. If this is so, then necessarily his action here again will be such that while it does not topple the system (this is reserved for God alone), it will noticeably challenge it. As the Word that the Christian accepts is the Word of God, who has united himself to man and man to himself, and as the Christian gives this Word the precedence in God's choosing and willing, his action will in all circumstances be characterized by its moving within the limits denoted thereby.

It will be an action in which he keeps God before him and also considers that first and in a very different way God keeps him before himself. It will be an action in whose fulfilment there is ruled out the practical atheism that still competes with the knowledge of God in the world. In what he does he will present himself to the others with whom he knows he is in solidarity as a person for whom God is the God of man and man the man of God, for whom, therefore, God's existence is the self-evident presupposition of his own, who in a striking way cannot in fact be an atheist, who cannot take part in that vacillation between knowledge and ignorance of God.

Just as necessarily his action will be one that is determined by the supremacy of God (the God of man) over man (the man of God). The Christian will so think and speak and act that he respects the freedom with which God rules and speaks from on high as the basis of his own freedom, and therefore in his own freedom he wills to be man only in his own place in responsibility to God. As he gives and allows the Word the precedence that is its due, his action necessarily fits into the irreversible order in which God is the Lord and man is simply the servant who must hear and obey him. Hence he can have no practical use for enterprises that still compete with the knowledge of God in the world, nor for the alternative that still offers itself of an equation of God and world and world and God. In this regard he is and will be a new man in relation to others.

The final and decisive thing is this. The whole injustice and evil of the system which rules the world—that of the ambivalence of its knowledge and ignorance of God—comes to expression in the unceasing vacillation between the humanity and inhumanity of his thoughts and words and works. When Christians pray for the hallowing of God's name by God himself, they are praying concretely that he will put an end to this abominable vacillation. For the holy name of God which is desecrated in the world is unequivocally the name of him who is not without or against man but *for* man, the God who liberates and thus rules man, the God who loves him. If, then, the Christian's action follows this petition, necessarily it will be action not only in the presupposed coexistence with God but also in the coexistence with man that results directly from it. More interesting, demanding, and binding than all things, even than ever so lofty ideas and principles, even and especially than the Christian himself, are people as such, and concretely the people with whom he has dealings in his place and time. The God whom the Christian confronts is the true God who is also true man. Confronting him, man is confronted by his creature, the neighbor, the fellow man who is God's child with him and hence his own brother. As he confronts God and is in covenant with him and responsible to him, not only atheism and religiosity and nostrification but also the inhumanity which in the world can compete so strangely with the knowledge of God, and therefore with humanity, can be no alternative for him. In his acts he simply cannot take part in the great vacillation between his being without or against his fellows and his being for them. It is thus most striking that he presents himself to other men of the world as a nonconformist, as one who is zealous for God's honor, as a witness to what he, who is also a man of the world, has to advocate to others of his kind. He does this by offering to them the image of a strangely human person.

§78

THE STRUGGLE FOR HUMAN RIGHTEOUSNESS

Christians pray to God that he will cause his righteousness to appear and dwell on a new earth under a new heaven. Meanwhile they act in accordance with their prayer as people who are responsible for the rule of human righteousness, that is, for the preservation and renewal, the deepening and extending, of the divinely ordained human safeguards of human rights, human freedom, and human peace on earth.[1]

1. REVOLT AGAINST DISORDER

The genuineness of human zeal for God's honor needs testing. Christians pray, "Hallowed be thy name." Calling upon God their Father, they recognize that they for their part are commanded to be zealous for his honor. But Christians are human, and their zeal for God's honor according to God's command will always be a human action and therefore a dubious one. It might be zeal without the passion required of them, the zeal of a very impure passion. It has to be tested. Whether and how far it is tested before God's eyes and according to his judgment, we cannot say. But testing its genuineness, that is, its character as obedience to God's command, comes within the sphere of ethical discussion, for we may critically compare what Christians do in zeal for God's honor with the obedient action that is demanded of them when they invoke God as their Father. The one thing that they must recognize to be commanded of them when they invoke him is manifold in itself. Whether their action corresponds to one of the elements of God's command and is obedient in this regard may be measured by whether the same applies to it in relation to other elements of the command. Zeal for God's honor is one, but only *one*, of the elements of the command of God that is given to Christians, just as the first petition of the Lord's Prayer which we have considered first, asking about the command of God implied in it, is the first but not the only petition. In turning now to the second petition we shall turn to another element of the one command of God. It is not to be separated from the first, nor the first from it, so that, subject to what follows, the obedient character of Christian action, and especially the genuineness of Christian zeal for God's honor, will show itself

[1]The opening sentences in the typescript, later excised, run as follows: "Christians have been given the certainty that God has taken in hand and actualized order in his creation for the good of man and that he will finally manifest and enforce it in its perfection. They thus revolt against all the oppression and suppression of man by the lordship of lordless powers."

by being obedient action also in relation to this other element of the one command of God. We call this other element of the command, or the corresponding action of Christians, their "struggle for human righteousness." There will certainly be no struggle, or only a poor one, when Christian action is not also and primarily zeal for God's honor. Our emphasis now, however, is different. Zeal for God's honor can be good, obedient, and full of promise only when it is directly accompanied by the struggle for human righteousness. In this first subsection we shall attempt a short introduction to the new problem denoted by this title.

Christians are summoned by God's command not only to zeal for God's honor but also to a simultaneous and related revolt, and therefore to entry into a conflict.

We are here using the concept of the Christian life as warfare in a pointed way which is not so evident in the New Testament. Behind the idea of the *militia Christi* there obviously stands a general recollection of the story of Gethsemane [Mk. 14:32ff. and par.], just as behind this there stands the story of Jacob-Israel who wrestled with God (Gen. 32:24ff.). In the New Testament, and especially the Epistles, the idea of conflict usually stands close to that of faith, to which it is related. It is a comprehensive term for the wrestling with inner and outer assaults on the existence and witness of the Christian — a wrestling that has to be militant and that carries with it effort, danger, and distress. The New Testament apostle and the New Testament community always have this struggle before them — it can also be called an athletic contest [cf. 1 Cor. 9:24ff.; 2 Tim. 2:5] — and it is thus ordained for them (προκείμενος, Heb. 12:1). To stand and conquer in this struggle, they must be armed with what is expressly described in Ephesians 6:11ff. as the πανοπλία τοῦ θεοῦ. Faithfully fought, it is their "good fight" (1 Tim. 6:12; 2 Tim. 4:7), the καλὸς ἀγών. A striking point to be gathered from the description of God's armor is that it seems to be viewed and understood as a defensive battle. We must "stand against the wiles of the devil" (Eph. 6:11), "withstand in the evil day," and "having done all . . . stand" (v. 13). "Take your share of suffering as a good soldier of Jesus Christ" (2 Tim. 2:3). We must keep this in mind as we here make rather more extensive use of the whole concept. But faith, in and for which we are to fight according to these sayings, is in itself and as such a spontaneous human action awakened by the Word of God. It does not exist for its own sake nor curve in upon itself but takes place in a movement of man out from and beyond himself, and therefore directly or indirectly in a challenge, in an attack on the dominion of unbelief. As this attack, it is itself attacked and has to maintain itself against the assault. Maintaining itself means standing in the attack that it has itself launched. It is on the defensive because it holds up its shield on the offensive. We shall follow this line and give specific examples: faith maintains and defends itself when it hurls itself against what Romans 1:18 calls all the ἀσέβεια and all the ἀδικία of men. It opposes their unrighteousness in relation to God and their resulting lack of human righteousness. That a consistent and concrete development of this thought is at least an application, if not an explication, of the New Testament prototype can hardly be contested.

Revolt or rebellion is more than the rejection of a particular possibility. Rejection can undoubtedly mean non-participation in actualizing the possibility. But it does not have to do so. One can obviously reject a possibility, that is, judge it negatively, and then for various reasons take part in its actualization. Furthermore, even the sharpest rejection does not in itself include within it one thing, namely, entry into the struggle for the actualization of a very different possibility opposed to the first one. In the thought, speech, and action demanded of Christians, the issue is not just that of rejecting what they see to be a bad possibility but that of rising up and revolting against its actualization: a revolt that has positive meaning and inner necessity because another possibility stands with such splendor before the eyes of the rebels that they cannot refrain from affirming and grasping it and entering into battle for its actualization. Their revolt against the first possibility is thus only the complement or the reverse side of their commanded struggle for this one. Because of this one it is unavoidable. In word and deed they say No here because they may and will say Yes there.

Christians thus exist under a binding requirement to engage in a specific uprising. The specific nature of the possibility for whose actualization they have to fight against the other is what makes the commanded revolt a specific one and differentiates it from other revolts. Like all others, they are, of course, acquainted with other revolts. Christians too can simply live and stand in some form of conflict for their free being. They can be in revolt against everything that would take their freedom away or restrict it: against painful conditions of life to which they are subject; against destinies which have led them or are about to lead them where they do not want to go [cf. Jn. 21:18]; primarily and supremely against tyrants, those by whom they find themselves browbeaten, defrauded, and oppressed, who encroach upon them, who intentionally or unintentionally hurt them and threaten to make life impossible for them. They may resist in matters such as this as well. Nevertheless, they are not just people; they are Christians, or at least they are seeking to be such. To the extent that they are Christians, or are engaged in becoming Christians, their life and its preservation, the possibility of their life and its actualization, cannot be strictly and seriously and primarily the thing for which they stand and rise up and fight. That against which they rebel as Christians cannot properly be that which threatens and imperils them in this regard. It cannot be this or that condition of life, however burdensome. It cannot be a blow of fate or a disposition of fate. It cannot be the persons who are so hostile, no matter how these oppress them. If revolts in such directions are not unfamiliar to them, if they have to admit that secretly or even very openly they often find themselves in revolts of this kind, they still see clearly that these are not their true revolt and that as Christians they can and may refrain from revolts of this kind, and in some circumstances will have to do so. The battles in which they entangle themselves and find themselves entangled along these lines are very different from the good fight of faith which is set before them [1 Tim. 6:12]. At any rate, in the fight of faith they may sometimes at least have to accept the renunciation of such revolts or struggles or to see that incipient revolts of this kind are postponed or minimized.

It is certainly no small thing to be afflicted by hardship, anxiety, persecution, hunger, nakedness, danger, and sword. Yet these things cannot separate the Christian from the love of Christ (Rom. 8:35). They are nothing compared with the glory that is to be revealed to us (Rom. 8:18). Indeed, they can and must work for good for those who love God (Rom. 8:28). Christians can and should glory in them because their point and effect can and should be to strengthen their perseverance, deepen their self-confirmation, and renew their hope (Rom. 5:3f.). "Humble yourselves therefore under the mighty hand of God, that in due time he may exalt you" (1 Pet. 5:6). Strictly speaking, rebellion, revolt, resistance, and conflict against assault do not come into question on this level, especially where (as in both Romans and 1 Peter) the affliction suffered comes from particular people. The picture of the crucified Lord is relevant here: "When he was reviled, he did not revile in return; when he suffered, he did not threaten, but he trusted to him who judges justly" (1 Pet. 2:23). So is the saying of the Lord in Matthew 5:39: "But I say to you, Do not resist one who is evil [or evil done to you by another]." The Old Testament law in Exodus 21:23ff., which demands repayment of like by like (an eye for an eye and a tooth for a tooth) is misunderstood if it is taken as a direction to the exaction of private vengeance. "Do not return evil for evil or reviling for reviling" (1 Pet. 3:9; 1 Thess. 5:15). There is an express warning against this in the Old Testament itself at Leviticus 19:18: "You shall not take vengeance or bear any grudge against the sons of your own people," and again at Proverbs 24:29: "Do not say, 'I will do to him as he has done to me; I will pay the man back for what he has done.' " In Romans 12:19ff., Paul takes from Deuteronomy 32:25 (LXX) the saying "Vengeance is mine, I will repay, says the Lord," but he goes beyond this Old Testament warning in a positive sense and writes: "Beloved, never avenge yourselves, but leave it to the wrath of God. . . . Do not be overcome by evil, but overcome evil with good." The continuation in 1 Thessalonians 5:15 is to the same effect: "Always seek to do good to one another and to all." Along the same lines, love is finally to be shown to the man in Corinth who wronged the apostle (2 Cor. 2:8). "Therefore let those who suffer according to God's will do right and entrust their souls to a faithful Creator" (1 Pet. 4:19). Those who take to the sword run the risk of perishing by the sword and incurring the divine judgment that it is not for them to fulfill (Mt. 26:52; Rev. 13:10).

A warlike march and attack of the children of light on the children of darkness like that expressly described in one of the Dead Sea Scrolls (1 QM) is never envisioned in the New Testament, not even as an eschatological possibility, nor in the Apocalypse. We certainly hear the cry of those who were slain for the Word of God (Rev. 6:9f.): "O Sovereign Lord, holy and true, how long before thou wilt judge and avenge our blood on those who dwell upon the earth." But we do not read of Christians playing any active part in the judgments passed on the world that is hostile to God and his people with the opening of the seven seals, the sounding of the seven trumpets, the pouring out of the seven vials of wrath, and finally the destruction of Babylon the Great [cf. Rev. 6:1ff.; 8:1ff.; 11:15ff.; 15—18]. Patience and faith are what the saints have to oppose to this world (Rev. 13:10; 14:12). Not they, but the angels are always the fighters.

The opposing teaching of the Qumran sect is even far below the level of what we read in the Psalms about the mind and conduct of the holy people, its king, and devout individuals in Israel in regard to their outer and inner enemies and adversaries who go by such names as the ungodly, fools, transgressors, blasphemers, liars, and men of violence. The concrete human figure of those who are thus designated remains remarkably obscure in the texts, so that attempts to localize and characterize them historically in Old Testament research will always be contested. Numerous people are obviously in view who with evil will and evil acts (especially in words) oppose the psalmists, or those for whom they speak. The wickedness of what they are and do is seen, however, in the mirror of what is said about them and against them in the Psalms. It is presented as the direct affliction of soul and body which it brings upon those whom they attack. It consists decisively of the distress they cause because their apparently uncontested and triumphant existence calls in question the authority, faithfulness, and power of the God of Israel and therewith the solidity of the covenant that he has made with his people and with each of its members. In this regard they are like howling dogs (Ps. 59:7), tearing lions (Ps. 17:12), or cunning fowlers (Ps. 124:7). This is why the faithful of Yahweh have such painful personal experiences with these people. This is why the words of abhorrence and even hatred with which they speak of them have such marked bitterness. This is what explains their characteristic attitude toward them. So far as I can see, however, only Psalm 18:34–47 speaks of those affected going to war against them, and here the fighting and victory is that of the king whom Yahweh has empowered for the task. For the rest the psalmists, or those for whom they speak, have no intention, as they also have no possibility, of avenging themselves on their oppressors or even of defending themselves against them. This is obviously because they realize that in the struggle with them the serious and final issue is the problem of theodicy, which it will be God's affair to answer and solve and not theirs. Hence they do not oppose their enemies with a front of their own. They bewail before the face of Yahweh the dark riddle of the existence and good fortune of the ungodly. They accuse them before him because of the injustice and pain that are done to them for his sake. They call upon *him*—praying that he will intervene as his own Defender and Avenger, and therefore as theirs too. Obviously, because they are personally abased and abused, their cry and complaint ring out passionately and even wildly. They are thus offensive to the abstract moral taste of the modern age. The Psalter says nothing here about the positive side of the New Testament admonition: about loving and blessing enemies and praying for them [Mt. 5:44; Lk. 6:27f., 35]; about overcoming the evil suffered at their hands by the good that is shown to them [Rom. 12:21]; about the solidarity of believers even with the ungodly [Rom. 4:5; 5:6]. Here the Old Testament is promise, not fulfilment. Yet a title like "Vengeance Psalms" for even the worst texts and passages of this kind is inexact and misleading to the extent that there is no mention—we must state this firmly—of demands or resolves to exact individual vengeance. We find no Maccabean or Zealot statements in the Psalter. From this standpoint also, the Old Testament is promise.

So much by way of delimitation. There is, however—and this is what concerns us here—a struggle that Christians cannot avoid, a revolt that is both permitted and also commanded. This begins at the very point where other conflicts and revolts in which human existence is at stake reach their limit and come to an end. Christians become and are free and fit for this revolt and conflict precisely to the degree that they have left behind them the more personal revolts and conflicts of that other kind, to the degree that they are willing and ready to integrate them into this one, to let them be sanctified and changed by it, to the degree that they use the freedom for life (cf. *CD* III,4 § 55) that their Creator has given them, not for themselves, but in an active dedication of their lives to his service and to preparation for it.

We must admit candidly that since Christians are human like all the rest, perfect purity is not in fact to be expected in their distinctive, because ordained, revolt and conflict. For all their serious concern to obey only the command that they are given and to fight only the fight of faith, in fact, as though the life of goods were supreme, they will often be very abstractly anxious about their life's possibility, as the psalmists obviously were, and they will always be more or less strongly motivated by the corresponding aims and feelings. To the extent that their thoughts and words and works are also determined by this intermingling of personal concerns — which cannot be their most proper concern as Christians — they will be disturbed, hampered, and weakened, and recourse will have to be had to God's sovereign grace to correct what they as only too human rebels and fighters cannot correct. Nevertheless, this reminder does not mean their release from the obedience required of them by the command of God. It does not mean the suppression of the principle that the obedience demanded must be pure and totally unadulterated. We shall thus lay aside the question of what more or less good thing does in fact result when Christians go to work and obey the command of God in their only too human humanity. We shall investigate instead the unalterable command that is given to them and the form of the obedience that is required of them.

The militant revolt demanded of Christians — and this distinguishes it from all kinds of other revolts — is not directed *against* any people: not even against the hosts of unbelievers, false believers, and the superstitious whom, for lack of the knowledge of God which they themselves have been given, they see taking totally different and corrupt and fatal paths, nor even, very generally, against the wicked on account of their wickedness and oppression or on account of what Christians have to suffer at their hands in coarser or more refined forms.

We have seen that those parts of the Old Testament Psalms which deal with "enemies" also do not refer to revolts and conflicts of this kind. Similarly, the lists of vices in the New Testament may sharply characterize non-Christians and anti-Christians, but they cannot be accused of privately issuing a summons to battle against the representatives of the vices either inside or outside the community. Similarly, neither Geneva nor Calvin encouraged the French Protestants of the sixteenth century to take part in the contemporary wars of religion — quite the contrary!

Where militant Christian fronts of this kind have arisen, where Christians have combined in parties to combat other parties, where they have even started military or moral and spiritual crusades against others, in the light of their origins this could take place only by mistake. They themselves were in the grip of error and deviation. They abandoned the revolt and conflict ordained for them. They thought and spoke and acted in evil — even more evil — opposition to the cause entrusted to them. They thus imperiled this cause more than those against whom they thought they should fight.

In terms of their commission — even though they will sometimes clash with all kinds of people in discharging it — they rebel and fight *for* all men, even, and in the last resort precisely, for those with whom they may clash. Their cause — the problem of the *militia Christi* and therefore of the *ecclesia militans* — is the cause of man precisely because it is the cause of God. Thinking, speaking, and acting in a friend-foe relationship, that is, in favor of some people and to the detriment of others, can never be their purpose. As Christians, they are from the very first the friends of all. They are commanded to work as such, to seek in all circumstances what is truly best for man. They see all people, like themselves, in a plight that is far greater than that which others could bring upon them personally and which will in any event concern them more strongly than anything that they personally might have to suffer at other hands. They see and understand this as the plight of humanity under which all in their own ways suffer as they do, and they suffer as all do. And they see and understand it as a plight for which people themselves are guilty. They see how it is continually brought about by all people — themselves as well as others. They see how people continually bring it upon one another. Solidarity in this general and self-incurred human plight binds them to all others and claims them more strongly than the distinction and antithesis which within this plight there may be between themselves and many of the rest. What they are commanded to do is to move against this plight, to enter into conflict with it. They are thus commanded to realize that it ought not to oppress people. This is not proper for it. It is no part of human nature. It is not a fate inevitably bound up with human existence. It is against nature. It is an alien dominion to which people themselves have appealed — this is their guilt — and to whose service they have given themselves. Hence it does not really have the dignity and legitimacy and therefore the ineluctability of a divine decree. From the pressure of this plight, people, if they are not free, can and should become free again. It does not correspond at all to God's will for them but contradicts it. People who know God's will — and Christians should be such people — cannot in any circumstances accept this plight as an unalterable reality, even though no people, not even Christians, can overcome it or rescue humanity from the pressure of its rule. In all circumstances the Christian is summoned and is in a position to rebel against this plight, to rise up against it, to enter into conflict with it. This and not men, this plight which is caused by all, for which all are responsible, and which oppresses all, is the enemy between whom and Christians — whose cause is God's and therefore man's — there can and may be no reconciliation or peace. If Christianity were not the *militia Christi*, the *ecclesia militans*, engaged in a struggle with the human plight, it would not be Christianity or the church of Jesus Christ.

The general plight against which Christians are commanded to revolt and fight is the disorder which both inwardly and outwardly controls and penetrates and poisons and disrupts all human relations and interconnections. Disorder arises and consists in deviation from order. The human race exists in such deviation. The order from which it deviates is the form of an obedient life of people in fellowship with God which includes as such the corresponding form — the guarantee of human right, freedom, and peace — of a life of people in fellowship with one another. The former includes the latter because God is not an egoistic supreme being remote and alien from man and ruling over him as fate. He is the God of man, his Creator, Lord, Helper, and Judge. Furthermore, man for his part does not belong to anybody or to any powers. He belongs to God and is the man of God as God is the God of man. In the revelation of this order, in the declaration of its divine righteousness as the basis and guarantee of human righteousness, God is the One he is, the God who is gracious to man as such, who affirms all men, and who in so doing works all things together for their good. The disorder, which is the great plight under whose pressure people have to suffer, arises and consists — and this is the guilt of mankind as it is also his plight — in the ignoring and transgressing of this order. It arises and consists in the unrighteousness of the fall of people from God which as such ineluctably carries with it their fall from one another, the changing of their being with one another, which corresponds to their being with God, into a general being without and against one another. In offending God they can only offend one another as well. They cannot deal righteously with one another, nor be liberal with one another, nor live at peace with one another. In and with the sin of Adam, who wanted to be as God, there is already enclosed the sin of Cain, the murderer of his brother [cf. Gen. 3:5; 4:8]. World history is the confirmation and repetition of this twofold history. Where all are against God, the hand of each can only be against that of others [cf. Zec. 14:13]. Man can only become a wolf in relationship to man. The useless, unworthy, unholy, and disastrous struggle for life [cf. C. Darwin, *On the Origin of the Species by means of Natural Selection*, or *The Preservation of favoured Races in the Struggle for Life*, London, 1859] can only begin in all refined, crude, and crudest forms. Christians are commanded to oppose this disorder by hearing the proclamation of the righteousness of God and in and with it the proclamation of the order of right, freedom, and peace which is given to man. They are to oppose it by keeping this in their ears and therefore by keeping before their eyes the possibility and necessity of human righteousness as well. They cannot acquiesce, then, in the dominant disorder. For them this is not a final reality that cannot be altered. Instead, it is a powerful phantom that is destined to disappear. Hence, even though they cannot do away with it, in all circumstances they must swim against its current. If we call the continually new development of great disorder a revolution, we might say that even though Christians participate in it and share the guilt for the resulting plight, they are at the same time born counterrevolutionaries. In their hearts and lives and therefore in their acts they can and will find no rest in face of the great disorder around them. In this light one can see why it is that their revolt and conflict cannot in any circumstances be a fight against other people. If it were, then no matter how just their cause, they would be confirming and increasing the disorder that arises in the opposition of man and man which brings about the common plight. It is unfortunately true that again and again they will do this. Not without some connection to this, it is also true that with their unrest they will earn no thanks from others but only ingratitude. They will not be able to escape their destiny of coming under attack themselves. In their function as peacemakers (Mt. 5:9) and as champions of the cause of all people — wise and foolish, good and bad — they must never let themselves be led astray either by the guilt of others toward them or by the idea that they themselves have no guilt whatever toward others.

The decisive action of their revolt against disorder, which, correctly understood, includes within itself all others, is their calling upon God in the second petition of the Lord's Prayer: "Thy kingdom come." The kingdom of God (also called the kingdom of heaven in Matthew) is awaited and comes from God, from above, from heaven. It is the universal and definitive revelation of the righteousness of God which judges and establishes humanity. It is the institution of his perfect lordship in human relations and interconnections. It is the setting up of his salutary order in human life and fellowship. The kingdom of God is God himself in the act of normalizing human existence. It is thus God himself in the victorious act of overcoming the disorder which still rules humanity. Christians have the freedom to pray that God's kingdom, God himself in this act, will appear and come — will come to us, from heaven to earth. Their use of this freedom, their sighing, calling, and crying "Thy kingdom come," is, when they say it and mean it comprehensively, their demanded revolt against disorder. Invocation of God in and with this prayer, obedient human action in this vertical direction, implies (as the same obedient human action) the horizontal of a corresponding human, and therefore provisional, attitude and mode of conduct in the sphere of the freedom which, as they pray for the coming of the kingdom, is already given to them here and now on this side of the fulfilment of the prayer. Thus to pray the prayer does not excuse them from provisionally rebelling and battling the disorder in their own human thoughts and words and works. On the contrary, they cannot pray the prayer aright without in so doing being projected into this corresponding action of their own which is provisional but nonetheless serious in this particular sphere. Oriented in this prayer to the coming of the kingdom, and thus made fellows of the kingdom, Christians cannot possibly refrain from a coming of their own [cf. J. Rist's hymn, "Auf, auf, ihr Reichsgenossen"]. They come by going to meet the coming kingdom of God, by seeing and grasping the possibilities which are provisionally present or which offer themselves not for divine but for human righteousness and order, by being concerned to actualize these within the limits of their weak ability and above all of their continually errant and perverted will. What kind of seeking first God's kingdom and righteousness would that be (Mt. 6:33), what kind of hungering and thirsting after it (Mt. 5:6), what kind of waiting for the new heaven and the new earth in which it dwells (2 Pet. 3:13), what kind of praying that prayer, if we were not motivated thereby to do resolutely what we can here and now on this side in orientation and with a view to God's side, to the great there and then of his kingdom, and to do this without claim or illusion, not trying to anticipate what only God could begin and only he can finish, but rising up to fight for human righteousness and order in the midst of disorder and in opposition to it? Where free praying of the second petition is a living and powerful event in the great hope of God's future, there the vitality and force of little hopes for the present of a person and of people will not be lacking: the free and responsible advocacy, actualized in little steps, of that which in the light of the act which God has commenced and will complete can be called human right, human freedom, and human peace, of that which very provisionally and incompletely can already be these things. Hence the second petition and its ethical implications must be our next theme.

2. THE LORDLESS POWERS

In this second subsection we have to consider the manner and nature of the evil which Christians call upon God to set aside in the second petition and which is also the enemy against whom, obedient to God's command, they have to rebel and contend within the limits of their human understanding and ability. We have described this adversary first as the great disorder that controls and characterizes the state and course of human things. It is the human unrighteousness that contradicts and opposes the salutary order and righteousness of God. It is the plight that plagues and disrupts and devastates humanity, in which Christians too find themselves and for which they share some guilt, and in recognition of which they have the freedom and are called upon to pray and also to work. But at this point, if we are to be clear in what follows, we must look more closely and speak more precisely.

It may be presupposed that man's fall and alienation from God is the root of all evil and therefore of this evil too. This is the final and true basis of the disorder. Indeed, it is itself the original disorder, the true unrighteousness which darkens and burdens human life and fellowship. Man's alienation from God at once carries with it his self-alienation: the denaturalizing of the humanity and fellow humanity of his own existence, the contradiction of the determination, inalienably given to him as God's creature, that he should belong to God and have in him his Lord, the beginning of thought, speech, action, and therefore existence, which are headstrong because they have no Lord. Naturally, man's being without a Lord, without God, cannot alter in the slightest the fact that God is his God and that in reality and truth he does have God as his Lord. He cannot escape from God: "If I ascend to heaven, thou art there! If I make my bed in Sheol, thou art there also!" (Ps. 139:8). It would be unthinkably terrible if this were not so, if God allowed man to tread his evil way to the bitter end, if he ceased on his side too to be man's God and Lord. It is bad enough for man, and fateful enough, that he can at least attempt this alienation from God, this flight from his Spirit and countenance into the lordlessness of those heights or depths, that in a dreadful "as if," and in contradiction of his true determination, he can exist "absolutely." In no case does he achieve more than an imagined godlessness and lordlessness, a pseudo-absolute being and existence, a thought, speech, and act "as if" he were without God and without a Lord. Nevertheless, even this has catastrophic consequences for man, which we must now consider.

When man, alienated from God, tries to live a lordless life, in no case does this result in his becoming the lord and master of the possibilities of his own life. The "You will be like God" (Gen. 3:5), "you will be your own lords and masters," was from the very first the promise he thought he should grasp when he started on this path. In fact, however, there never has been, is, or will be any fulfilment of this promise. In the foolish and hopeless attempt to escape from the sphere of God's lordship, it is not so simple for man to become and be even a little God and Lord with the implied approximation to God's supremacy and controlling power in the fashioning of human existence. Even a partially free control has always been everywhere the myth, but only the myth and illusion, of the person who thinks and claims that he has come of age and is now sovereign and autonomous. In thinking this—and the more self-consciously and emphatically he does so, the more—he is overtaken by the opposite. He ceases to be the free lord and master he could and should have been in the sphere of God's lordship if, instead of fleeing from God, he had oriented himself to him. Parallel to the history of his emancipation from God there runs that of the emancipation of his own possibilities of life from himself: the history of the overpowering of his desires, aspirations, and will by the power, the superpower, of his ability. His capacities when he uses them, as Goethe describes so vividly and with such frightening profundity in his poem *The Sorcerer's Apprentice*, become spirits with a life and activity of their own, lordless indwelling forces. To be sure, he thinks he can take them in hand, control them, and direct them as he pleases, for they are undoubtedly the forces of his own possibilities and capacities, of his own ability. In reality, however, they escape from him, they have already escaped from him. They are entities with their own right and dignity. They are long since alienated from him. They act at their own pleasure, as absolutes, without him, behind him, over him, and against him, according to the law by which they arose, in exact correspondence to the law by which man himself thought that he should flee from God. As he did to God, so the different forms of his own capacity now do to him. In reality, he does not control them but they him. They do not serve him but he must serve them. He is the more their football and prisoner the less he is aware of the reversal that has long since taken place between him and them, and the more he still rocks himself in the illusion of his lordship and mastery over them. If we are to see the disorder and unrighteousness which corrupt human life and fellowship, we must not only not deny, but consider very seriously, not merely man's rebellion against God, but also the rebellion unleashed by it, that of human abilities, exalting themselves as lordless forces, against man himself.

To be sure, these are nothing but man's own abilities loaned to his creaturely nature and peculiar to it. For this reason, even though in consequence of man's emancipation of himself from God these abilities emancipate themselves from man and thus acquire the character of entities with some kind of existence and dominion of their own, only a pseudo-objective reality and efficacy can be possessed by them and ascribed to them. If man himself cannot escape the sphere of God's lordship, neither can the alienated forces of man. No matter how bad their effects may be, they cannot be ontologically godless forces. Indeed, God is not just their frontier; he is at liberty to make use of them in the fulfilment of his will. They may pretend to be absolute, but they cannot be so, nor can they be effectively lordless (even their multiplicity forbids this). For God is their Creator, they are his creatures, and they stand at his disposal. Something of the same may also be said of their relationship to man. They are in rebellion against him but even in this rebellion, in their assumed and apparent independence of him, they are still his. There can be no question of an emancipation of these abilities from him that is finally valid, effective, and irreversible. They might play the role of unalterably given presuppositions, of gods or fate, in relation to him, but in the last resort they are not these things even for him. They clearly are not, for they are really given to him and belong to him as his own powers, abilities, and possibilities of life. They derive power and lordship over him because of the disintegration of his relationship to God. He cannot deny their power or shake it off. Nevertheless, it is not ruled out that he can be liberated from them and protect and defend himself against their dominion. Hence they are not necessary determinations of his being and existence. Troublesome though they are, they are only contingent and relative determinations. Related to this relativity of their relationship to both God and man is the obscurity, ambivalence, and unintelligibility of their reality and efficacy. Also related to it is the wraithlike transitoriness with which they manifest themselves, one appearing here and another there, then disappearing or retreating to give place to another, then appearing again. Related to it also is the variety of the forms in which they arise in the different periods and cultural circles of human life and in the lives of individuals. Related to it again is the necessity with which—corresponding to the fact that there always seem to be unknown as well as known powers and possibilities of human life—we have to reckon not only with some very familiar but also with some new and unfamiliar forms of this kind. Related to it finally is the difficulty of finding clear and suitable names and concepts with which to denote them properly and describe them vividly, the truth being that, because they do not and cannot have more than pseudo-objective reality, we can speak of them only in consciously mythological terms.

We must not be led astray, however, by the reservations just adduced. We have to speak about these powers. We have to do so because we see them and know about them and have to take their reality and efficacy into account. We have to do so because in all their strangeness they *are* real and efficacious. World history, being the history of man and humanity, of Adamic humanity which has fallen from God, is also the history of innumerable absolutisms of different kinds, of forces that are truly and properly man's own but that have won a certain autonomy, independence, and even superiority in relation to him. There they are, powerful enough in and in spite of their impotence to be too much for the one who can and should be their lord and to take him to task, to master him who should master them, influencing, determining, and controlling his thought and speech and also his purposes and enterprises for himself and in his common life with others. If they are only pseudo-objective realities, strangely enough they are still powerful realities which make a fine display of their lying objectivity. If their power is only a usurped and creaturely one, and therefore relative and limited, nevertheless even in its relativity and limitation it is a highly effective one in its outward penetration and expansion. If they work only "as if" they were legitimate, this "as if" is clear and convincing and even forceful enough to fill man with respect for them and continually to deliver him up to their authority. No adjuring of human freedom, no overlooking, forgetting, or denying, is any help here. They are not just the supports but the motors of society. They are the secret guarantee of man's great and small conventions, customs, habits, traditions, and institutions. They are the hidden wirepullers in man's great and small enterprises, movements, achievements, and revolutions. They are not just the potencies but the real factors and agents of human progress, regress, and stagnation in politics, economics, scholarship, technology, and art, and also of the evolutions and retardations in all the personal life of the individual. It is not really people who do things, whether leaders or the masses. Through mankind's fault, things are invisibly done without and above man, even above the human individual in all his uniqueness, by the host of absolutisms, of powers that seek to be lordless and that make an impressive enough attempt to exhibit and present themselves as such.

In this matter we have one of the not infrequent cases in which it has to be said that not all people, but some to whom a so-called magical view of the world is now ascribed, have in fact, apart from occasional hocus-pocus, seen more, seen more clearly, and come much closer to the reality in their thought and speech, than those of us who are happy possessors of a rational and scientific view of things, for whom the resultant clear (but perhaps not wholly clear) distinction between truth and illusion has become almost unconsciously the criterion of all that is possible and real.

The world picture held by the New Testament community and therefore by the authors of the New Testament writings can obviously be described as a "magical" one and therefore as one that does not have that clarity. What is, perhaps, more important is that they were less hindered than we are by the world picture of their contemporaries, which was also their own, from taking freely into account the strange reality and efficacy of the lordless powers that are our present concern. This is what they actually did.

It would be best, of course, not to talk of their "belief" in these powers. The pagan world around them believed in the powers, and to a large extent so did the Jewish world. The New Testament, however, did not make them the content and theme of faith and proclamation, and since they are not fit subjects for this, we would do well to follow its example. Nevertheless, precisely in regard to the one true content and theme of faith and proclamation, the New Testament did not refuse to see and think and speak about the existence of these powers. Without developing any doctrine concerning them, it exhibited and named them as the negative presupposition, the target, of Christian faith and proclamation. Named and listed with differences of fullness and order in the New Testament Epistles, they are called δυνάμεις (capabilities, powers, forces, Rom. 8:38; 1 Cor. 15:24; Eph. 1:21), ἐξουσίαι (full sovereignties, 1 Cor. 15:24; Eph. 1:21; 3:10; 6:12; Col. 1:16; 2:10, 15), πνευματικά (influential spiritual beings, Eph. 6:12), κυριότητες (centers and spheres of dominion, Eph. 1:21; Col. 1:16; cf. 2 Pet. 2:10; Jude 8), more personally κύριοι (1 Cor. 8:5), also ἀρχαί (authorities, Rom. 8:38; 1 Cor. 15:24; Eph. 1:21; 3:10; 6:12; Col. 1:16; 2:10, 15), again personally, ἄρχοντες (1 Cor. 2:8; Eph. 2:2; cf. 1 Cor. 2:6), κοσμοκράτορες (world rulers, Eph. 6:12), once (Col. 1:16) very finely, θρόνοι, empty chairs that point very effectively to the majesties that fill the vacuum but are absent—one is reminded of the empty throne in the English House of Lords to which members bow on entry! Once (1 Pet. 3:22) they are even called ἄγγελοι, presumably in analogy to 2 Corinthians 11:14, where the factors of this pseudo-objectively real and efficacious kind clothe themselves in the garments of the angels of God and imitate their work. In Ephesians 2:2 they are all represented and personified in the figure of an ἄρχων τῆς ἐξουσίας, of the πνεῦμα νῦν ἐνεργοῦν, whose dwelling is the air, which has the same material sense as the common designation τά ἀόρατα in Colossians 1:16. According to Romans 8:38f. and Ephesians 1:21, these lists do not pretend to be exhaustive. Colossians 1:16 makes the obvious point that though these powers may sometimes appear and be described as κύριοι and even θεοί (1 Cor. 8:5), they belong to the creaturely world. From all the names, which remind us of familiar human possibilities and functions, it may be gathered that those who bear them are related especially to humans. They are more than life-size realizations of man's powers, but they stand in relative autonomy and even opposition to him. They are for him suspect, dangerous, and corrupting forces: not the last enemy like death (1 Cor. 15:26), but penultimate enemies which are to be taken very seriously, which are well armed (Col. 2:15), which present a serious threat, which are active adversaries of man and therefore of God. They rule in the darkness (Eph. 6:12). The day of their dominion is an evil day (Eph. 6:13). It was they who crucified the Lord of glory (1 Cor. 2:8). But their power is limited in relation to man as well as God; in almost every New Testament passage the one who limits it is called Jesus Christ. Ephesians 3:10f. says boldly enough that the church of Christians has to display not merely to the human world but also to these background forces, which rule, suppress, and oppress it, the fulfilment in Jesus Christ of the counsel of God and therefore their definitive limit—that the days of their lordship are numbered. Jesus Christ is far above these forces (Eph. 1:21). He is their limit from the very basis of their existence. Like the ὁρατά (Col. 1:16), as originally human forces, they belong to the totality of the reality distinct from God, being created in and by and to Jesus Christ and therefore subject to his sovereignty from the very first. In his history he has factually shown himself the victor and overcomer in opposition to their work (1 Pet. 3:22). He has triumphed over them at the very point where they seemed to triumph over him, namely, in his crucifixion (Col. 2:14f.). Their merited end will be their destruction in the consummation of his *parousia*, when even their pseudo-reality, the appearance of autonomy in which they now live and have their being, will be abolished (1 Cor. 15:24). Hence they cannot separate believers from the love of God in Christ Jesus any more than the afflictions can which come to them from the sphere of the visible creation and especially from hostile people (Rom. 8:39; cf. v. 35). Nevertheless, it is the clear meaning of the New Testament statements or hints adduced here that even within the limits that are set for them by the counsel of God and its fulfilment, by Jesus Christ who has come already and is present and will come again, these forces do still live and have their evil being, constantly persuading, assailing, and influencing Christians as they do all men. This obscure but very real and always actual problem is probably the issue in the most emphatic Synoptic accounts not only of the victorious encounter of Jesus with demons [Mk. 1:23ff. and par.] — once a whole legion of them dwelling in a single man [Mk. 5:9; Lk. 8:30] — but also of the commission and power that he gave his disciples to cast them out [Mk. 6:7 and par.]. It should be noted that the New Testament never shows any direct interest in these forces. It is directly interested only in the encounter of Jesus and his disciples with them and in their expulsion. But this means an indirect interest in them too. As the New Testament sees and understands people, they are pushed as well as pushing, moved as well as moving. This is another reason why there can be no place here for the formation of Christian fronts against others. Without questioning human responsibility and guilt, it sees behind and before people — who are self-alienated in their alienation from God and therefore no match for them — those impalpable but supremely efficacious potencies, factors, and agents, those imaginary gods and lords that are so active in their imaginary character. While asserting and not denying man's responsibility, it sees and understands the irrational and harmful nature of human attitudes and acts in terms of man's having fallen under the binding sway of these factors and agents. As the message of God's freeing of man from this bondage it constantly proclaims to all what God has done for them, and will do, in Jesus Christ. It thus proclaims to them faith in him, not (even incidentally) as faith in these forces, but as resolute unbelief in their reality and efficacy, even though these may not be denied but have to be taken soberly into account.

It would be better for us if we were to learn again with the same fearlessness and freedom to see and to reckon with the fact that even today we still live in a world that has been basically dedemonized already in Jesus Christ, and will be so fully one day. But in the meantime it still needs a good deal of dedemonizing, because even up to our own time it is largely demon-possessed, possessed, that is, by the existence and lordship of similar or, at times, obviously the same lordless forces which the people of the New Testament knew and which have plainly not been broken or even affected, but in many ways intensified and strengthened, by the fact that our view of the world has since those days become a rational and scientific one. Into this clear picture of the world which is ours, there thrust themselves, palpable for all their impalpability in every morning and evening newspaper in every corner of the globe, the great impersonal absolutes in their astonishing wilfulness and autonomy, in their dynamic, which with such alien superiority dominates not only the masses but also human personalities, and not just the small ones but also the great. We do not merely note but we know on how many of these we exist in dependence, not just some people but all of us — in dependence on powers whose unreality, if we try to envision them, seems obvious, but which in fact are incomparably more real and effective than the known or knowable factors of historical life and society. It would be better, however, if we noted and knew what they are really doing to us, not merely because, if we ignore or deny these great unknowns, what is known or knowable will be puzzling and exposed to every kind of misinterpretation, but especially because in this case we do not know what we are doing when we pray "Thy kingdom come," namely, that, negatively at least, we are asking for the gracious unmasking, overcoming, and ultimate abolition of these absolutisms that rule us *per nefas*.

A magical picture of the world? Might it be that our fellow Christians from the younger churches of Asia and Africa, who come with a fresher outlook in this regard, can help us here? We hope at least that they will not be too impressed by our view of the world and thus be afflicted by the eye disease from which we ourselves suffer in this matter.

But we must look a little more closely. In general, the authors of the New Testament refrained from naming or even describing those lordless forces, possibly because they could assume that they were already clear enough to their readers. In fact, they are there before our own eyes too, yet not perhaps with such clarity that it is not advisable to mention at least some of them and give a brief account of their nature and activity.

One thing is sure. The terms used to denote them in the New Testament, and especially the concept of the kingdom of God as a term for the superior authority opposing them, point unequivocally to the fact that the reference is, if not solely, then additionally and, it would seem, primarily, to all kinds of political absolutisms such as the first Christian communities saw at work behind and above the attitudes and acts of the great and little potentates, the highly diversified governments of their day. They were not concerned, as we are not, with the problem of the government of human existence as such. As is well known — we shall return to this in the last subsection — the New Testament regards this as a salutary divine order which Christians should neither evade nor oppose but to which they should adjust as subjects, not under compulsion, but consciously and conscientiously. It was and is, however, a question of the demonic which is visibly at work in all politics.

Government is not just the establishment and exercise of the right among men but also, for the sake of this, the establishment of sovereignty and dominion and the exercise of power and force by man over man. Now if power breaks loose from law, if the one who should be active in the service of the divine order chooses to value and love as such his sovereignty and dominion, his power and force over others, if he undertakes to establish and exercise these things for their own sake, as the man does who emancipates himself from God, then inasmuch as they too emancipate themselves from him and become his master, the demonism of politics arises. Law or right is no longer the order which helps man, which safeguards his life, which gives him freedom and peace. It is the establishment and strengthening of the power which is seized and exercised by some in the subjugation of others. Power no longer protects the right, nor finds in it its determination and limit. It subjects the right to itself and makes triumphant use of it. The state no longer serves man; man, both ruled and ruling, has to serve the state. The demonism of politics consists in the idea of "empire," which is always inhuman as such. This can be a monarchical, aristocratic, democratic, nationalistic, or socialistic idea. As this idea it is inhuman, and in virtue of its content it is always so as such. It stands behind and above all government, although never totally so, but only approximately even in the worst of cases.

It is the *myth* of the state which can be described only in mythological language, as it is in Revelation 13:1-8: "And I saw a beast rising out of the sea, with ten horns and seven heads, with ten diadems upon its horns and a blasphemous name upon its heads. And the beast that I saw was like a leopard, its feet were like a bear's, and its mouth was like a lion's mouth. And to it the dragon gave his power and his throne and great authority . . . and the whole earth followed the beast with wonder. Men worshipped the dragon, for he had given his authority to the beast, and they worshipped the beast, saying, 'Who is like the beast, and who can fight against it!' And the beast was given a mouth uttering haughty and blasphemous words, and it was allowed to exercise authority for forty-two months. . . . And authority was given it over every tribe and people and tongue and nation, and all who dwell on earth will worship it, every one whose name has not been written before the foundation of the world in the book of life of the Lamb that was slain."

We may now offer a remarkable illustration of this chapter and also of the whole problem of political absolutism. At the beginning of the modern period in the West, recapitulating and transcending all the absolutist theory and practice of the Renaissance, a book called *Leviathan* was published in 1651, written by the English philosopher Thomas Hobbes. Not for nothing has E. Hirsch hailed Hobbes as typical modern man, man-come-of-age, unencumbered by any world behind or above the present one [E. Hirsch, *Geschichte der neuern evangelischen Theologie im Zusammenhang mit den allgemeinen Bewegungen des europäischen Denkens*, Gütersloh, 1968[4], I, 142, 153-57]. Who and what is Leviathan? According to Hobbes' strictly inductive and deductive insight and construction, he is the epitome of the rise and existence, the past, present, and future, the essence and reality of the all-wise, all-knowing, all-powerful, and, in its way, all-good commonwealth or state as the only earthly potentate and sovereign with one or more heads (and preferably with only one). In hopeless fear of the war of all against all that would be the result of the individual possession and exercise of power, people have handed over and entrusted to it all their political, social, economic, intellectual, and even ethical and religious freedoms, possibilities, and rights. By their consent, not actually given but to be presupposed a priori, Leviathan is safeguarded against every possible protest; he therefore rules in their place and over them, teaching, instructing, directing, using, and expending them according to his own incontestable good pleasure. They are not his meaning and purpose; he is theirs. In this regard their life can be no more than a functioning in his honor and service. For Hobbes this construct was "artificial man" in terms of its rise and "earthly God" in terms of its existence, dignity, and authority. Along the lines of the polemic which was the purpose of his book he might easily have called it the true God-man. Leviathan's opponent, Behemoth, whose resistance is the point of the work, is the Christian church of all confessions to the extent that in its teaching and its life it should not just be one of the organs of the state but should champion the very different omnipotence of a very different God-man. A myth certainly — but who can deny that the underlying reality of all ancient, medieval, and not least of all modern political history was what Hobbes saw with the sharp glance of a visionary and expressed with great philosophical composure but also proclaimed with the suppressed passion of a prophet as not just reality but as truth, as *the* truth? Nor did he remain its only theoretical witness. Karl Marx and the social theoreticians who followed him seem to have seen Leviathan from various angles. After World War I, more dilettantish but for that reason all the more excited and exciting writers like Oswald Spengler and Ernst Jünger also saw Leviathan in their hellish visions of the coming iron age, Prussianism and Socialism, the eternal soldier, and all the rest [cf. O. Spengler, *Preussentum und Sozialismus*, Munich, 1920; E. Jünger, *Der Arbeiter, Herrschaft und Gestalt*, Hamburg, 1932, esp. p. 17]. But beyond literature, both serious and less serious, and apart from what Hobbes might have seen in his own age and the ages before him, we unmistakably find the most varied approximations in the period after him: in the state of Louis XIV, who as the sun-king equated the state with himself ("L'état c'est moi" [not of certain attestation]), in the enlightened despotism of Frederick the Great, in the lesser form of the absolute principalities and republics of the rest of the eighteenth century, in the Revolutionary Terror in France, in the Slavic regime of the Russian tsars, and in the empire of Napoleon I, which on the presupposition of a hundred glorious battles promised and claimed that it would bring peace [cf. the later statement of Napoleon III, "L'empire, c'est la paix," Bordeaux, 10/9/1852]. Finally, of course, Leviathan may be seen in the so-called totalitarian states or dictatorships of our own century — Fascism, National Socialism, and Stalinism. For all the dissimilarities, these highly remarkable figures resemble the quiet scholar of Malmesbury in this regard — and this is the secret of their political magic — that without having read a word of Hobbes they were intoxicated, possessed, fascinated, and demonized by the Leviathan that he perceived and proclaimed, and for this reason they were able to fascinate and demonize those around them. The idea of absolute and lordless power concentrated at one point in one hand (it is not without reason that J. Burckhardt, *Weltgeschichtliche Betrachtungen, Gesammelte Werke*, IV [Darmstadt, 1956], p. 25, has called it an evil one), the idea of the state as a machine for the production, safeguarding, and extension of power (Golo Mann, *Deutsche Geschichte, 1919-1945*, p. 137), the idea of a polity which leaves only the options of intoxication with its mad principle, or actual assimilation to its structure and program, or law-breaking opposition — this idea was the force that fascinated and demonized those leaders and through them countless multitudes, a lordless force because they were not in any sense its lord but were instead possessed by it. The step from the possibility of adult man to the reality of man under age and under tutelage has proved to be a frighteningly small one in our own century. We need to realize that no state of any kind is or has or will be immune to the tendency to become at least a little Leviathan. The threat of a change from the might of right to the right of might couches at the door of every polity. It has never been actualized in more than an approximate form and never can be. But it is evil and harmful enough in these approximations. Thomas Hobbes affirmed, demanded, taught, and proclaimed it. Greater than the horror his strange kerygma arouses is the praise he deserves for not being blind and stupid in this matter but for his vision and knowledge. From the reverse standpoint it should be part of Christian vigilance to see and know what he saw and knew.

Another of the lordless powers is in fact given a specific name in the New Testament. This is Mammon. The origin of the word seems to be obscure. What is certain is that somewhat mythologically, yet not unrealistically, it refers to the material possessions, property, and resources that have become the idol of man, or rather his very mobile demon. The word "resources," with its double sense, is especially instructive at this point. At the beginning the reference is to resources which are part of man's nature, which are neutral, which are even good in themselves, which can be used by him in freedom. They are the power of man displayed in his control of certain material goods and valuables, to guarantee and secure a livelihood. But what happens when he uses this power as the man who is emancipated from God? Who ensures or guarantees what resources are now in play? His own? Or, apart from him, the power of his resources, the means which is supposed to guarantee and secure his livelihood but which now confronts him with imperious claims in its tendency to become an end, the thing which has accrued to him or been created and won by him, but which now has its own weight, majesty, and worth, the great or little barns, with the great or little that is stored up in them for the future (Lk. 12:16ff.), which profoundly disturb him because they promise, but only promise, that he may be at rest and of good courage? Can he trust their promises? Does he really own what he has? Supposing that for a long time it has really owned him? It causes him unavoidable anxiety: is it really his and will it remain his? Since it might slip out of his grasp, should he not strengthen and consolidate the guarantee and security it seems to offer by adding to it more things of the same kind? Must he not look out for such things and exert himself to create or acquire them? If his resources are to be faithful to him, to serve him and give him comfort, does he not have to be faithful to them and serve them? When he perceives this and acts accordingly, then in a very harmless form here or in greater measure there they acquire power over him. Mammon, the close relative of Leviathan, is born. It mounts its throne. The worship of it begins, whether wittingly or unwittingly, openly or discreetly, cheerfully or sighingly. Along with the many other things that it is, powerful not in one or other evil alone but in and over all people, the spirit of this world is also the spirit of Mammon, the spirit of our resources or possessions attempting self-absolutization.

In Matthew 6:24 and Luke 16:13 Mammon is presented as a second κύριος (lord) competing with God, and we are told that love and devotion and service cannot be shown at one and the same time to God and it and it and God—an unheard of suggestion, for who would think of such a thing? The unrighteous Mammon or the Mammon of unrighteousness (Lk. 16:9, 11) is what it is called in the light of and with reference to its being "another's" (Lk. 16:12) in the life of man which responds with no sure loyalty to loyalty, and thus grants no true guarantee or security, since man may seem to have it today and it can slip away tomorrow (Lk. 16:4, 9). Its treasures can also fall victim to moth and rust or burglars and thieves (Mt. 6:19). In this connection we also read [Lk. 16:1ff.] that its lordship is not as absolute as it pretends to be. One who is πιστός (faithful) — why does it not say "a believer"? — may have dealings with it, the unrighteous one. This one can play a trick on it by so disposing of it as no longer to dispose of it, simply giving it away in order to share the true good (ἀληθινά). This is what the steward does whom Jesus called a prudent man in Luke 16:8. Yet from what we read about him in Luke 16:1ff. this steward does not embody an ethical possibility but one that is to be realized with the coming of the kingdom of God. On this side of its coming we people are not free in relation to Mammon. It is even a great thing if there are those who pray for liberation from it and at least make some honest efforts to move in this direction.

In our own thinking and language Mammon is more directly connected than it is in the New Testament — although this aspect is present there — with the concept of money, which is certainly a familiar one in both the Old Testament and the New Testament. It is part of the slippery nature of the matter that the definition of money seems to be difficult and even to this day a matter of controversy among those versed in the subject. What is incontestable is that money as such is not a good which directly serves the support of human life. At most, gold and silver could and can come into the picture as raw materials out of which to make articles of adornment; but who, with some exceptions, either would or does think of using gold or silver money for this purpose? Even as a material good, money had and has only symbolic value. Without any real value in and of itself, money is the classic representation of real values on the basis of certain conventions. Money in the hands of its possessor is a publicly and generally recognized, though numerically limited, pointer to certain commodities available to and desired by him, to participation, within the limits of its numerical signifi-cance and the available supply, in the possessions or products of the society around him. With his money he can buy something from it, or from one of its members, as though the money were real achievement. A person's money, as the symbol of his ability, is for himself and others, by a conventional fiction, his measurable economic capacity. Economically speaking, he is worth what money he either has, or earns through his work, or has prospects of (e.g., by inheritance). In short, he *is* to the degree that he can pay, that he is credit-worthy. The thing that makes him this when he has resources under his control is no longer measured in terms of barns and their contents, or these only insofar as they have a monetary sale value. What really counts, the things that he controls, is his smaller or greater amount of money, stored up in a drawer or stocking, or better still, credited to him in a bank and there, whether as his account or in the form of shares or notes, quietly and agreeably increasing without any cooperation on his part, like the seed that grows of itself in the gospel [cf. Mk. 4:26ff.] — so long as the bank does not crash and both capital and interest are lost.

Man's relationship to God and neighbor would have to be different if he were not mildly or wildly fascinated by this. It is clear that Mammon in the form of money, which stirs and excites the speculative imagination in a very different way from barns and their contents, can be and is much more intensive Mammon, the lordless power of material resources that holds absolute sway over man and men and humanity. In all its inner worthlessness, revealed in the glorious discovery of paper money and especially in purely book transactions, money is, if not *the*, at least *a* capital epitome and standard not merely of economic values but of all human values, for what can one not buy for money? Money is a flexible but powerful instrument which, supposedly handled by man, in reality follows its own law. In a thousand ways it can establish some opinions and even convictions and suppress others. It can also create brutal facts. It can cause the market to rise and then to fall again. It can arrest this crisis and cause another. It can serve peace yet pursue cold war even in the midst of peace. It can make ready for a bloody war and finally bring it about. It can bring provisional paradise here and the corresponding provisional hell there. It does not have to do all these things, but it can. It can and does: not money as such, but the money that man thinks he possesses, although in truth it possesses him, and it does so because he wants to have it without God and thus creates a vacuum in which this intrinsically harmless but useful fiction becomes an absolutist demon, and man himself can only be its football and slave. Mammon, then, is no reality, and yet it is one — and what a reality! — not to mention what happens when Mammon meets and joins and comes to terms with that other demon Leviathan, political absolutism.

Since a full and systematic survey is not possible here, let us at least try to take a quick glance at two other typical groups of the lordless powers that rule man instead of serving him.

A particularly prominent and, to some extent, noble group is made up of intellectual constructs, or ideologies as they are usually called. How do these come into existence and seize power?

Man has the remarkable ability to grasp in the form of concepts his conscious perceptions of his own inner life, that of his fellow men, and finally that of the whole of the outside world. He can put these together in definite pictures. He can arrange his impressions and ideas in thoughts and groups of thoughts. He can make these into more or less exact knowledge and then bring this into inner connection with, and put it in the service of, that which he himself thinks he should will and be as a person both for himself and in society with others. He can convince himself, or let himself be convinced, of the need to begin with certain theoretical and practical ideas in all that he knows, wills, thinks, says, and does individually and concretely, to make these ideas for the time being the solid presuppositions or preliminary sketches underlying his actions, to approach problems and their solutions with the mind and reflection determined by them. So far, so good.

But supposing that it is the man who has fallen from God who makes use of this wonderful ability, this power of spirit! In this spirit of his, which makes itself independent of the living Spirit of God, there will then arise at once, and at the decisive point, a distinctive numbness, hardening, and

2. *The Lordless Powers*

rigidity, and therefore an inertia in which he will cease to be a free spirit. This comes about as he thinks he can and should ascribe to the presuppositions and sketches he has achieved by this remarkable ability, not just a provisional and transitory but a permanent normativity, not just one that is relative but one that is absolute, not just one that is human but one that is quasi-divine. His hypotheses become for him theses behind which he no longer ventures to go back with seeking, questioning, and researching. He thinks that they can be thought and formulated definitively as thoughts that are not merely useful but intrinsically true and therefore binding. His ideal becomes an idol. He thinks that he knows only unshakable principles and among them a basic principle in relation to which he must coordinate and develop them as a whole, combining them all, and with them his perceptions and concepts, into a system, making of his ideas an ideology. Here again the reins slip out of his hands. This creature of his, the ideology, seems to be so wonderfully glorious and exerts on him such a fascination that he thinks he should move and think and act more and more within its framework and under its direction, since salvation can be achieved only through the works of its law. This ideology becomes the object of his reflection, the backbone and norm of his disposition, the guiding star of his action. All his calculations, exertions, and efforts are now predestined by it. They roll toward its further confirmation and triumph like balls on a steep slope. Man's whole loyalty is loyalty to the line demanded by it. He thinks that he possesses it, but in truth it already possesses him. In relation to it he is no longer the free man who thought he had found it in its glory and should help to put it on the throne. He now ventures to ask and answer only within its schema. He must now orient himself to it. He must represent it as its more or less authentic witness and go to work as its great or small priest and prophet. At root he no longer has anything of his own to say. He can only mouth the piece dictated to him as intelligibly as he can, and perhaps like a mere parrot. His own face threatens already to disappear behind the mask that he must wear as its representative. He already measures and evaluates others only from the standpoint of whether they are supporters of this ideology, or whether they might become such, or whether they might at least be useful to it even without their consent, or whether they must be fought as its enemies. Its glory has already become for him the solution not only to the personal problem of his own life but to each and all of the problems of the world.

It is a good thing that there never has been, nor can nor will be, an ideology that is able to realize its absolute claim, to fill people, or even a single person, totally and exclusively and definitively, to make him no more than its functionary. Man does not live only as he thinks. Even as he thinks, he is wittingly or unwittingly engaged in a quiet movement from old ideas to new, and therefore in transition from one ideology to another, so that one ideology can fascinate him only in specific times and places and only to a specific degree. It is bad enough, however, that in specific times and places in both individual and social life ideologies can rise up like monstrous bubbles in all their changing colors and have their fascinating effect on the minds of humans, not as omnipotent intellectual forces but as very potent ones that do not merely accompany human history but to some extent make it, partly in concurrence with Leviathan and Mammon, partly in competition with them.

The presence and activity of ideologies may be seen linguistically in the ending "ism," which may praise or blame intrinsically harmless terms and concepts pointing to some element of creaturely being, but which are in any case connected with a mysterious hissing. Thus ideas are systematized as idealism, the corresponding phenomena as phenomenalism, the related reality as realism, which may present itself as spiritualism here, naturalism or even materialism there. History gives us historicism and existence existentialism. Freedom when clarified or obscured ideologically becomes liberalism, society becomes, as a term of praise or opprobrium, socialism or communism, private ownership of the means of production capitalism, holding on to what is old and tested conservatism, resolute advanced progressivism, and even radicalism. Faithfulness to the Bible is extolled or censured as biblicism, faithfulness to the confessions as confessionalism, piety as pietism, and Christian discipline as methodism. In place of the recognition of Christ, that is, when this is changed into a principle, there now enters what is called christocentrism. In relation to God, the same process gives us, according to taste and purpose, deism, theism, monotheism, pantheism, or even atheism. As is well known, "ism" can also be conjoined to the names of people, so that we have Hegelianism, Marxism, Stalinism, and so forth, and the disciples of these people are then usually called "ians" or "ists." In every field "ism" shows that one view, one concept, one figure in the field of human life, one possibility of human outlook and action, has assumed the role of regulator and dictator in relation to all the rest, and that round this principle a system has developed in face of which man is more or less on the point of losing his freedom or has already lost it. Wherever we find "ism" there lurks an ideology, and it is as well to be on guard if it is not already too late.

A second sign of the presence and activity of ideologies is the occurrence of slogans or catchwords. It is no accident that ideologies should rely on phrases that have such an expressly menacing ring. These phrases are deliberately thought out, spoken, and written or printed with a view to striking, stabbing, and finally snaring. They do not enter into conversation with the other but speak about him in a massive surprise attack. The slogan is not designed to teach, instruct, or convince the hearer or reader. It aims to exert a drum-roll influence on people by awakening associations, engendering ideas and the associated feelings, and issuing marching orders. It does not initiate or permit any reflection or discussion, but it hammers home an axiom that must precede and underlie any possible reflection and discussion. It can do this in the form of direct or indirect imperatives: "Workers of the world unite," or "Germany, wake up," or "Make way for the strong," or "Equal rights for all," or "Africa for the Africans." It can also seem to be objective, yet be all the more demanding by associating the noun with a significant adjective, for example, "presuppositionless science," or "indigenous art," or "the free world," or "the American way of life," or "biblical reformed insight," or "historical-critical method," or "relevant preaching." Some catchwords can be given a better interpretation since they are concentrates of the insights and intentions expressed in them. Others, however, are neither clear nor precise and seek to exert pressure only in one direction, so that it is no use looking for their exact meaning among those who shout them the loudest and receive them the most enthusiastically, nor even perhaps among those who invent them. Slogans are simply vents with whose help ideologies surface and in the form of loud whistles call for general applause and acknowledgment. Let us not be deceived: we all listen to the most varied catchwords, we all use them more or less merrily, and in so doing we show that we ourselves are people who have been struck and stabbed and snared by systematized ideologies.

The third sign of ideologies is the propaganda which they all have to put out, and usually put out with a swing, each on its own behalf and with varying degrees of force, against all the others. Along with much else, a mouth to speak great things is given not only to the beast of Revelation 13 but to most of his associates and especially to ideologies. This mouth is propaganda, and to serve it the Third Reich set up a special ministry of propaganda. It is a necessity and also a typical expression of these lordless powers of the spirit. These powers seek as such not only to strike and stab and snare the human spirits to whose fall from God they owe their existence but also to put them reliably and securely in their service by integrating them into their own thinking as though they came to think this way on their own: "Advertising helps it happen." They have to win them over. They want to do so. They have thus to commend themselves and make themselves clear to them. This means that they have to proceed apologetically and polemically. They thus engage in propaganda. Propaganda is putting things in black and white — the particular art and masterwork of ideologies. What they have to push systematically is their own excellence and usefulness, and by way of background they must show how utterly valueless and harmful their rivals and opponents are. Words of propaganda may be fruitfully combined with acts of propaganda. Propaganda can be direct or indirect, the crude work of the village smith or the refined work of the skilled mechanic, totally ingenuous and well-meaning but also poisoned and bitter, skillful on the one hand and unskillful on the other. If there has always been propaganda in some form, from the time of the modest newspapers of the seventeenth century it has developed with a new speed and to a new degree, as new and more effective instruments have been found and brought into use. One should note that the truth needs no propaganda and does not engage in it. As the truth, it simply speaks for itself and opposes falsehood. Propaganda is a sure sign that what is at issue is not the truth but an ideology which needs it, to whose nature it corresponds, and which is not ashamed to make use of it, as we see today in the propaganda of furtive anti-Semitism, of communism and anticommunism, and also of moral rearmament, which expressly boasts that it champions and proclaims an ideology and will cause it to triumph. If only we could say of the church that it does not engage in propaganda! To the extent that it does it makes itself unworthy of the truth to which it must bear witness by obviously confusing it with an ideology and thinking it can handle it as such. It would be as well for all of us to realize that as we are daily washed around by so much open and hidden propaganda, we too are undoubtedly caught in the snares of more than one of these distinctive powers of the spirit.

Along with the spiritual forces — and we now turn to the second group of lordless powers that concern us — there are also those that in contrast might be treated together as *chthonic* forces. Even as man forms pictures and concepts, thinks in ideas, and coordinates these relatively or absolutely, he does not exist in an empty or separate sphere of the spirit. As a being that is pervasively determined, shaped, and gifted physically as well, he also exists in the physical sphere of the created cosmos, in the corporeal world which in practice is to a large degree visible to him and under his control, and in the known and unknown energies of this sphere as the realm of his own experiences and activity. In the Bible this sphere is called earth, in distinction from heaven, which is in principle invisible and outside his

control. As man himself is not separately soul and body, but the soul of his
body, he never looks and strives only upward, as it might seem in the act
of perception and thought, but always downward as well. He does the
former only that he may the more strongly do the latter, thus making true
the great saying in Genesis 1:28 that he is to have dominion over the earth,
which on the biblical view includes the so-called universe. He is to make
the earth his own world, to shape it as the theater and tool of his historical
existence. He realizes the possibility and freedom which is given him for
this purpose and which is basically unlimited in this field. He lives in and
by using it. Outwardly as well as inwardly, in work as well as thought, he
disposes and triumphs over the forces of his own nature and that around
him, over the spirits of the earth [cf. J. W. Goethe, *Faust*, V, 460ff.]. He
investigates them, makes them usable by him, and puts them in his service
as their lord. This is what he has learned to do, and has done, with increasingly astonishing range from the distant past. So far, so good, we may again
say: good to the extent that he does this as real man, that is, as man loved
by God, created good by him, and ordained by him to do this work in the
freedom that he owes to the grace of the free God and as he himself stands
in the service of him who has given him this dominion, the lord of nature
who is at the same time the servant of God.

If, however, he slips out of this service, he thereby forfeits the lordship
that should be his. In the sudden or gradual movement with which man
breaks free from God, he revolutionizes the natural forces that are coordinated with him and subordinated to him, first those that slumber and then
awaken in himself, then the spirits of the earth that are first concealed in
the surrounding cosmos but are then discovered and unleashed by his keen-
sightedness and skill. It is he who frees and automatizes these spirits to
satisfy his own wants and to achieve his own practical goals. He is the one
who discovers them and sees how useful they can be in his service. It is his
spirit that triumphs in their exploitation. It is he who is at the helm, who
pulls the levers, who presses the knobs. Nevertheless, they automatically
and autonomously rumble and work and roll and roar and clatter outside
him, without him, past him, and over him. He finds that he himself is
subject to their law, which he has foreseen, and to their power, which he
has released. Turning aside from God, he is himself displaced, that is, jerked
out of his proper position in relation to these forces into one that is unworthy
of him. Still his slaves, they now confront him as robots which he himself
has to serve, and not without being forced to fear their possible pranks. In
satisfying his earlier wants, they fill and excite him with new ones which
he never experienced before but which he cannot deny or suppress in view
of the enticing possibility of meeting them. In simplifying and easing his
life, they also complicate it and make it more difficult. They take away his
little anxieties but create new and bigger ones. They seem to promise him
courage and a greater zest for life, but increased worry about life is the
fulfilment of their promise. Like the spiritual forces, but in a way that is
felt much more directly, the chthonic powers, which for a change draw
downward instead of up, serve in and of themselves to bind the man who

has broken free from God, to put him under obligation, to tyrannize him, to lead him where he does not want to go [cf. Jn. 21:18], to rob him of his freedom under the pretext and appearance of granting every kind of freedom. Their lordship is certainly not an unconditional one. It has only a limited sphere. But like the sphere of Leviathan and Mammon and the ideologies, this sphere is as big as the sphere of life of fallen man as such. In the here and now in which we all are, there is every cause to turn to their existence and action, absurd though it is, and to examine it fearlessly but closely.

Among these lordless powers of earth that lord it over us, we must certainly consider that of technology, which urgently dominates the field today, but not that alone. We may begin with a harmless — but not totally harmless — example. Who or what really determines fashion — the fashion to which man thinks he must obediently subject clothes, headgear, and hairstyle, the alternation of assurance and then of exposure first to the rather sympathetic astonishment and then to the horror and amusement of those who think they must follow the new fashion? How is it that women's fashions change so much more quickly and solemnly and intensively than men's? Why does it seem to be to even the most sensible women, if not an act of lese majesty, at least an impossibility to be old-fashioned? Who wants it this way? The particular industry that tirelessly makes money out of it and whose kings, we are told, reside especially in Paris? But who has made these people the kings? What is it that has always made this industry so lucrative? How has it come about that since the end of the eighteenth century men's clothing has become so monotonous and uninteresting? Conversely, how has it come about that world history might be presented from the standpoint of the sequence in which men have thought that they should shave or not shave their faces or adorn them with the boldest or most hideous arrangements of hair? Who inspires and directs these processes, which are not a matter of indifference to the feeling for life and all that it implies? If it is a matter of rapidly changing taste, what released spirit of the earth pulls the strings so that this fancy passes, another which is anxiously watched by millions comes and prevails, and then after a while it too departs? The example of fashion may seem to be a trivial one. The same questions arise at a higher level in regard to difference and change in styles of painting, sculpture, music, and poetry in different times and places. It is usually said that these express the changing feeling for time and nature, but why precisely this expression and not another one?

Today what is called sport seems to have become the playground of a particular earth-spirit. In most cases the old and honest saying "A healthy mind in a healthy body" (Juvenal, *Satires*, X, 356) can no longer be invoked today as a rational explanation of what motivates active sporting figures. From the pictures of some of them, for example, some great boxers, one cannot conclude that they are particularly noble people. But what has made sport to a large extent a public matter of the first rank, first in ancient Greece and Rome, and then again today? What is behind the enthusiasm of millions of sporting fans who watch the players with such passionate and often frenzied excitement? What has made the industrializing and commercializing of sport so clearly remunerative? Why is the Sunday evening paper so infinitely more important to countless numbers of people because of the late news it gives about football scores rather than accounts of the most astounding and momentous things that might have happened in the arena of world politics? After the soccer championship games in Sweden in 1958, what led Brazil, the home of the victorious team, to establish a new national holiday, and what was it that brought the prodigy

Pélé, then seventeen years old, not only a good deal of money and many other good things but also no fewer than five hundred offers of marriage, while on the same occasion Germany, for the opposite reason, threatened to plunge into a kind of irritated national mourning with all kinds of accompanying phenomena? Why all this fuss and fury? What is the real glory (*doxa*) of the winner of the Tour of France or Switzerland? Is there a measure of representation here? Is it a matter of the primitive need to make heroes of those who prove themselves and triumph over all others in some contest, whether in climbing the north face of the Eiger or winning auto races or being successful matadors, because we would all like to be these people, and can thus find ourselves in them and, jealous of all rivals, can accompany them, rejoicing when they succeed and weeping when they fall? But who dictates this need to man, and who says that it is to be met in this ultimately rather primitive form? What is the majesty that has brought to the Olympic games the regular cultic form of worship, praise, laud, and thanksgiving? So many facts, questions, and riddles! It should be obvious that we have here a special form of derangement. Man has lost and continually loses his true majesty. It is thus inevitable that, in this matter too, sense should change into nonsense.

We may also put the general question of what really happens when, after or alongside his necessary work, man seems to want pleasure and seems able to have it. There have always been means to provide pleasure, and there is a whole host of such today. Ultimately they are much the same: companionship in a room or out in the open, satisfaction of curiosity about foreign and preferably very distant places and countries, a certain amount of sport, today some jazz, cinema, and television, at a higher level reading, a little (and sometimes more than a little) alcohol, not to forget a little (and sometimes more than a little) sex. But does what is offered really stand the test of the goal that is obviously in view with the use of all these means, with the endless sequence of great and little entertainments and celebrations? If it did, then why should they not take place, why should not all or some of these means be open to discussion, why should we not be able to have sufficient festivals? The real point, however, is that in order to have the enjoyment sought in them, people have to be joyous. Are they? If they are not — and how can they be when they want to loose themselves from God? — then how can anything they crave and grasp to make them joyous really achieve enjoyment for them? If they found pleasure, then they would not have to desire and chase increasingly refined and massive means of providing pleasure, and we should find satisfied faces at the larger and smaller places of entertainment and amusement. The various exertions that have to go toward the providing of pleasure, the means that are needed to give it, the over-assiduous talk devoted to the pleasure expected from them — are not all these signs that bode no good for the pleasure that will eventually be derived, since they suggest that any enjoyment they offer will be uneasy, tense, and hectic? Why is it that after the event such a dull, if not a sour or bitter, taste is left on the palate? Is it not true that to the tumult of the desire for enjoyment there corresponds only too closely in the enjoyment itself a thirst for desire? What is wrong? Why is this so? Is it not that in the form of more or less everything in which man seeks pleasure, and thinks he can find it, a special kind of earth-spirit has long since been at work, one of those lordless powers? These forces can and should serve man. As their cheerful lord, man can and should make use of them. But supposing the relationship has long since been reversed, so that man is no longer their cheerful lord and he must serve them, not possessing them but possessed, driven, and obsessed by them? Supposing that since he means and does nothing good by God, they mean and do nothing good by him, and instead of providing him with entertainment, all things considered, they can only pervert all his entertainment at the very root?

We shall now consider a last example taken from the host of typically chthonic powers and forces. What has happened to us — with unparalleled and increasingly astonishing extension and intensity today — in the field of transportation, the fulfilment of the very simple expression of life involved when we move from one place to another? How has it come about that, no longer content with walking, carriages, galleys, and sailing ships, nor with the good old steam locomotive that seemed like a mythical monster to the surprised D. F. Strauss (*Ausgewählte Briefe*, ed. E. Zeller, Bonn, 1895, p.103 [Letter to E. Rapp, May 24, 1841]), we have sought, and obviously had to seek, increasingly rapid movement by land, air, and sea with the use of more effective automobiles, jets, and diesels? And how does it stand with the brilliant successes in which we may rejoice, and the new prospects they continually open up before us? There undoubtedly seemed and seems to be a great rationalization and simplification of our coming and going, and above all an increasing acceleration with the consequent saving of time and energy. Furthermore, the irksome distances between the countries and inhabitants of our planet have been reduced to a minimum. So far, so good! If only one could say why all these people rushing by so quickly are in such a hurry, why it is that they are so terribly pressed, as may be seen very forcibly today on every street! What do they propose to do with the time and energy saved? When people of such different places and localities are so surprisingly brought together, what do they think of saying to one another? How far is the enhanced speed of our movements to and fro really necessary or rewarding? Are people in such a hurry because they are afraid of something? What are they afraid of? Be that as it may, what have the automobile, the airplane, and the rocket brought about in human life that is not just different but better as compared with the time of walking and the stagecoach, better, that is to say, in terms of true pleasantness, the understanding and mastering of serious problems and needs, the real relations between people? Have they given us a more open, profound, fruitful, beautiful, and kindly view of the cosmos around us, a more vital one than that of Goethe? Do not modern travelers rush undeviatingly past a hundred noteworthy things, blind where their forefathers could see, and perhaps flying over them altogether up in the void? Has life really become easier and not harder through our happily achieved accelerations? Or are we expecting that all this will come with increased speed, with the help of atomically propelled vehicles or the development of cosmic carriages when the moon itself will not be worth looking at by those who are on the way to Venus? Meanwhile, we suppress the common complaint of the pedestrian of what is to become of him (initially because he lets himself be given a ride so gladly). We note with concern how so many homeless motorcars are choking our overcrowded roads and streets. We have noted the evening lines of traffic moving slowly enough on the roads leading into and out of our cities. We ask ourselves timidly whether the increasing traffic, making a mock of highway planning and its many devices, will not finally prove to be the biggest obstacle to efficient transportation, and whether in the near future the same problem might not arise in the air as well. And how can we fail to note the daily lists of traffic accidents and their victims, whose total numbers (in 1960, 65,000 in Europe) have already reached and even surpassed the number of those lost in war? We regard it as very dubious comfort that their growth is not so bad in relation to the increase in the number of vehicles now on the roads. We also note the devastation of the countryside as freeways cut ruthlessly through arable land, pastures, and whole villages. We ask whether the speed that motorized man is allowed is not bought too dearly in view of its obvious hostility to life. But what is the good of all this noting and questioning? What does it accomplish apart from making the backwoodsman opponent of modern transport a mere figure of fun? The wheel of time cannot be stopped, let alone reversed. The wheel, the wheel! What kind of wheel is this? If there is any unfettered and palpably lordless chthonic power today, which eludes every effort to predict and control its future and evades protest, it is the powerful instinct, violently aroused in all its rational irrationality, which ineluctably invites man, regardless of whether he can or should, to hurry as quickly as possible, and then even more quickly, through the space that is his, pushing and forcing him to do so whether he wants to or not. The bondage of the will! People have to do this, *we* have to do it, even though we do not know why, even though we do not know where the propulsion of the earth-spirit in this form will lead us. Yet we must add to this: No, they do not have to do it, we do not really have to do it, the person who rests in God and is moved by him is sovereign in relation to this very primitive thing, namely, his movement in space, whether in a car or on foot, whether with greater or lesser speed, and he can order it and carry it out meaningfully — and knowing what he is doing. It is, however, one of the strangest symptoms of the basically perverted beginning of our existence, and of the existence of the powers that anonymously control us, that we seem *not* to be free to do this.

We pause for a moment. What has been said about Leviathan and Mammon, and about the spiritual and chthonic powers, has been said by way of sampling to show clearly that the New Testament was not romancing but taking a very realistic view of the human situation, which we should not ignore because of our very different picture of the world, when it spoke about the lordless forces which in and with the fall of man have broken away from God, which now hold sway over man, which come between him and God, and which impel him apart from and even against his own knowledge and will. There are such powers. Their false lights cannot be overlooked. The rumor of them cannot be missed. There can be no mistaking the perverted nature of their being and the deep lack of seriousness of their activity. To talk of them more seriously than has been done here is not to take them seriously as befits them but to give evidence of falling doubly victim to them. We have had to speak of them, because as a result of the fall of man it is they that bring human existence and history, both as a whole and in detail, into the disorder against which the Christian who prays the second petition of the Lord's Prayer is commanded to rebel; the disorder which is man's fault, since it is he who unleashes those powers, but under which he has to suffer, since they prove to be stronger than he is; the disorder in face of which he is referred to the mercy of our Father in heaven, to calling upon him, but which he himself is also summoned to resist to the utmost of his strength. The powers are very different from one another. At first glance they seem to be unrelated and even contradictory in their effects. Yet they have one thing in common. As remarkable protuberances of the ability loaned to man as the creature of God, they do not work for man but against him. In spite of all his dreams and expectations, they bring him no help. He promises himself that they will give liberation, strength, ease, simplification, and enrichment, but they do not. They do not mean good by him. On the contrary, they break away from him even as he breaks away from God. They are thus inhuman. Indeed, to the extent that he himself, having broken away from God, is God's enemy, the powers are hostile to man and are man's enemy. They disrupt his life. They would inevitably destroy him if they were allowed to work without restriction, if a limit were not imposed on them. When they are still in the process of development, they pretend that they will develop and safeguard his freedom, that they will shape his inner and outer resources and desires, that they will bring mighty fulfilments and extensions and deepenings of his creaturely being. They attract and force him to venture upon continually new experiments and enterprises with them. But it is not for nothing that they are the fictions, the illusions, the lying spirits they are. They can only confuse and unsettle him. In varying degrees, this is what they do. Inevitably, in the form of the forces which he has unleashed and which have become lordless, his own strength turns not only away from him but against him. They rob people of the freedom which they have misused and thus forfeited in advance. They oppress people. They move them according to the laws of their own dynamics and mechanics. They make them subjects, parrots, puppets, or even robots. In so doing they afflict and oppress and harass them. Under their lordship people necessarily become "people of disorder" [cf. G. Staewen-Ordemann, "Menschen der Unordnung," *Studien zur Religionssoziologie und Sozialpsychologie*, Vol. III, Berlin, 1933]. As people are estranged from God, so they are from themselves and their neighbors, alienated from God and themselves and their fellows. As the powers tear apart the individual, so — because there are so many of them and in such competition — they tear apart society also. Giving rights to no one, they make it impossible for any to grant mutual rights. As the human dignity of those who are in some way ridden and spurred and whipped by demons is fundamentally compromised, just so the dignity of others can signify no lasting obligation to them. In the realm of Leviathan and Mammon, of the ideologies, and especially of the chthonic powers, none of them can have any rest or peace, and they can spread no rest or peace around them. The lordship of these powers, which are all of them no more than exponents of the rebellion that separates man from God, is synonymous with the destruction and ruin of both the individual and society. This dominion reveals, though it does not constitute, the plight of man, the profound unrighteousness in which we people exist — each alone and in mutual relation — because of the basic unrighteousness of our relationship to God, the unrighteousness in which, each for himself and all for all others, we inevitably make life more or less difficult. What would we be, what would happen to the world, what would it have become long ago, if the river of the unrighteousness that triumphs in the lordship of the lordless forces had not come up against an unshakable dam? But such a dam does resist it. Over against the kingdom of human disorder stands the kingdom of the divine order.

3. THY KINGDOM COME

Man would like to break free from God, to make himself independent of him, to posit himself absolutely. In so doing, however, he overreaches

himself. He cannot and will not succeed. Nor will the powers that he re-
leases and that make themselves out to be lordless. "He who sits in the
heavens laughs; the Lord has them in derision" (Ps. 2:4). He does that to
us. He would not be God if the unrighteousness and disorder that man has
brought on his individual and social existence, the lordship of the lordless
powers, and the suffering that man causes himself and has to endure under
their lordship, did not find a limit in him.

That they have this limit may be seen already in their own sphere in
the simple fact that the Christian and the Christian community pray "Thy
kingdom come." The fact that along with everything else that happens it
also happens that people can and will and, in all their weakness and confusion, do pray this proves the majesty and might of another kingdom,
which as God's kingdom is very different from the kingdom of disorder, the
lordship of the lordless powers to which the Christian and also the church
are painfully enough exposed and even subject. Within the sphere of these
powers, that other kingdom is obviously if inconceivably confessed and
known. There is an open looking in its direction. A calling for it is heard,
an invocation of God as its Lord and King. Among all other human acts,
and in all humanity, the act of this invocation is to be noted too, and in it
may be seen the limit which is set for the kingdom of human disorder — set
by that other kingdom which in the form of the prayer for its coming is not
only distant but also near and already present.

This is the special thing about the freedom that Christianity has for this
act. This is what makes it a sign that neither man's breaking away from
God, nor the unrighteousness and disorder of his existence, nor the manifestation of this in the lordship of the powers which he has unleashed and
which oppress and afflict him, can establish a definitive situation or represent an ineluctable fate. The freedom to call upon God is authentic freedom, not one of the inauthentic freedoms that man usually arrogates to
himself and grasps and steals in his rebellion against God. It is not contrived
or achieved by Christians. It is given to them as the freedom for obedience
to the command received by them, the command of God from which they
have turned aside but which turns to them with the order to pray "Thy
kingdom come," and in so doing awakens them and keeps them awake to
know this kingdom even in the midst of the kingdom of disorder, to look
toward it and to call for it. As they use the freedom for this prayer that is
given them with the command, they already stand on a rock even here and
now, when everything around them and everything in their own hearts and
lives and consciences is tottering and falling [cf. E. M. Arndt's hymn: "Ich
weiss, woran ich glaube"]. In simply obeying this command they become
and are members and fellows and citizens and witnesses to themselves and
others of this kingdom for whose coming they pray. The fact that they call
upon God with this prayer becomes and is a proof that he, God, resists the
torrent of human injustice and evil, and therefore that they as people cannot
cease to oppose it as well in their own place and manner. The fundamental
and comprehensive form in which this takes place consists, however, in

their using the freedom they have been given to call upon him, "Thy king-dom come." What do they pray for when they call upon God in this way?

Our primary contention is that the second petition that Jesus put on the lips of his disciples looks and points, as does the first, to an act of God which, although it embraces all times and places in its compass, is a once-for-all act that had not taken place before and neither needs to be nor can be repeated. It points to the occurrence of a specific history that is to be specifically inaugurated anew and brought to its goal by the Father in heaven, upon whom the petition calls. In the sphere of human unrighteous-ness and disorder, and under the lordship of the lordless powers, this is what is constantly taking place everywhere and far too often is basically the same even if in many variations. Though this might seem to be interesting, the sphere is finally a boring one to the extent that events in it, as Qoheleth knew and said [Eccl. 1:2-11, etc.], do not constitute any new history but are a cyclic history with constant repetition of the same things, like the famous snake which bites its tail and waits to see what will finally happen when it continues its meal. As God's act, the kingdom of God for which we long and wait and pray in the second petition does not take place in the contin-uation of a dubious cycle, nor as a repetition or variation of the same thing. No, we look for the dawn of the beautiful morning light which is not the old morning that recurs each day [cf. M. v. Schenkendorf's hymn: "Brich an, du schönes Morgenlicht"]. In its concrete content and compass, what is prayed for is not like any other event. It is not something that has already happened before. From the standpoint of the possibility of all other events, it is absolutely unexpected and inconceivable. It comes down directly from above and breaks through the level of all that has taken place thus far. It thus demands and creates freedom for human thought and volition in a new dimension. In this way, in this majesty, it is the limit of the disorder that is both the guilt and the pain of man. It also opposes the kingdom of demons. It was not for nothing that we could not speak of the demonic kingdom with final seriousness but only, as it were, with a wink. For it is in opposing this kingdom that the Lord laughs and has it in derision, doing what those who fear him ask him to do in this petition. The Lord does not reason or discuss or debate with either demons or the men to whose help he hastens in doing what he does here. He does not ask for their opinion or advice. He does not have to explain himself to them or justify himself before them. He does not link up with their own achievements. He does not concur or collaborate with them. He simply goes his own way, the way of his own honor and our salvation. That he should and will act thus is the promise that is given to Christians, and it is as such the summons and command to call upon him and to pray "Thy kingdom come." He snatches them up on high: "Lift up your hearts." The fact that Christianity in free obedience prays thus in answer to his command is not itself the new thing but the reflection of the great new thing of the kingdom of God within and over against the disorder and demonization of human life. It is itself already a prophetic sign of the limit that is set for this.

We have to remember especially, then, that when the kingdom of God is proclaimed in the New Testament, as in the second petition of the Lord's Prayer, we do not have the same old story but the striking up of the new song of Psalm 33:3, Psalm 40:3, and so forth. The Galileans believed that they had been given a new teaching by Jesus (Mk. 1:27), and the Athenians correctly thought that they had received the same from Paul (Acts 17:19). A new man (Eph. 2:15; Col. 3:10) came on the scene with the reality proclaimed in the gospel. It is instructive to compare with this some passages in Deutero-Isaiah that deal with the intimated restoration of Israel, an antitype of what the New Testament calls the kingdom of God. "From this time forth I will make you hear new things, hidden things which you have not known. They are created now, not long ago; before today you have never heard of them, lest you should say, 'Behold, I knew them.' You have never heard, you have never known, from of old your ear has not been opened" (Isa. 48:6ff.). "Remember not the former things, nor consider the things of old. Behold, I am doing a new thing; now it springs forth, do you not perceive it?" (43:18f.). And in a passage from Trito-Isaiah, which is adopted in Revelation 21:1 and 2 Peter 3:13, we read: "For behold, I create new heavens and a new earth; and the former things shall not be remembered or come into mind. But be glad and rejoice for ever in that which I create" (Isa. 65:17f.). No piece of new cloth is sewn here on the old garment, no new wine poured into old wineskins (Mk. 2:21f.). The previous idea that old wine is better than new (Lk. 5:39) is no longer applicable. A new commandment comes into force (Jn. 13:34; 1 Jn. 2:8). The continuity between what goes and what comes can consist and be known only in the κτίσις, the creation of the one God who is faithful to his creature (Gal. 6:15; 2 Cor. 5:17). But God does not stand still nor move backward. "Behold, I make all things new," says he who sits on the throne (Rev. 21:5).

How could God himself not be new to us people each morning, new in all that he is and wills and does, new also over against all that we believe we have already heard of him and ought to know and think of him, new not only to unbelief and half-belief, but also to sincere belief in him, new not only to his enemies but also to his most loyal friends and servants? All kinds of traditional or self-won ideas about him may not be new, may be already old, or quickly enough becoming so. God himself, however, will always be new to us. God's kingdom is God himself and — wonder of wonders, Marcion was right here — it is God himself as he not merely *is* somewhere and somehow (not even in the highest height or as the God beyond God of Paul Tillich) but as he *comes*. The concern of the second petition is precisely with this coming. As God's kingdom is God himself, so God is his kingdom in his own coming: his coming to meet man, to meet the whole of the reality distinct from himself. The second petition looks toward this special dynamic reality, to the coming of God's kingdom as the coming God himself, to its breaking forth and breaking through and breaking into the place where those who pray the petition are, to encounter with them and therefore with all creation. God comes — this is why his coming is the coming of his kingdom — as the legitimate King and almighty Lord of the human world which belongs to him and in whose midst Christians pray thus. He does not come as a self-disclosing numen to give them material for religious ideologies and the corresponding cults. He does not come to reveal and impart to them this or that morality. He does not come with a purpose whose execution depends, if not totally, then at least partially on the action, or at any rate the cooperation of Christians. He comes in the deed in which he acts and deals on and for and with them as their Lord and King, in which he acts directly as such and proves himself to be such. In coming he illumines, establishes, asserts, and protects his questioned, obscured, and threatened right to man and therefore man's own right, his right to life, which is negated apart from God's own right as Lord and King. He comes as the Holy One who is also the Merciful One, the Merciful One who is also the Holy One. He comes and creates righteousness, zealous for his honor as Creator and burning with love for his creature. He creates the righteousness which is the right order of the world that belongs to him. He comes and in creating righteousness he abolishes the unrighteousness of people both in their relationship to him and also in their relationships to one another. He comes and sets aside not only unrighteousness but also the lordship of the lordless powers, scattering them to the winds like the mists of the hypostatized fictions that they are, restoring to man the freedom over his abilities of which they had robbed him, reinstituting him as the lord of the earth which he may and should be as the servant of God. He comes and with him comes that "peace on earth among men with whom he is pleased" (Lk. 2:14), that is, among those who are elected, created, loved, saved, and kept by him. This peace on earth, actualized when God himself comes as King and Lord and creates and establishes it, is the kingdom of God.

One can only describe this kingdom approximately. And what does "describe" mean in this context? Almost all the elements in the description need further elucidation, and even were we to give this — or try to give it — as accurately as possible, we should still have to admit at the last that we had not by a long way covered what is denoted but only at best given a more or less exact indication and paraphrase. The kingdom of God is the great new thing on the margin — yet outside and not inside the margin of the horizon of all the perceptions and conceptions of us people, who are people of disorder, who have fallen wholly and utterly under the lordship of the lordless powers. All errors at this point have their source in a failure to see that the kingdom of God is inconceivable and incomprehensible to us, or, as we must freely say, it is an unthinkable thought, higher than all our thoughts as heaven is higher than earth (Isa. 55:9). Or, to put it positively, all errors at this point have their source in the idea that we are able by analogy to get some picture and concept of the kingdom of God, understanding, or thinking we understand, what is meant by the terms "God" and "kingdom" and "coming." The kingdom of God defies expression. It is real only as God himself comes as King and Lord, establishes righteousness in our relationship to him and to one another, and thus creates peace on earth. It is true, that is, it may be known to be real, only as God himself reveals himself in this his coming, speaking to people and being received by them. Our own experiences, pictures, thoughts, and concepts may relate to this reality and truth of his. It is as well for us if they do. In and of themselves, however, they are all empty shells. When people speak of an idea of the kingdom of God, as constantly happens in modern exegetical and dogmatic theology [cf. J. Weiss, *Die Idee des Reiches Gottes in der Theologie*, Giessen, 1901], they are really speaking past it. Only in the reality and truth of God's own coming does that beautiful morning light dawn on the margin of the horizon of our own experiences and thoughts. If it is not known in this, it is not known at all. The second petition looks toward this.

Not for nothing does Mark 4:11 (and par.) speak of the *mystery* of the kingdom of God that is given to the disciples (obviously in its self-disclosure), whereas to those outside, although everything belongs (τὰ πάντα γίνεται) and is present objectively, it is present only in parables without disclosing itself to them. In speaking about the being and nature of the kingdom, access to it, its order, its value as the supreme good, its growth and effects, Jesus, according to the Synoptists, spoke both to those outside and also to those inside in parables, in veils which yet unveiled what was denoted, veiling it even as they unveiled it. The call to all of them was this: "He who has ears to hear, let him hear" [cf. Mt. 11:15; Mk. 4:9 and par.]. Where in the New Testament can the word of the kingdom (Mt. 13:19) be received as a doctrine or as an unfolding of the concept? Jesus and the primitive community certainly did not accomplish in this form their κηρύσσειν, εὐαγγελίζεσθαι, διαγγέλειν, or διαμαρτύρεσθαι of the kingdom (Acts 28:23). The mighty works that accompanied this proclamation could not be, and were not meant to be, more than signs of the kingdom (Mk. 16:20). In this light, is it not open to suspicion that Lohmeyer (*Das Vater-Unser*, Göttingen, 1962⁵, p. 64) should speak of a perceptible structure of the concept of the kingdom in which three constructs of thought have come together as one? None of the three that he adduces is in fact perceptible.

To be sure, the kingdom of God is in many passages (1) a place, a house in which are many dwellings (Jn. 14:2) with keys that can open and shut them, and where children, and guests invited by the master of the house, have or acquire the right to be, into which people can enter and come, where they can sit at table and eat and drink, and from which they can be ejected with shame. But the New Testament itself does not pursue this line. The decisive thing in the passages controlled by it, to the extent that they speak of the kingdom of God, is not the place as such, but the figure of the father or the master of the house to whom it belongs, and the reciprocal dealings between him and the original or added residents, either present or future. While the prodigal son undoubtedly longed for his father's house, he did not rise up, as is often said, simply to go back home but rather to go back to his father (Lk. 15:18). And when instead of the houseowner we find the owner of a vineyard or a businessman on a journey, and their dealings with their workers, the question of the house or other place where these dealings took place is obviously an indifferent one regarding the purpose of the parable.

We may undoubtedly agree with Lohmeyer that another group of passages may be distinguished which, as he puts it, bursts through the first idea and presents the kingdom of-God as (2) the future world of God, the new Jerusalem which comes down from heaven, the new earth under the new heaven. It is now the place where many will come from the east and the west and recline at table with Abraham, Isaac, and Jacob while those who belonged to this table, the "sons of the kingdom," will be shut out (Mt. 8:11f.). The kingdom is now the inheritance that is given to the righteous (Gal. 5:21; 1 Cor. 6:9f.; 15:50). In it they will eat and drink and sit on thrones, judging the twelve tribes of Israel (Lk. 22:30) and shining as the sun (Mt.

13:43). In the same context, however, Lohmeyer (p. 66) calls the kingdom a treasure on which one can suddenly stumble (Mt. 13:44) but which one can also seek and find and, by giving up all else, win — a force that is already at work like leaven (Mt. 13:33), a seed or principle of life that in all secrecy grows to the maximum extent (Mt. 13:31f.), a net cast in the sea in which fish of all kinds are brought together (Mt. 13:47). We reach here a point at which the mystery of the kingdom of God is greatest. It is an event which has already come but is still to be expected, which is still to be expected precisely because it has already come. All this is true, and yet in the light of what seems to be this insoluble contradiction in the second construct of thought, one can hardly point to a consistent view or one that can serve as a stone in the "structure" of the concept.

Finally, we have a line of thought (3) which is closest to the literal meaning, that is, that of God's royal action in the history of his people. Yahweh is the true King of Israel and remains so in spite of Saul's kingship or David's. Because he is King in the history of his people, he is King also in that of all other peoples and that of the human world as a whole. Hence the kingdom of God is a demonstration of the truth of Exodus 15:18: "The Lord will reign for ever and ever." But what are we saying if we translate the kingdom of God by the royal dominion of God, or, more precisely, his royal dominion which comes, which will break in, but which has already come and broken in, and is thus real and true in this double sense? For according to Luke 17:20f., it does not come with observation. It is not the object of empirical study. It cannot be established and recorded and analyzed as an historical fact. Every "Look here!" or "Look there!" points past it into the void. It cannot even be found "within us" (according to Luther's mistranslation of ἐντός ὑμῶν). It is indeed among us in supreme and incontrovertible reality and truth, yet not in eating and drinking (Rom. 14:17), not in the observance or nonobservance of ordinances, but in righteousness, peace, and joy in the Holy Spirit, and in the comprehensive sense of 1 Corinthians 4:20: "Not in talk, but in power." What are we saying, then, when we speak of the royal dominion of God?

There can also be no question of a "structure" of the three constructs of thought when even Lohmeyer himself (p. 67) says that the third is separated from the second by a deep gulf, and might not the same be said of the second in relation to the first? A structure implies a system. But there is no system of the kingdom of God — certainly not in the New Testament — and people in every age should not have let themselves try to reduce God's kingdom to a system. To be sure, we are dealing with one thing here, but not in the form of certain intersecting human views and conceptions. Of such one can only say that, as their elements and they themselves cannot be reduced to a common denominator, they bear witness to the fact that they relate to something that is uniquely and incomparably one. They bear witness to the power and fullness with which this one thing presents itself and speaks for itself, and they thus give irresistible and inexhaustible reason to think of this one thing. They also bear witness to the majesty with which it forbids us from trying to comprise and comprehend it in a picture. This one thing always presents and reveals itself as the wholly new thing in face of which (cf. D. Bonhoeffer, *Dein Reich komme*, ed. E. Bethge, Hamburg, 1957, p.10) we must be clearly aware, in reflecting on it honestly and seriously, that we cannot make it into a utopia. If only there had been a clear awareness of this! The kingdom of God is that one thing in its mystery, in its self-disclosing mystery, yet still in its mystery and not otherwise. The second petition points to this one thing that is wholly new.

This has the following implication for the practical understanding of the second petition. In its coming as the act of God himself, the kingdom of God escapes all intellectual systematizing. It must be known as a unique reality and truth with its own nature and power. It is thus independent of human will and act and different from all the human works and achievements into whose sphere it enters. It is God's own independent action which limits all human history from outside, which is sovereign in relation to it, and which thus determines and controls it. Man can and may attempt many things, but he cannot bring in the kingdom of God. This kingdom and its righteousness are certainly to be sought. They are to be sought above all the other things that man may seek (Mt. 6:33; 13:45). But like the treasure in the field (Mt. 13:44), it is there even before it is sought or found by anybody. It certainly calls for human righteousness and order amid all human unrighteousness and disorder. It does this, however, as its own righteousness and order confront even the most perfect human righteousness and order and are as different from it as heaven is from earth, so that human righteousness and order can follow and respond to it only as the act and work of human obedience, and man is in no position to grab them like a robber and make them his own, as described in Mt. 11:12. The kingdom would still be what it is even if there were never any such following and response anywhere. As it is prayed for in the second petition, the kingdom is not a kind of continuing, prolonging, excelling, and completing of what people may, as commanded, attempt and undertake in a more or less rich understanding of their relationship to it or in some other form of reflection on what is good. It is instead the new thing that precedes the beginning of all such action if the latter is to be well done. It is the new thing that crowns — crowns with grace and mercy (Ps. 103:4) — all such completed action if it is to remain well done. It is not a refining or strengthening or intensifying or qualifying of such action which supposedly gives to it the character of a quasi-divine action. It is instead God's own action, which does not merge into the best of human action, for example, that of Christian faith or the Christian church, which does not mingle with it, let alone identify itself with it, which remains free and independent over against it, and which in its purity and freedom is God's gracious, reconciling, and finally redeeming action. As such it is to be gratefully, joyfully, and humbly affirmed in Christian faith and boldly and strongly proclaimed by the Christian church, but without being equated with either the work of faith or that of the church. Conversely, then, it is not a divine work for whose commencement, continuation, and completion some human cooperation has to be considered and postulated and which could have no standing or being without the assistance of certain people. It is God's work alone, which as it is revealed to them can be known by people in faith, gratefully hailed and extolled by them, and then attested and proclaimed, but which cannot in any circumstances be made their own operation or promoted, augmented, or perhaps improved by their action.

"The kingdom of God is as if a man should scatter seed upon the ground, and should sleep and rise night and day, and the seed should sprout and grow, he knows not how. The earth produces of itself (αὐτομάτη), first the blade, then the ear, then the full grain in the ear. But when the grain is ripe, at once he puts in the sickle, because the harvest has come" (Mk. 4:26ff.). At this point, as in the first petition, we necessarily part company with Reformation exegesis in important respects.

Luther explained in his Small Catechism that the point of the second petition is that the kingdom of God, whose coming is certain even without our prayer, should come to us. Linguistically, he took this from the *adveniat* of the Vulgate, which may go back to a variant of Codex D in the Lucan test: ἐφ' ἡμᾶς ἐλθέτω . . . , but which disrupts the most ancient wording inasmuch as the relation to "us" is typical and important in the last three petitions, whereas a characteristic of the first three (Lohmeyer, p. 59) is that the three verbal forms (including ἐλθάτω) have no relations, and thus emphasize the objectivity of the event envisioned. Luther's exposition is also open to question when, in continuing, he says that the coming of God's kingdom to us takes place when the heavenly Father gives us his Holy Spirit so that by his grace we may believe his holy Word and live godly lives both here in time and there in eternity. This again corresponds to a variant form in Luke (11:2), where the prayer for the kingdom is replaced by the very different request for the Holy Spirit: ἐλθέτω τὸ ἅγιον πνεῦμά σου ἐφ' ἡμᾶς καὶ καθαρισάτω ἡμᾶς. This is, of course, a good and necessary prayer, but it is not an apt replacement for the second petition nor an explanation of it, because the kingdom of God in its coming as the concrete appearing of God himself and therefore of his righteousness and order on earth goes beyond the event in which the Holy Spirit brings about, in retrospect and prospect of the act, our sanctification, that is, our faith in God's Word and the corresponding life. The same constriction of the second petition takes place in Luther's Large Catechism. Very truly and beautifully — we shall return to this — God's kingdom is here equated quite simply with the fact that God sent his Son Christ our Lord into the world, and he redeemed and freed us from the power of the devil, brought us to himself, and ruled us as a King of righteousness, life, and salvation. Even here, however, the accent does not fall on the doing of this act of God as such, but on its relation to us or our relation to it, that is, on the gift of the Holy Spirit which follows the act, on God's visiting us by his holy Word and enlightening and strengthening us in faith through its power. Hence we are to pray here that this may be a work of power in us so that we who have received it may remain and daily increase in it, and that it may win the adherence of others and make its way mightily through the world. This too is a fine prayer, but as a paraphrase of the second petition it is a sorry merger and inclusion of the event of the kingdom in what can take place in the history of Christians and Christianity only secondarily and relatively on the presupposition of the history of Jesus Christ and as its consequence. Thus the superiority and independence of the divine action which are envisioned in the second petition are obscured over against all human history, and this history in particular. Conversely, independence is given to this particular history of Christians and Christianity, and there takes place a hypostatizing of faith and the church — think what it means if the coming of the kingdom is to be seen in these! — which not only makes it superfluous to look backward and forward to the coming of the kingdom in the history of Jesus Christ but threatens to prevent this backward and forward look altogether.

The same deviation may be seen even more clearly in the expositions of the Lord's Prayer offered by Calvin in the Geneva Catechism, in his *Commentary on the Synoptic Gospels*, and in the *Institutes* (III, 20, 35-47). According to Calvin, the coming of God's kingdom means the increasing extension and triumph of God's lordship among us people who resist him, until at the last day it will achieve unrestricted sway, and God will be all in all [1 Cor. 15:28]. The victory of God in and over the world that contradicts him, a victory which has begun already and will finally reach its goal, takes place in two forms. His kingdom comes first in the gathering, ruling, and sanctifying of his elect; in the subjection of their minds, hearts, impulses, and desires to his will and law as this is brought about by his Word and Spirit, or, from their standpoint, in their self-denial; in the negation of their old and natural man; in a new life begun in free obedience; in the bearing of the cross that is placed upon them; and in the expectation of the glory of the life to come. On the presupposition of the inner change of individual Christians, then, the kingdom of God comes in the event of the establishment, increase, and order of the church on the basis and under the direction of the Holy Spirit and his gifts, and then in a successive reordering of confused human relationships through the ministry of the church. The other form of the coming of the kingdom is the negative one: the power of the truth of God, demonstrated in its victorious march, to overthrow and destroy those who resist God and the church and all their hostile plans and enterprises. For these people, the reprobate, the kingdom of God means that the resistance they will not abandon will be smashed. In any case, this resistance will be set aside. We thus pray that one way or another in human history, whether in goodness or severity, there may be no power that will finally withstand God's power. We pray that he may win the field, whether here in grace or there in judgment. In the specifically Calvinistic force of its conception and wording, this too is a notable and, properly understood, appropriate prayer. But as an exposition of the second petition of the Lord's Prayer, recapitulated fairly exactly in Question 123 of the Heidelberg Catechism, though without the predestinarian climax, it represents a disturbing de-eschatologizing and legalizing of the content of the petition, a dissolving of the mystery of the kingdom in the wonderful history of Christians and Christianity which it inaugurates, with a shadowy counterpart in the terrible history of those who are shut out. According to Calvin, what those who pray the prayer have before them by way of promise and hope is that the battle in this world between light and darkness, faith and unbelief, human righteousness and unrighteousness, the church as the city of God and the world as the city of the devil [cf. Augustine, *De civitate Dei*, XXX, I], and, unfortunately, the elect and the reprobate, must and will move on increasingly to its goal in the expected final victory, certainly as God's mighty act, but not as his once-for-all and concrete deed in its newness and sovereignty over against—and in favor of!—the totality of what people do, and do not do, and do well or badly in their history. What is to be asked for, according to Calvin, is God's gradual seizure of power and final triumph *within* this history, in the changing of bad persons into good, the glory of the people, and the removal of the opposition of some definitively bad persons. The second petition, however, looks to a mighty act that limits and determines from outside the whole of human history with its brighter and darker elements, its advances, halts, and setbacks. It looks to an unequivocal act of the grace of God, to the mystery of the kingdom of God which encounters all that history and limits it in its totality as its hope.

Not in detail but in basic features this Reformation view of the kingdom of God has until recently remained normative in modern theology in spite of every change. Certainly pietism and the later awakening did not see the coming of the kingdom or its beginning in the official church and Christianity but in the more or less marginal movements for the inner renewing and deepening of the Christian life and the activities these stimulated in the spheres of mission, social concern, and philanthropy. Even today it is thus customary in these circles to speak of works of the kingdom of God and workers in the kingdom of God without bothering about the inner contradictions this might involve (cf. J. J. Moser, *Altes und Neues aus dem Reich Gottes* . . . , Frankfurt and Leipzig, 1733-1736; J. H. Wichern, *Der Beruf der Nichtgeistlichen für die Arbeiten im Reiche Gottes und den Bau der Gemeinde*, *Sämtliche Werke*, III, Berlin and Hamburg, 1969; H. Brandenburg, "Reichsgottesarbeiter," *RGG*³, V, 931f.). More dryly, but with little material difference, the Enlightenment regarded the kingdom of God as a brotherhood which Jesus intentionally set up, international in scope, for the establishment of harmony between morality and nature (cf. F. V. Reinhard, *Versuch über den Plan* . . . [1781¹], Wittenberg and Zerbst, 1798⁴, pp. 53, 62ff., 123ff.; also *Consilium* . . . [1780] in *Opuscula academica*, I [Leipzig, 1808], 234-267; J. Gottschick, "Reich Gottes," *RE*, XVI, 783-806). According to Kant, the kingdom of God is a world in which rational beings dedicate themselves with all their hearts to the moral law, a world ordered by this law (cf. *Kritik der praktischen Vernunft*, 1788, pp. 231f.). According to Herder, it is the elevation of the whole race to true humanity in accordance with the law of nature, that is, of the goodness, power, and wisdom of God (cf. *Ideen zur Philosophie der Geschichte der Menschheit*, Preface, *Sämtliche Werke*, B. Suphan, XIII [Berlin, 1887], 10). According to Schleiermacher, it is the quintessence of the total moral life that is engendered by the redemption effected in Jesus, in which the creation of human nature is completed at its highest level, but which is actualized in the individual in continually renewed volition (*Der christliche Glaube*, esp. § 89 and § 121). According to R. Rothe, it is the fellowship of redemption that at first takes shape as the church but then gradually discards this unsuitable form and with the merging of the sacred into the profane, so that the profane becomes sacred, finds fulfilment in the organism and life of the state (*Theologische Ethik*, III [Wittenberg, 1870²], 174f.). According to A. Ritschl, it is the task, progressively fulfilled by joint human activity, of achieving a fellowship of love which includes, transcends, and changes all specific bonds and which is as such both God's own goal and also the goal that he has appointed for the world (cf. *Die christliche Lehre von der Rechtfertigung und Versöhnung*, III [Bonn, 1895⁴], 266f.). It is not true that the so-called religious socialism of the first two decades of the twentieth century, which is associated especially with L. Ragaz, equated the kingdom of God with the future socialist state. It is true enough, however, that in that movement, expectation of the kingdom of God was never clearly differentiated from enthusiastic hopes for a better world beyond the sway of capitalism, nationalism, militarism, alcohol, and so forth, so that in such circles there was a good deal of misguided if zealous talk of fighting for the kingdom of God, and the movement undoubtedly has to be mentioned in this series (cf. L. Ragaz, *Weltreich, Religion und Gottesherrschaft*, 2 vols., Erlenbach-Zurich, Munich and Leipzig, 1922; also *Der Kampf um das Reich Gottes in Blumhardt, Vater und Sohn —und weiter!*, Erlenbach-Zurich, Munich and Leipzig, 1922). Rather oddly, much the same may be said about many sermons on the Lord's Prayer later in the century, for example, those of W. Lüthi (*Das Unservater*, Basel, pp. 28-40), F. Buri (*Gebot und Gebet*, Zollikon, 1960, pp. 105-111), R. Bohren (*Das Unser Vater —heute*, Zurich/Stuttgart, 1960², pp. 41-50), and even D. Bonhoeffer's exposition of the second petition (*Dein Reich komme* . . . , Hamburg, 1957, pp. 5-20). The Reformation understanding, the relating of the coming of the kingdom to what is done, or should be done, in Christian faith and the Christian church in service to the world, has been surprisingly little shaken or even affected by its contradiction in modern exegesis and has continued to exercise a dominant influence.

Nor can it be denied that in its main features it can appeal to the continuation of a tradition going back to at least the end of the second century. Origen took the second petition to mean that the soul should let itself be ruled by God and become obedient to his spiritual law (*On Prayer*, XXV, 1). In obvious dependence on the frequently adduced 2 Timothy 2:12 ("If we endure, we shall also reign with him"), Chrysostom supplemented this interpretation with the reverse consideration that the soul which lets itself be ruled by God as its King, itself becomes a king ([Ps.-] Chrysostom, *Homily on the Lord's Prayer*). Already in Augustine, this ruling with God had become more important than being ruled by God. To be sure, God always had the initiative as the one who acts first but only in such a way that his work triggers the independent if divinely supported work of man, so that the kingdom of God becomes the task of man. Followed by many others, Augustine could speak of a building up (*aedificare*) of the kingdom in the preaching of the church and its administration of the sacraments, and although in the eternal consummation of the kingdom this work would be replaced by the pure contemplation and fruition of God, nevertheless in relation to its temporal form the momentous equation of the kingdom and the church becomes possible and necessary and is thus ventured (cf. Augustine, *On the Sermon on the Mount*, I, 2, 9; *Sermon LVII*, V, 5; *Tractate in John's Gospel*, *CXXIV*, LXVIII, 2; *On Psalm CXXVI*, 2; *On the Trinity*, XV,i; *Sermon CCLI*, IV, 3; *De civ. Dei*, XXII, xx, 8). Along mystical lines, but with no material change, Bernard of Clairvaux (*Opera*, IV, ed. J. Leclercq and H. Rochais, Rome, 1966, p. 48, ll. 21-23) and Bonaventura (*Opera omnia*, V, Quaracchi, MDCCCXCI, pp. 539-553) took the kingdom of God to be the divine indwelling of the soul brought about by man's free surrender to God. Tauler went even further and regarded it as man's essential unity with the Godhead, to which he opens the door by a sequence of acts designed to produce stillness and indifference in all his thinking, willing, and doing. When he performs these acts, the divine abyss inclines to the pure ground of the soul which is turned to it, changing this from a created being into an uncreated being. God then rules and is enthroned, and the kingdom of God is in him, or, rather, he himself has become the kingdom of God (cf. *Die Predigten Taulers*, ed. F. Vetter, *Deutsche Texte des Mittelalters*, Vol. XI, Berlin, 1910 [reprint Dublin/Zurich, 1968], pp. 362f.). The Reformers did not speak like this. Nevertheless, the older or oldest interpretation of the second petition prevailed in their understanding just as theirs did in the theology of the centuries that followed.

We are thus parting company with an imposing ecclesiastical consensus when we state that at this point the so-called historico-critical biblical study of the modern age, with J. Weiss, A. Schweitzer, and F. Overbeck as pioneers, has rendered a not yet fully appreciated service to theological knowledge with its discovery of the eschatological character of the New Testament in general and the message of the kingdom of God in particular. We have to take seriously what is clearly to be learned from it in this respect. Whether in the early church, the Reformers, more modern or even the most recent authors, exposition of the second petition has constantly suppressed the point that the kingdom of God is a unique entity or factor not only in relation to the world but also in relation to the Christian world. It is the new thing of Deutero- and Trito-Isaiah which transcends history even though it is immanent in and takes place within it. The kingdom of God is God himself, who in the act and revelation of his own divine righteousness certainly frees man and calls him to a being in human righteousness but who still remains free over against all the inner and outer works of human righteousness, who does not merge into any of them so that people might say, "Lo, it is here or here" (Lk. 17:21), who can thus free all people for such works, and call them to them, precisely in his indestructible sovereignty.

We can sum up all that has been said thus far in the simple statement that the prayer for the coming of the kingdom, like that for the hallowing of God's name, is in the more literal sense just that — a pure prayer. Pure prayer takes place only — but here it does take place — in the relationship of the children of God to their Father in heaven. Conversely, prayer in this relationship finds the criterion of its authenticity as invocation of the Father by his children in the fact that it is pure prayer.

The prayer for the coming of the kingdom is pure prayer first (1) because it cannot be omitted. It is absolutely unavoidable that God should be invoked with this prayer. It is not unavoidable just because the suffering and distress in the world of the unrighteousness of men in their relationship to God and to one another are so great that they have to cry to God. That they do this is true enough. It is not self-evident, however, that this crying should be or has to be a prayer to God. The "should," the supreme "must," which makes calling upon God with the prayer "Thy kingdom come" unavoidable, arises because the Father in heaven frees his children — and therefore imperiously summons them — to turn to him with this prayer. If it is pure prayer, then those who call upon God with it do not venture it because they snatch at it as a last resort in face of the confusion and distress of the human situation. They venture it in the freedom of obedience to pray to God thus.

It is also a pure prayer (2) because in it they turn to God, with whom alone it rests that his kingdom should come, that is, that he himself should come as King and Lord, by his intervention putting an end to human unrighteousness in both its dimensions, destroying the lordship of demons, and creating peace on earth among men of his pleasure [Lk. 2:14]. That we should ask and request from God more, even a good deal more, reason, equity, and humanity in human conduct and relations against the background of a proper fear of God is one thing, and it is no little thing, and prayer certainly ought to be made for it. We cannot say, however, that it rests only with God that this should come about, that it should only be prayed for, that we ourselves can do nothing toward it, for example, by way of appropriate efforts to give better instruction and education to the human race. The prayer for the coming of the kingdom, however, looks directly and exclusively beyond all that people can and should do for the betterment of the human situation to the change which it can be God's business alone to effect.

Finally it is pure prayer (3) because it carries with it[2] the unreserved certainty of being heard. In its twofold determination it is not an experiment, a flight in the void, but an action that achieves its goal and is directed straight toward this. It would necessarily be afflicted by doubts and therefore be an uncertain enterprise if it were simply an expression of human distress and perhaps of tired resignation in face of all the possibilities of

---

[2]The TS had here the following parenthesis (later excised): "— as it is (1) not ventured capriciously but in obedience to God and the freedom he has given for it, and as it (2) prays for that which can be expected only from God—"

human action and conflict, if it were no more than a despairing cry in the dark. That kind of prayer could obviously have no greater confidence than any other "Baal, hear us" [1 K. 18:26]. Necessarily, too, it would be tormented by well-founded doubts if it were asking merely for the divine supporting and strengthening of human efforts to better the human situation. But as it is made in obedience to God's command as a prayer for the new thing which is to be expected from God alone, it has an objectively and subjectively solid basis that is protected against all doubt. When God wills and commands that something should be expected and requested from him alone, he does this thing and it takes place for certain, without any "ifs" or "buts," without any "perhaps and perhaps not." The prayer and the answer are two different things even when the prayer is pure prayer, for the prayer is man's and the answer is God's. Nevertheless it is inevitable that in the sense described, the pure prayer "Thy kingdom come" should anticipate and reflect, without ceasing to be human prayer, the answer of the reality and truth of the coming of God's kingdom. As in the first and second senses, so now in the third, pure prayer reflects what it prays for, the sovereignty of God. There is no other way to this knowledge. The royal way which in all circumstances leads to this knowledge is pure prayer for its coming.

Obviously, however, we have to posit the further question of where and how it comes about that this pure prayer takes place, and in it the knowledge of the coming of God's kingdom. Where and how does it enter the hearts and lips of Christians? Where and how does the Christian community receive the impulse, the courage, and the power prophetically to go ahead of the world, whose most proper concern it is, with this petition? Where and how is this commanded of it by God, and therefore categorically and irrefutably, as the request for the act which can be only his? Where and how does there disclose itself to it, as it is obedient to this command, this prospect — the sure and certain and incontestable prospect — of this future, of the coming of God's kingdom and its righteousness in their radical and victorious opposition to all human unrighteousness and to the lordship of the lordless powers? Where is the Archimedian point from which Christianity not only counts on this imminent coming and intervention of God but gratefully and patiently waits for it, yet impatiently also, because it waits with restless yearning and since its waiting cannot be idle, prays, "Thy kingdom come"? If we cannot say something about this, what have we been talking about all this time? Would we not have been blowing bubbles? And should we not be left in darkness as to the extent to which, as we pray for the dawning of God's righteousness, we find ourselves summoned to take up resolutely, if relatively, provisionally, and feebly, the struggle for human righteousness too? With the meaning of the prayer as such, its ethical relevance is at stake as we look for an answer to this further question.

We recall especially that the second petition, like the Lord's Prayer as a whole, belongs to the context of the New Testament witness. It is to be understood in this context. In it we find information concerning the place from which the Christian community and each individual Christian as a member of it calls upon God in this petition, and information also on the way in which that prayer arises and is possible and actual in the hearts and on the lips of Christians. From the New Testament context we derive in the first instance two basic things. The first is that it has a strictly eschatological content and character, that is, that it looks toward an act of God as the goal and end of all human history and of all the history of faith and the church within it. The second is that it has its basis and meaning in the totality of this history, but in a definite event within it, in a specific, once-for-all, and unique history within that history. Coming from this specific history, Christians pray, "Thy kingdom come." Hence their prayer is not — the New Testament gives us not the slightest reason for this view — the expression of a hope manufactured by people and cherished by the human race as such, the hope of a final solution of the complicated problems of world history which takes place in more or less pure transcendence. It is not the exponent of wishful thinking, whether metaphysically speculative or mythologizing.

Seen in the New Testament context, the future, the world to come, the last thing to which the petition undoubtedly looks, has already encountered those who call upon God in it here in the present, in this world. It already stands before their eyes, knowable and known by them, as the first thing. It is before them as they know it to be already behind them. They have already been confronted by the new thing for which they pray. It already speaks to them and already claims them. It already terrifies them as judgment and already comforts them as grace. Already a pure and free act of God, which they have not performed, over which they acquire and have no control, encounters them there and is encountered by them there. They have to do with the future in the present, the world to come in this world, the last thing in the first. Thus it is already an event here and now but is still to be awaited then and there. They are near to it but distant. They live in its perfect today, but they must also yearn and look for its tomorrow and pray for its coming. Both as future, world to come, and last thing — but also as present, this world, and first thing — it is the new thing of God which is not in their hand or power, so that even as it takes place before their eyes they must call upon God for it to take place. They were and are liberated, authorized, and imperiously required to do this as it takes place before their eyes. This is how it is, generally speaking, with the prayer for the coming of God's kingdom in the context of the New Testament witness.

We must see and emphasize first that the prayer finds its basis in the fact that the coming is not just ahead but is already an event. Not from an alien or neutral place but from the enacted and present coming, the New Testament community looks for the future coming. It is in the light of its knowledge of God's new thing that it truly calls upon God for its manifestation.

The New Testament has good news concerning the kingdom of God. It preaches, proclaims, and bears witness to its reality and truth. Its coming is to be expected and prayed for (Mk. 1:15 and par.) because it has drawn near. The time is fulfilled. All that has taken place or does and will take place in it has reached its goal and end. The whole of the New Testament message derives from this coming of the kingdom. It may explicitly point back to it or point forward to it, but it is to be understood as both a future and also a present saying, future because present. "The Kingdom is at hand" means that the kingdom and its invasion and intervention are not just future. They are the most immediate future of all men today. Whether people notice it or not, the kingdom has come right up to them. Whether they know it or not, in its own unique and inconceivable way, yet irrevocably and irrefutably, it has become concrete history, unique history yet still history, this history in the midst of all other history. We have already seen that it is "among you," not μετὰ παρατηρή σεως, not in such a way that it can be observed, registered, or analyzed. Note that this is the answer Jesus gives to the question of when the kingdom will come (Lk. 17:20f.). In another place we read that it "has come upon you" (Mt. 12:28; Lk. 11:20). This is what his disciples have to say: "The kingdom of God has come near to you" (Lk. 10:9)—obviously everything else in and with this one thing. It can be seen yet not perceived, heard yet not understood (Mk. 4:12)—otherwise it would not be the kingdom of God. Note that it is not said to be invisible or inaudible. It is not just intellectually perceptible like an idea. There are eyes and ears that are called blessed because they perceive as well as see and receive as well as hear (Mt. 13:16). A person may show by his conduct whether or not he is fit (εὔθετος) for the kingdom of God (Lk. 9:62). Even a scribe (γραμματεύς, Mt. 13:52) may be interested and taught and trained (μαθητευθείς) not only for his beloved letters but also for the kingdom of heaven. In modern terms, he may study Scripture not just historically but with a concern for the history to which it bears witness. There are also those, the children of Mark 10:14, or the people of the πτωχοί or πτωχοὶ τῷ πνεύματι (Lk. 6:20; Mt. 5:3), or those who are persecuted for righteousness' sake (Mt. 5:10) to whom the kingdom can be promised, of whom it may be said that it is theirs. One can enter or not enter this kingdom (Mt. 5:20, etc.). There can be no greatest in it, but there can be great and small (Mt. 5:19). It can be occupied by force, as by robbers (Mt. 11:12, this rather obscure passage may be part of a polemic against the followers of John the Baptist, or against some of them). According to Romans 14:17, it may be confused with a rigorous or liberal attitude to some observance, or with a λόγος, a theology of the kingdom of God (according to 1 Cor. 4:20). The saying about entrusting the keys to the apostles (Mt. 16:19) speaks of the kingdom of heaven as a present reality, and Paul does the same in Colossians 4:10f., where he names Aristarchus, Mark, and Jesus Justus as fellow workers (who comfort him), not ἐν τῇ, but εἰς τὴν βασιλείαν τοῦ θεοῦ. The same applies in 2 Thessalonians 1:5, where suffering for God's kingdom is in view, and also in Revelation 1:9, with its reference to a companion in tribulation (θλῖψις) and the kingdom (βασιλεία). In more than one of these passages one may ask whether there is not an ambivalent reference to both the present and also the future of the kingdom. In their totality, however, they show that in the New Testament the kingdom is with some breadth the treasure that is hidden in the field and already present [Mt. 13:44], the costly pearl that is already waiting for its buyer [Mt. 13:45f.], the net that is already cast [Mt. 13:47f.], the seed that is already sown on good soil and less good [Mk. 4:1ff. and par.].

Only one satisfactory answer can be given to the obvious question: what is meant in the New Testament by the presence of the kingdom of God, by its coming as already an event? What is meant is the center, the whence and whither, the basis, theme, and content of all the New Testament sayings, namely, the history of Jesus Christ, the words and deeds and suffering and death of the one Son of the one God as the Messiah of Israel and the savior of the Gentiles, as the One in giving whom God loved the world, in whom, given up for it, he loves and will love it, in whom he has reconciled it to himself [cf. 1 Tim. 2:5; Jn. 3:16; 2 Cor. 5:19]. "The kingdom of God is at hand" means "the Word was made flesh and dwelt among us" (Jn. 1:14). In him the divine righteousness and order contest, defeat, overcome, and set aside human unrighteousness and disorder. The first disciples found themselves confronted already in their own lifetime with the kingdom of God as God revealed and declared Christ to be the One he was in his resurrection from the dead, as he, the Crucified and Slain, appeared and met them as the Living One, and as they thus found themselves confronted with Jesus. Similarly, people of all times find themselves confronted already with the mystery of the absolutely new and inconceivable and incomparable thing of the kingdom of God as in the power of his Holy Spirit they find themselves confronted with this Living One as their Lord, as the Lord of all lords [Rev. 17:14; 19:16].

That this is so seems at a first glance to be deducible from the New Testament texts only to the extent that in fact all its positive statements about what God does to his own honor and our salvation derive explicitly or implicitly, directly or indirectly, from the seeing and hearing of the history of Jesus Christ, from the knowledge of him who "for us men and for our salvation came down from heaven, and was incarnate," and who in this knowledge is to be proclaimed as the One who "shall come again." Furthermore, there is in the New Testament no trace of any statements about God's work and word which refer to a kingdom of God that has come or is to be expected apart from the history of Jesus Christ. "Are you he who is to come, or shall we look for another?" is the question that John sends to Jesus from prison. In all its indirectness, the answer is clear: "The blind receive their sight and the lame walk, lepers are cleansed and the deaf hear, and the poor have good news preached to them." This means that the kingdom of God is an event. "Blessed is he who takes no offense at me," who does not ignore me and look for someone else who will bring and reveal another kingdom (Mt. 11:2ff.). According to the whole meaning of the New Testament, the Baptist's question can be understood only as one that leads into the void. In its circle of vision there can be no other bringer and revealer of any other kingdom. "All authority in heaven and on earth has been given to me" (Mt. 28:18). Of what other kingdom of God could we think meaningfully at some later stage? When people have tried to do it, they always have moved into fantasies and utopias and been lost in them.

Nor is it the case, in the New Testament at any rate, that the history of Jesus Christ is the one adequate manifestation of God's kingdom but coincides with it only as a good copy can be said to do so to the original. This relationship may help to clarify the one between the kerygma and dogma of the Christian community and its object and content. The proclamation of the kingdom of God by Jesus, however, is not the proclamation of a reality and truth differing from himself as its Proclaimer, from his being and life. In the history of his prophecy, the reality and truth of the kingdom are not just indicated in the sense that there is a coming somewhere behind and above his own words and works and suffering and death, he himself being merely the precursor and herald of the kingdom. The precursor and herald of the kingdom that has come and comes is John the Baptist, with his finger pointing away from himself, and with John the whole activity of the community from the days of the apostles to our own, its preaching, teaching, and instruction, its baptism and holy communion, its pastoral care and diaconate in the narrower and broader senses of these concepts. All this is one great signifying. The mystery of the proclamation of Jesus Christ himself, however, is that in officiating as the prophet and preacher of the gospel of God (Mk. 1:14), of the King and Lord of his kingdom, he himself is the Son of God, so that his person and work and word cannot be distinguished from the person and work and word of God; and God's kingdom is his, the kingdom of the Son no less than the Father. Here — and only here — signifying and being (*significare* and *esse*) are not two things but one. Not just in virtue of his coming but as he comes, not just as surely as he comes but — Luther's formula is legitimate and even necessary here — "in, with, and under" (cf. Luther's Large Catechism) his coming, the kingdom of God comes in full present reality.

It is worth noting, of course, that the New Testament expressly speaks of this identity only with some restraint. The phrase "the kingdom of Christ and of God" is undoubtedly used but occurs only at Ephesians 5:5 and refers there to its future form. Its presence is clearly at issue when Colossians 1:13 says that the Father has snatched us away from the power of darkness and put us in the kingdom of his beloved Son. With an equally plain reference to its present reality, Jesus says in John 18:36, "My kingdom is not of this world," though "my kingdom" in Luke 22:30, "thy kingdom" in Matthew 20:21 and Luke 23:42, and "his kingdom" in Matthew 16:28 and 2 Timothy 4:1, 18 refer clearly again to the future. The wording of Ephesians 5:5 warns us against viewing Christ's kingdom as a different one alongside God's or as a smaller part of God's, or against identifying Christ's kingdom with the church (all these interpretations have been attempted; cf. J. Weiss, *Die Idee des Reiches Gottes in der Theologie*, Giessen, 1901). Nor is there support anywhere for this kind of differentiation. No ground for it may be found even in the famous passage 1 Corinthians 15:24-28, where Christ at his final parousia will hand over the kingdom to the Father and having overcome all hostile forces will himself be subject to God, who has subjected all things to him. Zinzendorf took terrible offense at Paul over this, chalked it up as an error, flatly refused to recognize it as binding, and ventured the bold hypothesis that because of it Paul was punished with the "thorn in the flesh" mentioned in 2 Corinthians 12:7 (cf. N. L. v. Zinzendorf, *Ein und zwanzig Discurse* . . . , pp. 96f., in *Hauptschriften*, ed. E. Beyreuther and G. Meyer, Vol. VI, Hildesheim, 1963). One has only to compare it with Philippians 2:6ff., however, to be spared such vexation. This passage says that in its future and definitive manifestation, in the form in which we are still to expect it, the kingdom of God will be revealed as the kingdom whose warring, victorious, and triumphant King and Lord is the Son of God and therefore Jesus Christ, the Son of God, however, who does not advance his own cause as distinct from the Father's, but who subjects himself to the Father, is obedient to him, and acts in his service and in fulfilment of his will and work. If, then, he is manifested in the last form of his parousia in this subjection and servanthood, if his kingdom is manifested as that of the Servant of the Lord, this implies no later restriction but is the authentic interpretation of his action as King and Lord in the kingdom of God as his own kingdom. His passion was itself his action as the Lord. It is the very thing that proves and confirms the identity of his kingdom with God's. Precisely in his humility as the Son of the Father, he has overcome the world and reconciled it to God. Precisely in relation to it, then, there can be no talk of the limitation of his kingdom by God's or of the end of his kingdom. No, in it "God has highly exalted him and bestowed on him the name which is above every name" (Phil. 2:9). In it he is the One of whose kingdom there will be no end (Nicene Creed with reference to Dan. 7:14; Lk. 1:33), for as God's kingdom it is everlasting. Before taking the opposite view, should we not consider and remember (in expounding 1 Cor. 15:24ff.) that in most of the (comparatively few) passages in which the kingdom is expressly called Christ's kingdom (mine, thy, his kingdom), the reference is to the future in which there is supposedly a limitation or even a disappearance of Christ's kingdom in favor of God's, according to a poor exposition of 1 Corinthians 15:24ff.? In this future there will be a final and universal disclosure of the mystery that his kingdom (the "kingdom of the cross," according to Zinzendorf; cf. *Des Ordinarii fratrum Berlinische Reden* . . . , pp. 154ff., *Hauptwerke*, Vol. I) is the kingdom of God.

For the rest, it could well be that the unmistakable restraint with which the New Testament authors speak explicitly about Christ's kingdom has its basis in a recollection of the basic pillar of New Testament christology, namely, that the Humbled is the Exalted, the Crucified the Living One, the Servant the Lord. One might then go on to ask whether today it might not be better to exercise a similar restraint with respect to the current phrases, such as Christ's "royal dominion," correct though the concept undoubtedly is.

In itself it certainly is correct, and if we fail to see this, we cannot understand what the New Testament says about the kingdom of God and hence we cannot understand the second petition. There is in the New Testament texts no lack of indirect and implicit attestation to the identity of God's kingdom with Christ's. The confession "Jesus is Lord" (κύριος 'Ιησοῦς) — the exemplary form of an inspired human word according to 1 Corinthians 12:3 — is used in innumerable places in the Synoptists, John, and the Epistles either as an address to Jesus, in statements about him, or as a standing attribute of his name. It is probably also the New Testament basis of the whole credal structure of the church. But what does it tell us? Lord (κύριος), which may be viewed as a borrowing from the surrounding Hellenistic world, but which may also be (and probably better) explained in terms of the Old Testament, does not point to someone who confirms the lordship of another or bears witness to it as his prophet; it points to one who in doing this is himself Lord, King, and Sovereign in a sphere of lordship of his own. But what other kingdom than God's can be at issue when Jesus is addressed as Lord? Again, what other kingdom does he embody and reveal according tc the Synoptists when he heals the sick, casts out demons, indeed, when with his "I say unto you . . ." [Mt. 5:22, 28, 32, 34, 39, 44] he states, expounds, and applies the law of the covenant with all the authority of Yahweh who gave it to Israel, indeed, when he does what obviously only God can do (Mk. 2:7), forgiving sinners and moving in and out among Pharisees and publicans as if he were acting in the place of the Father in heaven who causes his sun to shine on the good and the bad and his rain to fall on the righteous and the unrighteous (Mt. 5:45)? To what does he call the weary and heavy-laden when, in order that they might find rest, he calls them to himself without hesitating or considering that they should be able to find it only with God (Mt. 11:28ff.)? [It should be noted that in this passage he calls them to himself as the One who is lowly in heart (ταπεινὸς τῇ καρδίᾳ)!] And what is Jesus saying in John when in an increasingly alienating way he calls himself (ἐγώ εἰμι . . .) the light of the world [Jn. 8:12], the bread from heaven [6:41, 51, 58], his flesh the true food and his blood the true drink [6:55], himself the door [10:7, 9], the shepherd [10:11], the way, the truth, and the life [14:6], and even the resurrection [11:25]? This is not even to speak of what we are constantly told in this Gospel about the unity of his will and work with those of the Father. What does it mean that just before his death (Jn. 19:28) he knew and said that "all is now finished" (ὅτι ἤδη πάντα τετέλεσται)? What can Paul mean when he writes in 2 Corinthians 5:21 that in Christ, the sinless One who was made sin for us, God has ordained us to be the righteousness of God, or when he calls Christ the "hope of glory" in Colossians 1:27, "our hope" in 1 Timothy 1:1, and "our peace" in Ephesians 2:14? All this means that in him, in his history, God himself acted and spoke, acts and speaks, ruled and rules in his own most proper cause— not just in heaven but also on earth, in our midst. All these things, materially if not explicitly, are equivalents to references to the imminent kingdom of God, which in the view of the New Testament is obviously no other than the mighty work of Jesus of Nazareth which winds up time and all that happened, happens, and will happen in it: the kingdom of the Lord who as the Son of the Father became and was the Servant of mankind in order that he might be as such the true Lord; the kingdom in proclaiming which he in fact proclaimed himself. The succinct saying of Tertullian is right: "In the gospel Christ Himself is the kingdom of God" (Adv. Marc., IV, xxxiii, 8).

Jesus Christ is the new thing. He is the mystery that cannot be imprisoned in any system of human conceptuality but can be revealed and known only in parables. He is God acting concretely within human history. He is the One who calls those who know him to obedient willing and doing but who is and remains free from all human willing and doing, even from that of devout and earnest Christians, even from the word and work of the Christian church, of whose witness to the world he as the free Lord is the basis, theme, and content. He is the total and definitive limitation of human unrighteousness and disorder, of the interim demonic world of unchained powers: the conqueror of this world, the victorious enemy of all the enmity of men against God, one another, and themselves.[3] He at that time was in his history, on the path that he trod to the end in his time, the imminent kingdom of God.

We must emphasize the "he"—not, then, an it, however lofty or profound; not a transcendent [TS: transcendental] world of light; not an original and finally binding moral law; not a self-resting and self-moved ground of being as the origin and goal of all being; not a new philosophy, pedagogy, or politics asserting itself as better or the best; not a quintessence of personal human life either exemplary in love, purity, humility, and so forth, or fascinating in its originality; and finally, not a Christian dogmatics triumphantly proclaiming the triumph of grace, not a doctrine about him, not a christology, not a doctrine of the kingdom of God. Simply and solely he himself: accomplishing and completing God's work for the salvation of the world, that is, its reconciliation to God; speaking without reservation or

---

[3]The MS had here a fragmentary fine print section, later excised, which opened by quoting Jn. 20:19f.

subtraction God's Word to all people without exception; *he*, this man in the history of his life and word and work and passion and death. Whoever knew and loved and proclaimed him knew and loved and proclaimed the imminent kingdom of God. Speaking about God's kingdom could only mean telling his story.

Note the verb ἔρχεσθαι, which all four evangelists use in their (differing) accounts of the beginning of Jesus' public life. "Jesus came to Galilee" (Mk. 1:14), "came to Capernaum" (Mt. 4:13), "came to Nazareth" (Lk. 4:16), was seen by John the Baptist "coming" to him (Jn. 1:29). What follows in the Gospels is the developing story of this coming of his in and with which no less and no other than the kingdom of God comes. This is why the third evangelist wanted to "follow all things closely" (Lk. 1:3) and give an account of "all that Jesus began to do and teach" (Acts 1:1). This is why the fourth evangelist ends by saying: "But there are also many other things which Jesus did; were every one of them to be written, I suppose that the world itself could not contain the books that would be written" (Jn. 21:25). This might sound like a criticism of what Luke says. But why should not both statements be right in their own contexts? How could the evangelists not *want* to be complete? But how *could* they be when what was at issue was an account of the history of Jesus Christ and therefore news of the kingdom of God drawn near?

The New Testament writings — not just the Epistles but also the Gospels and among the authors not just those who collect and pass on what is handed down by the eyewitnesses, but also those who speak as eyewitnesses themselves — and with the New Testament writings the New Testament community, all look back to the past of the history of the coming of Jesus and to the past of the drawing near of the kingdom of God as to an incomparably and uniquely great *then*, which brings light to their present, which is at work in it, and which cannot therefore be forgotten but has to be passed on as faithfully as possible and always borne in mind. The *then* which in its inexhaustibility they keep before them either directly or indirectly as they look back to it is the presupposition of the prayer "Thy kingdom come." They could at any rate pray this prayer to the extent that they could know what they were saying in it because the kingdom and its coming were not empty words to them but were a known factor as they looked back to this *then*.

They were known as the history of Jesus Christ which took place then was known, the history of his words and deeds and passion and death expounded and illustrated and crowned by the history of his appearances as the one who had risen from the dead. This concrete starting point, and with it the concrete orientation of the petition, may be seen very clearly in the simple form of the petition in 1 Corinthians 16:22: "Our Lord, come" — which obviously means the same thing — or in Revelation 22:20: "Come, Lord Jesus." That Paul could use the Aramaic form (*Maranatha*) even in dealing with the Corinthians, who were so distant from the Palestinian world, shows that this version of the second petition of the Lord's Prayer is not a later interpretation but is an ancient and even, it would seem, a particularly venerable tradition.

We must, if possible, look more closely. Two things here are not at all self-evident but most astonishing. The first is that the past act of the coming of Jesus and the drawing near of the kingdom had the power to present itself to the Christians who looked back to it as also their future, and the future of the whole world. The past act obviously did not allow them merely to look back and merely to comment on it but commanded them to see the great *then* as also a *one day* that was still ahead. The past act was the very thing that obviously caused, summoned, compelled, and freed them to pray the forward-looking prayer "Thy kingdom come," "Our Lord, come," "Come again in thy great *one day* as thou hast already come, and as the One who has already come, in thy great *then*." How are we to explain this? Nor is the second thing—the other side of the same coin—any less astonishing, namely, that the first Christians, who as people living and thinking in their own time were just like all others before and alongside and after them, were still able to find a place for and to follow the impulse, demand, and constraint that came to them from that past history, making a turn of 180 degrees and therefore looking toward that past act as the future not only of their own lives but also of all world occurrence, and moving toward it with the second petition in their hearts and on their lips. There can be no doubting the twofold fact as such. On the one hand, the kingdom of God did present itself to the first community as present but also future in the history of Jesus Christ, Jesus Christ being its beginning, he who was, and also its goal, he who is to come [Rev. 1:8; 21:6; 22:13]. On the other hand, the first community did live at one and the same time in both the recollection and the expectation of his coming and the coming of God's kingdom, looking backward and then in a turn of 180 degrees looking forward, thinking with total gratitude of what had already taken place perfectly and praying with total hope that it would take place no less perfectly again. The New Testament offers us no explicit explanation of the double riddle of the unmistakable fact of this highly distinctive sense of time which is obviously determined by its whole content. The first Christians lived too directly by and in the solution to this riddle to experience any need or desire to account for it in any detail. Since we cannot say the same about ourselves, however, we are required at this point to interpose a discussion of it. In this regard the answer to the question which is at least to be indicated according to the sense of the New Testament is not in doubt.

If we ask (1) how it is possible that the coming of Jesus Christ and in and with it that of God's kingdom could present itself to the first disciples and the apostolic communities as one which was already perfectly past but still perfectly future, then, abandoning any attempt to understand the New Testament better than it understood itself,[4] our simple answer must be that

---

[4]Cf. J. G. Herder, *Sämmtliche Werke* (ed. B. Suphan), XI, 163; F. Schleiermacher, *Sämmtliche Werke* (ed. F. Lücke), VII, 32, 45.

this apparent impossibility became an actuality in the Easter history which expounds, illustrates, and crowns the history of Jesus Christ. We can only sketch here what must be thought and said about this in the present context. What took place in the appearances to the first disciples of the Jesus who had just been crucified, dead, and buried meant in any event the knowability of Jesus to them in the future of his completed history. He lived and spoke and acted before them as the subject, snatched from death, of the history toward which they had only been looking back as though, being complete, it were now ended, as though with its completion it had become part of the past. Even as eyewitnesses of the Easter event they could not stop looking back to this history and remembering what Jesus had said and done in it. But now they were prevented from merely looking back. Jesus had now met them, not as another person but as the same person in a totally different way. They for their part had not found him to be another person but the same one who had lived among them, spoken to them and the people, cast out demons, suffered under Pontius Pilate, died, and been buried: the same, but in a totally different way, in the future of his completed history. The future of his completed history as the disciples now came to see it in the Easter days was the revelation of Jesus as the One who had been in that history but who had been hidden from their eyes from the cradle to the cross: in relationship to God, the only Son of this Father of his, glorious, knowable, and known by them in the fullness of the grace and truth proper to him as such (Jn. 1:14); and in relation to the creature and its history, the Lord whom all creatures in heaven, on the earth, and under the earth must worship and confess to the glory of God his Father (Phil. 2:10f.). The One revealed and knowable to them as this Son and Lord was Jesus raised again from the dead — the same in a totally different way — who appeared to them in the Easter days, who met them in the Easter days: he in the future of his history now revealed to them and not concealed, the kingdom of God in what was now revealed to them as the universal future of its hitherto particular and to that extent concealed coming. A purely abstract and exclusive looking back to his previous history and to the coming of God's kingdom in it was obviously now forbidden to the disciples, and made completely impossible, by this his appearance and their encounter with him in it, by reason of the Easter event. The door thrust open in this event could not be shut again. After Easter the turning of 180 degrees had to be made. Looking back to his previous history, to the *then* of the coming of God's kingdom, had to become at once looking forward to his future. It was impossible to look back to the risen Jesus, the revealed Son and Lord, the kingdom known as universal and not just particular in him. One could only look and move forward to this Jesus. It had and has to be said of the Easter history — this is the self-evident presupposition of the whole of the New Testament — that he *comes* who came, Jesus the Lord, and that it *comes* that came, the kingdom of God.

If we ask (2) how it was possible — humanly possible, we should say — that the first disciples, the apostolic communities, and all later Christians who did not participate directly in the Easter event could and can make the turn from pure recollection of Jesus and the kingdom to their expectation, from great gratitude for that completed history to great hope for the future, then again, avoiding all pragmatic considerations that are alien to the sense of the New Testament, we must give the simple answer that this took place in the apostolic communities, and still takes place in Christians up to our own day, in virtue of the gift and in the doing of the work of the Holy Spirit. We are not referred here to the existence and function of human eyewitnesses of the history of Jesus which shines forth in the Easter history as the revelation of its future. We are referred to the power of God to open blind eyes to see this light. This power of God is the Holy Spirit. The Holy Spirit certainly did and does make use of the eyewitnesses, but he is not limited to them or their mediating force. It is he who effected and effects both grateful recollection of that history in human hearts and heads and also hopeful expectation of its future, knowledge of the kingdom of God that came then in particular and will come one day universally. The Holy Spirit liberated and commanded them to turn to that beginning and in so doing to turn to this end, thus entering into the Easter event and no less definitely and certainly than the first disciples seeing Jesus and God's kingdom in the future of his history and therefore in his revelation as the Son of God and the Lord of all creation. Apart from the Holy Spirit, apart from being liberated and empowered by him, no one has called Jesus Lord and no one can (1 Cor. 12:3). The Holy Spirit is the *forward* which majestically awakens, enlightens, leads, pushes, and impels, which God has spoken in the resurrection of Jesus from the dead, which he has spoken and still speaks to the world of humanity: *forward* to the new coming of Jesus and the kingdom. The Spirit is the *Holy* Spirit because, coming from the Father and given by the Son as the power of the Father and the Son, he is God himself in the same act in which in the Easter event he confessed his completed work in the history of Jesus Christ with the promise that he will confess it again universally and definitively. Endowed and equipped with freedom for this, Christians grasp this promise, look and move forward, and pray, "Thy kingdom come," "Come, Lord Jesus."

Without a reference to Easter and Pentecost, it is impossible to give an answer, at least in the New Testament sense, to the question of the possibility of the turning which took place for and in the New Testament community from the past of the history of Jesus Christ and the coming of God's kingdom to their future.

It would be ungrateful if we did not conclude this subsection with an historical statement. The present view of the kingdom of God and its coming may sound new, but it can and will lay no claim to complete originality. We could not have spoken or tried to speak as we did if, quite apart from the academic theology of their days, the two Württembergers J. C. Blumhardt (1805-1880) and his son, C. Blumhardt (1842-1919) of Möttlingen, and then Bad Boll, had not in sermons and devotional and edificatory utterances, not only taught the reality denoted by the term the "kingdom of God," but with much greater theological relevance attested and proclaimed it. What has been presented here rests on personal exegetical reflection and theological deliberation. If something is now being said about the Blumhardts, it is not with the intention of summoning them as subsequent star witnesses for what has been developed. In fact, it could not have been stated and developed as it has without the impulse they gave and their influence through other mediations and modifications. This is what must be expressly confirmed here in expansion of what has already been said in *CD* IV,3, pp. 168-171.

Emphasis has already been placed on the services rendered in this matter — in the sphere of "regular" theology — by the forerunners and first representatives of the so-called "history of religion" school toward the end of the nineteenth century. Their rediscovery of the eschatological dimension of the New Testament message of the kingdom of God had primarily the significance of a critical clarification over against the ancient "this-sidedness" of the concept, and especially of the second petition of the Lord's Prayer, which unfortunately not even the Reformers had overcome. It was the work of the two Blumhardts, however, to fill out the concept positively with a living view of the reality denoted and to bring it into modern Christianity and the world as a truth that was wholly new to it. In 1920, I wrote a little essay on F. Overbeck ("Unerledigte Anfragen an die heute Theologie," in K. Barth and E. Thurneysen, *Zur inneren Lage der Christenheit*, Munich, 1920, pp. 3-24) in which I advanced the bold and hotly contested thesis that to do justice to this scholar one must see him back to back with his contemporary, the younger Blumhardt. The two lived in very different worlds. They hardly knew each other, and if they had they would have been objects of considerable astonishment to one another. But I would still say, perhaps even more definitely, that what underlay a certain movement in academic theology at the end of the nineteenth century must be seen together with what was championed most unacademically but very positively by the two Blumhardts, father and son. This is why we should think of them briefly at this point.

The phenomenon, in its way unique, of the proclamation of God's kingdom by the two Blumhardts confronts us, of course, with a complex problem. They are clearly distinguished from that tradition which goes back to the second century, and also, offensively enough even to our own day, from the ecclesiastical and pietistic Christianity around them, by their very definite opposition to the identification of the kingdom of God with the life and work of the church and of special Christian groups either inside or outside it. When they spoke about the kingdom of God, they looked far beyond everything, even the best, that had already taken place, or might still take place, inside all church or chapel walls. Yet they were themselves heirs of that tradition to the extent that they thought they could discern the dawning of the kingdom in certain temporal and historical changes and events which, as they saw it, had already occurred or were to be anticipated. Along these lines the elder Blumhardt, to his life's end, could continually look back to the extraordinary happenings he had witnessed in Möttlingen and then in Boll, and he could look forward in hope to a general outpouring of the Holy Spirit that would awaken to new life the dead bones of contemporary Christianity [Ezk. 27:1ff.]. Similarly, the younger Blumhardt in his middle years thought that he had discovered more than natural lights in the concept of evolution in modern science, in which he had a passionate interest, also in social democracy, with which he declared his solidarity for a time (up to the acceptance of a mandate in the Württemberg Assembly), and then in temporary association with the activity of his son-in-law, Richard Wilhelm (cf. his *Christus in der Welt. Briefe an R. Wilhelm*, ed. A. Rich, Zurich, 1958), even in the religions of the Orient. A certain inclination to ascribe to the world what he increasingly would not ascribe to Christianity as such, not with the corrosive sharpness of Kierkegaard, but materially no less decisively, may be clearly seen in him. But one must add at once that in his final period he became very quiet about these discoveries, and, in distinction from many of his followers and successors, he never systematized them or presented them as dogmas or laws binding on others, but worked them out and proposed them more as necessary and promising experiments for the hour. In the same way his father, although he was constantly occupied with the miracles that he had experienced, never gave outward publicity to any of them, even the healing of Gottliebin Dittus, but emphatically warned against all sensation-seeking or self-aggrandizement along these lines, soberly if sorrowfully accepting the passing of the great penitential movement at Möttlingen and teaching the same restraint to those around him in Boll. The Blumhardts did not lack vitality, dynamism, or a healthy self-awareness. In their sermons and pastoral work, speaking with authority and not as the scribes [cf. Mt. 7:29 and par.], they could be very categorical both in the indicative and the imperative. But one thing we certainly cannot accuse them of is the investing of their own persons, achievements, or followings with any prophetic or priestly glory. Both of them constantly pointed beyond themselves and beyond everything connected with Möttlingen and Boll, which from the very first stood under some threat in this regard. They knew the frailty of all that men will and think and do, themselves included. "I am buried in misery," the father could exclaim at the height of his life and work (cf. F. Zündel, *Pfarrer Johann Christoph Blumhardt* . . . , Zurich/Heilbronn, 1881[2], p. 465). And the saying of the son just after the death of his father, "Die that Jesus may live" (the original form is "Die and so Jesus will live,"; cf. C. Blumhardt, *Eine Auswahl aus seinen Predigten, Andachten und Schriften*, ed. R. Lejeune, Vol. II, Erlenbach-Zurich and Leipzig, 1925, esp. p. 78 and pp. 585-591; also pp. 113, 119, 122), does not refer to dying to the wicked world, nor to the pious flesh of church folk and pietists, but directly to self and to all who were in danger of seeing in what they found and did in Möttlingen and Boll a little bit of the kingdom of heaven on earth and of thus becoming like others — not those who wait and hasten on, but those who have arrived, not those who hunger and thirst but those who are in happy possession. "Do not deny the Savior by being content with what you have" (cf. C. Blumhardt, *Haus-Andachten nach Losungen und Lehrtexten der Brüdergemeine*, Stuttgart/Basel, 1916, p. 65. [The original, however, runs as follows: "Do not deny the Savior by not being content with what you have." For a possible explanation of Barth's lapse of memory here, see the German edition, *Das christliche Leben*, Zurich, 1976, p. 446, n. 115]). A remarkable discontent with all that they had known and experienced — a discontent which increased at some periods and declined at others — may be seen unmistakably in the old age of both the Blumhardts; they did not think that they had led their lambs into the desert!

It was thus a mistake when someone who should have known better wrote at a later date (E. Jäckh, "Blumhardt . . . ," *RGG*[2], I, 1152-54; cf. also E. Jäckh, *Blumhardt Vater und Sohn und ihre Botschaft*, Berlin, 1925[2], p. 7) that the kingdom of God as they proclaimed it is to be understood as an "organism which comes into being through God's action and which embraces both this world and the world to come." The "little point" to which the younger Blumhardt sometimes referred (C. Blumhardt, *op. cit.*, p. 25) as that which he really had in mind, and which everyone must see to understand him correctly, was certainly not an organism embracing this world and the world to come but was rather, if we are to use that kind of terminology, the world to come intervening from outside and from first to last, not just limiting or even illumining this world, but with superior severity and goodness storming and smashing it in all its dimensions. The gaze of both Blumhardts did not *rest* upon this world to come, and therefore it did not *rest* upon what they perceived more or less certainly to be its reflections in this world. The world to come to which they looked was not a being but an action and event, or, rather, a being engaged in an action and event, in a coming. How could either it or its reflections allow human eyes to rest upon it? The gaze of the two Blumhardts gratefully and yearningly followed its movement, which is absolutely superior to all movements in this world, which precedes them all and transcends them all. Too much emphasis cannot be placed on the fact that the two Blumhardts were seriously and finally interested in it and that it was for this reason that they were also interested in the reflections of it they thought they saw in this world, though they were interested in these only secondarily, only to some extent incidentally and therefore unsystematically, and without establishing either themselves or others on them. Their true theme — and for those who know them there is no doubt about this — was the world to come, which they did not just perceive in those reflections but saw in faith and hope as an action and event at the beginning and end of the whole of this world. But what is this world to come? When the two Blumhardts did not speak of the kingdom of God indirectly, in experiments, or with only penultimate seriousness, but directly, thetically, and with ultimate seriousness, then with astounding simplicity and directness they pronounced the name of Jesus which illumines and infinitely outshines all the miracles at Möttlingen and the experiences at Boll, all the expected new outpouring of the Spirit, all the later possibilities which may be noted in science or religion or accepted in politics. Without being polemical in this regard, what they had in view was neither the God-man of early christology nor the so-called historical Jesus for whom their age already had such a lively concern. Very naively, but with axiomatic certainty, they were thinking of the reality of the risen and living Jesus himself, acting and speaking as a distinctive factor no less actual today than yesterday: the Jesus who is self-evidently, as in the primitive church, both the beginning and also the end [Rev. 21:6; 22:13]; the Jesus who has already come and will come again, and who is thus present to his people and — unknown to it — the world. "As often as I write the name of Jesus, a holy light fills me with a joyful fervor of thanksgiving that I may know Him mine. What we have in Him I now know properly for the first time" (so the elder Blumhardt on a portrait used by Zündel in his biography, *op. cit.*, before p. I, though Blumhardt wrote *Schauer* [awe] not *Schein* [light] and also underscored the last sentence). It is true that in the younger Blumhardt this name is often pushed into the background by a strong and joyful but general reference to God, for which he probably had his reasons. But in him too it continually shines out so brightly that it unquestionably limited and dominated his field of vision both behind and before. Some examples may be given from his *Hausandachten* (1916): "What men begin perishes, but what God purposes (Isa. 46:10) stands. He sends a Savior, a prince, and will help man to all eternity. Thus the counsel of God stands now in Jesus Christ. Truth and righteousness are to be in him that good and bad must separate from one another" (p. 55). There is "a compulsion in Jesus Christ given him by God, granted to him by the Almighty" (p. 19). "Then the good Lord can point out and say, Look, before you thought of Me, when you were still a stupid, stupid man, I sent thee the Savior who died for thee" (p. 91). "Whenever one hears about him, it has to be said that he is truly risen and his words and deeds have power. He thus remains a light shining on dying humanity" (p. 101; the original has "it remains"). "The light which shines on the cradle of Jesus Christ should be to us a promise: He comes; He is near . . . a Lord and King of righteousness that heaven and earth may become new and finally men too" (p. 389). Nor may we forget that the whole Blumhardt history stood under the sign of the saying: "Jesus is Victor." Regarding this, the father told how one December day in 1843 he had received the saying in an audition that he experienced in a wood along with several witnesses. Then to his astonishment he heard it again on the lips of the sister of Gottliebin Dittus, who was torn by the unhappy girl's affliction. As the pastoral battle that Blumhardt had fought was reaching its climax, it now sounded forth like the teeth-gnashing admission of defeat by the demons. It was not, then, a doctrine or a definition but an unmistakable cry from the heights and the depths: "Jesus — is — Victor," in which, to understand it as Blumhardt did, we must grant and accede to each of the three words its own special force. We should also take note of an explanatory text which is accessible to everybody, the familiar, poetically modest, but materially most instructive verse of a hymn by which the older Blumhardt himself interpreted the cry: "Jesus is the victorious hero who has defeated all his foes," a summary of what has already been done and effected and established in the life and death and resurrection of Jesus; then, looking forward with confidence from that point: "Jesus is He who will soon have the whole world at His feet," with which one may compare the memorable and more positive saying of the father shortly before his death: "The Lord will lay His gentle hand in mercy on all peoples" (cf. Zündel, *op. cit.*, p. 535); and finally something that is not yet seen but may be awaited with unconditional assurance in the light of the starting point: "Jesus is He who comes with pomp (revealing Himself in glory as the One He was and is) and leads out of the night to the light." This is, for those who have ears to hear [Mt. 11:15; 13:9 and par.], the movement of thought of the two Blumhardts, their theology in brief, their message of the kingdom, whose specific force will not be easily evaded by those who perceive it even if only from a distance, notwithstanding all the personal and historical factors which conditioned it.

4. FIAT IUSTITIA

"Behold, the days are coming, says the Lord, when I shall raise up for David a righteous Branch, and he shall reign as king and deal wisely, and shall execute justice and righteousness in the land. In his days Judah will be saved, and Israel will dwell securely. And this is the name by which he will be called: *Yahweh zidkenu* (the Lord our Righteousness, Jer. 23:5f.). Christians are folks who know this one: the Son of David, the King and his reign and right and righteousness. They have their origin in his time, in what took place in it as he did it. They are thus Judah who is saved and Israel who dwells securely. Victims, like all others, of the ongoing course of the world, and under obligation to it, even within the still persisting time of human unrighteousness and disorder, even within the sphere of lordship of the lordless powers, they have the freedom and joy, and also hear the command, to lift up their heads [Lk. 21:28], to look ahead, to look and move toward the same *Yahweh zidkenu* and his time and work, to look and move on from the Christmas of the old year to the Advent of the new. They truly call upon him now, in and with the kingdom that has already drawn near: "Thy kingdom come," "Come, Lord Jesus."

Their obedience to this command, their humble but vigorous use of the freedom to call upon God in this way, is the true and essential thing about the revolt to which they are called and summoned as we saw at the beginning of the section: their revolt against the unrighteousness and disorder in whose sphere they find themselves and indeed whose guilt they share (with a sharper sting than others) and whose consequences they also suffer (again with a livelier awareness than others). As they pray for the coming of the kingdom of God, they call upon God to accept and have mercy on erring and confused humanity by establishing right and righteousness in the land in the definitive manifestation and revelation of the King raised up by him — his own divine and incontestable righteousness, his indubitable righteousness which is total, not partial, and definitive, not provisional. They expect and pray that God will bring about this end of all his ways. That they expect and pray it is the core and star of the very modest contribution that can be made on the human side in the battle against disorder. In all its modesty, however, this is the most authentic, powerful, and effective thing that can be done on the human side, even by them. All else that might come into question here does not reach up to Christian expectation and prayer because even at best it can be aimed only at shifts of emphasis within the world, at contestable, partial, and provisional corrections of the human situation, but above all because the undoubtedly modest expectation and prayer of Christians is secretly distinguished by its coming from, and being sustained and impelled by, the point where the kingdom has already come in the person of the King whom God has raised up, where all righteousness has already been fulfilled, where all that can be done for mankind has already been accomplished. The prayer which this King himself has laid on the lips of Christians, even as and though it too is a wholly human and therefore feeble action, surpasses — as it comes from that point — all other possibilities of human revolt against disorder, pressing on to the place from which there may be expected, and expected as the fulfilment of the demanded request, the help that is not just apparent, partial, and inadequate, but genuine, complete, and effective. As Christians call upon God with this petition, they do what is qualitatively more and better than the best that all other movements for the establishment of human righteousness can do, their own efforts included. If only they knew what a task and what power were entrusted to them when as the children of God they are freed and summoned to hasten to their Father with this prayer to him! If only they knew what a debt they incur to him and themselves and the whole world which they have to represent with this petition if they neglect to do this! If only they knew finally with what profoundest rest and joy they can withstand the inner and outer assaults of the course of the world with all the things that are so unseemly and intolerable and monstrous and impossible in it, looking ahead to its end and goal, when they do not grow indolent and slothful but persist cheerfully and industriously in the by no means heroic action of praying "Thy kingdom come."

This is not indeed an heroic action but a very unassuming one. If it is to be heroic, this will not be in any sense through the heroism of the Christians who pray but solely through the power of the intercession which the one true Hero made and still makes for them and for the whole world in Gethsemane, on the cross, and as the One who prayed first the six petitions of the Lord's Prayer — the Hero in fellowship with whom they may then pray for their part, mirroring his intercession in their own prayer. Again, if the action is to be more than unassuming, it will not be by the depth and fervor of their prayer but solely by the holiness of the Spirit of God who helps their weakness and glorifies not them, but himself in them [Rom. 8:26]. At this point we must emphasize that in the prayer "Thy kingdom come," when prayed as an act of obedience to God's command, we have an action that for good or ill is performed by Christians as people in human fashion. If it were not this, the prayer would not be prayed. It could be just an inner sigh, coming and going as a passive feeling in which nothing happens and nothing is in fact done. Like many another devout word of prayer and confession, it could be just a liturgical formula with whose more or less solemn or mechanical recitation nothing again happens and nothing is in fact done. In the hearts and on the lips of Christians the prayer for the kingdom may have been in millions of cases no more than this kind of useless sigh or liturgical formula with whose utterance nothing has happened and nothing has been done. But how do we know? Just as often, and perhaps more so, in spite of the weakness of the praying Christians, with God understanding them better than they do themselves, it might have been prayed in the freedom of obedience as a prayer of serious need and demand, and thus a seriously open, ready, and willing prayer, and at its heart a brave prayer. When it was a brave prayer, however, something happened. Something was in fact done by the people who prayed it, who directed it to God as pure petition. When people turn bravely to God with this petition — and we assume that there are some who do — then necessarily with their hearts and lips, caught up by what they pray, their whole life and thought and word and deed are set in motion, oriented to the point to which they look with the petition. They necessarily establish themselves on that for which they there pray to God — for which they can only pray, but can pray bravely. They would be making a game of it if this did not happen, if they did not do this. They find, however, that they are not allowed to make a game of it, to pray as if they did not pray. Praying bravely for that which they request in the second petition, they therewith take part, as we have seen, in the movement that characterizes the being, thought, and action of the apostles and their communities. In the power of Jesus Christ who rose again and lives for them too, and as the work of the Holy Spirit who enlightens and impels them, there takes place and has already come about in their life and history that turning of 180 degrees from the appearance of the Lord that has taken place already to that which is awaited in the future, from the kingdom of God that has already drawn near to that which is still to come in its final, universal, and definitive revelation. Praying the second petition bravely means following this movement and turning, having no other choice but to look ahead and also to live and think and speak and act ahead, to run from the beginning, the history of Jesus Christ first revealed in his resurrection, to the goal, its final manifestation, the coming kingdom of God — to run toward this with all one's soul and all one's powers like one who is running a race, as Paul puts it in 1 Corinthians 9:24ff. and Philippians 3:12ff. The heart of the Christian ethos is that those

who are freed and summoned to pray "Thy kingdom come" are also freed
and summoned to use their freedom to obey the command that is given
therewith and to live for their part with a view to the coming kingdom.

The coming of the kingdom of God is the appearing of God's righteousness on a new earth and under a new heaven [cf. Isa. 65:17; 2 Pet. 3:13; Rev.
21:1]. It is the setting up of his ordering of human life and life together, of
his order of life, right, freedom, peace, and joy which is good for man as
his creature, covenant partner, and child, which saves and keeps him. In
Jesus Christ and the power of his Spirit this order is fully present already
to those who know and love him. It is also fully revealed in him. In its
majesty, as the grace and benefit addressed to all in him, but also as the
judgment executed on *all* human unrighteousness and disorder, it is their
hope, but it is not yet revealed even to them. Its revelation in this majesty —
Jesus Christ as the sun of righteousness [Mal. 4:2], as the sun of grace
which lightens all people, Christians and non-Christians, good and bad,
which also illumines and enlightens them — is the new coming of the kingdom of God that is still awaited. Christians live toward this, toward its
day, as they live from its first coming. To bring in this day, to cause it to
dawn, to reveal God's righteousness in its majesty, cannot be the affair of
any person, and therefore it cannot be the affair of the Christian, for example, through the lights entrusted to him, just as the coming into being
of light on the first day of creation was not the work of the creature but
solely that of its Creator, and just as the first day of Jesus Christ, the coming
of the kingdom in his history and in the Easter event, was not initiated by
humans, not even by God's chosen Israel among them, nor by the faith of
the disciples, but solely by the free mercy of God. Nevertheless, for those
who in the power of the resurrection of Jesus Christ from the dead, enlightened by the Holy Spirit of the Father and the Son, look ahead from that
beginning to this end, this cannot possibly mean that they are commanded
or even permitted to be idle in the meantime; to acquiesce for the time being
in human unrighteousness and disorder and their consequences, in the mortal imperiling of life, freedom, peace, and joy on earth under the lordship
of the lordless powers; so far as possible to adjust themselves during the
interim to the status quo; to establish themselves on this; and perhaps even
with gloomy skeptical speculation to find comfort in the thought that until
God's final and decisive intervention, the course of events will necessarily
be not only as bad as previously but increasingly worse. No, they *wait* and
hasten toward the dawn of God's day, the appearing of his righteousness,
the parousia of Jesus Christ (2 Pet. 3:12). They not only wait but also hasten.
They wait by hastening. Their waiting takes place in the hastening. Aiming
at God's kingdom, established on its coming and not on the status quo, they
do not just look toward it but run toward it as fast as their feet will carry
them. This is inevitable if in their hearts and on their lips the petition "Thy
kingdom come" is not an indolent and despondent prayer but one that is
zealous and brave.

But what has to happen when the prayer is prayed? What does running
mean? What is the orientation and direction of Christian life and thought

and word and work that corresponds to what is requested? The answer is —
and along the lines that we have followed thus far no other answer is
possible — *Fiat iustitia*. That is to say, Christians are claimed for action in
the effort and struggle for human righteousness. At issue is human, not
divine righteousness. That the latter should come, intervene, assert itself,
reign, and triumph can never be the affair of any human action. Those who
know the reality of the kingdom, Christians, can never have anything to do
with the arrogant and foolhardy enterprise of trying to bring in and build
up by human hands a religious, cultic, moral, or political kingdom of God
on earth. God's righteousness is the affair of God's own act, which has
already been accomplished and is still awaited. God's righteousness took
place in the history of Jesus Christ, and it will take place again, comprehensively and definitively, in his final manifestation. The time between that
beginning and that end, our time as the time of the presence of Jesus Christ
in the Holy Spirit, is for Christians the space for gratitude, hope, and prayer,
and also the time of responsibility for the occurrence of human righteousness. They have to be concerned about the doing of this righteousness. On
no pretext can they escape responsibility for it: not on that of the gratitude
and hope with which they look to God and wait for his action; not on that
of their prayer for the coming of his kingdom. For if they are really grateful
and really hope, if their prayer is a brave prayer, then they are claimed for
a corresponding inner and outer action which is also brave. If they draw
back here, or even want to, then there is serious reason to ask whether and
how far their gratitude, hope, and prayer are to be taken seriously.

The phrase *Fiat iustitia* supposedly comes from the Hapsburg emperor Ferdi-
nand I, the younger brother of Charles V. Though that counterreformation potentate
did not intend it in this sense, we put a good construction on it here. We are thus
letting the continuation *et pereat mundus* sink into the oblivion to which it belongs.
A righteousness that could and would mean the perishing of the world would not
be either divine or human righteousness but simply the righteousness of the devil.
We shall not replace that bad conclusion, however, with *et vivat mundus*. The
righteousness that brings life to the world can only be that of the kingdom of God.
Where people, especially Christians, practice this or introduce it, where they try to
proclaim, define, and exercise a divine right instead of simply believing in the coming
of God's kingdom and praying for it, there they are enslaved to a titanism whose
only result can be all kinds of greater and smaller monstrosities, wild illusions,
oppressions and suppressions of all kinds, and finally witch hunts, murder, and
killing. The world might very well perish in consequence of an attempt to carry
through this undertaking. It is true not only that divine righteousness cannot be
brought in by Christians but also that for the sake of God's honor and the protection
of themselves and the whole world from the greatest evil, they are prevented and
prohibited from trying to bring it in. What they are commanded to do — and as in
all simplicity they give thanks and hope and pray they cannot escape this command — is to work for human righteousness. In this sense then: *Fiat iustitia*.

Human righteousness! We shall not develop at length here the self-
evident point that, measured by God's righteousness and in unconquerable

distinction from it, this will always be, even at best, an imperfect, fragile, and highly problematical righteousness. Others may deceive themselves in this regard, but to those who have the prayer for the kingdom in their hearts and on their lips it is indeed self-evident. Nevertheless, it is not so important that they can refrain from doing what they have to do in this relativity. We Protestants have always had a certain inclination to find it too important. We should break free from this. Those who pray that prayer start off with the thesis that the perfect righteousness of God's kingdom is not their own doing, that they can only seek it (Mt. 6:33), as is appropriate, in gratitude for its reality, in hope of its manifestation, in prayer that it may come. This means, however, that any concern for the imperfection of all human action, their own included, is taken from them as idle and pointless. They are also forbidden the lazy excuse of all lazy servants that since all they can do will always be imperfect anyway it is not worth exerting themselves and growing weary in the causes of petty human righteousness. No, precisely because perfect righteousness stands before them as God's work, precisely because they are duly forbidden to attempt the impossible, precisely because all experiments in this direction are prevented and prohibited, they are with great strictness required and with great kindness freed and empowered to do what they can do in the sphere of the relative possibilities assigned to them, to do it very imperfectly yet heartily, quietly, and cheerfully. They are absolved from wasting time and energy sighing over the impassable limits of their sphere of action and thus missing the opportunities that present themselves in this sphere. They may and can and should rise up and accept responsibility to the utmost of their power for the doing of the little righteousness. The only concern should be their awareness of how far they fall short in this sphere of what is not only commanded but also possible for them. But they can quickly rid themselves of this concern by setting to work to snatch the available possibilities of doing what is commanded and thus catching up in God's name where they are in arrears. A little righteousness and holiness of works — there will certainly never be a great deal! — does not have to be an illusion or a danger here. The only danger arising out of the (ill-founded) anxiety that one might become too righteous and too holy, a man of works, is the temptation to remain passive where what is required, with a full sense of one's limitations, is to become active.

It is not self-evident, of course, that in the sphere of human activity, alongside and far below divine righteousness, there should be in all seriousness a human righteousness which Christians are freed to do and for whose occurrence they are made responsible. It is not self-evident that the same lofty concept of righteousness, denoting on the one hand perfect divine action and on the other most imperfect human action, should be appropriate or necessary in this context. In relation to human action as such and in general, the analogy is in truth an impossible one. Here, however, we are referring to the obedience of the action of those whom God has freed and summoned to call upon him for the coming of his kingdom and the doing of righteousness. In relation to the action of these people, it cannot be denied that in all its imperfection this action stands related to the kingdom of God, and therefore to the perfect righteousness of God, inasmuch as it derives from the event of the kingdom in Jesus Christ and hastens toward its manifestation in Jesus Christ. Obviously, this whence and whither mean that it cannot be alien to it but is given a determination which it does not have in itself and cannot give itself but which it acquires, which it cannot escape as it takes place in that relation, and which cannot be denied to it. The determination that it acquires and has in that relation is that it can take place only in correspondence with its whence and whither and therefore with God's kingdom and righteousness. If it never can or will be like this, and should not try to aim at equality with it, neither can it be or remain totally unlike it. There is a third possibility. The action of those who pray for the coming of God's kingdom and therefore for the taking place of his righteousness will be *kingdom-like*, and therefore on a lower level and within its impassable limits it will be *righteous* action. Certainly we should not say too much here, yet we should not say too little either. Done in that relation, under that determination, and therefore in that correspondence, the action of Christians may in its own way and within the limits of its own sphere be called and be a righteous action. This is the one talent that is entrusted to Christians, who are neither angels nor archangels but only people, and they must not wrap it in a cloth or bury it anywhere, as did the stupid fellow in Luke 19:20 and Matthew 25:25. Following their prayer, their action can and should be kingdom-like, righteous in its own place and manner. There is not the shadow of a serious reason to contest this.

What do we mean, however, by kingdom-likeness and therefore by the human righteousness of Christian life and thought and speech and action in correspondence with the object of the petition? Anticipating the answer, we may say that according to the measure of what is possible for them, their action must in all circumstances take place with a view to people, in address to people, and with the aim of helping people. The concern of Christians in the coming of the kingdom for which they pray is with doing the perfect righteousness of the God who seeks and magnifies his honor by thinking of men, by taking them to himself, by establishing their right as their Creator, Father, Judge, and Deliverer, by creating and giving to them perfect life, freedom, peace, and joy. On the other hand, in the city of the devil, the kingdom of human unrighteousness and disorder which defies God, what is at issue is the work of human hostility in which people fight with one another for their right to live, to live in freedom, peace, and joy, in which they thus deprive themselves of this right, their human right and dignity being constantly overlooked, forgotten, broken, and trampled under the lordship of the released and lordless powers. Praying for the coming of the kingdom of God and his righteousness, and thus empowered, instructed, and summoned to fight against human unrighteousness, Christians can look only where they see God looking and try to live with no other purpose than that with which God acts in Jesus Christ. This means, however, that the true and serious and finally important object of their attention, love, and will, and therefore of their thought, speech, and action, in agreement with their prayer and in correspondence with what they pray for, can only be man: man as the one whose brother God himself willed to become and became; for whom Jesus Christ lived, died, and rose again; to whom he has promised the Holy Spirit; whose cause he will conduct to its goal in his final manifestation. "We are not our own but God's" (Calvin, *Inst.*, III, 7, 1). "We do not belong to ourselves but to the Lord." But because the Lord is the Father, Son, and Holy Spirit who bound and obligated himself to man, Christians also belong to mankind and in this concrete sense they belong to themselves. They cannot be for man as God was nor do for him what God does; they should not presume to try to be, for him or act for him in this way. But they can and should be witnesses of what God is for man and does for him. Christians may and can and should reflect and practice God's being and acting for man, the distinction with which he treats him, by making man the special object of their own interest. What they do therewith — giving and allowing him precedence among all the other things that interest them — is little enough to deprive them of any ground for boasting. As they do it, however, they practice the appropriate human righteousness corresponding to the great divine righteousness. That this should be done and occur (*fiat*) in what they think and speak and do, that it should be the orientation and basis of their lives, is the responsibility they are given.

We do not forget that they are made responsible within the world of unrighteousness and disorder and therefore in the sphere of dominion of these powers and forces. They are made responsible, then, as those who have both a passive and an active share in the evil and corruption of this world, in the unchaining of those demonic factors in world occurrence, in the silent or gloriously tumultuous enterprise of their deification. The only point is that in spite of their situation of shared guilt and oppression they have been required and empowered to pray for the coming of the kingdom. This is what differentiates them from all other people. So too, of course, does their commitment to oppose, resist, and revolt against human corruption in their own sphere, which it is not their affair to transcend. Not led astray by necessity, they have to swim manfully against the stream regardless of the cost or consequences. They do this by looking past and beyond all other things to man, whom God loved in spite of all his corruption and misery, by making man the proper object of their interest, by making man's right and life and freedom and joy their theme. In this way they fight the fight for human righteousness against human unrighteousness. Since they still move in the sphere of human unrighteousness, and their fight can never be wholly free from it, they are well advised not to make extravagant gestures nor to make too big a song about what they do. But if they look solely at man, they are obeying the command that is unquestioningly given them as they may pray for the coming of the kingdom. It is enough if they really do this. In doing it they are in all humility righteous people — sinners, but righteous sinners.

Their concern is with man. From the very start they are "humanists." They are not interested in any cause as such. In regard to every cause, they simply look and ask whether and how far it will relatively and provisionally serve or hurt the cause of man and his right and worth. No idea, no principle, no traditional or newly established institution or organization, no old or new form of economy, state, or culture, no so-called patrimony, no prevailing habit, custom, or moral system, no ideal of education and up-bringing, no form of the church, can be for them the a priori of what they think and speak and will, nor can any negation or contesting of certain other ideas and the social constructs corresponding to them. Their a priori is not a cause, however great, necessary, or splendid it may appear to be or is. It is the righteousness of God in Jesus Christ and therefore, in cor-respondence with this, the man who is loved by God, his right and worth — solely and simply man. Certainly in relation to man — perhaps temporarily or more permanently, perhaps joyfully or anxiously — they will have to say Yes or No, and say it resolutely, to current ideas and life-forms. Certainly in relation to him they will not be afraid of taking sides for and against. But in so doing they will think and speak in terms of theses and not prin-ciples. In this field there can be no absolute Yes or No carrying an absolute commitment. One reason for this is that an absolute guarantee of human right and worth cannot be expected from the rule of any idea or the power of any life-form. From one standpoint or another, every idea or life-form will sooner or later prove a threat to man. Hence Christians, looking always to the only problem that seriously and finally interests them, must allow themselves the liberty in certain circumstances of saying only a partial Yes or No where a total one is expected, or a total Yes or No where a partial one is expected, or of saying Yes today where they said No yesterday, and vice versa. Their total and definitive decision is for man and not for any cause. They will never let themselves be addressed as prisoners of their own decisions or slaves of any sacrosanct consistency. Their Yes and No in this sphere can always be only a relative Yes and No, supremely because if it were more they would be affirming and acknowledging the existence of those absolute or lordless powers, canonizing their deification, and instead of resisting the true and most dangerous enemies of man and his right, life, and worth, offering them the most hazardous and fateful help. It is another question that they do not topple them, that they do not liberate people from their rule, that they feel their power themselves, and that they can only look on helplessly as countless others fall under their wheels. But how can they confirm them as they would do if they were to indulge in absolute affirmations and negations in this sphere? Christians must resolutely refuse to swallow some of the strengthenings they are offered in order that they may go through world history with a stiffened backbone. In so doing, they will show that they have real backbone. They must not do this because they are themselves possessed by a principial nonconformism, but because they realize that the people about whom they are concerned cannot be helped (even relatively) by such strengthenings, that is, by principles that are enun-ciated and venerated as divine, that these are rather the works and products of human perversion which can only increase the evil which suppresses and oppresses people. Where do we meet one another more like wolves swal-lowing one another up than when we come in the name of absolutes and therefore as champions of pseudo-deities, no matter what we call them?

Because Christians are dealing with people, they can say to all principles only a relative Yes or No, and they must resist as such all principles that claim to be irrefutable.

As only God himself can be at issue in the prayer of Christians for the coming of the kingdom, so only man can be at issue in their other thinking and speech and action. Man himself is he whom God loved, for whom Jesus died and rose again, and for whom he will come again as Judge and Redeemer. To him as such Christians owe righteousness, their whole attention and concern, and mercy. They do not believe at all that clothes make the man. They cannot be impressed, or deceived, then, by the Sunday clothes or working clothes or fool's clothes in which they will often enough meet him. They will not fear him because of the armor and cut-and-thrust weapons with which he tries to impress them and behind which he simply hides his anxiety, and they certainly will not fear him because his coat has too many holes to conceal effectively the emptiness of his vanity and his real need. They will not see him as political or economic or ecclesiastical man — the less so the more he claims to be a high priest. They will not see him as the member of this or that country or sociological stratum, nor as the type of this or that psychological category, nor as one who believes in this or that doctrine of salvation or perdition. They will not see him as a good citizen or a convict, as the representative of a conviction or party that they find agreeable or painful, as a Christian or a non-Christian, as a good or bad, a practicing or non-practicing Christian. Naturally, they will on occasion see him also as the bearer of one or many of these garbs or masks. It will be no accident that he bears them and that he bears this or that particular one of the many that are available. To see him it may be helpful to see him also in these disguises, as man at work, man at play, business man, organization man, or so-called modern man. All this is good and right and relevant, but Christians cannot stop here, looking only at mankind in these disguises. These are not man himself. He himself may act as though he wanted to be addressed in terms of his garbs and masks, but he cannot really be addressed thus. He cannot be nailed to these and judged and treated accordingly. In, with, and under all the apparatus by which he is surrounded and with which he surrounds himself and usually hides himself, he himself is the being who, whether he knows that God is on his side or not, is to achieve his right, live in dignity, and enjoy freedom, peace, and joy, but who behaves with terrible ineptitude and even wickedness in this area, chooses crooked and dubious paths — why take the simple course when a complicated one is also available? — acts either with total lack of humor or total lack of seriousness, is either as timorous as a gazelle or as relentless as a buffalo, and in any case does not achieve his purpose, being unable to find again what he intends and seeks in what he thinks he sometimes finds. Man himself *suffers*, and he fights tooth and nail against admitting this even to himself, let alone to others. He acts — this is the point of his disguises — as if he does not suffer. This one who suffers is man himself whom God loves. The task of little righteousness which Christians are given when they may pray for the coming of God's kingdom is to see and understand man in this plight from which he cannot rescue himself, but only God can rescue him, to turn to him openly and willingly, to meet him with mercy. What does man need on this side of the deliverance that can be only the work of God? Being hopeless, he needs hope. He thus needs — this is the mercy that is to be shown to him — the promise that what he intends and seeks is really there and is there for him. Christians know and have this promise. They know the God who has already created, and in glory will still create, right, worth, freedom, peace, and joy for man. They may hope, and they live by their hope. To bid man hope, and thus to mediate to him the promise that he needs, is their task. Concern for this is their conflict. In it they practice the little righteousness which is their affair and portion, in contrast and yet also in correspondence with the great righteousness that God has practiced, practices, and will still practice.

As Christians, obedient to the command that they are given, busy themselves with this task, whose execution can begin only with the merciful seeing and understanding of man himself, they confess solidarity at every point with man himself, they show themselves to be his companions and friends without worrying about his garb or mask, and they make his cause their own. Knowing what he for the most part does not know, namely, that those who hunger and thirst after righteousness, that those who, however mistakenly or strangely or impotently, ask after and seek the right and dignity of man, have God on their side and will be satisfied [Mt. 5:6], they cannot separate this from him no matter what name he bears or what kind of man he is. It binds them and puts them under obligation to him. They know what they themselves need. They themselves, who as humans are also hidden in all kinds of robes and uniforms and rags, go through life wanting their right, though not demanding it by their own efforts. They do not live by the better, which does not wholly evade them and which they may sometimes achieve in favor of others. They live solely by hope and therefore by the promise that human right, worth, freedom, peace, and joy are not a chimera but have already been actualized by God in Jesus Christ and will finally and ultimately be revealed in their actualization. They have to be witnesses, shining lights of hope, to all men. They have to make the promise known to them in its direct wording and sense as a call to faith. There arises here the missionary task of the Christian community in the narrower sense, a task in which each individual Christian will naturally have to have a part. But Christians cannot be content with this. This call needs a practical commentary in the acts of those who issue it to men — just as Jesus Christ himself proclaimed the kingdom of God not only with words but also with significatory acts. Man is right in wanting to see the good works of Christians in order to praise their heavenly Father (Mt. 5:16). They also have to be witnesses to him by resolutely being there — and not as the last on the scene — when on this side of the deliverance that God has begun and will complete, in relative antithesis to human disorder and the lordship of demons, there is wrestling and fighting and suffering for a provisional bit of human right. Not with good words alone, not even the best, can they be companions and friends of the man who suffers because he seeks and cannot find, but who in fact, whether he knows it or not, may always and everywhere hope, and therefore cries out for the promise. In order that the promise may not merely be uttered but ring out loudly, Christians must draw alongside man. Nor must they do this as weary skeptics. As they may live by the great hope, they must stand by him even in little things, in hope venturing and taking with him little steps to relative improvements wherever he attempts them, even at the risk of often going astray and being disappointed with him. They should not be afraid, then, to say Yes here and No there in solidarity with him—a relative but still a definite Yes or No. Sometimes in so doing—and there will be plenty of occasion for this—they may really know better and be able to do better, and therefore they can criticize, correct, and instruct. Sometimes they may think or speak or do the same thing but in a slightly or even a very different way. It is more important, however, that in coming to his side they should give him the courage not to be content with the corruption and evil of the world but even within this horizon to look ahead and not back. Shame on them if they let him surpass them in courage for this! The experience, however difficult, of hoping seriously, joyfully, and actively in little things, of doing the relatively better relatively well, will not only be salutary for them but will drive them truly to the great hope, to new prayer that God will take his great step not merely to the better but to the best: "Come, Lord Jesus." But in so praying they may not and cannot abandon man, man himself in spite of all his disguises. They will always see in him a fellow man and not just a future brother, and they must treat him as such. They must assist him in full commitment in this time between the times and thus bring him the promise and be for him credible witnesses that God, like themselves, has not abandoned him and will not do so, that his kingdom, the kingdom of the Father, Son, and Holy Spirit, has come and will come even for him, that Jesus Christ is his hope too.

APPENDIX
NOTES ON THE APPENDIX

GENERAL NOTE

The passages in the Appendix follow the manuscript apart from the ampersand, abbreviations of biblical books, dittographies, and obvious mistakes in punctuation and orthography. Stylistic changes marked by Barth at one point for dictation are carried through in the whole sentence. Editorial additions are in brackets [ ], while words not fully decipherable are put in brackets with a question mark. The editors have furnished the titles.

NOTE ON THE FIRST VERSION OF THE CONCLUSION OF §74

The basic reworking of the conclusion of §74 relates to pages 51-69 of the typescript. Barth did not go back to the original (MS pp. 20-28) but left it unaltered. Of the nineteen pages of the typescript in its older version, he worked five into the new version without change. He used another five after considerable shortening. Thus he cut out all but four lines of one page. He dropped nine pages altogether and replaced them with nine new ones. He also added one page (53a). If there was a manuscript version of the nine new pages, it has not survived.

The first version of the conclusion of §74 is thus to be found only in the manuscript version. Of the typescript version (with dictation changes and handwritten corrections and extensions) only nine pages are retained in the revision.

In the text that follows we must distinguish:

1. passages that were adopted in the final version so that they are in the main text but are printed according to the typescript; these are introduced by "cf. p. . . .";

2. passages that Barth cut out but that remained in the typescript along with passages that he retained; these are placed in double parentheses—(( ))—while typescript extensions of the manuscript are denoted by single quotation marks, and all other alterations, apart from very minor ones, are indicated in the notes (in which italics denote emphasized words, of which there are many more in the TS);

3. passages that have been replaced in the final version and are not in the typescript; to the extent that these seem to be related to heavily revised parts of the final version, they carry the reference "cf. the final version p. . . ."

NOTES ON THE FIRST VERSION OF THE
DISCUSSION OF ATHEISM (§77)

No parts of this first version have been incorporated unaltered in the final text (pp. 209ff.), which in the manuscript comes directly after the excised first version. Barth at this point, in regard to the two pages of the typescript of the eliminated version, on which there are no other parts of the text, has the note: "454-55 out." Thus only a short fragment of the dictated form of this version has survived. This is denoted by parentheses. In it simple extensions of the typescript version are denoted by single quotation marks, and all other changes are indicated in the notes.

FIRST VERSION OF THE
CONCLUSION OF §74

That[1] the command of God is in all cases the command of Jesus Christ and therefore the form of grace is the mark by which this command is distinguished from all the other imperatives that may also seem to be, or really are, both serious and urgent. But we must now derive from it its content, what man is commanded in it, and first the general directive by which to know what God demands of man and what man must always do in obedience to God. We must inquire into this general directive in this last part of the introduction. Understanding it will give us the relevant structure of this part of special ethics.[2]

((Apart from the multiplicity of very concrete applications in which it is given to individuals and concerning which ethics can make no statements, the command of God as the command of God the Reconciler has many[3] and varied[4] forms that at first glance point in the most varied and 'apparently' contradictory directions. It is a command that retains its unity but does not immediately display it,[5] being multiform,[6] not uniform. We shall allow for its multiplicity as clearly as possible and establish it as fully[7] as possible. At a first glance, however, it might seem to be somewhat confusing.

We go back to the New Testament and contrast, naturally only by way of example, the following passages. Christians according to Mark 9:50 are to have salt in themselves and[8] are also to be at peace with one another. According to Matthew 10:16, they are to be as wise as serpents and also as harmless as doves. In Matthew 24:42, and so forth, they are addressed as people who are awake and are to remain[9] awake, but in Ephesians 5:14 as sleepers who are to wake up.[10] According to James 1:22, they are not to be hearers only but doers of the Word; but Mary is praised in Luke 10:39f[f.] because, in distinction from her busy sister, she is ready to sit at

---

[1]Cf. p. 36.
[2]This sentence was first erased in the TS, then restored.
[3]*"many"*
[4]*"varied"*
[5]"is not immediately visible in its unity"
[6]*"multiform"*
[7]"carefully"
[8]*"and"*
[9]*"remain"*
[10]*"wake up"*

Jesus' feet and hear his Word.[11] According to John 13:34f., they are to keep the new commandment to love one another, but according to Matthew 7:13,[12] they are 'very tritely' to keep the general and familiar golden rule to do to others as they would that others should do to them. They are to love their brethren united with them in the community (this is almost always the point of the command to love one's neighbor); yet according to Matthew 5:43f[f.] (is this a breaking of the rule or an interpretative extension?), they are not only to love their brethren, as Gentiles might also do, but as the children of their Father and in imitation of his perfect goodness, they are to love even their enemies and persecutors. According to Ephesians 5:25, 28, 33, they are to love their wives as their own bodies,[13] but according to 1 Corinthians 7:29, they are to be married as though they were not. According to Romans 12:2, they are not to be conformed to this aeon, but according to Philippians 4:8 (where Paul is probably[14] referring to the best moral concepts of the current world around the community), they are to think on "what is true, honest, just, pure, lovely, and of good report, on whatever may be virtue and whatever may be worthy of praise." According to 1 Peter 2:17, ' —how can all this be put together? —' they are to honor all men (especially the emperor),[15] love the brotherhood, and fear God. According to John 14:1, they are to believe steadfastly in God and Jesus, but according to Philippians 2:12, they are to work out their salvation, and to do so in fear and trembling. According to Philippians 3:1 'and' 4:2,[16] they are to rejoice, but[17] according to Matthew 5:4, those who mourn are called blessed. These are obviously many[18] different and not readily compatible[19] forms of the one command, which are neither to be harmonized nor to be left 'and asserted' in their difference but are to be understood as different forms of the *one*[20] command growing from the same root.

We thus need to find the red thread which runs through all these things, the common meaning in which they do not contradict one another but hang together and are thus to be understood, not individually, but in concert.)) What[21] is the one thing in the midst of the real and not just apparent many things that the gracious God commands man and man is commanded by God? In the face of the unity of the commanding God on the one side and of responsible man in all his different times, places, and situations on the other, or, decisively, in the face of the unity of the living Mediator between God and man, we have to presuppose that all along the line this one thing is at issue. We are now asking what is the most relevant term for this one thing, the most appropriate concept in which it can be understood as the

[11]*"was ready"*
[12]Mt. 7:12
[13]"as the life of their own bodies"
[14]"obviously"
[15]"all men and the emperor in particular"
[16]Phil. 4:4
[17]"yet"
[18]"many" erased in TS.
[19]"these are different"
[20]Not underscored in TS.
[21]Cf. pp. 36f.

basis of all our further deliberations. Various possibilities suggest themselves. A choice has to be made. It must not be made arbitrarily. As we venture it, we cannot keep in sharp enough focus the point at issue. The choice will always be a venture that can vindicate itself only when it is made, for of the concepts in question, there is none that does not commend itself from some standpoints and none that imposes itself as absolutely necessary to the exclusion of all others. We can seek only a relative and not an absolute concept, only the one that characterizes the matter at issue, and embraces it in all its multiplicity, with what seems to be approximately the greatest clarity.

The[22] basic concept in *CD* III,4, the first part of the special ethics developed as the final part of the doctrine of creation, was the concept of "freedom." It was especially adapted to play a dominant role there because our task at that point was to describe the command and obedience in relationship to the determinations of human existence, which, as we learned from the Word of God, are posited at creation. It is such a rich and beautiful and fruitful concept, and it occurs in such important places in the basic discussions of God and man in the covenant of grace that are just behind us, that one might well ask whether we are not permitted and commanded to continue along the same lines, to put ethics as the crown of the doctrine of reconciliation under the same promising sign, to develop ethics here too, if with a rather different application, as the ethics of freedom. In theology, however, there must be no tyranny of concepts. For this reason alone, to avoid any danger or even any harmful appearance in this direction, it is advisable to look for a new basic concept for this second part of special ethics. A decisive reason, however, is that while the concept of freedom is, as we have seen, illuminating enough as a term for the matter at issue, the command of the gracious God and the obedience of the man responsible to him, it does not adequately bring out its special characteristics. We shall have to keep it in mind and time and again give it its due. But in the present context we need to find a more precise basic concept.

Not[23] a little might be said in favor of the concept of "repentance," which in the New Testament is such an important one in denoting what God requires and man must do under the sign of the imminent kingdom of God. In this context we are thinking of repentance as the *conversion* which is grounded, and has to be carried through, in an awareness of the situation: conversion from an old manner and orientation of life, which has been overtaken and outdated in this situation, to a new one which corresponds to it better. The radical and universal nature of the divine command, and of the human obedience for which it calls, is brought out with classical clarity in this concept, so long as it is understood with sufficient depth and comprehensiveness. It might undoubtedly be the concept we seek. We shall also have to keep it in mind, and time and again recall it. If we widen our

[22]Cf. pp. 37f.
[23]Cf. pp. 37f.

search and pass by, without wholly neglecting, a related concept that is so precious to the existential theological thinking of our time, that of the "decision" which is constantly demanded and has constantly to be made in new ventures, this is because, while it excellently brings out the formal point that the question of the nature and content of the command and obedience is left open, what we want is not just a formally clear concept, but one that is filled out materially, one that tells us what is the conversion that is according to God's will, what is the decision to which man is summoned by it.

Why,[24] then, do we not adopt the great and simple concept of "faith"? Is faith not the Alpha and Omega of what God expects and requires of man? Is it not the imperative of all imperatives? Can decision mean anything other than the decision of faith? When this concept is expounded as man's venture of trust and obedience in relationship to the God revealed to him by his Word in his act, does it not embrace everything that God wants done by the man who knows him in his goodness? We certainly do better not to join Luther in praising faith as the "creator of divinity," since this might easily be stated and understood in proximity to Feuerbach. But who can oppose Luther when elsewhere he more prudently describes faith as the "captain" of all good works? Is it not that? Can an ethics that is specifically oriented to God and man in the covenant of grace want anything other or better than to be an ethics of faith? But does there not threaten here a new tyranny of concepts deriving from the special opposition to Judaizing in Galatians and Romans and its interpretation by Luther and his generation, and in modern times especially by the existentialists? Against the elevation of faith as the central ethical concept do we not also have to say of faith as well that it describes what God commands and man must do only formally and not materially, so that it has to be filled out in a specific way if it is to say something that has ethical content?

1 Corinthians 13[25] could not easily be changed from a hymn in praise of love to a hymn in praise of faith. The same may be said of the statement of Paul that love is the fulfilment of the law (Rom. 13:10), which reminds us clearly of what is called the "new commandment" in the Johannine writings (Jn. 13:34; 1 Jn. 2:8). If faith is to be the central ethical concept, do we not have to bear in mind the misunderstanding to which, as "mere" faith, it was already exposed in the New Testament communities (Jas. 2:14f[f.]), and has always been exposed since? But do we not have to understand it more precisely, along the lines of the saying that occurs already in Galatians (5:6), as the faith that works by love:

Certainly[26] in all that we say about our theme it must never be forgotten that there can be no other obedience than that of faith. Nevertheless, it is still not advisable to think that our question is disposed of by pointing to this concept.

[24]Cf. pp. 38f.
[25]Cf. p. 38.
[26]Cf. p. 39.

As[27] another fine possibility, why not "thanksgiving"? To give thanks is to recognize an unobligated and unmerited favor. It is to show that one recognizes the favor as a favor, as a free one at that. It is to express this in act and attitude toward the one who does the favor. As a concept that is both formally clear and materially important, standing as it does in excellent relation to man's encounter with God in the covenant of grace, this seems to be fairly exactly the concept we are seeking.

A[28] good linguistic argument supports the choice of this concept, namely, the obvious correspondence and analogy between εὐχαριστία and χάρις, gratitude and grace. There is also an historical argument, for if we adopt the concept, we shall be following the material and linguistic example of the Heidelberg Catechism, whose third — ethical — section, which is so typical of the Reformed side of the Reformation, bears the familiar title "Of Gratitude." Christ, who has bought us with his blood, renews us by his Holy Spirit, "so that in our whole life we may show ourselves grateful to God for his blessings and he may be praised through us" (Q. 86).

We[29] might accept this rich and living concept joyfully and with no reserve. Gratitude or, more concretely, thanksgiving, does in fact give us precise and exhaustive information about what is commanded of man in his relationship to the gracious God, and therefore about what is decisively and comprehensively commanded of him. ((Yet the relationship of man to God at once and most decidedly includes also his relationship to his brother and also his relationship to himself and his relationship to the world. And if what is commanded of man in these three other relationships can and must be understood formally as his rendering of thanks to God, it is impossible[30] to regard what is commanded of him in these other relationships as thanksgiving that is to be rendered to his *brother*,[31] *himself*,[32] and the *world*.[33] In regard to all that follows, then, we must be content simply to emphasize the content and dignity of this concept and look around for another one that will perhaps prove to be more suitable with respect to the subordinate dimensions of the command.

As one that meets all the claims advanced thus far, we might 'very simply' consider the concept of the "Christian life.")) This[34] whole part of special ethics might in fact be regarded as a tractate on the life of the Christian (Calvin, *Inst.*, III, 6). If it is, the hardworn, heavily freighted, and ambivalent adjective "Christian" will have to carry the sense of grounded in the knowledge of God in Jesus Christ and oriented to the justification, sanctification, and vocation of man effected in him. ((A life in faith in him, love for him, and hope in him is the Christian life. God the Reconciler

[27]Cf. p. 39.
[28]Cf. p. 39.
[29]Cf. p. 39.
[30]TS: "it might give rise to misunderstanding."
[31]Not underscored in TS.
[32]Not underscored in TS.
[33]Not underscored in TS.
[34]Cf. p. 37.

demands it of man. Man has to live such a life in obedience to him. God does not demand it only of Christians.)) Whether recognized or not, God's command has always and everywhere this content. And wherever and whenever a person's life is lived in obedience to God, it is consciously or unconsciously a Christian life. ((Only by way of example does God demand it specifically of Christians. Only by way of example can Christians be obedient to him in a Christian life. Certainly in distinction from [that] of conversion or even that of faith, one cannot say that this concept is a purely formal one. And in distinction from that of gratitude, it embraces all four dimensions and not just the first, decisive, and controlling one of man's relationship to God. So long as it is presupposed that by the Christian life one really means the life of man from, under, and with J[esus] C[hrist], this concept includes the fullness of the one thing necessary. It embraces man in the totality of his relationship to God and therefore in his relationship, as to God, so also to his brother, himself, and the world.

Now this concept of the Christian life — and all the other concepts that we have considered along with it — can be summed up in the briefest interpretation in that of faithfulness.)) What[35] the God who activates his divine faithfulness in J[esus] C[hrist] wills and requires of man is that he be faithful in return to him, and because to him, so also to his brother, to himself, and to the world. Faithfulness is a steady and lasting persistence and endurance, renewed constantly in a series of acts, in an obligation that is grounded and accepted in reciprocity. The concept may be preferred here to others because it represents such a significant elucidation and deepening of the concept of ((freedom[36] under which we have understood the command of God as the command of God the Creator. Freedom and faithfulness do not contradict one another. The command of God is one. It is thus necessary as well as possible to interpret faithfulness by freedom and freedom by faithfulness.)) [Excised marginal notes (cf. pp. 281f.): A further advantage of the concept of faithfulness, perhaps, is that in it one may see the original meaning of the word faith, at least if we have in mind its Greek equivalent and its origin and object in the πίστις of God himself.] ((The decisive reason for choosing faithfulness as a guiding concept instead of all other possibilities is that this term brings out most precisely what is now before us, the situation of the covenant, indeed, the covenant of grace,[37] between God and man and therefore the Christian life as the will of God which man must obediently do. The reconciliation of the world with God enacted in J[esus] C[hrist] is for God's relationship to man and man's to him a once-for-all, decisive, and basic act of his faithfulness,[38] deriving from his determination to be toward the man the One 'he' is even to the very end. God confirms himself, 'acts in faithfulness to himself, as in spite of all that speaks against him' he binds, gives, and pledges himself to be in J[esus] C[hrist] the God

---

[35]Cf. the slightly different text, pp. 39f.
[36]*"freedom"*
[37]*"grace"*
[38]*"faithfulness"*

of man, to be for him in his own person Servant, Lord, and Witness —
Priest, King, and Prophet — his righteousness, sanctification, and wisdom.[39]
In being this, however, he also commands man to be faithful to himself,
that is, not to be other than what he is as God binds, gives, and pledges
himself to him;[40] to 'show himself to be' and to remain this man. The
Christian life[41] is a human life in which the circle which begins with God's
action for and to man[42] closes with an action of man which corresponds,
conforms, and is analogous to God's action, and man meets faithfulness
with faithfulness.))[43]

Faithfulness,[44] deeply linked to the concepts of truth, righteousness, and mercy,
is the basic category in which the Old Testament understands and presents both the
being and action of Yahweh in his covenant with the people elected and called by
him, and also that which he expects of this people, its commitment. "Yahweh your
God is God, the faithful God who keeps covenant and steadfast love with those who
love him and keep his commandments, to a thousand generations" (Dt. 7:9). He
always remains himself in his relationship to this people: himself (with the same goal
of salvation) as the God of the progenitor Abraham, but also of Isaac and of Jacob
and his descendants, the God who does not merely perform the unique act of power
in the exodus from Egypt with which the common history of Yahweh and this people
begins, but continues it in its existence as the wilderness people, in the complicated
events of the conquest on both sides of the Jordan, in the hard struggle to maintain
it, and then in the leading of David and his house. This faithful action of his,
perceived and proclaimed by Moses and the prophets, is the Word in which he
commands Israel to become and to be and to remain faithful to him in its own
response of faithfulness. Israel does this only in a transitory way. It displays it
concretely only in certain very fragile forms. Its history as a whole is that of ever-
new forms of unfaithfulness, a long history, from the standpoint of its acts and
attitudes, of defection from the covenant of Yahweh. Nevertheless, Yahweh, not
Israel, set up this covenant, so that Israel can neither destroy [?] nor evade it. What
can Israel's unfaithfulness accomplish over against God's faithfulness? Only that
Yahweh's ongoing direction takes on a predominantly and even exclusively penal
character. Yet Yahweh still loves his people even when he accuses and condemns
and smites it. It is because he loves it so much that he deals with it so severely. In
so doing he does not cease to bear witness that he watches over it, that he has not
turned from it in weariness and disenchantment. He does not accept its unfaithfulness. As though nothing had happened, he continues to call it back to the only
appropriate stance of faithfulness and therefore to remind it of the salvation he still
purposes for it. His eyes, the eyes of the faithful God, still look with favor on the
faithful in the land (Ps. 101:6).

Again,[45] if we are to understand the New Testament concept of faith, it is
important to remember that the adjective πιστός (also the noun πίστις in Rom. 3:3)

[39]TS: "wisdom, righteousness, sanctification, and redemption" (1 Cor. 1:30).

[40]TS: "what he is in virtue of the fact that God bound, gave, and pledged himself to him.
God commands him. . . ."

[41]*"Christian life"*

[42]"and to him" not in TS.

[43]*"faithfulness with faithfulness"*

[44]Cf. p. 40.

[45]Cf. pp. 40f.

can often denote a quality or attribute of God. He first has shown himself constant and persistent in what he has done for the world and everyman in J[esus] C[hrist]. Thus, πίστις in its usual sense as a term for the human act, and the verb πιστεύειν, notwithstanding its meaning elsewhere, are to be understood basically as the faithfulness of man responding to this faithfulness of God. In faith man sticks it out with God because he sees that God as his God, and to his advantage, first willed to stick it out with him, and did in fact do so. As this human faithfulness which responds and corresponds to the faithfulness of God, faith is obedience, the venture of trust in God. Is not perhaps this readiness of the human partner to stick it out with the divine partner the meaning and nerve of all the other New Testament imperatives? Do not these speak frequently and urgently of the command that Christians must endure, remain, stand fast, be established, hold on, and persevere, as though absolutely everything depended on this? That they should begin and continue with this trust, that there should be this response of human to divine faithfulness, is, of course, taken for granted in the New Testament sphere when the acts of Christians are in view. Why, then, do we find that the awakening of faith and the entry into freedom to persevere with God seem to be surrounded with an aspect of the extraordinary? Why do we find exhortations in which there is a continual summons to the required response of faithfulness and therefore to holding fast to God? Why is there continual reference to the obviously not yet attained perfection of perseverance? Failure at this decisive point, that is, unfaithfulness, is obviously a danger that seriously threatens Christians and even the apostle, and to avert it the elect, the called, believers stand in need of intercession and must call on God themselves. One decisive change, however, has come about in the New Testament as compared with the Old Testament, and this alters the whole picture. The open contradiction in the Old Testament between the faithfulness of God and the unfaithfulness of man has now been removed at a central point and hence at all others. In one person the covenant of grace has been confirmed[46] on man's side. Staying by God, πίστις and πιστεύειν, has become unequivocally an event of human obedience. Constantly threatened by the possibility that they might fail and become unfaithful like continually unfaithful Israel, πιστεύοντες look, and their πίστις refers, to the one person in whom the covenant of grace is kept and established, not only as God's act but also as man's in faithfulness on both sides: to the "pioneer and perfecter of our faith" (Heb. 12:2), who is set before them as the firstborn Brother who has persevered for all of them, who has been faithful in their place. Believing now means—and this makes the requirement imperious but also liberating—not only staying with God but also staying, because with God, with this one man too, in fellowship with God: believing in Jesus Christ. This is the new thing in the demand for faithfulness and therefore in the central ethical problem in the New Testament.

((The[47] faithfulness of God, which as such imperiously calls for man's counter-faithfulness, is the faithfulness that he has granted and maintains absolutely freely in his grace, moved thereto only of and by himself. It is thus unconditional and unshakable, as may be shown already in the relationship between Yahweh and Israel but fulfilled in the circle of the covenant closed in the person of J[esus] C[hrist]. It could vacillate and vanish only if God were unfaithful to himself and thus ceased to be God. It would be

---

[46]MS, in error, repeats "removed" from previous sentence (*beseitigt* for *bestätigt*).
[47]Cf. p. 41.

blasphemy even to think such a thing. It would thus be blasphemy to believe that God could become and be unfaithful to man. His pertinacity in the covenant with man has no end, though it[48] might mean damnation and hell for man. God's faithfulness is also total faithfulness, with no reservations or second thoughts. It is not an engagement[49] that he has entered into only partially and incidentally so that alongside and behind it[50] there is a non-engaged being and willing and action of God, 'a dark background,' an uncertain factor in God, of which one might suspect and fear that one day it would with the same divine sovereignty, unconditionality, and unshakability end up with the dropping rather than the upholding of man. The acts and promises[51] of God in the Old Testament sphere — if they had not received in J[esus] C[hrist] the seal of his Yes and Amen they might have been understood by us with the same abstraction as even to this day they are necessarily understood in the synagogue — might be misunderstood along these lines. Risking the totality of his divine being, willing, and action, God in J[esus] C[hrist] has 'unmistakably' become the God of man. — [52] To all this there corresponds, however, the nature and character of the command of faithfulness[53] that he has given to man.[54] The point is, this is what God wills from man,[55] that man should persevere with God in relation to[56] and according to the measure and manner of God's first persisting with him)): freely, that is, without compulsion, urged and moved thereto by himself; unconditionally, that is, without claim, without any 'ifs' and 'buts' whereby man might try to lay down the law for God so as to become and be and remain faithful to him; unshakably, that is, without even considering, let alone permitting himself any limitation; and last of all totally, without staking out any reserved areas in his being in view of which he might become and be unfaithful, ceasing to persist with God with an appeal to some other freedom. This is what the gracious God has in mind in his command to man. This is what he wants from him. What he requires is not inappropriate but is simply that as a clear mirror he should encounter him as he, God, encounters man.

But[57] that God must demand this, that he must imperiously say what he wants from man as appropriate, presupposes and shows that it is not self-evident that man should answer God's faithfulness with faithfulness. He does not just do this. That God has pledged himself to him in faithfulness, and that he is the covenant partner of this faithful God, may be guiltily or innocently hidden from him or unknown to him. He may once have heard it and taken it to heart and then forgotten it again. His knowledge

---

[48]TS: "even though"
[49]TS: "obligation"
[50]TS: *ihr* (not *ihm*)
[51]TS: "the promises"
[52]New para. in TS
[53]TS: "men"
[54]TS: *"Treue-Gebotes"* for *"Treuegebotes"*
[55]TS: "(this is what God wills from man)"
[56]TS: *im Blick darauf* for *daraufhin*
[57]Cf. pp. 41f.

of God, and his knowledge of himself on this basis, may still be obscure to him or have been obscured again. It may be that he does not want to know what he knows. It may be that he wants and tries to escape the validity of the law by which he must be faithful to God as God is faithful to him. It may be that he refuses the free, unconditional, unshakable, and total practical observance with which alone it can be fulfilled, that he is ready and willing to accord it obedience only with deductions and withdrawals. Account is obviously taken of this man when the faithfulness corresponding to that law is imperatively commanded, when he must be summoned and admonished to achieve it, when the order of the covenant, the Christian life, must be brought to his remembrance as a duty, when it must be continually brought before him as something new. When does he believe as he should and must believe? Even the man reconciled to God in J[esus] C[hrist] is not yet redeemed and perfected man. Even he is still on the way and even he can falter, stumble, and fall on the path marked out for him and already entered upon by him. Even he is still in a battle in which he can suffer defeat and often does. Sin still couches at his door, he still has a desire for it (Gen. 4:7), it still "dwells" in him (Rom. 7:17, 20). The faithfulness with which he is faithful to God is thus quite unlike the faithfulness with which God turns to him. He still needs the divine word of command which calls for adjustment, the word of command of the God who is gracious to him. He still needs *paraclesis*, the recollection which bitterly accuses him, which urgently admonishes and binds him to new action and conduct. God's faithfulness must still mean claim, decision, and judgment for man. Ethics from the standpoint of grace, reconciliation, and the covenant, the ethics of faithfulness which now confronts us as a task, reckons with that inequality, and its problem is that of the adjustment that God demands.

We certainly must not let ourselves be guilty of diminutions of the majesty of the command, weakenings of its character as a strict order, or softenings of the danger in which sinful man finds himself and from whose sphere the command seeks to call him. Even less, however, should we permit any obscuring of the absolutely decisive point that the command is that of the gracious God who is faithful in his grace, faithful to himself, but faithful also to unfaithful man. It is God's faithfulness to man that makes imperious his command to man to be faithful to him in return. It would be the worst dishonoring and defusing of God's command to take it out of this context. For the sake of respect for the majesty of the divine command we must not on any pretext, not even that of supposedly greater seriousness, go behind the situation between God and man which has been created and exists in J[esus] C[hrist]. There must be no construction of a command which is not the command that God has given to man in this situation. As the command of the gracious God who is faithful in his grace, constant in himself, and persevering in relation to us men, it summons us to the Christian life and is generally binding as the demand for faithfulness, as the true determination, order, and limitation of the action of sinful man as such, which it is our task to investigate in detail in what follows. Our only remaining task is to understand the order of procedure.

One point is clear from the outset. Faithfulness to the faithful God is the one total thing that is required of man as the Christian life. But always faithfulness to God is also a specific orientation of the conduct required of man, a content of the divine command that is concretely emphasized precisely in its general range. God's own faithfulness as the source, authority, and power has also a specific form in which it comes to man as the awakening, quickening, and enlightening work of his Holy Spirit. Thus the commitment to counter-faithfulness which it lays upon man consists primarily and decisively of the openness which is expected of him to God's instruction, of the readiness and willingness that is required of him for guidance by the Spirit of God. An inescapable mark of all good conduct will always be that it takes place in this very special openness, readiness, and willingness. But to be faithful to the Spirit of God — this is the second point to concern us — is commanded of him, certainly as this or that individual, but also as a brother among brothers, as an individual member of the community which God has elected for his service in the world and called and gathered from all nations by his Spirit. Thus we shall at once have to understand and describe the Christian life which is required of man as also in its own way and in accordance with its special task the faithfulness which must be shown in the life and work of the community in relation to its many members. The Christian's conduct will be called good when, and only when, this horizontal direction is peculiar to it as and because it has the vertical dimension. All the same, what God in the word of his Holy Spirit demands and expects of the Christian as a member of his people is his wholly personal action, faithfulness in the form of a very definite inner and outer attitude, the display of a very definite character, namely, that which is appropriate to him as a man who is confronted with the faithfulness of the God who is gracious precisely to him. A third point has to be considered also. If his conduct is good because it is obedient to the divine command, it will always be marked by the attitude that is characteristic of such a man. Faithfulness to the Spirit of God, faithfulness in the community, and faithfulness in this characteristic attitude, are to be achieved and displayed however — here is a fourth orientation of his conduct — in the world which has been reconciled in J[esus] C[hrist] with God and with [?] itself, and which even though it is not yet redeemed, exists in the light of its coming redemption. They are to be achieved and displayed in deep solidarity with this world's misery and hope, also under severe attack by it, but above all in humble but resolute witness in and to it. His action, if it is well done, has to measure up to this criterion: God orders him to be faithful to him in the ever so threatened world which was nevertheless created by him and effectively enough loved by him in J[esus] C[hrist]. These are the four directions in which human life must be lived as the Christian life that God commands. Fundamentally, it must be lived in all four directions *at once*, but practically in continual and multiple *transitions* from the one to the other, the first, that is, that of faithfulness or obedience to the Spirit of God, representing in its particularity a kind of pivot for all the movements that man is commanded and permitted to make.

The four sections whose specific themes are indicated thereby will form the chief and central portion of that part of special ethics which is now before us. In this totality, however, there is missing the answer to a twofold question without which everything is left enigmatically and uncertainly up in the air. Our concern at every point will be with the demand for faithfulness which is issued by God to man in the covenant of grace and with the display of the demanded faithfulness by man. In other words, we have to do with a reciprocal act of God and man and therefore with their common *history* seen here from the specifically ethical angle. In the occurrence of this history both the divine commanding and the human attitude and action which corresponds (or should correspond) to it both unfold in those four directions, fundamentally in all of them at once, but practically in the whole fullness of every possible transition from the one to the other. It[58] is by no means self-evident, however, that this history should take place at all in the life of man, that it should become his own history, that the encounter between God and man should come about with all the problems it raises, that the common way of the commanding God and responsible man should in fact be entered upon and followed. How does this history arise? The question is a double one, and in both its forms it has two sides, a divine and a human. Its first form is this: how does it come about that God's faithfulness in its validity and power extends not only to all people and therefore to each individual person but becomes in the life of a specific individual a word that is concretely directed to him and received by him, an event in his life, striking roots, as it were, in him, acquiring for him the significance and efficacy of a factor in his life which cannot be denied or set aside but which is constant, controlling, and normative for his entire future? Thus far in relation to the grace of God addressed to him. And in relation to the faithfulness of man that is awakened and commanded by the word of faithfulness, when that new and controlling factor comes into his existence, what is he expected to do once and for all as the first thing, the act of his commencing obedience? What is his own beginning corresponding to the beginning that God has made with him, his direct confirmation, normative for all that follows, of the new birth that God has worked for him? The second form of the question is this: once this history, the Christian life of this man, has begun, how can it and will it continue? In regard to the faithfulness of God, how will the word and command effected [?] by it maintain the actuality they have attained for him? How will the factor that has newly come into his existence persist with the same significance and efficacy? What will be the necessary food of the one who is born anew in that event? Then in relation to the faithfulness commanded of this man, what will he have to keep on doing for his part in the light of the ensuing demonstrations of the faithfulness of God, in looking forward to them and back upon them — in the light of the constantly displayed and living power of that new and controlling factor? In what movement can and should he follow and correspond to the ongoing movement in which God's faithfulness precedes him, so that he for his part may be and remain newly faithful [to it?]?

58Cf. pp. 45ff.

Ethics in the context of the doctrine of reconciliation obviously has to take up these two questions, and both of them in their twofold form. The first is the question of the foundation of the Christian life, of the God who is faithful to man and commands him in his grace and of the man who is responsible to this God and owes him counter-faithfulness. The second is the question of the necessary and expected renewal of the Christian life in relation once again both to the commanding God and also to the man who is responsible to him. We shall put the answer to the question of foundation before the series of individual discussions of the various orientations. We shall place the answer to the question of renewal after this series in the form of a conclusion to the whole.

In the introduction we shall be dealing with baptism, and in the conclusion with the Lord's Supper. Both the giving and receiving of baptism and the celebration of the Lord's Supper rest on emphatic orders. They thus belong to ethics as this is developed in the specific light of God's reconciling action. To each, then, a special place must be assigned. In accordance with their specific meanings baptism is related to the foundation of the Christian life, and thus comes in the introduction to the whole, and the Lord's Supper is related to the renewal of the Christian life, and has thus to be dealt with in the conclusion. Neither is to be put, however, at the place where we are thinking of the initial and ongoing demonstration of God's faithfulness as the ontic and noetic basis of the faithfulness required of man. The righteousness and power of God's saving work effected in J[esus] C[hrist] and the dignity and force of his Word spoken by the Holy Spirit, God will not share with any other, whether it be with the bibl[ical] prophets and apostles, the church, its officebearers, its preaching and other ministries, or baptism and the Lord's Supper. With what he does and says, God raises up and fashions witnesses of his grace, not its vicars, representatives, or guarantors, not instruments, vehicles, channels, or means of grace. It is always his own affair to show man his faithfulness, to effect and reveal man's salvation. Baptism and the Lord's Supper are not emanations, repetitions, or continuations of his work and word, nor actualizations and mediations of it, nor its warranties and seals. They are not additional and more or less self-evidently related forms, events, or revelations of salvation. They belong at a specific point to the divinely permitted and commanded attestation and proclamation of the one event of salvation accomplished in the one Mediator (1 Tim. 2:5f.), who in the power of the Holy Spirit directly presents, represents, reflects, and manifests himself. Baptism and the Lord's Supper are also actions of the obedience for which he has freed and made responsible the community as such and its members in particular. Like the whole being and work of the community and each individual Christian, as actions of obedience they live by the work which God himself alone has done in the birth and passion and death of J[esus] C[hrist], by the Word of the revelation of this work which goes forth from his mouth alone. As actions of this obedience, they are related to God's work and word and therefore to the demonstration of his faithfulness and therefore to the foundation and renewal of the Christian life, to the origin of the faithfulness which is required of man for his part. Not in and by themselves, not by the work done by the church or the Christian, but by the work done by God in Jesus Christ through the Holy Spirit, as the human response to this one saving and illuminating work, they have the promise of the divine good-pleasure and are well done as holy and fruitful acts. Their light is the reflection of what they have to bear witness to at their appointed and prominent place in the context of the whole life of the community and the individual Christian. Baptism is the solemn Christian act in face of the divine foundation of the required faithfulness of man and therefore of the Christian life, while the Lord's Supper is the solemn Christian act in face of its divine renewal.

Altogether six discussions are thus demanded. We have to deal (1) with the foundation of Christian faithfulness and therefore with baptism as the first and unique human act confirming the divine foundation; (2) with the Christian's faithfulness to the Holy Spirit which determines and limits all that follows; (3) with his faithfulness in the community; (4) with his faithfulness to himself; (5) with his faithfulness in the world; and (6) with the renewal of Christian faithfulness and with the Lord's Supper as the human action in which the Christian may and should continually confirm its divine renewal. Perhaps for once we may be permitted to describe the divinely willed and commanded Christian life expounded in points 2-5 as man's path from the divine foundation to the divine renewal of his required faithfulness, and in this connection as his path from baptism to the Lord's Supper.

FIRST VERSION OF THE
DISCUSSION OF ATHEISM (§77)

((Among the forms of the ignorance of God in the world, we mention first the attempt[1] to *deny*, as it is said, God himself,[2] that is, to dispute[3] the statement that he *is*, which is enclosed in the knowledge of God, to understand God[4] as a construct of thought, with no essential basis or context, which has been invented by some people for various ideal or less ideal reasons, and which has been uncritically accepted and affirmed[5] by others who have not perceived its [fictional] origin and character. This attempt is [as a rule] made with the appeal to a prefabricated and supposedly scientific[6] world view in which no place is seen for God and with the arguments which may be easily derived from this. Its true presupposition, however, is not this world view, and its true motive is not the holy zeal to make it watertight. It could be attempted without that world view and without that holy zeal. Atheism, as the attempt is called, is the mighty ignorance of God, enigmatically ruling in the world,)) in the polemical and to that extent unprotected form ((which corresponds only too well to its negative nature even though it is not recognized and practiced by all.))[7] In "atheism" this ignorance shows that it lives by its antithesis to the knowledge of God in the world and that it has to defend itself against this opponent. In "atheism" it also betrays its inner weakness by the primitive nature of its defense, namely, that there can be no such codeterminative(?) knowledge of God because the God who supposedly makes himself known and is known is a fictional and not a real God. What a cogent self-demonstration of the same world which can escape neither the knowledge of God nor the distinctive ignorance of God! What a poor and particularly gross and wild and uninterruptedly(?) sensational eruption of this ignorance! What a shocking desecration of the holy name of God! The only thing is that its undoubtedly dreadful form should not lead us astray but show us clearly that atheism is simply one variety of the great ungodliness of the world alongside which there are others, and that in virtue of the relative honesty with which this ungodliness

[1] Marginal note in the TS, later excised: "the attempt (made not only in modern times but also in ancient and indeed the very earliest times)"
[2] TS does not have "himself."
[3] TS: "*dispute*"
[4] TS: "him"
[5] Following TS
[6] TS: "(prefabricated and supposedly scientific)"
[7] TS: "and clearly practiced as such by all"

expresses itself in it, it is not perhaps the worst variety. If only the atheist
were not insincere in the fact that he usually arms himself with that ad hoc
constructed world view and fights with arguments derived from it! If only
he would also stop indulging in a kind of godless mysticism and morality
so as not to be called a seriously ungodly person. If he would confess frankly
and freely without any such camouflage that as and because he does not
know God, yet is profoundly disquieted by the undeniable knowledge of
God in the world and must be rid of this opponent at all costs, he says, and
thinks he must say, in his heart, "There is no God" (Ps. 14:1; 53:1). With
the atheist who simply and without circumlocution makes the ignorance of
God in the world his cause along with the necessary defense against the
threatening knowledge of God, one can debate, and one can even draw
alongside him, with an equally simple confession of faith in God and an
expression, without claim, of the confession of his knowledge. With such
a one it is possible to agree at least on who or what he is trying to deny.
Does he have in mind the God of a philosophy or metaphysics? Or the God
that he regards as the common coefficient of all the religions known to him?
Or the God whom he remembers as a shadowy figure in some Christian
church and theology — perhaps because this has badly proclaimed God to
him or he has badly understood it? But with the atheist who will not simply
confess his ignorance of God but who arms himself with a world view and
moves in the direction of mysticism, it is difficult to debate, or get alongside
him, because as such he will not listen to the equally simple confession of
faith in the true God of man in his unity with the true man of God, because
it will be hard to make clear to him that with his denial of one of the gods
or all the gods he might be denying the one true God who is the true source
of the disquiet which he is trying to guard against but that he can as little
deny him as anyone else can, and that he must give up, therefore, trying
to do so. It is obviously part of the problem of the ambivalence of the
knowledge and ignorance of God which characterizes the world's situation
that even among the apparently most consistent representatives of the ignorance of God, among atheists, one looks in vain for simple confessors of
their cause. But this is perhaps connected with the intrinsic impracticability
of the matter which makes an honest and simple confession of it impossible,
so that there can be no real confrontation of faith with faith (or at least with
believing unbelief).

SMALL FRAGMENT OF AN ATTEMPT TO REVISE THE EXISTING TEXT OF *CD* IV,4[1]

CHAPTER XVII

THE COMMAND OF GOD THE RECONCILER

§74

ETHICS IN THE CONTEXT OF THE DOCTRINE OF RECONCILIATION

The Word of God's free grace, effective and revealed in Jesus Christ, is his command to each person and all people in which he calls for the response of their obedience in the thought, speech, and action of their free gratitude.

The doctrine of reconciliation, like the doctrine of creation, should conclude with an ethical chapter. Knowledge of God's reconciliation of the world to himself in Jesus Christ, and therefore of his covenant with man set up and fulfilled in Jesus Christ, embraces knowledge of the human action which corresponds to this divine action and which may to that extent be seriously called good. The Word of God's free grace liberates man to be obedient to God in free gratitude. It asks, demands, and calls for this appropriate response. That this is so could not be hidden from us at any point in our development of the doctrine of reconciliation thus far. It was expressly intimated when at the end of each of the three parts we had to speak about

[1]Attached to this single MS page is a sheet with the thesis and headings in blue biro on the one side and on the other a description of the text and a note in black biro with vertical red markings.

The thesis is as in the text except for one small difference in wording and the shorter ending: "the response of their obedience in acts of their gratitude."

The headings are as follows:

Horizon: God
    Man
    Situation
    Command — Obedience

The description on the back reads: "this is the small fragment of a new attempt c. 1964 to revise the whole of the existing text of *CD* IV,4."

The note is to the effect that there was not to be any material alteration of §75 on baptism.

the work of the Holy Spirit in the gathering, upbuilding, and sending of the community and also about the faith, love, and hope of the individual Christian. To the extent that dogmatics already in the prolegomenon and then throughout has had to have in view and to bring to light this special form of the relationship and dealings between God and man it has everywhere been ethics too, an attempt to answer the question as to the human thought and speech and act which is made possible and commanded by God and is therefore right before him. To emphasize this and expound it in detail was the point of the fourth part of the doctrine of creation and is now the point of the fourth part of the doctrine of reconciliation.

There is only one God, and so there is only one command of God addressed to each person and all people, and only one obedience of man to it. Nevertheless, as God is the one God in the different modes of being of the Father and the Son, so without prejudice to its unity there are different forms of his Word and command insofar as they refer on the one side to his relationship as Creator to man as his creature and on the other side to his relationship as Reconciler to the sinful man reconciled to him in Jesus Christ. There are also correspondingly different forms of the one obedience which is made possible for all men and commanded from all men. The second form of the divine command and human obedience will concern us now, namely, the problem of ethics in the special light and context of the doctrine of reconciliation.

INDEXES

I. SCRIPTURE REFERENCES

II. NAMES

III. SUBJECTS